South Asia Economic and Policy Studies

The Series aims to address evolving and new challenges and policy actions that may be needed in the South Asian Region in the 21st century. It ventures niche and makes critical assessment to evolve a coherent understanding of the nature of challenges and allow/facilitate dialogue among scholars and policymakers from the region working with the common purpose of exploring and strengthening new ways to implement regional cooperation. The series is multidisciplinary in its orientation and invites contributions from academicians, policy makers, practitioners, consultants working in the broad fields of regional cooperation; trade and investment; finance; economic growth and development; industry and technology; agriculture; services; environment, resources and climate change; demography and migration; disaster management, globalization and institutions among others.

More information about this series at http://www.springer.com/series/15400

Muhammed Muqtada
Editor

Quest for Inclusive Growth in Bangladesh

An Employment-focused Strategy

Springer

Editor
Muhammed Muqtada
Consultant Economist and Visiting Fellow
Centre for Policy Dialogue (CPD)
Dhaka, Bangladesh

ISSN 2522-5502 ISSN 2522-5510 (electronic)
South Asia Economic and Policy Studies
ISBN 978-981-15-7613-3 ISBN 978-981-15-7614-0 (eBook)
https://doi.org/10.1007/978-981-15-7614-0

This Springer imprint is published by the registered company Springer Nature Singapore Pte Ltd.
The registered company address is: 152 Beach Road, #21-01/04 Gateway East, Singapore 189721, Singapore

To

Professor Rehman Sobhan

Our mentor, who has been a leading champion for building an inclusive democratic society

Foreword

No society can surely be flourishing and happy, of which the far greater part of the members are poor and miserable

Adam Smith

(An Inquiry into the Nature and Causes of the Wealth of Nations, 1776, p. 96)

In his magnum opus, *The Wealth of Nations*, Adam Smith challenged the view that a higher standard of living of the poor would result in their desire for luxury or make them lazy. He argued that the real yardstick of socio-economic progress was not the advancement of the few, but rather the advancement of the many. In a prosperous society, farmers who feed others must themselves be well-fed, tailors who clothe others must themselves be well-clothed and builders who shelter others must themselves be well-sheltered. Hence, economic growth only has meaning as long as it is inclusive, and creates a meaningful difference to the lives of every individual in the society.

It is in this spirit that the Centre for Policy Dialogue (CPD) undertook a study on inclusive growth in Bangladesh a few years back under its flagship research programme, the *Independent Review of Bangladesh's Development (IRBD)*. This book is the culmination of diverse research carried out by the Centre during the recent past to promote an inclusive growth strategy for Bangladesh. CPD had also invited Dr. Muhammed Muqtada, a former Director (Policy Planning, Employment Sector) of the International Labour Organization (ILO), Geneva, to be the guest editor of this volume. Dr. Muqtada helped us conceptualise the central theme of the book, contributed chapters and tied all articles together so that they all collectively echo a consistent message.

Broadly, this book highlights the importance of inclusive growth, describes the components of it and outlines how growth may be made inclusive in practice in the context of Bangladesh. Each chapter uses a different entry point into inclusive growth, and discusses a distinctive element which is crucial to reach the goal of inclusive growth. The distinguishing feature of this book is its central emphasis on employment as a vehicle for reaching growth outcomes which are inclusive. It is hoped that this book will be useful for policymakers in Bangladesh as well as in developing and least developed countries for devising growth strategies which will benefit all.

July 2020

Fahmida Khatun
Executive Director
Centre for Policy Dialogue (CPD)
Dhaka, Bangladesh

Editor's Preface

In recent times, especially since the beginning of this century, there has been a flurry of interest among researchers and policymakers to explore and pursue an inclusive growth strategy. A sense of urgency for this is underscored by the growing scepticism over a single-minded pursuit of GDP growth that has left many economies with a lagging state of social and human development. These trends are even more brazenly exposed during economic downturns and crises, such as seen in the aftermath of the recent COVID-19 pandemic, and earlier, during the global financial crisis of 2008–09; equally, these crises expose the inadequacy of policies and the fragility of institutions that aim to arrest growing vulnerability and social exclusion. The enunciation of the United Nations' 2030 Agenda for Sustainable Development, which is widely seen as a blueprint for inclusive and sustainable growth, and to which countries across the world are now committed, can be arguably seen as the collective global expression of these growing concerns.

The present study attempts to explore and review the growing call for adopting an inclusive growth strategy, and to identify the critical issues and goals at stake. Given that the latter are many, and can potentially lead to an unwieldy policy canvas, the study argues in favour of pursuing an inclusive growth strategy through the goal of full employment, one that would have maximum catalytic effects on several other goals, which would likely effect inclusion both in the outcomes and processes of growth.

This study is admittedly not a comprehensive account of all goals and issues of inclusive growth; it contains a collection of essays on selected policy themes that are interrelated and central to the building up of the strategy framework suggested at the outset. Queries raised, and reforms suggested, on existing policies are expected to provide an impulse and a direction towards the design of an inclusive growth strategy. While Bangladesh is the focus of the study, the analytical issues and policy recommendations are expected to be equally pertinent for the developing countries of South Asia, and beyond.

The chapters of the volume, and the thematic issues addressed, are an outcome of extensive in-house discussions among researchers at the Centre for Policy Dialogue (CPD), a leading think tank, which has initiated the book project. The essays have been prepared through collaborative and intense empirical research by senior research staff at the institution. I am honoured to have been invited by the CPD to develop the themes of these essays, and to anchor and steer the research.

Geneva, Switzerland
July 2020

Muhammed Muqtada
Development economist; formerly a Director in the Employment Sector of the International Labour Organization (ILO), Geneva, and a Visiting Fellow, Centre for Policy Dialogue, Dhaka, Bangladesh

Authors' Acknowledgements

The authors of the book would like to extend their sincere gratitude towards a few individuals and organisations, without whose involvement and diligent contribution, the successful completion of this project would not have been possible.

The concept of carrying out a set of thematic studies on employment as a strategy for attaining inclusive growth in Bangladesh, and of bringing them out as a compendium, was initially developed at the Centre for Policy Dialogue (CPD) as part of its flagship programme *Independent Review of Bangladesh's Development (IRBD)*. The authors would like to express their sincere appreciation to Dr. Debapriya Bhattacharya and Prof. Mustafizur Rahman, Distinguished Fellows of CPD, for their valuable suggestions and overall support to the study teams throughout the volume preparation phase.

An expert group meeting was held at an early stage of the project, where the concept and outline of the volume were presented before a number of sector specialists. The authors would like to thank all the participants for their constructive inputs. The authors are particularly indebted to the three anonymous reviewers whose valuable comments and feedback have enriched the papers.

Taking this opportunity, generous support from the Department for International Development (DFID) Bangladesh office in carrying out this research programme is also acknowledged.

CPD colleagues across the divisions—Research, Dialogue & Communication and Administration & Finance—have extended their fullest cooperation in bringing out this book. Colleagues at the Publication unit played an instrumental role in proposal development and the final shaping of the book.

Thanks are also due to the Springer Nature Singapore Pte Ltd for showing interest to publish the book and for taking it forward to the wider readership.

Lastly, the authors have taken this opportunity to express their deepest gratitude to the founding Chairman of CPD, Prof. Rehman Sobhan, an esteemed economist of the Asian region, whose lifetime work has been the inspiration behind this collective study.

Contents

Editor and Contributors

About the Editor

Dr. Muhammed Muqtada a development economist and policy analyst, is best known for his work on growth, poverty, employment and labour market issues. He had been associated with the International Labour Organization (ILO), Geneva, for nearly two and a half decades, and had held several top management positions at the ILO. He led, and participated, in various fact-finding, programming and employment review missions in various countries across all regions. As Director of Policy Planning, he coordinated and directed the research programmes of the ILO's Employment Sector, Geneva. Prior to joining the ILO, he taught macroeconomics, economic development and planning at the University of Dhaka. Among his co-edited titles, are—Employment Expansion and Macroeconomic Stability in an Era of Increasing Globalization (from MacMillan, London); and Bangladesh: Economic and Social Challenges of Globalization (from The University Press Limited, Dhaka). At present, Dr. Muqtada is involved in applied research and consultancy services and to date, has provided expert advisory services to governments, international organisations and other stakeholders within and beyond Bangladesh. He has also been a Visiting Fellow at the Centre for Policy Dialogue (CPD) in Dhaka, Bangladesh. Dr. Muqtada was educated at the University of Cambridge, UK (PhD in Economics, 1980), and the University of Dhaka, Bangladesh (MA and BA in Economics).

Contributors

Muntaseer Kamal Senior Research Associate, Centre for Policy Dialogue (CPD), Dhaka, Bangladesh

Towfiqul Islam Khan Senior Research Fellow, Centre for Policy Dialogue (CPD), Dhaka, Bangladesh

Fahmida Khatun Executive Director, Centre for Policy Dialogue (CPD), Dhaka, Bangladesh

Khondaker Golam Moazzem Research Director, Centre for Policy Dialogue (CPD), Dhaka, Bangladesh

Muhammed Muqtada Development Economist; Formerly a Director in the Employment Sector of the International Labour Organization (ILO) Geneva and a Visiting Fellow, Centre for Policy Dialogue, Geneva, Dhaka, Bangladesh

Md. Minhaz M. Reza International Initiative for Impact Evaluation (3ie), New Delhi, India;
Formerly Research Associate, Centre for Policy Dialogue (CPD), Dhaka, Bangladesh

Syed Yusuf Saadat Senior Research Associate, Centre for Policy Dialogue (CPD), Dhaka, Bangladesh

Mostafa Amir Sabbih Senior Research Associate, Centre for Policy Dialogue (CPD), Dhaka, Bangladesh

Acronyms

7FYP	Seventh Five Year Plan
8FYP	Eighth Five Year Plan
ACC	Anti-Corruption Commission
ADB	Asian Development Bank
ADP	Annual Development Programme
AFD	French Development Agency
AIT	Advance Income Tax
ALMP	Active Labour Market Policy
ASEAN	Association of Southeast Asian Nations
ATV	Advance Trade VAT
BBS	Bangladesh Bureau of Statistics
BDT	Bangladeshi Taka
BGMEA	Bangladesh Garment Manufacturers and Exporters Association
BIDS	Bangladesh Institute of Development Studies
BIGD	BRAC Institute of Governance and Development
BMET	Bureau of Manpower Employment and Training
BoP	Balance of Payments
CAR	Capital Adequacy Ratio
CD	Customs Duty
CMSME	Cottage, Micro, Small and Medium Enterprise
CPD	Centre for Policy Dialogue
CPI	Corruption Perceptions Index
CSR	Corporate Social Responsibility
DFID	Department for International Development
ECI	Export Concentration Index
EDF	Equity Development Fund
EEF	Equity Entrepreneurship Fund
EGHP	Employment Generation for Hardcore Poor
EGP	Employment Generation Programme
EGPP	Employment Generation Programme for the Poorest
EOI	Export-oriented Industrialisation
EPI	Expanded Programme of Immunization

ERP	Effective Rate of Protection
EU	European Union
EVI	Economic Vulnerability Index
FDI	Foreign Direct Investment
FFW	Food for Work
FI	Financial Inclusion
GCC	Gulf Cooperation Council
GDP	Gross Domestic Product
GFC	Global Financial Crisis
GNI	Gross National Income
GoB	Government of Bangladesh
GPI	Gender Parity Index
GR	Gratuitous Relief
GTZ	German Technical Cooperation Agency
HAI	Human Assets Index
HDI	Human Development Index
HEI	Highly Export-oriented (manufacturing) Industry
HHI	Herfindahl-Hirschman Index
HIES	Household Income and Expenditure Survey
HLPF	High-Level Political Forum
HPAE	High-performing Asian Economies
HPNSDP	Health, Population and Nutrition Sector Development Programme
HS	Harmonized System (of coding)
HYV	High-yielding Variety
ICOR	Incremental Capital–Output Ratio
ICRG	International Country Risk Guide
ICT	Information and Communications Technology
IDRC	International Development Research Centre
ILO	International Labour Organization
IMF	International Monetary Fund
InM	Institute of Microfinance
IRRI	International Rice Research Institute
ISI	Import-substituting Industrialisation
ISS	Informal Sector Survey
IT	Information Technology
LDC	Least Developed Country
LEI	Low Export-oriented (manufacturing) Industry
LFS	Labour Force Survey
LIC	Low-income Country
LMIC	Lower Middle-income Country
M&E	Monitoring and Evaluation
M2	Broad Money
MDG	Millennium Development Goal
MEI	Moderately Export-oriented (manufacturing) Industry
MFA	Multi Fibre Arrangement

MFI	Microfinance Institution
MFS	Mobile Financial Services
MGNREGA	Mahatma Gandhi National Rural Employment Guarantee Act
MIC	Middle-income Country
MLT	Medium- to Long-term
MoF	Ministry of Finance
MP	Member of Parliament
MPI	Multidimensional Poverty Index
MRA	Microcredit Regulatory Authority
NBR	National Board of Revenue
NGO	Non-government Organisation
NNP	National Nutrition Programme
NPL	Non-performing Loan
NSC	National Savings Certificate
NSD	National Savings Directorate
NSSS	National Social Security Strategy
ODA	Official Development Assistance
OLS	Ordinary Least Squares
OMS	Open Market Sales
OOP	Out-of-Pocket
PCB	Private Commercial Bank
PKSF	Palli Karma-Sahayak Foundation
POSH	Postponability of Social Change and Human Development
PPG	Pro-Poor Growth
PPP	Purchasing Power Parity
PRI	Policy Research Institute of Bangladesh
PRSP	Poverty Reduction Strategy Paper
PUSH	Political Unreadiness for Speedy Human Rights
RD	Regulatory Duty
REER	Real Effective Exchange Rate
RERMP	Rural Employment and Road Maintenance Programme
RM	Reserve Money
RMG	Readymade Garments
RMP	Rural Maintenance Programme
RNA	Rural Non-farm Activity
RNF	Rural Non-farm
ROSC	Reaching Out-of-School Children
RPO	Representation of the People's Order
RTI	Right to Information
RWG	Redistribution with Growth
SCB	State-owned Commercial Bank
SD	Supplementary Duty
SDG	Sustainable Development Goal
SME	Small and Medium-sized Enterprise
SMI	Survey of Manufacturing Industries

SPF	Social Protection Floor
SSA	Sub-Saharan Africa
SSNP	Social Safety Net Programme
TFP	Total Factor Productivity
TFR	Total Fertility Rate
TIB	Transparency International Bangladesh
TR	Test Relief
TTI	Total Tax Incidence
TUP	Targeted Ultra Poor
UK	United Kingdom
UMIC	Upper Middle-income Country
UN	United Nations
UNDP	United Nations Development Programme
US	United States
USD	United States Dollar
VAT	Value Added Tax
VGD	Vulnerable Group Development
VGF	Vulnerable Group Feeding
WDI	World Development Indicators
WEF	World Economic Forum
WGI	Worldwide Governance Indicators
WIDER	World Institute for Development Economics Research

Chapter 1
Inclusive Growth: Background Considerations and Key Themes

Muhammed Muqtada

Abstract The introductory chapter provides brief commentaries on the background issues that shed light on the rationale and design of the book. These background issues relate to an understanding of the evolving concerns of development planning in reducing poverty, unemployment and inequality. The study provides a summary account of three such regimes (viz. overwhelming faith in growth; changing the patterns of growth; and a focused pro-poor growth) and how the limitations of these have led analysts and development partners to seek an alternative inclusive growth strategy. Such a strategy depends not only on the traditional redistributive measures and access to opportunities, but also on social systems that safeguard job entitlements and ensure social security and participation. The study notes that as was true of past crises, the current economic upheaval following the COVID-19 pandemic has exposed the weaknesses of the social systems. This chapter lays out the book plan, and sketches an overview of the essays of the book whose themes are expected to contribute to the design of an inclusive growth strategy.

1.1 Evolving Significance of Social Inclusion in Development Planning

During the past two decades there has been a burgeoning literature on inclusive growth and its importance in development planning. This study attempts to provide an understanding of why there has been a growing attention to inclusive growth during this period, both at the conceptual and policy levels; what the crucial ingredients are in constituting inclusive growth; and how a strategy could be contoured to approach such a growth. These issues, which require some introspection and details, are treated in the various chapters of the study. The first part of this introduction is a synoptic

M. Muqtada (✉)
Development Economist; Formerly a Director in the Employment Sector of the International Labour Organization (ILO) Geneva and a Visiting Fellow,
Centre for Policy Dialogue, Dhaka, Bangladesh
e-mail: muqtada1@gmail.com

M. Muqtada (ed.), *Quest for Inclusive Growth in Bangladesh*,
South Asia Economic and Policy Studies,
https://doi.org/10.1007/978-981-15-7614-0_1

recapitulation of some of the background considerations, purported to provide a rationale and significance of the study, through brief reflections on themes that are associated with the evolving quest for inclusive growth. The second part of the chapter provides the book plan and a sneak peek into the various chapters, and thereby, an overview of the book.

It must be emphasised, unequivocally, that although the term *inclusive growth* was sparingly used in past development planning, there existed nonetheless programmes and policy measures that were intended to address particular issues and aspects of social inclusion. In particular, in the developing countries, in the post-colonial milieu of mass poverty, deprivation and dire shortfall in human capabilities, there has been a gradual introduction of diverse policies and strategies to balance economic growth with broader imperatives of human development. The extent and size of interventions varied according to the urgency of the issues and the resources at the disposal of individual countries. There was thus a perceptible growth of programmes and measures across the developing countries that were intended to achieve accelerated rate of poverty reduction and employment generation, beyond what growth was able to achieve on its own. These ranged from micro-level interventions to nationwide programmes, such as the well-known Mahatma Gandhi National Rural Employment Guarantee Act (MGNREGA) in India and Bolsa Familia in Brazil. In many countries, the non-government organisations (NGOs) played a major role in supporting incomes and entitlements of the poor, e.g. the Grameen Bank and BRAC in Bangladesh.[1] Unfortunately, these interventions, notwithstanding their merit and intention, were found inadequate, and often subordinated, to *growth-first* objective. Especially during the 1980s and 1990s, developing countries across the world were impelled to adopt stabilisation and structural adjustment measures that arguably tended to conditionalise a neo-liberal approach to growth. While some of these reforms helped countries to acquire fiscal and monetary discipline, drastic cuts in public expenditure and sectoral austerities inevitably led to the slowing down of pro-poor interventions, and to rising inequality and vulnerability. Subsequently, while growth resumed in many countries, there were growing concerns over the latter, nationally and internationally.[2] It may be argued that these were the precursors to an evolving emphasis and renewed pledge to equitable sharing and social inclusion, which found expression in national planning[3] as well as in international development fora.[4] As mentioned in the beginning, there has since been a surge in the literature on the urgency of inclusive growth, propelled further by an increasing critique, expressed by many influential thinkers, of a single-minded pursuit of gross domestic product (GDP) growth.[5]

---

[1] See for example, Khan (2015) for reflections on the relative importance of the NGOs in the success story of Bangladesh.

[2] See for example, the Copenhagen Declaration that was reached at the World Summit on Social Development, Copenhagen, 1995 (UN 1995).

[3] See for example, Dev (2010).

[4] See World Bank (2008).

[5] See for example, Stiglitz et al. (2019).

1.1.1 The Euphoria of Growthmanship

There has been for decades a universal tendency among countries, in both the developing and developed world, to pursue growth of GDP as the ultimate yardstick for measuring economic progress. It would be fair to suggest that ever since gaining independence from colonial rule, i.e. during the 1950s and 1960s, developing countries were, out of necessity, largely preoccupied with growth of the economy, the success of which was measured by the growth of GDP.

The primacy of economic growth in the development process has naturally led to the choice of per capita GDP as the most significant indicator of a country's growth and prosperity. It was assumed by analysts and practitioners that high growth of the total product would automatically raise the levels of living through the *trickle-down* mechanism. Even if the trickle-down process took time to have its anticipated effect, the goal of growthmanship was nevertheless considered desirable since there would eventually be a larger *cake* which could better address issues of relative and absolute poverty in developing countries. However, as the empirical literature unfolded, a larger cake did not always lead to a better or bigger slice for all, i.e. higher per capita growth did not equate with benefits of growth for all.

Besides, there exist a large body of literature which contends how and to what extent per capita GDP is an inadequate, often an inaccurate, measure of a nation's prosperity and progress.[6] After all, GDP is essentially a numerisation of all economic activities/transactions in an economy, and often fails to capture various activities carried out at the household level, or by unpaid family members, whose incidence is significant in the developing countries. Furthermore, it fails to capture the consumption and production biases that reinforce, and are influenced by, existing inequalities.

Although Kuznets and others acknowledged, as early as the 1930s, that a nation's well-being cannot be judged by simply measuring national income, the GDP indicator continued to rule supreme, especially with the Bretton Woods institutions giving primacy to growth in the post-World War II era.[7]

The presumption behind this overwhelming preoccupation is that GDP growth will generate jobs, reduce poverty and induce higher levels of living and welfare for a country's population. There are complex arguments, without necessarily a full conviction, on whether and how higher GDP would enhance welfare of the population. While GDP growth is a necessary and primary condition to achieve that, it is neither sufficient nor automatic.[8] Even within discourses on the successful growth

---

[6]Stiglitz et al. (2019).

[7]In 1990, the United Nations Development Programme (UNDP) launched its Human Development Index (HDI) as an alternative to per capita GDP, to monitor a country's development. The formulation of the index is attributed to Mahbub Ul Huq and Amartya Sen.

[8]Note, the 2030 Agenda for Sustainable Development also calls upon countries for a stepped-up growth of GDP (see Goal 8) to achieve higher employment and structural transformation. However, the targets and indicators of Sustainable Development Goals (SDGs) together provide an elaborate blueprint for what may be termed as sustainable and inclusive growth.

stories of the four Asian tigers, often dubbed as the Asian miracle countries, there remain unresolved debates on the relative roles of free markets and public interventions, and the policy details that allowed better productive and remunerative engagement of the workforce and relatively less inequality in these economies.[9]

While pursuit of higher GDP growth and wealth generation has generally concerned means and ends of material progress, enhancing prosperity enveloped broader concerns of well-being of the nation's people.[10] Sen (1983),[11] Stiglitz et al. (2019), among many others, have persistently argued how GDP fetishism has kept the planning focus away from crucial issues that enhance well-being, such as through addressing the crises of climate change, inequality and democratic institutions. Incidentally, these are also key goals of the 2030 Agenda for Sustainable Development. The wealth of nations and the well-being of population, are arguably inseparable (Acemoglu and Robinson 2013). The critical and unresolved question is to what extent policymakers can foster a relationship between the two to yield inclusive growth. During the past two decades, barring the global financial crisis period of 2008–2010, there has been substantial GDP growth in many developing countries, particularly in Asia; however, the many *elements* of what would constitute a good *economic performance*, or inclusive growth, received inadequate attention. If planning is fixated on narrow objectives (e.g. only GDP growth), the outcome is likely to be narrower than the objectives of inclusive growth.

1.1.2 Patterns of Growth

The optimism that greeted the output maximising strategy for development rested on "…the incorrect belief that rapid growth will be, broadly, and after time lags, at least proportionate in all sectors and income levels" (Stewart and Streeten 1976, p. 390). Country experiences have brought out diverse results; largely incomes have grown over time, often erratically, but poverty remained fairly high until the more recent decades. Thanks to the spurt of growth in some of the most populous countries (e.g. India, China, Bangladesh and Indonesia) where the incidence of poverty has declined rapidly, and which has substantially contributed to the overall decline in global poverty. The world *on average* has been able to meet the Millennium Development Goal (MDG) target of halving poverty incidence by 2015, although, as the evidence show, large variations exist among regions and among countries.

[9]See for example, World Bank (1993), Khan (2015).

[10]For a succinct view of the various paradigms, from old and new generations, on growth and development, see Meier (2001). Others have argued to look beyond the growth and development framework. Hamilton (2004) in fact writes powerfully not only on the need to abandon growth fetishism, but equally to reflect on *post-growth* societies.

[11]"Perhaps the most important thematic deficiency of traditional development economics is its concentration on national product, aggregate income and total supply of particular goods rather than on 'entitlements' of people and the 'capabilities' these entitlements generate" (Sen 1983, p. 754).

While extreme poverty has declined considerably, the living standard of the bottom 40% is actually declining.[12] Thus, while the average income grew steadily in some developing countries, most other experiences include a wide array of trajectories, involving unsteady and erratic performance in terms of average real income (Ranieri and Ramos 2013). Sub-Saharan Africa (SSA) as a region continues to register a high incidence of poverty, of more than 40% (World Bank 2018).

Given that growth on its own may not be enough to attain various development goals, and that growth can entail social costs, there was a shift of attention to *patterns of growth*, i.e. one that could simultaneously optimise economic and social benefits. The conventional wisdom has been that rising inequality would accompany, and be almost a necessary condition for, growth; and that high growth, in turn, following the logic of Kuznet's U-shaped growth-inequality curve, would subsequently moderate relative inequality and alleviate poverty. Much of the experiences of the developing countries show that growth generally has not necessarily produced a turning point beyond which the initial inequality trend has been reversed.[13] In fact Milanovic (2016) has argued that the growth–inequality relationship can be seen, instead of an established U-shaped curve, as *Kuznets waves*, i.e. a situation where inequality rises, falls, and rises, perhaps endlessly. Various studies have failed to establish any robust relationship between per capita GDP growth and inequality, implying that there may be various other factors that contribute to growing inequality, including structural factors.[14] Moreover, in various decomposition analyses, while poverty reduction has been attributed largely to the growth factor, a rising inequality appears to have adversely contributed, often significantly, to mitigation of poverty. This has invigorated further the debates on the distributional consequences of growth (see Chap. 2). In the subsequent development literature, inequality became a critical issue and considerable effort has gone into designing policies that could produce a more egalitarian growth pattern consistent with the existing socio-political framework of the individual countries. A major focus was on employment-intensive growth which was an important factor in the egalitarian growth among the East Asian countries.

It was during the 1970s that the inequality syndrome had started to emerge as a critical concern in development planning. The World Bank's *redistribution with growth* (RWG) strategy[15] could be seen as an important forerunner of a policy agenda that supported an *inclusion* campaign, i.e. one that tried to set a pattern of growth and not simply confined to state welfare programmes and transfers. As is well known, the RWG strategy focused on measures that could support an accelerated growth of income of the poorest quintile relative to the others, which, in turn, implied that the poor required access to assets of various sorts to generate a sustained flow of income. Such measures were deemed politically non-feasible, and failed to move the agenda forward since it required a major change in the existing asset-structure in the

[12]See World Bank (2018).

[13]See Ravallion (2001, 2005) among many others.

[14]See Piketty (2006). He contends that inequality was intrinsically related to policies and institutions that various governments undertook.

[15]See Chenery et al. (1974).

form of land reform and/or other forms of wealth redistribution. The RWG strategy and related policy discussions on egalitarian growth soon came to be relegated by the vigorous return to neo-liberal growth strategy, enforced by the introduction of stabilisation and structural adjustment reforms since the 1980s. The so-called counterrevolution period (1980s and 1990s) had its own value judgment, deeply embedded in the neo-liberal paradigm (Patnaik 2016), that sought to restore price and balance of payments stability. These reforms also saw a return to primacy of growth, and the *trickle-down* advocacy of distributive justice. Developing countries in particular had to adopt draconian measures to cut fiscal and current account deficits, which, at least initially, adversely affected employment and other social indicators. The revival of *trickle-down* approach to growth together with enforced fiscal austerity, not only shelved attention to equitable growth, but also failed to make marked improvements in the well-being of the poor.

1.1.3 Pro-poor Growth

The designing of pro-poor growth strategy is inherently an outgrowth of the discourses on the patterns of growth, and the concept gained momentum particularly during the 1990s, when the massive stabilisation reforms apparently failed to generate adequate growth and to reduce poverty. Intuitively, pro-poor growth is a focus on a pattern of growth that would bring clear benefits to the poor. The attention to pro-poor growth was significantly reinforced by the persistence of mass poverty during the 1990s.

One can observe two emerging and competing definitions of pro-poor growth. One is the *absolute definition*, whereby growth is considered to be pro-poor as long as the poor people benefit in absolute terms, as reflected in some agreed measure of poverty (Ravallion and Chen 2003). On one hand, this definition provides a straightforward conceptualisation which captures the most fundamental aspects of poverty, while on the other, it ignores the distributional aspects of income, which allows income of the wealthier to grow much more than that of the poor, and that further can cause a distributional shift carrying potential political-economic implications by dis-favouring the poor and possibly harnessing social problems affecting society at large.[16]

In contrast, the *relative definition* states that, growth is pro-poor if the incomes of poor people grow faster than those of the population as a whole, i.e. inequality declines. Different understanding of such relative improvement produced different versions of the definition. One of the versions states simply that the poor people's income needs to grow at a higher rate than that of the average income (White and Anderson 2001); others proposed a definition, whereby the more the redistribution associated with the growth (i.e. the greater the inequality effect), the more pro-poor growth it will be (Kakwani and Pernia 2000). Adding complexity to the debate, other

[16]See Chap. 2 for further details.

studies have incorporated non-income dimensions to the exercise of conceptualising and measuring pro-poor growth (Kakwani and Silber 2008). These also focus on the multidimensional aspects of poverty and incorporate measures that are seen as central to developing human capabilities (such as education, health, nutrition and general welfare) in the assessment of pro-poor growth. These are further treated in Chap. 2.

Alongside the emerging analytical literature on why and how growth needed to do more for the poor, various strategies and programmes at the country level were being designed. One such approach was labelled and promoted by the World Bank and other development partners as the Pro-Poor Growth (PPG) strategies.[17] The broad contention was that policy instruments would be geared towards ensuring that growth would be pro-poor, such that it reduced inequality. Furthermore, should there be a negative relationship between inequality and growth (as several influential experts have contended),[18] any reduction in inequality would foster growth in the long-run and set up a relatively egalitarian growth process.[19] Such measures would involve policies on productive and remunerative job growth as well as greater public policy attention. These were intended to go beyond simple pro-poor public interventions to exploring avenues where the poor could benefit from and *participate* in the growth process.[20] Besides pro-poor policies, the PPG strategy would also include programme interventions with varying targets and resource bases. These can have various objectives, such as those entailed in MGNREGA in India, Bolsa Familia in Brazil or other conditional and unconditional cash transfers that are linked to strengthening the poor's entitlements. These strategies thus make a distinction between static reduction of income inequality and raising the growth of income of the poor. The latter takes the form of providing investment resources to the poor (e.g. protection against dis-savings; better education, health as well as employment entitlements, etc.) that can support a relatively permanent source of income. It must be noted that major pro-poor interventions during the late 1990s and subsequent period (e.g. Poverty Reduction Strategy Papers (PRSPs)) measures brought about a significant reduction in global poverty, although even until 2015, nearly 735 million people were estimated to be living below the World Bank threshold of USD 1.90 per day (measured in 2011 Purchasing Power Parity (PPP) terms).[21] On the other hand, intra-country inequality has remained stubbornly high, or increasing.[22] Nevertheless, the PPG strategies were intended to provide significant attention to the poor, and were arguably the early attempts in recognising the significance and possibilities of inclusive growth.

---

[17] See World Bank (2005).

[18] See for example, Milanovic (2016).

[19] Bourguignon (2004).

[20] See World Bank (2005).

[21] World Bank (2018).

[22] Cf. Milanovic (2016).

1.1.4 Inclusive Growth and the Employment Approach

The discourses on the various patterns of growth indicate common concerns over the unsatisfactory trends in the *quality* of growth, especially in emphasising that growth by itself will not automatically reduce inequality and vulnerability in the economy, and that public action and interventions are needed.

It is not surprising that the starting point of inclusive growth, according to several recent studies, is the need to address inequality, primarily to increase the poor's share in the benefits of growth. Reducing inequality was also likely to have a favourable impact on poverty alleviation. There are serious debates on how far enhancing the share of income/benefits of the poor could be done and through what policies and reforms, viewing that growth itself, in the recent period was largely associated with growing inequality. During the past two decades, individual studies and analysts and international organisations floated arguments and issues regarding the conceptualisation and practice of inclusive growth. In these, some of the emphases has been on broadening the perceptions on poverty and inequality, especially on their multi-dimensionalities. For instance, South Asian countries have done well to reduce poverty incidence by the USD 1.90 per day threshold (12.4% in 2015),[23] but relative deprivation and vulnerability are increasing.[24]

Furthermore, a significant contention in the literature with regard to inclusive growth is on how to ensure participation of *all classes* of people, both in the *outcome*, as well as the in *process* of growth. The present study contends that, for the underprivileged, the outcome and process dimensions are interrelated. Should growth lead to expansion of work opportunities, there must not only be the means to gain access to these opportunities (e.g. education, skills and jobs), but also in ensuring their participation and rights at work. A fair participation and voice of the poor in the process of inclusive growth, in turn, can hardly be ensured without appropriate reforms of institutions and governance structure.[25] The concepts and characterisation of inclusive growth are further detailed in Chap. 2.

A key concern in the discourses on inclusive growth, irrespective of the varying shades of opinion, is the objective of seeking a meaningful balance between growth and human well-being. In the post-World War II period, the United Kingdom (UK), and subsequently other advanced economies, moved towards a commitment to building a full employment society, which can be arguably seen as a precursor of inclusive growth, and which also ushered in stepped up public action, state welfarism and related institutional reforms. Moreover, historically, countries which have successfully eradicated poverty are also largely the ones that have attained full employment or near full employment.[26] The significance of full employment goal as a key mechanism to ensure inclusive growth, in both developed and developing countries, is aptly recognised as a major goal of the 2030 Agenda. In an inclusive

[23]World Bank (2018).

[24]See Chap. 2 of this volume.

[25]See Sobhan (2010) on structural flaws in governance structure in South Asian countries.

[26]The advanced economies as well as the East Asian emerging economies are cases in point.

growth pursuit, it is important to note that productive, remunerative employment not only tends to alleviate poverty and inequality (Atkinson 2015),[27] but can also potentially foster participation and empowerment of the jobless and/or vulnerable population. The present study perceives employment as a central metric of inclusive growth, as well as a catalyst for achieving many of its diverse elements.[28]

Incidentally, the 2030 Agenda provides a guidance and a pathway towards a more inclusive and equal world for the future generations, committed to its central pledge of tackling inequality and envisaging a world where opportunities and benefits will be more equitably distributed among the population. One must note that the SDG Agenda is a sequel to the MDGs which were framed by the United Nations (UN) to apply greater attention and resources for the upliftment of crucial social indicators, the lacunae of which are particularly exposed during various crises. The current COVID-19 pandemic has truly done so, especially exposing, in many countries, the blatant inequality, vulnerability and lack of any meaningful social protection. The 2030 SDG Agenda, and a call to pursuing inclusive growth, has become even more relevant.

1.1.5 Inclusive Growth, the COVID-19 Pandemic and Economic Crises

The ongoing pandemic is an unprecedented phenomenon, one that has already taken more lives than any other catastrophe, natural or man-made, since World War II.[29] It has compelled countries to undertake draconian measures to lock down people and economic activities, apparently to prevent transmission of the virus through social distancing. Both through the supply-side disruptions and demand-side shocks, these measures have had severe cascading effects, with sharp contractions in output and a surge in the incidence of unemployment, poverty and vulnerability. The International Monetary Fund (IMF) in its recent estimates has projected that global growth during 2020 will decline to (−) 3%, with advanced economies declining to (−) 6%.[30] Such contractions have already led to enormous deterioration in unemployment and working conditions. According to the International Labour Organization (ILO), there has already been a 10.7% loss in working hours during the second quarter of 2020, an equivalent of 305 million jobs.[31] In Bangladesh, the numbers of new poor have swelled, and according to some initial estimates, poverty incidence

[27]For an analysis of empirical studies on the employment–poverty nexus, see Khan (2005).

[28]See Chap. 2.

[29]At the time of writing this, more than 50 million people have been infected globally by the COVID-19 virus, and over 1.25 million people have already died.

[30]IMF (2020).

[31]Cf. ILO (2020).

has likely increased from the existing 20.5% to nearly 35%.[32] The pandemic has further brought to the fore the rising inequality and increased vulnerability of not only those below the poverty threshold, but also huge numbers hovering above the poverty line.[33] Countries are currently engaged in assessing the damages to lives and livelihoods, and have embarked on unprecedented stimulus packages[34] to support income/security for the vulnerable, and to help businesses to restart.

It must be noted that the COVID-19 virus is still raging on and new infections are continuing to rise, for which impact assessments of the depth of the crisis and the required policy and resource management are in a fluid state. While the impact of the pandemic on lives and livelihoods has been sudden, and in many countries overwhelming, it has also brought to fore the inherent weaknesses of the social safety systems, such as coordinated transfer programmes to cushion livelihoods in times of crises, health insurance, etc. These have been most pronounced in developing countries where the informal sector is very large, and where social systems have received inadequate attention despite growth and prosperity over the past years. The pandemic is, in effect, a wake-up call for a thorough review of policy and institutional measures, which if appropriately designed, can cushion the population against joblessness, vulnerability and insecurity. It is usually during big crises that planners are reminded of an economy's weak framework, conditions of jobs and entitlements, and the need to build up institutions to ensure social protection. Starting with the Great Depression to the global financial crisis of 2008–09, crises have reminded countries of the need for such a social system, including the progression to a full employment society and social inclusion. Now, the COVID-19 pandemic, with its severe impacts on economic and social indicators, is underlining the significance of inclusive growth once again.

1.2 The Plan and an Overview of the Book

1.2.1 A Case Study on Bangladesh

The study proposes to take Bangladesh as a case study to reflect how far a country with considerable economic growth can potentially help achieve social and human development, and yet may fall well short of an inclusive growth. Bangladesh, during the recent past, has made enormous strides with respect to economic growth. From being an economy of only USD 37.9 billion in 1995, its GDP has grown more than nine-folds in 2019, and it has scaled up to 39th position in the global GDP

---

[32]For estimates regarding Bangladesh, see CPD (2020); for alternative assessments see Osmani (2020).

[33]Ibid.

[34]Stimulus packages announced so far range from a whopping 21% of GDP in Japan, to 3.7% of GDP in Bangladesh.

ranking.[35] Nevertheless, growth has not been equitable and vast numbers of the population are still in extreme poverty. Inequality has risen continuously during the past two decades and various groups and regions have become increasingly more vulnerable. This experience demonstrates the oversight in the pursuit of inclusive growth since a significant proportion of the population remains prone to chronic and transient poverty resulting from external shocks and adverse fluctuations in income. This oversight is founded in the failure to address the inequitable distribution of economic and political resources across the nation (Sobhan 2010). Furthermore, reforms of institutions and governance structures have had little favourable impact on the underprivileged classes to gain access to public goods and participation (Sen 1999). The current pandemic which has led to severe economic downturns has also exposed the fragile nature of the social protection and social delivery systems.[36]

There are hardly any empirical study focused specifically on inclusive growth in Bangladesh, although studies exist on individual elements that are used to indicate inclusive growth. In fact, this study would likely be among the first forays on the subject in the context of Bangladesh. To this end, the study charts out a strategy for operationalising inclusive growth with specific reference to Bangladesh. It provides an eminent case study where the chapters are designed to address the key analytical and policy issues of such a strategy.

1.2.2 Some Considerations

There has been in the recent times a flurry of interest, both among national and international practitioners and a burgeoning literature on the urgency of designing an inclusive growth strategy. However, no clear definition or characterisations exist that are universally accepted, though there is consensus on some core goals (see Chap. 2). Meanwhile, countries across the world have vigorously embarked on the UN's 2030 Agenda, which with its panoply of goals and targets, promises a path to inclusive and sustainable growth.[37] Several countries, like Bangladesh, have integrated the Agenda into their national development and budget plans. However, the Agenda does not distinguish priorities, and relies on the individual countries to design and implement strategies to attain these goals and targets. While, regarding the latter, a degree of ambivalence will continue to exist and to give rise to debates, the present study contends that priorities have to be chosen in a pragmatic manner that, given constraints of time and resources, are likely to register the maximum impact. The present study also argues that such priorities are best profiled at the national level. The book explores the currently held perceptions on inclusive growth, in an attempt

[35]This is according to IMF database.

[36]See CPD (2020), Osmani (2020).

[37]The 2030 Agenda, which includes 17 SDGs and 169 indicators that are purported to foster inclusive growth, does not indicate which ones, at what pace of progress, would indeed affirm progress toward inclusive growth.

to delimit what it is that ensures tangible progress toward inclusive growth. In this context, the book draws on the implicit inclusive growth narrative of the UN's 2030 Agenda that is best pursued through selected goals, particularly Goal 8 (*promote sustained, inclusive and sustainable economic growth, full and productive employment and decent work for all*)—and provides a rationale why full employment should ideally be a central yardstick for measuring and monitoring progress towards inclusive growth. This goal is critically affiliated to several other SDGs, related, inter alia, to growth and transformation; reduction of hunger, extreme poverty, unemployment and inequality; social protection; inclusionary governance and institutions.

The study argues for a rethink of traditional policies, and provides arguments and ways to reorient these towards inclusive growth and better social inclusion. These involve a dedicated focus on employment and inclusion in the design of macroeconomic policies, such as monetary and fiscal policies; trade and industrial policies; policies towards rural non-farm (RNF) employment; social protection and safety net strategy; and finally, in the nature of institutional and governance reforms which are imperative for ensuring better social inclusion, especially through enhancing participation of the underprivileged in the growth process. These essays would, admittedly, not provide a comprehensive inclusive growth strategy, but show approaches to building one.

1.2.3 The Themes: An Overview

The themes of the chapters are selective and are interrelated; yet each chapter has its particular rationale, and methodologies, findings and conclusions. In lieu of a concluding essay in this study, the following provides an overview of the key issues and findings of the individual chapters. In fact, the chapters can be read as independent standalone essays, which, at the same time, share issues and evidence that reinforce the contentions of the volume on inclusive growth strategy. The ongoing COVID-19 pandemic and its impact are certain to affect many of the issues discussed in this study. However, given that data and assessments are in a fluid state, the chapters, where relevant, attempt to provide some tentative observations. The themes of the chapters are the following.

The Quest for an Inclusive Growth Strategy. This essay traces some of the antecedent factors that has led to the emergence of inclusive growth; reviews the growing literature and debates on concepts, contextualising these for pragmatic policy-making such as the need to factor in structural factors and multidimensionality of poverty and inequality; puts out a rationale for the full employment as a central running theme in an inclusive growth strategy; and based on the above, sums up seven priority goals, and provides the contours of an inclusive growth strategy.

The chapter analyses some of the conceptual nuances of the definitions and/or characterisations of inclusive growth, and argues these may not be adequate to capture ground realities. Furthermore, some may reflect variants of earlier concepts of growth and redistribution, such as expansion of and access to opportunities. An important recognition in the study is the involvement of all classes in *outcome* and *process* dimensions of inclusive growth, which warrants that the underprivileged acquire voice and participation. The study contends that the latter, which would require key governance and institutional reforms, needs to be factored in defining inclusive growth.

The chapter also provides a brief discourse on the trade-offs in the well-known poverty–growth–inequality nexus. While growth may be considered *good for the poor* (Dollar and Kraay 2002), the study cites several conceptual and empirical work to suggest that reducing inequality would not only lower further the poverty incidence, but is good for growth. Some argue that *inequality-averse growth* is feasible (Khan 2015), and that growth and equality, with appropriate policies, could also be seen as complements (Stiglitz 2016). In this context, the causalities and multidimensionalities of inequality and poverty are important and need to be further explored.

The study provides a rationale for conceptualising full employment as a central and running theme in the pursuit of inclusive growth, and states a few interrelated goals which are also among the major goals of the 2030 Agenda. While promoting an inclusive growth strategy would require multiple policy interventions, the book calls for a careful articulation of policy priorities, and refrains from a comprehensive approach that would obfuscate the relative weights of the goals and related policies. Hence, the emphasis of the book is on *approaches* to inclusive growth. These approaches, which are considered as policy priorities and form key themes of the chapters, are subsumed within a simple strategy framework.

Inclusive Growth in Bangladesh: Evidence and Issues. The study provides a thorough and independent examination of whether and how far the rapid growth in Bangladesh has been inclusive in nature. During the past two decades Bangladesh has been growing relatively quite rapidly; in fact, lately, the growth of Bangladesh in terms of per capita GDP has been among the highest in the world. Equally, there has been strong progress in selected social indicators, such as life expectancy, fertility rates, infant mortality and gender parity in primary and secondary school enrolment. The severe economic downturn caused by the ongoing pandemic has not only disrupted progress on the above, but has brought on additional challenges of addressing the massive new poverty, unemployment and vulnerability, especially in the informal sector. The duration of the epidemic and its continuing adverse effects are still unknown, but what appears clear is that a well-defined active labour market and social protection policy could better cushion and support the vulnerable groups during crises.

The essay explores how far growth in Bangladesh has been inclusive, in both comparative as well as in intertemporal terms. Following what the study considers as critical goals and pillars of inclusive growth (viz. poverty and inequality, growth and structural transformation, employment, access to infrastructure and public services, health and education, gender equality, and governance and institutions), this chapter provides a detailed empirical enquiry into Bangladesh's progress on inclusive growth by tracking various proximate indicators for each goal. Selected countries of South and Southeast Asia are used to gauge the relative strength of this performance. In this context, it also constructs an *inclusive growth index* with reference to these goals and indicators that are significantly associated with an employment-focused approach to inclusive growth.

The above approach, i.e. intertemporal and comparative, allows one to identify which indicators need to be improved, and hence, to reprioritise policy options. Thus, evidently Bangladesh has grown impressively in terms of its GDP growth, but it has not, comparatively speaking, brought about desired structural transformation. The empirical trends of some of the indicators, e.g. share of manufacturing in total employment, share of private investment, or growth in agricultural productivity have lagged behind those observed in the comparator countries. Similarly, while headcount poverty has declined appreciably, the rate of poverty reduction has been slower than its peer countries. One indicator, viz. public expenditure on social protection is among the lowest in the group of countries, which could be a partial explanatory factor. Moreover, inequality and vulnerability (the reduction of which is a key measure of inclusive growth) is rising consistently during the past decade and half.

Regarding the other goals, Bangladesh has performed reasonably well in enhancing gender parity, especially in primary and secondary school enrolment. Nevertheless, serious concerns exist on other indicators of gender parity, especially wages disparity and lower women's share in wage-employment, etc. Various indicators of governance show that the economy is beset with high levels of corruption and various other governance deficits.

The intertemporal and comparative pattern of the estimates on a large number of indicators provide a sobering assessment of the relative progress of Bangladesh towards the seven goals. The chapter constructs a composite *inclusive growth index*, in which Bangladesh has shown average performance, but has consistently lagged behind India, Sri Lanka and Vietnam. The chapter, with its elaborate empirical findings, provides the key rationale of the book and the platform to deliberate upon themes intrinsically tied to inclusive growth.

Macroeconomic Policy, Price Stability and Inclusive Growth. This essay argues that macroeconomic policy must be in the forefront of a pursuit of inclusive growth. During the past two decades, the economy of Bangladesh achieved a fairly substantial and steady growth in GDP. This was also a period which witnessed, apart from the global financial period of 2008–09, an almost uninterrupted stretch of macroeconomic stability. This chapter examines the past growth-stability trends, and observes that, generally, a conservative macroeconomic policy stance, supported by some fortuitous circumstances, helped Bangladesh to keep budget and current account deficits as well as debt–GDP ratio well-below internationally recognised threshold levels.

Although macroeconomic stability has helped Bangladesh to maintain a growth momentum, there are key challenges ahead to pursue an inclusive growth strategy as pledged in the Seventh Five Year Plan (7FYP). In particular, the following challenges are pointed out: (i) how to step up private investment, which has remained sluggish during the recent past; (ii) in view of planned growth targets to attain status of an upper middle-income country (UMIC) by 2031, how to sustain price stability while maintaining expected high-growth momentum, and accommodating concomitant rise in demand for public services; (iii) the need for reorienting macroeconomic policy framework towards its broader objectives, especially to reduce unemployment, inequality and vulnerability as part of its commitment to inclusive growth and the 2030 Agenda; (iv) the need for effecting structural transformation through a pattern of growth embodying the goal of full, productive employment that would facilitate labour to move to more productive manufacturing and services sector. It is contended that the macroeconomic policy-making would require a rethink in order to meet the above challenges.[38]

To this intent, the paper explores the critical role of monetary, fiscal, external and financial inclusion policies, and contends that a relatively more expansionary monetary and fiscal stance would be needed towards stepped-up investment, job growth and reduction of inequality and vulnerability. The existing monetary policy needs to move beyond its overwhelming preoccupation in containing price stability, and support greater financial deepening and financial inclusion initiatives. Similarly, the fiscal stance has to move out of its existing disconcertingly low revenue–expenditure equilibrium, and seek greater fiscal space to deliver growing imperatives of structural change and social inclusion.

Growth of Manufacturing Employment in the Changing Context of Trade and Trade-Related Policies. This chapter, and the next, are two essays in this book that focus on two key sectors which have the potential to generate employment and incomes significantly: manufacturing and RNF. This chapter focuses on the impact of the manufacturing sector on the generation of productive employment, and the support provided by trade policies towards industrialisation and export. The analysis of government policies reveal that focus has been largely on fostering trade-led growth of the manufacturing sector, which would contribute to employment generation, almost on a similar strategy adopted in some East and Southeast Asian countries. In Bangladesh, the Five Year Plans, industrial policy, export policy and import policy orders, small and medium-sized enterprise (SME) policy, etc. have more or less similar objectives in terms of labour-intensive and export-oriented industrialisation. Using both aggregate and sub-industry-level manufacturing data, the chapter provides some insights on the broad outcomes (and deviations from intended effects) of various trade-related policies.

---

[38]There are several leading analysts who have advocated alternative perceptions of macroeconomic policy framework to promote a job-centred approach to inclusion that would reduce inequality and vulnerability. See among others, Stiglitz et al. (2006), Bhaduri (2019). "For an alternative macroeconomic policy paradigm, the defining issue for more equitable and inclusive development requires viewing output growth as the outcome of decentralized high employment growth, rather than employment growth as the outcome of high output growth" (Bhaduri 2019, p. 235).

The chapter follows the analytical frame proposed by Jenkins and Sen (2006) under which trade affects manufacturing employment in three ways: (a) impact on output of the manufacturing sector, thereby positively impacting employment (called *scale effect*); (b) rise in output of exportables by replacing output of importables, thereby positively contributing to employment (called *composition effect*); and (c) changes in labour coefficients within industries, thereby positively impacting employment (called *process effect*).

The chapter further categorises the manufacturing sector into highly export-oriented industries (HEIs); moderately export-oriented industries (MEIs); and low export-oriented or domestic-market-oriented industries (LEIs). The empirical exercises show that HEIs comprise both labour- and capital-intensive industries, and growth in employment in both categories of industries has been relatively high. In case of MEIs, growth in employment is largely low, except in electrical equipment and other manufacturing industries which are labour-intensive. In contrast, the employment performance in different labour- and capital-intensive industries under LEIs is mixed. The chapter essentially contends that overall, trade (i.e. export-orientation) influences employment in both labour and capital-intensive industries through a *combined* effect of *size*, *composition* and *process* related to trade. However, impact of non-trade-related issues on growth in employment, particularly in a few domestic-market-oriented industries, needs further analysis.

A major critique of government policy support is that selected products under different sub-sectors, whether domestic-market-oriented or export-oriented is largely influenced by different pressure groups, which affect the rationality and the efficacy of the support mechanism. In other words, given the limited scope of public expenditure in Bangladesh, these biased support to some sub-sectors deprive various other important sub-sectors which might have a higher potential to contribute to export and employment. The chapter thus argues that the existing protection/support framework has not necessarily been job creating, and that more support needs to be provided to small and medium industries. Hence, it would be necessary to recalibrate tariff regime to remove anti-export bias, and simultaneously support industries with high employment and/or their productivity prospects.

In the backdrop of different kinds of market failures and problems of governance, the choice of policies with regard to enhancing employment should be well-calibrated with policy priorities to increase productivity and export with appropriate emphasis on both domestic-market- and export-oriented industries. Attempts to create *exports at any cost* or to overly protect domestic industries are likely to engender policy biases, rent-seeking and corruption. Bangladesh would need to explore its own *golden mean*.

Alternative Approaches to Full Employment in Bangladesh: Role of the Non-farm Sector. In Bangladesh, the agriculture sector continues to be saddled with high surplus labour (largely in the form of underemployment), while it is the services sector which has grown the fastest, and in most cases accounts for the bulk of employment growth. On the contrary, the growth in the share of employment in industry/manufacturing (implicitly marking transfer of labour from agriculture to industry), has been relatively low, contrary to growth patterns predicted by Clark-Fisher hypothesis. There is thus widespread scepticism on how far, and how quickly, Bangladesh economy could productively absorb its large pool of surplus labour, and attain full employment. In this context, and following Ranis and Stewart (1993), the chapter reengages in, and examines the potential role of rural non-farm activity (RNA), at least in overcoming rural unemployment and underemployment, as it did in the case of some East Asian countries.

This chapter, with all the limitations and caveats of available data, explores the extent and pattern of RNA growth in Bangladesh, its impact on jobs and incomes, as well as on labour market formations. The study argues that RNF activities and employment, though always a significant feature of the rural economy of Bangladesh, have vastly increased in importance in the recent two decades; e.g. the share of non-farm employment increased from around 37% in 2000 to more than 48% during 2016–17. More recent studies and evidence on the growth of RNA continue to support such a contention. Employment in non-farm which was growing around 8% till the 1990s (Hossain et al. 1994), maintained its growth momentum during the subsequent decades. The broad and limited data on the relevant indicators suggest a fairly distinct upward trend in the growth of non-farm enterprises and employment.

The chapter notes that rapid changes in pace and pattern of RNA have also been reflected in labour market structure and mobility. Estimates show that there has been distinctly positive increase in average employment size of rural enterprises; growth in permanent enterprises; marked increase in the incidence of the *employer* and *own account worker* categories. More significantly, a striking feature of the changes in occupational structure is the changing patterns of women participation in the rural economy. The study contends that changes in rural labour market are often not reflected as structural change due to the presence of informality within the three traditional sectors.

The chapter further explores pathways to enhance RNF employment and assesses the prospects of reaching full employment. The potential of three such pathways are examined: increase in agricultural productivity; rise in RNF productivity and earnings; changing patterns of household income and demand for RNF goods and services. To realise the full potential of RNA towards a possible rural full employment, Bangladesh would require a comprehensive policy framework and coordinated strategy that could enhance growth of higher productivity jobs, household incomes and aggregate demand.

Role of Social Protection in Ensuring Inclusive Growth in Bangladesh. The inadequate growth of productive, remunerative jobs, noted in various chapters above, and the consequent slack in the labour market, have given way to economic and social insecurity in Bangladesh, especially in the informal sector. Hence, since 1971, when Bangladesh was in the grip of mass poverty, deprivation and famine, there emerged a plethora of anti-poverty programmes and multi-pronged measures directed towards disaster rehabilitation and towards creating income and employment opportunities. Subsequently, these evolved into social safety net programmes (SSNPs) which till today are continuing to grow sporadically at local, regional and national levels.

There is very scant information in Bangladesh on the precise impact of SSNPs on the various dimensions of inclusive growth, such as on growth and structural transformation, inequality and poverty. In broad average national terms, it has been observed that the extent of per household benefits from SSNPs has been pretty small, and in some cases negligible (Osmani 2014). Yet at the local level, specific programmes with proper targeting and implementation have produced tangible results, especially in relation to alleviating poverty and hunger.

The chapter points out a number of shortcomings of the SSNPs in Bangladesh. Among these, the most commonly observed are the inadequacy of allocation, weaknesses in targetting, leakages, lack of coordination among the implementing agencies, high administrative costs and inefficiencies, and absence of any impact evaluation framework. Many of these programmes do not have concrete targets, or detailed exit strategies for beneficiaries. Tackling error, fraud, and corruption in social protection programmes of Bangladesh is difficult since none of these terms are clearly defined in the first place; only a few merit expansion and consolidation. For example, the initiation of Employment Generation for Hardcore Poor (EGHP) in FY2009–10, a flagship SSNP in continuation of 100-day Employment Generation Programme (EGP), has been a significant step towards a more focused and targetted attention to providing employment to the poorest section of the society. The study argues that this programme, modified along the MGNREGA in India, could provide a quasi-social security to a vast number of underemployed and vulnerable people.

A total, systematic and coordinated approach to social security is yet to evolve—a primary reason being the extent to which fiscal space can be extended to accommodate a universal system of social security and a pension scheme. Equally, there exists the formidable challenge of extending social protection to the vast informal economy workers, which is likely to create dualism in the social protection system. For the *informal* sector, there are various programmes, of varying scale and coverage, both within the framework of government budget and NGO support.

The chapter argues in favour of creating a framework and a process to build a social protection floor (SPF), through identification and categorisation of the needs and priorities of social assistance and insurance. The recently developed National Social Security Strategy (NSSS) presents such a potential mechanism according to different life-cycle groups. The chapter contends that the current SSNPs, and the entire gamut of transfer programmes which lack a framework, must be closely reviewed on an NSSS-coordinated platform. One needs to balance priorities to address and build on processes that would reinforce the SPF goals, and move the NSSS framework towards targetted universal goals, and less contingent on random discretionary SSNPs.

Governance, Growth and Social Inclusion. This chapter brings together further reflections on the critical importance of governance and institutions in attaining inclusive growth (Chap. 2), especially in addressing what Sen (1999) refers to as lack of economic choices, protection and de facto political rights. The chapter explores and emphasises the need for urgent attention to some critical aspects of governance which are likely to pose threats and challenges to future growth, and to prospects of social inclusion. This paper examines trends in some of the widely-accepted governance indicators in Bangladesh, based on the Worldwide Governance Indicators (WGI) database on six broad dimensions of governance (Kaufmann et al. 2005) which include: *voice and accountability*, *political stability and absence of violence*, *government effectiveness*, *regulatory quality*, *rule of law* and *control of corruption*. Estimates on each of these indicators, except political stability, show a deterioration, or at best a stagnation, over time. In particular, low voice and accountability and rule of law are likely to be associated with rise in rent-seeking and corruption (Sobhan 2010), and which have contributed to unequal sharing of income. The chapter also explores the governance–growth relationship, and observes that overall, the per capita GDP growth has hardly influenced the governance ranking in any significant way, nor has governance score, which has remained low and largely unchanged, thus far affected per capita growth. The chapter, however, argues that, in the long-run, low governance indicators (especially *rule of law*) are likely to increase transaction costs that could significantly affect growth of private investment.

In the context of social inclusion, the chapter argues that improving governance and institutions is critical, as emphasised in the SDG 16 of the 2030 Agenda. In particular, in order to foster social inclusion, governance would require additional considerations beyond the traditional indicators and goals of inclusive growth. The study contends that this would imply better progress in the dispensation of rights, representation and rule of law. These could facilitate the participation of the under-privileged in a process of inclusive growth, and thereby in its outcomes (see Chap. 2). While this is tall order, the paper contends that these can be pursued, perhaps in small measures, through for example, choosing the "wrongs and rights in development" (Sen 1995).[39] In this context, the chapter suggests, by way of examples, three measures: potentially feasible redistributive measures; empowering the poor through, inter alia, employment and decent work; expanding public policy and public goods such that inclusion is not handicapped by market failures.

References

Acemoglu, D., & Robinson, J. E. (2013). *Why nations fail: The origins of power, prosperity and poverty*. London: Profile Books Ltd.

Atkinson, A. B. (2015). *Inequality: What can be done?* London: Harvard University Press.

Bhaduri, A. (2019). Macroeconomic perspective on development. In D. Nayyar (Ed.), *Asian transformations: An inquiry into the development of nations* (pp. 216–239). Oxford: Oxford University Press.

Bourguignon, F. (2004, February 4). The poverty-growth-inequality triangle. Paper presented at the Indian Council for Research on International Economic Relations, New Delhi, India.

Chenery, H., Ahluwalia, M. S., Bell, C. L. G., Duloy, J. H., & Jolly, R. (1974). *Redistribution with growth*. Oxford: Oxford University Press.

CPD. (2020, June 7). *Challenges of policymaking in times of pandemics: State of the Bangladesh Economy in FY2020*. Issue paper prepared for a virtual media briefing, organised by the Centre for Policy Dialogue (CPD), Dhaka, Bangladesh.

[39]This is taken from the title of the article Sen (1995).

Dev, S. M. (2010). *Inclusive growth in India: Agriculture, poverty and human development*. New Delhi: Oxford University Press.

Dollar, D., & Kraay, A. (2002). Growth is good for the poor. *Journal of Economic Growth, 7*, 195–225.

Hamilton, C. (2004). *Growth fetish*. London: Pluto Press.

Hossain, M., Rahman, M., & Bayes, A. (1994). *Rural non-farm economy in Bangladesh: A dynamic sector or a sponge of absorbing surplus labour*. New Delhi: International Labour Organization (ILO)/South Asia Multidisciplinary Advisory Team (SAAT).

ILO. (2020). *ILO Monitor: COVID-19 and the world of work* (4th edn.). Geneva: International Labour Organization (ILO).

IMF. (2020). *World Economic Outlook, April 2020: The great lockdown*. Washington, DC: International Monetary Fund (IMF).

Jenkins, R., & Sen, K. (2006). International trade and manufacturing employment in the South: Four country case studies. *Oxford Development Studies, 34*(3), 299–322.

Kakwani, N., & Pernia, E. (2000). What is pro-poor growth? *Asian Development Review: Studies of Asian and Pacific Economic Issues, 18*(1), 1–16.

Kakwani, N., & Silber, J. (2008). Introduction: Multidimensional poverty analysis: Conceptual issues, empirical illustrations, and policy implications. *World Development, 36*(6), 987–991.

Kaufmann, D., Kraay, A., & Mastruzzi, M. (2005). *Governance Matters IV: Governance indicators for 1996–2004*. World Bank Policy Research Working Paper 3630. Washington, DC: The World Bank.

Khan, A. R. (2005). *Growth, employment and poverty: An analysis of the vital nexus based on some recent UNDP and ILO/SIDA studies*. Issues in Employment and Poverty Discussion Paper 19. Geneva: International Labour Organization (ILO).

Khan, A. R. (2015). *The economy of Bangladesh: A quarter century of development*. Basingstoke: Palgrave Macmillan UK.

Meier, G. M. (2001). The old generation of development economists and the new. In G. M. Meier & J. E. Stiglitz (Eds.), *Frontiers of development economics* (pp. 13–50). Washington, DC: The World Bank and Oxford University Press.

Milanovic, B. (2016). *Global inequality: A new approach for the age of globalization*. Cambridge, USA: Harvard University Press.

Osmani, S. R. (2014). *Designing social protection for the rural poor: Learning from lessons on the ground*. InM Working Paper No. 31. Dhaka: Institute of Microfinance (InM).

Osmani, S. R. (2020). *Coping with COVID: The case of Bangladesh*. Dhaka: BRAC Institute of Governance and Development (BIGD). Mimeo.

Patnaik, P. (2016, January 17). Growth through redistribution. *People's democracy*.

Piketty, T. (2006). The Kuznets curve: Yesterday and tomorrow. In A. V. Banerjee, R. Bénabou, & D. Mookherjee (Eds.), *Understanding poverty* (pp. 63–72). Oxford: Oxford University Press.

Ranieri, R., & Ramos, R. A. (2013). *Inclusive growth: Building up a concept*. IPC-IG Working Paper No. 104. Brasília: International Policy Centre for Inclusive Growth (IPC-IG).

Ranis, G., & Stewart, F. (1993). Rural nonagricultural activities in development: Theory and application. *Journal of Development Economics, 40*(1), 75–101.

Ravallion, M. (2001). Growth, inequality and poverty: Looking behind the averages. *World Development, 29*(11), 1803–1815.

Ravallion, M. (2005). *Inequality is bad for the poor*. Policy Research Working Paper Series 3677. Washington, DC: The World Bank.

Ravallion, M., & Chen, S. (2003). Measuring pro-poor growth. *Economics Letters, 78*(1), 93–99.

Sen, A. (1983). Development: Which way now? *The Economic Journal, 93*(December), 745–762.

Sen, A. (1995, October 20). Wrongs and rights in development. *Prospect*.

Sen, A. (1999). *Development as freedom*. Oxford: Oxford University Press.

Sobhan, R. (2010). *Challenging the injustice of poverty: Agendas for inclusive development in South Asia*. New Delhi: Sage Publications.

Stewart, F., & Streeten, P. (1976). New strategies for development: Poverty, income distribution and growth. *Oxford Economic Papers, 28*(3), 380–405.

Stiglitz, J. E. (2016). Inequality and economic growth. In M. Jacobs & M. Mazzucato (Eds.), *Rethinking capitalism: Economics and policy for sustainable and inclusive growth* (pp. 134–155). New Jersey: Wiley-Blackwell.

Stiglitz, J. E., Fitoussi, J.-P., & Durand, M. (2019). *Measuring what counts: The global movement for well-being*. New York: The New Press.

Stiglitz, J. E., Ocampo, J. A., Spiegel, S., Ffrench-Davis, R., & Nayyar, D. (2006). *Stability with growth: Macroeconomics, liberalization, and development*. The Initiative for Policy Dialogue Series. New York: Oxford University Press.

UN. (1995, March 14). *Copenhagen declaration on social development*. A/CONF.166/9. New York: United Nations (UN).

White, H., & Anderson, E. (2001). Growth versus distribution: Does the pattern of growth matter? *Development Policy Review, 19*(3), 267–289.

World Bank. (1993). *The East Asian miracle: Economic growth and public policy*. Washington, DC: The World Bank.

World Bank. (2005). *Pro-poor growth in the 1990s: Lessons and insights from 14 countries*. Washington, DC: The World Bank.

World Bank. (2008). *The growth report: Strategies for sustained growth and inclusive development*. Washington, DC: Commission on Growth and Development, The World Bank.

World Bank. (2018). *Poverty and shared prosperity 2018: Piecing together the poverty puzzle*. Washington, DC: The World Bank.

Chapter 2
The Quest for an Inclusive Growth Strategy

Muhammed Muqtada and Fahmida Khatun

Abstract The chapter explores some key issues and concepts that have led to the emergence of inclusive growth as a development paradigm, and the considerations that need to be given in the design of an inclusive growth strategy. It reviews the literature, which does not provide a universally accepted definition, rather some consensus on its characterisations, such as the *outcome* and *process* dimensions of inclusive growth. The study argues that these dimensions are interrelated, and that achieving outcomes (e.g. a declining inequality) would be hard without appropriate participation and bargaining rights, especially of the poor and underprivileged. Institutions and governance reforms would be key to ensuring the latter; hence must be seen as an additional goal of inclusive growth. The study further argues that growth and equality can be complements, but that would require a policy framework to address the multidimensionality of poverty and inequality. Based on these perspectives, the study forwards seven key goals, subsumed within an employment-focused strategy, and which are also central to the UN's 2030 Agenda. It further suggests a simple strategy framework, with three interrelated sub-strategies, that could provide a platform to relate economic, structural and institutional policies for an approach to inclusive growth.

M. Muqtada (✉)
Development Economist; Formerly a Director in the Employment Sector of the International Labour Organization (ILO) Geneva and a Visiting Fellow, Centre for Policy Dialogue, Dhaka, Bangladesh
e-mail: muqtada1@gmail.com

F. Khatun
Executive Director, Centre for Policy Dialogue (CPD), Dhaka, Bangladesh
e-mail: fahmida@cpd.org.bd

M. Muqtada (ed.), *Quest for Inclusive Growth in Bangladesh*,
South Asia Economic and Policy Studies,
https://doi.org/10.1007/978-981-15-7614-0_2

2.1 The Emergence of Inclusive Growth

2.1.1 The Basic Considerations

It has now been well-documented that during the past quarter of a century, growth has led to substantial reduction in absolute poverty, even though many individual countries have failed to reach the Millennium Development Goals' (MDGs) poverty reduction target. At the same time, empirically established stylisations tend to underscore that fast growth has been generally accompanied by worsening inequality.[1] In his widely-acclaimed publication, Milanovic (2016) has contended that while global inequality has been trending downwards (although still high), inequality *within* countries is frequently seen to be increasing, especially in the developed countries. There have been several other past studies that tend to underscore the growing trends in inequality,[2] often attributed to the unleashing of neoliberal policy reforms adopted in the wake of stabilisation and structural adjustment during the 1980s and 1990s by most developing countries.[3] The acute concerns over stabilisation and the need to return to sustainable growth shelved all policy attention towards distribution. It is only during the more recent period, that inequality has reemerged, both in developing world as well in the advanced countries, as a significant policy issue not only in respect of mending social cohesion, but arguably also in terms of its negative effects on growth and poverty alleviation. The alarming rise in inequality has taken centre-stage in policy decisions across both developed and developing economies.[4] Reducing inequality *within* and *between* countries is a critical element in the 2030 Agenda for Sustainable Development, and its urgency is being reflected in national and international policy-making.

It must be emphasised that emerging and developing countries have continuously grappled with policy reforms to bridge *growth versus development* issues, and adopted varying measures to enhance the quality of growth. As noted in Chap. 1, these measures defined alternative patterns of growth (e.g. redistributive growth; pro-poor growth, etc.), that usually incorporated policies and programmes to reduce poverty and often targetted programmes for the poor and disadvantaged. Thus, the pervasive and widely practiced public works programmes, or innovative national programmes such as the Bolsa Familia in Brazil or other programmes in strengthening the entitlements and capabilities of the poor can be seen as elements of inclusion and social cohesion. However, as mentioned above, there was inadequate policy attention paid to rising inequality, and in particular, to many groups of people and regions that emerged as vulnerable.

---

[1] Dabla-Norris et al. (2015).

[2] Several studies of the World Institute for Development Economics Research (WIDER), based on extensive empirical work, tend to confirm the growing inequality within the developing countries, especially since the 1980s (see Cornia 2004).

[3] See Cornia et al. (1987).

[4] See among others, Berg and Ostry (2011), WEF (2015).

Despite the ambivalence surrounding what constitutes inclusive growth, there has recently been a huge surge of interest, and a growing campaign, regarding how to ensure that a country's growth is inclusive. Critical to the build-up of this new paradigm are broadly the following considerations:

- Poverty incidence has on average declined substantially around the globe. Overall, the absolute number of people below the poverty threshold has declined from 1.7 billion in 1996 to around 737 million in 2015. As Table 2.1 shows, according to the World Bank estimates, the greatest declines in poverty are observed in East Asia and the Pacific (including China), with the absolute number dropping from a high of 711 million in 1996 to about 28 million in 2018. This dramatic fall occurred mostly owing to the massive growth and development in China. On the contrary, in Sub-Saharan Africa (SSA), the absolute number of people living in poverty appears to have increased, from 354 million in 1996 to around 420 million in 2015. Though the average poverty incidence has gone down globally, in absolute numbers there is still an unacceptably high number of persons living in poverty today. Besides, in South Asia and SSA, more than three out of four workers are involved in vulnerable forms of employment, with women disproportionately affected compared to men. The eradication of poverty, especially extreme poverty and hunger, still remains a global challenge, and is among the pressing goals of the 2030 Agenda. This is equally a clear warning that although inclusive growth purports to broaden the scope of growth-sharing and growth-participation, the dominant focus on alleviating poverty and deprivation could not be ignored.
- An intrinsic pursuit of inclusive growth not only concerns the reduction of absolute poverty, but also a decline in relative impoverishment (Ostry et al. 2014). It is argued that the modern economic growth, the subsequent improvement in quality of life and the diffusion of knowledge have allowed us to avoid inequalities on an explosive scale. It is therefore comprehensible, that policy-making has evolved over time and has reinforced emphasis on social protection and safety nets to moderate the potential heightening of social tensions and upheavals. However, as Piketty (2014) points out that the main driver of inequality—the tendency of returns on capital to exceed the rate of economic growth, especially in the emerging and advanced economies—threatens to generate extreme inequalities that can stir discontent, and undermine social cohesion and democratic values.
- The above idea implies that the pursuit of inclusive growth, i.e. growth that benefits all stripes of society, including the poor, the near-poor, middle-income groups, and even the rich, becomes ever more pertinent (Klasen 2010). In fact, a major incorporation in the inclusive growth paradigm is the reckoning of the roles played by each of the income groups or social classes in the growth process. In this regard, it has been widely argued, especially in the emerging economies, that the expansion and deepening of the middle-income group/class carries immense potential for growth of the economy.[5] It is universally acknowledged that the growth of the middle-income class deepens and diversifies the domestic market,

[5] See Easterly (2000), among others.

Table 2.1 Number of poor people by region (million) living at USD 1.90 per day (2011 PPP)

Region	1996	1999	2002	2005	2008	2010	2011	2012	2013	2015	2018
East Asia & Pacific	711.3	692.9	549.7	357.0	296.0	219.3	167.5	143.1	71.5	47.0	27.8
Europe & Central Asia	32.7	36.9	28.0	22.9	13.3	11.7	10.2	9.4	8.1	7.8	5.9
Latin America & Caribbean	67.4	69.6	63.3	54.9	39.6	36.2	33.6	28.2	26.1	25.3	28.0
South Asia	519.0	N/A	556.0	510.0	468.8	403.7	331.7	304.9	275.4	N/A	N/A
SSA	353.7	378.7	388.3	386.4	394.6	404.9	403.4	403.3	405.3	419.6	N/A
World	1705.7	1728.3	1600.3	1346.0	1226.4	1088.0	960.5	903.3	801.5	736.7	N/A

Source World Bank (n.d.a)
Note PPP: Purchasing Power Parity; N/A implies not available

and is a proximate factor in the process of restructuring an economy. Although there is no universally accepted definition of middle-class income,[6] and whether one uses income or consumption yardstick, there is a prima facie economic rationale to support this group to boost aggregate demand, and affect structural changes through diversification of consumption and production.

- Inclusive growth would need to relate not only to all strata of society (Klasen 2010), but also must *leave no one behind*, which would imply targetted attention to specific groups and regions. This is in fact the clarion call from the 2030 Agenda, and as mentioned above, would need to ensure participation of all in growth process.[7] The emergence of the concept of inclusive growth can be seen as a realisation that growth processes may have different impacts not just across the distribution of income, but also among ethnic and gender groups and geographical regions (Ranieri and Ramos 2013).

2.1.2 Inclusive Growth: Definitions and Characterisations

The literature on inclusive growth stumbles on an accurate definition. Much of the attempts at defining it have hardly gone beyond a circular definition: inclusive growth is largely one where bulk of the country's population participates in the growth process, and one where all have a fair share in growth dividends. With an overwhelming concern over rising inequality, some have characterised it as simply growth with equality (or declining inequality).[8] There have been several studies in the recent period attempting to specify inclusive growth, although many of these have focused largely on characterisations related to *outcomes* and *process* sharing of growth. A brief review is provided below on the concepts and characterisations that are crucial and pertinent in the articulation and designing of a policy platform.

During the 1990s and thereafter, as the neo-liberal strategy of growth evidently failed to reduce inequality and unemployment, individual countries developed a purposive pro-poor growth framework, with various international agencies supporting its potential operationalisation.[9] Amidst the unfolding debate over pro-poor growth, the concept of inclusive growth came to light and started coexisting with the concept of pro-poor growth without a clear specification of their relationship. Hence, some definitions of inclusive growth are often interchangeable with definitions of pro-poor growth. However, opinion can also vary depending on whether one

[6]See Ravallion (2009) who places this group as those who earn between USD 2–USD 13 a day, warns that bulk of this population is often nearer the USD 2 dollar (median poverty threshold of developing countries), and often vulnerable to risks.

[7]UN Agenda 2030 for pledges, "As we embark on this great collective journey, we pledge that *no one will be left behind*" (UN 2015, p. 5, italics added).

[8]See for example, Rauniyar and Kanbur (2010).

[9]In particular, the World Bank, Department for International Development (DFID); French Development Agency (AFD) and German Technical Cooperation Agency (GTZ) were among the lead institutions.

takes the absolute or relative definitions of pro-poor growth. For instance, Habito (2009) defines inclusive growth as gross domestic product (GDP) growth that leads to significant poverty reduction, which is no different from absolute pro-poor growth. This view is also supported by Ianchovichina and Lundstrom (2009), but they argue that focusing on the relative definition of pro-poor growth can lead to suboptimal outcomes for both poor and non-poor households. Other definitions incorporate non-income dimensions while keeping the focus on *outcomes*, yet others put their attention on *process* and tend to emphasise more on the opportunities to participate in the process of growth.

A significant shift in the development literature can be marked after the Global Financial Crisis (GFC) of 2007–08. There has been a shift in the policy mindset driven by *mostly free-market*, growth-oriented ideologies to a *more managed market* version of growth. The post-crisis development agenda increasingly tended to express concerns over the human aspect of development, with both the World Bank and the International Monetary Fund (IMF) placing inequality as a major concern (Ostry et al. 2014).

The post-GFC literature, in relation to inclusive growth, includes a diverse range of elements, ranging from structural transformation to additional impetus on social safety nets and institutions. For example, Rauniyar and Kanbur (2010) adopted a definition tantamount to relative pro-poor growth, whereby inclusiveness is defined as increasing equity in the distribution of income. In their view, inclusiveness can be more or less pro-poor, depending on which income levels are more positively affected by growth. Therefore, focus of policy (for poverty reduction) must be on growth that increases the incomes of the lowest quintiles. Extending the discussion to incorporate non-income dimensions, Rauniyar and Kanbur (2010) distinguished between inclusive growth, referring to the distribution of increases in income, and inclusive development referring to the distribution of improvements along dimensions other than income. On the other hand, Dagdeviren et al. (2000) highlight the importance of inclusiveness with respect to the instrumental role of the distribution of income in poverty reduction. These variations are important towards a better understanding of the poverty–growth–inequality nexus which is crucial for setting the goals of inclusive growth (see Sect. 2.2).[10]

The eminence of inclusive growth and its incorporation in the development agendas was perceived and significantly underscored by several international organisations and donor agencies. Among the early reckonings was the emphasis given to it by the World Bank's Growth Commission Report.[11] Inclusive growth subsequently found special priority agendas in the United Nations (UN) formulation of the Sustainable Development Goals (SDGs); similarly increasing emphasis on inclusive growth came from several other development partners, viz. the World Bank, DFID, United Nations Development Programme (UNDP), etc. Recently the World Economic Forum (WEF) has gone a step further by introducing an analytical and empirical basis for assessing inclusive growth, and for monitoring and ranking individual

[10]See Bourguignon (2004) for a well-known treatment of the nexus.

[11]See World Bank (2008).

country performances.[12] The definition of inclusive growth advocated by World Bank puts emphasis on the pace and structure of economic growth (Ianchovichina and Lundstrom 2009). In this definition, inclusive growth would also involve long-term sustainability and structural transformation through economic diversification and competition, but broad-based across sectors and inclusive of the large part of the country's labour force, linking both the micro and macro determinants of growth. Such a perspective about growth, distribution and employment generation is also emphasised in Bhalla (2007); in addition, Bhalla proposed combining measures of productive employment (types and sectorial distribution of jobs created; productivity growth, especially in lower-income employment) with measures of poverty and malnutrition. The World Bank refrains from an explicit advocacy of a productive employment generation strategy as a cornerstone of the inclusive growth strategy; rather, the emphasis is on creating an environment that would open up opportunities for engaging the workforce.[13] Such a stance is likely to generate unease regarding whether inclusive growth would once again be all about growth, but perhaps with an added concern and emphasis on creation of opportunities for the poor.

The Asian Development Bank (ADB) has carried out extensive research, analytical and empirical, and it appears that there is no commonly agreed definition of inclusive growth and/or development. According to one of these reports, the term is understood to refer to growth coupled with equal opportunities, which has significant economic, social and institutional policy implications (Rauniyar and Kanbur 2010).[14] An alternative way to conceptualise inclusive growth involving distributional concern was proposed by Ali and Son (2007), who switched focus from outcomes to opportunities and proposed that inclusive growth was as much about creating new economic opportunities as ensuring equal access to these opportunities. The pursuit of equal opportunities stems from the belief that it is a basic human right to be treated equally in terms of access to opportunities. The study argues that equal access to opportunities increases growth potential; conversely, inequality in opportunities could potentially diminish growth and make it unsustainable. However, the study does not elaborate on how these opportunities and their distribution (or the poor's access to such opportunities) would be assessed. Furthermore, Ali (2007) argued that rising income inequalities pose a danger to social and political stability and the sustainability of the growth process itself.

These inequalities are often reflected in social exclusion, which public policy would need to address through investing in education, health and other social services. There are several other studies which have weighed in on understanding inclusive growth. Table 2.2 presents a comparison of selected propositions as noted by Klasen (2010).

From Table 2.2, and discussions of the various contributions on and characterisations of inclusive growth, it is fairly evident that there is no clear consensus either on a definition, or on a sacrosanct list of characteristics. Moreover, many of these

---

[12]Cf. WEF (2015).

[13]See for example, Islam and Islam (2015).

[14]Cf. ADB (2012).

Table 2.2 Comparing and contrasting inclusive growth concepts

Concept	Key ideas	Process/outcome	Income/non-income	Income growth necessary?	Ease of measurement	Innovation
Strategy 2020	Growth that creates opportunities and expands access	Largely process	Income	Yes	Unclear	Very close to Ali and Zhuang
Rauniyar and Kanbur	Growth and declining inequality	Outcome	Both possible	Yes (income dimension)	Straightforward	Nearly identical to relative pro-poor growth
Ali and Son	Pro-poor improvements in non-income dimensions	Outcome	Non-income	No	Straightforward	Close to non-income growth incidence curves
Ali and Zhuang	Growth that is based on and expands equal opportunities and access	Largely process	Both	Yes	Technically difficult	Close to extension of equality of opportunity concept
The World Bank	Growth that promotes productive employment	Largely process	Both	Yes	Difficult	Some relation to Ali and Zhuang approach
UNDP	Growth with equality	Process and outcome	Both	Not necessarily	Difficult	Some relation to many related concepts

Source Klasen (2010)

conceptual nuances are abstract, and it is unclear how to establish their relationship to ground realities, or to fix policies. The key concern that provides a common platform is that all the concepts of inclusive growth are, broadly speaking, ways of challenging the *quality* of growth. Nevertheless, one may begin to look for common grounds, which may well be an empirical issue at the country-level. These appear to encompass: (i) sustainable and shared growth through expansion of economic opportunities; (ii) secular decline in poverty; (iii) decline in inequality; (iv) various pro-poor interventions ranging from access to health, education, skills, etc.; and (v) social protection and safety nets. As goals of inclusive growth, these are further examined in Sect. 2.6.

Apart from these goals, the discussions so far point to some other dimensions of inclusive growth. For example, various studies, especially several conducted by the international agencies,[15] have emphasised the need to distinguish between the *outcome* and *process* dimensions of inclusive growth. On the *outcome* side, the focus is on the reduction of inequality. After all, it was the concern over the persistent rise in inequality, one that could not be explained simply as necessarily an outcome of capitalist mode of growth that challenged the quality of growth. The above discussion points out that inclusive growth is not simply about growth with a post-growth distribution framework. In other words, inequality needs to gradually decline with growth through an increasing share of the national income accruing to the poorest quintile(s). For this to happen, one has to strike a right balance in the poverty–growth–inequality nexus (discussed in the next Sect. 2.2).

On the *process* side, a vital emphasis is on how far various income and economic/social groups participate meaningfully in the growth process. The process dimension of inclusive growth is hugely complex and where the policy instruments may involve value judgments. Apparently, some instruments, e.g. *employment for all* may cater to both outcome (i.e. employment may reduce poverty, inequality) and process (workforce participation to enhance output). Various development organisations (ADB 2012), and individual studies (de Haan and Thorat 2013) characterise this process as one that creates opportunities (apparently through growth) and expands access (ostensibly through expanded provisions of health, education, skills, etc.). Despite such opportunities and provisions, growth can continue to widen inequalities, and a wider view of the *process* dimension would require an understanding inter alia of:

(i) the need to go beyond the *average* values of poverty and inequality. In many countries, average poverty has come down, often substantially, but large proportions of the people are bypassed by growth, and are still in extreme poverty and hunger;
(ii) the *multidimensionality of poverty and inequality*. As well-known, poverty and inequality cannot be all captured by income only. Similarly, policies may be framed to reduce unemployment, but there may still exist a high incidence of the *working poor* and vulnerability;

[15] See among others, ADB (2012), Klasen (2010), de Haan and Thorat (2013).

(iii) the *process dimensions for a fair participation*, that are likely to require interventions beyond expanding opportunities and access. Inclusive growth can be seen as a renewed invitation to probe into facets of structural inequality. An amelioration of it can be attempted, even if not by redistributing land or assets, at least by enabling greater access to opportunities, and an empowerment of the poor that allows them a fair participation. Amartya Sen (1999) in his seminal work 'Development as Freedom' alluded to not only lack of economic choices and protections, but also to de facto lack of political rights. Thus, for example, while opportunities and access can potentially allow workers to participate in labour market, these are unlikely to help them in the process of bargaining for fair wages, or for fundamental *workers' rights*.[16]

Inclusive growth, in other words, would need to reflect on policy issues that may not be considered in a purely *average* outcome approach. It would likely require incorporating policies and reforms to address causes and multidimensionality of poverty and inequality, etc. (see further details in Sect. 2.3). Thus, the present study argues that high levels of inequality, not only in terms of income, but also assets and wealth, would tend to exclude the poor from joining the party, i.e. participating in the processes of growth. In other words, limited access to land, education, credit, etc. makes it difficult for the poor to exploit new opportunities that are likely to be created by growth. Even if they can access new opportunities, they may still lack the voice and political rights to bargain a fair participation in the process of growth.

The observations above call for a further probing into the definitions and characterisations of inclusive growth. Inclusive growth is not only about reducing average poverty and inequality, but also about wider participation of all in the growth process; this, in turn, warrants attention to reducing disadvantages and discrimination that hinder equal access and equal participation.[17] The launch of the 2030 Agenda for Sustainable Development of the UN, which potentially provides a blue-print of inclusive growth through its 17 goals and 169 targets, strongly underscores both the outcome and process dimensions. For instance, Goal 16, which calls upon nations to build and foster inclusion institutions, and the Agenda's strong invitation to leave no one behind, underscores the importance of the participation in the process of inclusive growth.[18] Thus, the present study contends that the outcome and process dimensions are equally significant in fostering inclusion. This view of inclusive growth would, of necessity, require further reflections on and a better understanding of the interdependence of these two dimensions. Evidently, an inclusive growth strategy would need to articulate and incorporate a range of economic, structural and institutional issues.[19]

---

[16] See de Haan and Thorat (2013).

[17] See Klasen (2010) op. cit.

[18] See Acemoglu and Robinson (2013).

[19] Cf. Khan (2019); also see Chap. 8.

2.2 The Poverty–Growth–Inequality Nexus

As evident in the discussions above, recent studies appear to provide varying emphases on the goals of inclusive growth, agreeing in some, but without a clear consensus on any particular list. However, three critical elements, which arguably constitute the centre-piece of discourses on inclusive growth, are: (i) a sustained growth of the GDP; (ii) a decline in poverty incidence; (iii) and a reduction in inequality. Does the poverty–growth–inequality nexus pose an impossible trinity? Or, can all these three goals, largely reckoned as the outcomes of inclusive growth, be attained simultaneously?

The early discourses on the poverty–growth–inequality nexus, especially those that challenged growth fetishism, were largely concerned with how far growth contributed to reducing poverty and/or inequality. Much attention was drawn to Kuznets hypothesis, based on historical account of the United States (US), England and Germany, that inequality would tend to rise during the initial phases of growth, but would tend to decline as economies reach high per capita income levels. Various scholars, based on empirical constructs, challenged Kuznet's U-shaped hypothesis, arguing that there did not exist a systematic and robust relationship between growth and inequality, and that inequality did not necessarily decline as economies grew.[20] In fact, Milanovic (2016), in a global study, maintained that inequality within many countries was increasing. Others maintained that rising inequality could slow down the rate of poverty reduction.[21]

Several studies have attempted to identify drivers of inequality. One such contends that behind the increase or decline in inequality lies how an individual country harnesses, inter alia, the forces of globalisation, financial liberalisation, technology, and labour market reforms.[22] While globalisation, financial liberalisation and technology have opened up national boundaries to support generation of global wealth, such wealth has been unevenly distributed across countries, amongst various occupational categories, and between labour and capital. Therefore, it is no wonder that inequality, between and within countries, has emerged as a serious concern in the recent times.[23] In global terms, as we have noted, millions of people are still under the *extreme* poverty line, and millions are unemployed and/or underemployed. It is of equal concern that poverty, unemployment and squalor, and a lack of inclusiveness especially among the youth, is often alleged to be linked to the modern emergence of mass international migration. Global market reach has allowed even more unprecedented profits and power to big financial and industrial corporates. This has significantly skewed the income structure in most economies.[24]

[20]See McKinley (2009) for a summary account of the reasons that Kuznets forwarded to explain how and why inequality would decline as an economy attains higher growth.

[21]See Dabla-Norris et al. (2015).

[22]Ibid.

[23]Cf. Milanovic (2016).

[24]See Milanovic (2016) op. cit.

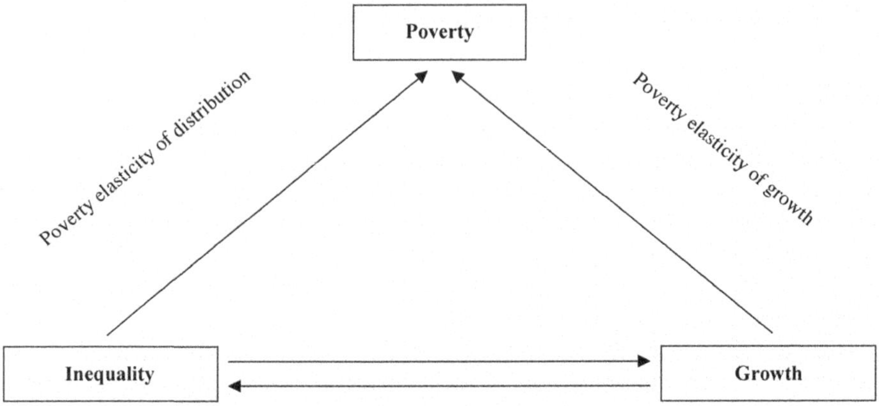

Diagram 2.1 Bourguignon's poverty–growth–inequality model. *Source* Adapted by the authors from Bourguignon (2004)

The concern with the adverse distributional implications of growth processes resulted in a vast array of literature with a key concern on how to ensure that the poor people actually benefit from growth. The poverty–growth–inequality nexus is underpinned by hugely complex and debatable relationships, which are as much value-based as statistical. In schematic terms, Bourguignon (2004) provides an attempt to unscramble the relationships behind the nexus, adapted through the Diagram 2.1.

He contended that poverty–inequality and poverty–growth relationships were essentially guided by their respective poverty elasticities (as shown in Diagram 2.1). These are, however, not necessarily straightforward, since the growth–inequality relationship (bottom of the triangle) is complex and contextual. While the former two relationships are often dubbed as *arithmetic*, the latter is conditional on an individual country's policy choices and its development strategies. Thus, assertions such as *growth is good for the poor* (Dollar and Kraay 2002)[25] and *inequality is bad for the poor* (Ravallion 2005),[26] tend to underscore the stark choices a country has to make to attain its desired outcomes on growth, poverty alleviation and reduction of inequality. While, in the long-run, growth is likely to be good for poverty alleviation, it would, in the short-run, depend on how growth translates into benefits (poverty-elasticities), but also on how far growth-to-poverty reduction is tempered by, say, a rising inequality. In other words, if poverty reduction were the overriding consideration in a developing country, it is likely that the country would chart out a pro-poor pattern of growth without necessarily reducing inequalities in income and economic opportunities. Using a simulation on Mexico, Bourguignon (2004) shows how a reduction of inequality (from a Gini of 0.55 to 0.45) could help bring down poverty by 15% in 10 years, which would take 30 years if inequality remained at the same level. There have been several other studies to support this view. For instance,

[25]This is the title of the article, Dollar and Kraay (2002).

[26]From the title in Ravallion (2005).

Wan and Wang (2019), in the context of some Asian countries, provides estimates of the cost of inequality, viz. how rising inequality has likely impeded the pace of poverty reduction.[27]

Thus, it is important to recognise that while the growth–poverty and inequality–poverty would tend to be determined by the respective poverty elasticities, there are likely to be parametric changes in the latter depending on how far growth itself affected inequality, and/or inequality affected growth (Wan and Wang 2019). Growth would tend to generate inequality when policies adversely affect wages and earnings, promote rent-seeking, or are biased against sector(s) where the poor are immobile and/or disadvantaged sectorally, regionally or skill-wise. Easterly (2000) contended that this was the case during the immediate period following the Structural Adjustment Programs (SAPs), which tended to reduce the poverty-elasticity of growth. As we have noted already, inequality is not necessarily an expected concomitant of early economic growth periods, as contended by Kuznets. Studies show that growth episode in developing countries are variously associated with either rising or slowing inequalities.[28] The critical issue is whether the initial inequality is unacceptably high, and is rising. This, as appears to be the recent experience in many developing countries, such as Bangladesh, is likely to reduce the *pace* of poverty alleviation in the economy.

On the other hand, high and persistent inequality could also adversely affect growth itself, as noted by individual researchers (Stiglitz 2016)[29] as well as organisations. Research at the IMF, for instance, has identified *high structural inequality* to be an impediment to economic growth.[30] The study further brings together evidence to contend that non-extreme redistribution, and the consequent reductions in inequality, are observed to be associated with higher and more durable growth.[31] The rising inequality in both developed and developing countries is not only likely to have adverse impact on future growth, but is also likely to lead to serious social and political upheavals. Hence, there is now a wider and more pervasive search on understanding the underlying causes of inequality.

Depending on how individual countries articulate their national policies with the above considerations in mind, would determine whether a pattern of growth can be designed where poverty would decline *and* the net redistributive effects would be positive. What is inadequately addressed in determining the patterns of growth are the key elements in the growth strategy itself that are causing inequality to rise significantly. The neo-liberal growth strategists do not find it necessary to do so. For instance, the claim by Dollar and Kraay (2002) that growth is good for the

---

[27] "In total, 248.4 million (under the US$3.20 poverty line) and 145.09 million (under the US$1.90 poverty line) Asians could have been lifted out of poverty but were not, due to rising inequality in the region. This cost largely came from China (212.57 million and 114.18 million), followed by India, Indonesia, and Bangladesh" (Wan and Wang 2019, p. 262).

[28] See Ravallion (2001).

[29] "…far from being either necessary or good for economic growth, excessive inequality tends to lead to weaker economic performance" (p. 134).

[30] Ostry et al. (2014).

[31] Ibid.

poor is based on the empirical findings that: (i) with growth in an economy, income of the poorest quintile increases proportionately to average income; and (ii) this is unaffected by policy interventions to benefit the poor. Such assertion, by extension, would imply that since *growth by itself* reduces poverty, pro-poor interventions would not be all that necessary. However, Ravallion (2001) points out that in the case of Latin American countries, which have attained high per capita income, there exists large numbers of poor people who are bypassed by the growth process. As discussed in the previous section, multiple studies by individuals and organisations have challenged and refuted this contention.

On the strategy front, while growth strategies were largely focused on the urgency of poverty alleviation, there was much less an articulated policy response on *reducing inequality*. It is important to recognise that redistribution is only part of the growth–inequality story. Often when growth itself tends to generate inequality (e.g. when policies adversely affect wages and earnings, and encourage rent-seeking, etc.) redistribution can be seen as an attempt on the margins to moderate inequality outcomes of growth, without necessarily addressing the root causes of inequality. Stiglitz (2016, p. 134) contends there is the need for "alternative explanations of inequality, with particular reference to the theory of rent-seeking and to the influence of institutional and political, which have shaped labour markets and patterns of remuneration." There are others who contend "that reasonably stable income distribution, with social mobility through measures like initial land reform, improved public health, and education, along with labour-intensive infrastructure for generating employment, created preconditions for high growth" (Bhaduri 2019, p. 235). In other words, a probing analysis and understanding of root causes of inequality would help design more appropriate policies that could potentially ensure that growth and equality are *complements*.[32]

Fundamentally, the poverty–growth–inequality triangle (Bourguignon 2004) and its cause–effect nexus is yet to be fully unscrambled, both in conceptual terms as well as the normative and policy connotations that are entailed. The nexus needs more detailed empirical probing in order to establish the *nature* and *direction* of causation and the nature of policies that need to be identified to address both poverty alleviation *and* inequality reduction. However, as the following section argues, strategy design has to go beyond aggregate statistics of growth, poverty and inequality, and extend to ground realities which in the first place shape these aggregates.

[32] Stiglitz (2016) op. cit.; similar views are expressed in Ali and Zhuang (2007).

2.3 Inclusive Growth and Multi-dimensionality of Poverty and Inequality: Few Ground Realities

2.3.1 *The Narrative*

In the context of the present study, to what extent and in what ways does the discussion above on the poverty–growth–inequality inform the quest for inclusive growth, and the design of a strategy? Foremost, the debates on the nexus certainly tend to challenge growth fetishism, and provide a sobering evaluation of the quality of growth, especially in countries which have earned political acclaim by drawing attention to their high GDP growth rates. China, India and Bangladesh are cases in point. Figure 2.1 on cross-country data from selected Asian countries tend to show a close association between higher GDP growth and inequality.

Rising inequality in many of these countries has led to disconcerting concerns and to the introduction of many distributive reforms. These well-known traditional distributive measures are intended to cushion and protect income and entitlements of the poorest quintiles. However, generally these measures are unlikely to constitute inclusive growth; these appear as complementary measures (even though some are fairly pervasive, e.g. Mahatma Gandhi National Rural Employment Guarantee Act (MGNREGA) in India) of social inclusion that tend to provide legitimacy to growth-centred planning.

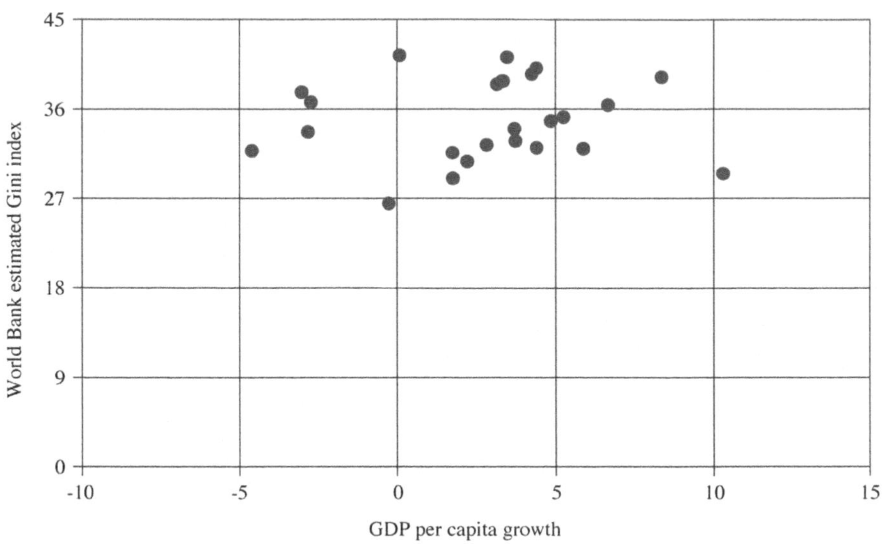

Fig. 2.1 Inequality and per capita GDP growth: Selected Asian countries. *Source* World Bank (n.d.b)

In charting a country's course towards inclusive growth, with all its complex elements, is there a tendency to divert attention away from the poor, especially the extreme poor? As noted in the discussion on the poverty–growth–inequality nexus above, stark choices would be needed on the weight to be given on the elements and the associated policies. The SDG 2030 Agenda's call to leave no one behind adds significant perceptions on inclusive growth; that it should probe beyond *average* poverty and inequality outcomes of growth, especially into their causes and multidimensionality. In other words, the emergence, and the propagation of inclusive growth would need to reassure that attention to pro-poor growth elements is not compromised (McKinley 2009). The following paragraphs provide some observations which would tend to challenge a deviation from this rationale.

2.3.2 Numbers, Norms and Multidimensionality

Given the overwhelming evidence that growth does not *automatically* reduce poverty and inequality, reductions in the latter (especially in countries where its incidence is high) are likely to require making hard choices on redistributive measures, and on coping with trade-offs in fiscal measures. We have cited above several studies that have suggested that growth with reduced inequality would likely support tangible reduction in poverty.[33] In other words, in developing countries with a high incidence of poverty, and with the poor who are the least beneficiaries of growth, policies need to be calibrated to ensure that *pro-poor* and *inclusive growth* are compatible. There are likely to be debates and trade-offs, but as we have maintained, redistributive measures need not be anti-growth.[34] However, for the latter to happen, it would require public persuasion in accepting values and norms in the planning process.

Let us recall our discussion earlier that growth in most parts of the world during the past two decades has significantly reduced poverty, but that it varies enormously by regions. Furthermore, if one were to take the absolute numbers of people that are poor, the numbers are very steep, especially in South Asia and Africa (see Table 2.1). If these are subjected to further scrutiny to find out the extremely poor, i.e. approximating the incidence of undernourished, the numbers are still staggering (as shown in Table 2.3). In fact, the numbers show an increase between 1999–01 and 2016–18 for South Asia and SSA. These features, i.e. degrees of undernourishment and hunger, and such other multidimensional facets, do not feature in the overall incidence of poverty. Several other indicators need to feature in a true measure of inclusive growth (see Chap. 3).

---

[33] See for example, Bourguignon (2004) op. cit. Ravallion (2005, p. 6) contends that even if there were no robust correlation between inequality and growth, this would not imply that, "policy makers aiming to fight poverty in any given country can safely focus on growth alone".

[34] McKinley (2009) raised concern whether inclusive growth may have a tendency to relax weights on policies that have been traditionally understood to be pro-poor.

Table 2.3 Number of people undernourished (millions) (3-year average)

Region	1999–01	2006–08	2009–11	2016–18
World	916.3	883.2	826.1	809.9
Southern Asia	272.4	303.7	293.7	277.7
SSA	182.0	178.3	181.2	229.9
Eastern Asia and South-eastern Asia	336.1	302.6	256.0	198.8
Latin America and the Caribbean	63.0	44.7	40.7	41.5

Source FAO (n.d.)

It is one thing to establish detailed and sophisticated estimates of poverty and inequality, but it is another to assess and understand *why* poor people are poor. In particular, the depth of poverty cannot be assessed simply by the income factor. It is widely known that they also have significantly unequal access to health and education resources. In this context, one may recall the norms underpinned in Sen's (1997) persuasive argument on the need to go beyond traditional *income* inequality and search for *economic* inequality thus: "The argument for shifting our attention from income inequality to economic inequality relates to the presence of *causal influences* on individual well-being and freedom that are economic in nature but that are not captured by the simple statistics of incomes and commodity holdings" (p. 384, italics added).[35]

Redressing the latter would warrant approaches beyond a growth strategy, more likely through an articulation of well-designed public policy as well as institutional reforms. Such a public policy is best served and informed by a detailed understanding of the multidimensionality, and causes of poverty and inequality. The UN 2030 Agenda, which has otherwise created a global platform for a socially just and sustainable society, fails to mention the need to identify the root causes of poverty and inequality and exclusion.

2.3.3 Beyond Averages[36]

Empirical analysis of the growth–poverty and growth–inequality relationships has largely been based on average cross-country or country-level trend values of poverty and inequality. However, single-statistic figures on the poverty incidence and the Gini cannot fully capture the wide range of deprivation and discrimination that exist within the poorest quintiles. A much closer probing to understand the proximate explanatory factors would support a more inclusive planning than one based on the average. For instance, Bangladesh has been, quite rightly, lauded for achieving the MDG of halving its *average* poverty incidence during the stipulated period 1990–2015.

[35]Cf. Sen (1997).

[36]See Ravallion (2001) for an exposition.

Table 2.4 Variations in poverty incidence within Bangladesh: Three districts with the highest incidence and three districts with the lowest incidence of poverty based on upper poverty line

Year	3 districts with highest incidence		3 districts with lowest incidence	
	District	Incidence (%)	District	Incidence (%)
2010	Kurigram	63.7	Chattogram	11.5
	Barishal	54.8	Noakhali	9.6
	Shariatpur	52.6	Kushtia	3.6
2016	Kurigram	70.8	Madaripur	3.7
	Dinajpur	64.3	Munshiganj	3.1
	Bandarban	63.2	Narayanganj	2.6

Source Household Income and Expenditure Survey (HIES), Bangladesh Bureau of Statistics (BBS) (various issues)

However, there are enormous differences of the incidence among various classes, occupational categories and ethnic groups. Furthermore, as Table 2.4 shows, there are yawning regional differences of poverty incidence.

Thus, while a country can rightly show progress on average growth and average social indicators, there can still exist a huge incidence of social exclusion. Similarly, policies need to be informed by detailed understanding of the processes that cause differential income impacts on various groups, and regions. Most countries often resort to employment generation measures as a means to reducing unemployment. However, unless complemented by other measures, these may not be an adequate response to existing poverty and inequality. Table 2.5 provides a broad view, regionally, of the extent to which open unemployment rates fail to capture how poor (*working poor*) and how vulnerable the working people are. Thus, jobs generation measures which are intended to reduce *average* unemployment may not by themselves be able to address the true challenges of vulnerability.

Most developing countries, especially during the 1980s and 1990s, had undertaken various economic reforms. In particular, the various labour market reforms, together with financial sector liberalisation, saw a growing asymmetry of power allocation

Table 2.5 Vulnerable employment across the regions

Region	Unemployment rate	Working poor	Vulnerable employment
SSA	7.4	34.3	69.9
Arab States (non-GCC)	15.2	38.0	34.2
Latin America and the Caribbean	6.5	8.2	31.2
Southeast Asia	4.4	8.4	54.1
South Asia	4.1	18.1	73.6

Source ILO (n.d.)
Note GCC: Gulf Cooperation Council

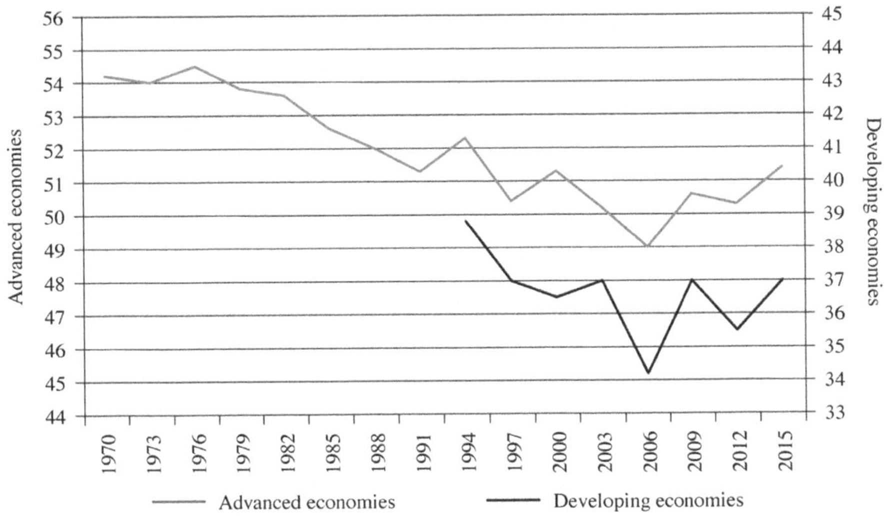

Fig. 2.2 Share of labour in national income. *Source* IMF (2017)

between labour and capital, a manifestation of which has been the relative repression of job creation and labour income, and growth of precarious and vulnerable jobs.[37]

2.3.4 Growth-Induced Inequality and Exclusion

Many countries are afflicted by growing inequality owing to declining wages vis-à-vis productivity growth, and consequently labour's share in national income has been declining. As noted in the IMF (2017), it was indeed since the 1980s that the share of labour's income in national income has been markedly falling (Fig. 2.2). The IMF report contends that this was largely due to technology and global integration which causes wages to grow slower than productivity, implying that an increasing portion of the productivity gains has gone to capital.

Furthermore, the capture of rents by a few as an underlying cause of inequality applies not just to developed countries, but also importantly to developing countries, where the growth and deregulation of the financial sector and changes in labour market policies have contributed to the rising trend of income inequality. Inequality is driven not only by unemployment, but also an increasing share of poorly paid jobs. Together with these, the decoupling of wage growth from productivity growth has contributed to the trend decline in the labour share in total national income. In a milieu of rising inequality, one observes a general decline in real wages across most regions, particularly since the global financial crisis (see Fig. 2.3). Thus, irrespective of productivity growth, real wages have not shown any marked improvements in

[37] See ILO (2009).

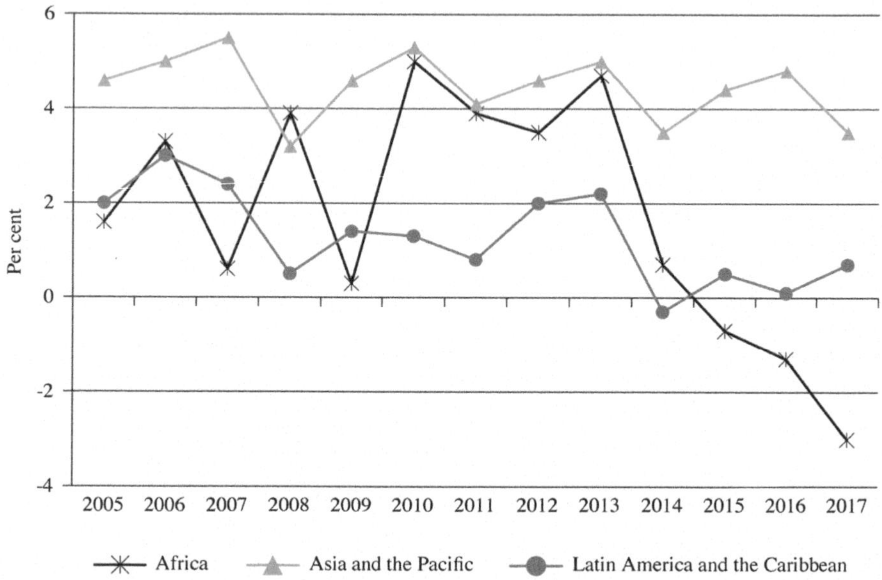

Fig. 2.3 Growth of real wage in different regions: 2005–2017. *Source* ILO (n.d.)

most countries. This also reflects on the weak bargaining position and participation of the workers in the growth process.

2.3.5 *Structural Factors*

It is important to reiterate that while rising inequality is now widely accepted as bad for the poor, and often bad for growth and its quality, the critical element is to ascertain, in terms of an individual country, the true *determinants* of such inequality. One may recall that in the case of East and some of the Southeast Asian countries, equitable growth was strongly facilitated by an *initial* asset distribution (especially through land reforms), together with substantial investment in physical and social infrastructures. The linkages between unequal income and unequal asset distributions are observed across countries, both in developed as well as developing countries. In Bangladesh, it is observed that wealth inequality is substantially higher than income inequality (see Chap. 3). In modern day development planning, redistribution of growth, to the extent that it is pursued, refrains from any serious discussions on redistribution of *physical* assets (such as land); instead the focus is increasingly toward other catalytic agents that potentially allow future stream of income generation, such as through enhancing access to education, skills and credit. These are significant measures to open up access to opportunities for the poor, but one has to still monitor the formation and changes in the asset structure (both mobile, and immobile), which may continue to widen income inequality.[38] Sobhan (2010), writing in the context of South Asian countries, contended that poverty alleviation was intricately related to structural injustices, including, inter alia, unequal access to assets, markets and participation.[39] Apart from promoting social capital, this would require, inter alia, institutional and policy reforms towards empowering of the marginalised people and workers so that they are able to express and bargain their share of growth benefits (e.g. decent work) through collective agency.

2.4 Does Inclusive Growth Subsume Pro-poor Growth[40]? a Strategy Perspective

Many of the recent efforts at designing a policy framework for inclusive growth do adhere to concerns of improving the lot of the poor. However, the policies that are advocated (see World Bank position in an early section) are still predominantly on growth and opening up of *opportunities* for the poor. In other words, in a strategy of growth-induced *opportunities*, the issues of how the poor would access them remain unclear. Klasen (2010), based on a number of studies by the ADB, distinguished between inclusive growth as outcome, and process-based (see Sect. 2.1). There are also others, e.g. International Development Research Centre (IDRC), which recognises the importance of the poor's access to growing economic opportunities, and its impact on reduction of inequality (de Haan and Thorat 2013).

Currently, the above inclusive growth stance does not spell out how the widening *relative inequality* observed in many countries would be addressed. Khan (2015) drawing on the experiences of early growth periods in East and Southeast Asian countries, has argued for an inequality-averse growth.[41] A widely accepted factor that tends to explain the inequality averse growth of the East Asian countries is the labour-intensive growth of manufacturing, bulk of which was export-led. Such growth propelled these economies towards full employment, with real wages rising along with increasing productivity. Such growth would be ideal for most developing countries. Several analysts have endorsed that such a stance was quite feasible, provided policies are consciously undertaken towards this end.[42]

In addition, unlike pro-poor growth which takes a consequentialist approach in a sense that outcome is the only imperative aspect, inclusive growth is concerned with whether and how people engage in the growth process. This would encompass a range of specific groups that constitute the underprivileged and underclass of the

[38]Piketty (2014).

[39]Sobhan (2010).

[40]See Chap. 1 for a brief discussion on pro-poor growth. Also see World Bank (2005).

[41]Khan (2015) maintained that, in the instance of Bangladesh, a relatively higher rate of poverty reduction would have been achieved if the rising inequality as observed over the past several years could have been moderated.

[42]See Bhaduri (2019).

society; the deprived women in and outside the workforce; people with disability; transgender groups; various ethnic groups and minorities who face discrimination, etc. Policy attention to expansion of opportunities need to be complemented by policies that would provide access for specific target groups. On the outcome dimension, a critical pursuit of an inclusive growth regime would thus, inter alia, lie in a vigorous campaign towards productive and remunerative employment generation; avoiding policies that ostensibly widen inequality and breed social exclusion; policies to enhance social inclusion through well-designed social protection and safety net systems (see Chap. 7). On the process dimension, policies to facilitate greater participation in the economy, especially of the extremely poor, would require a public policy regime and a governance structure to enhance capabilities and representation (see discussion in Chap. 8). Khan (2001, p. 27) emphasises that interventions would be necessary to ensure protection of "the weak members of the labour force, especially in an environment of unequal bargaining power."[43] This unequal bargaining power faced by the poor can hardly be redressed without institutional reforms towards enhancing their voice and representation. The latter are possibly a next best approach, no matter how unsatisfactory, in mitigating structural inequality that is so widely observed in developing countries.[44]

2.5 Full Employment as a Key Metric of Inclusive Growth

As abundantly clear from the previous discussions of the inclusive growth literature, innumerable issues have been raised on what constitutes inclusive growth, and on how to pursue inclusive growth. While various studies agree on some common goals, there is no defined approach on how to achieve these goals. In fact, it would be a misplaced exercise to design a comprehensive strategy when the goals and indicators are less than firmly established. The present study espouses a minimalist strategy framework, and contends that an effective inclusive growth strategy would be best pursued through articulating policies that address the priorities of the *individual* country, and through search for a common factor or a *glue* that interlinks these policy priorities.

In the absence of a crystallised and articulated strategy of inclusive growth, a prominent exposition comes from the goal of attaining full employment, a stance pursued by the Western European countries during the post-World War II period. Historically, the call for full employment as a goal emanated from these advanced economies, arguably following the Keynesian tradition. At the risk of some simplification, it may be contended that the advanced economies envisioned a balance between the goals of growth and *prosperity* of their population through the declared objective of attaining full employment, and through adoption of varying levels of state

[43] See Sobhan (2010), Stiglitz (2016).

[44] Piketty (2006), who maintained that inequality dynamics depend primarily on the policies and institutions adopted by governments.

interventions and an active role of public policy to sustain full employment. However, the goal of full employment, or even the objective of employment generation, fell from grace during the era of stabilisation that followed. Conservative institutions pioneered austerity drive and policies toward flexibilisation of labour markets, with adverse effects on job creation and poverty reduction. While a few international organisations such as the UN, International Labour Organization (ILO), etc. and international conferences[45] campaigned to uphold the goal of full employment, it was perhaps the GFC of 2007–08 and the subsequent years during which employment and labour conditions worsened, that provided the impulses to reinvoke job creation as a central tenet of policy-making.[46] The current global economic downturn caused by the COVID-19 pandemic has equally emphatically brought to fore the critical issues of job entitlements and job security for all.

As noted in Sects. 2.2 and 2.3 of this study, inclusive growth recognises that the factors that contribute to the poverty–growth–inequality nexus are closely linked to each other; indeed capabilities of the poor are limited not only by the personal heterogeneities (such as age, disability, gender), but also by variations in social opportunities. The present chapter contends, in the same vein as with the authors of many global campaigns,[47] that inclusive growth must involve, among others, the creation of decent jobs, which will ensure fair income, social protection for families, workplace security and better prospects for personal development and social integration.

Poverty and inequality and exclusion are inherently linked to the widespread persistence of unfavourable trends in the labour market variables, such as the pervasive existence of surplus labour, youth and female unemployment, workplace discrimination and insecurity, etc. With the utterly slow pace of growth of jobs and wages over the last two decades, the stiff employment challenges are abundantly clear from an empirical reading of the widely accepted indicators, viz. high unemployment rates, especially among the youth workforce. What is more disconcerting is that, barring the performances in a few countries, there is on an average, a stubborn persistence of these trends in various regions (Fig. 2.4).

Thus, there is currently a surge of attention diverted towards placing employment on top of the policy agenda. Furthermore, there is now overwhelming support for the contention, including from the Bretton Woods institutions that, "development happens through jobs" (World Bank 2012, p. 22). The present study contends that pursuing the goal of full, productive employment and decent work provides a focused approach, and an organising policy theme that can well-articulate the priority concerns of an inclusive growth strategy: especially with respect to such key considerations as sustained growth, reduction in poverty and inequality, and maximum

[45]For example, World Summit on Social Development, 1995; the MDGs in 2000, etc.

[46]ILO (2010), op. cit.

[47]Many national and international development strategies have embraced the call for attaining the goal of full employment and decent work. A global call to such a commitment, which was made at the ILO Philadelphia Declaration 1944, was renewed at the World Social Summit (Copenhagen Declaration 1995), and yet again in the 2030 Agenda for Sustainable Development.

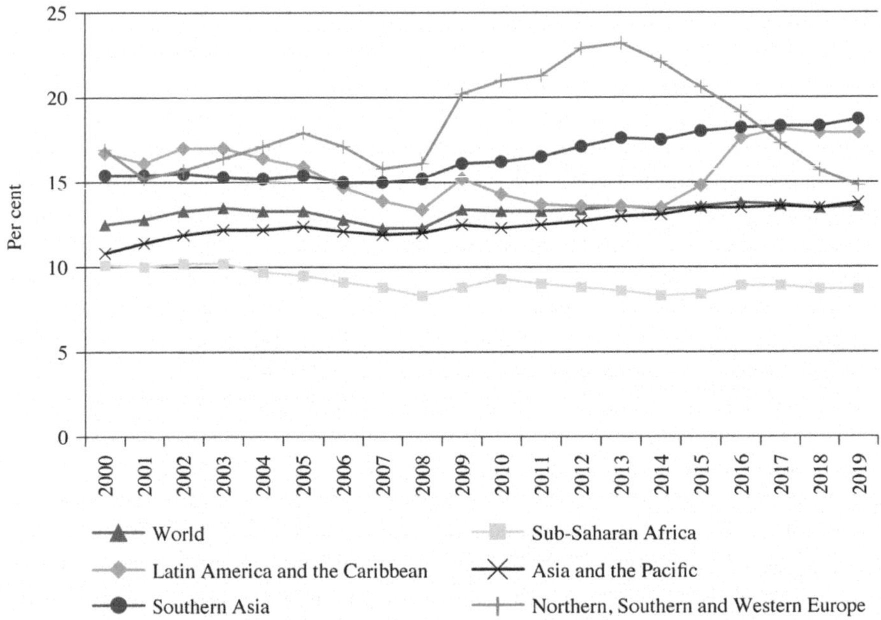

Fig. 2.4 Youth unemployment trends: Selected regions. *Source* ILO (n.d.)

participation.[48] Apart from the fact that attainment of a full employment society is a worthy goal in itself, *jobs for all* can equally serve as an economically sensible and politically expedient objective.[49] Several analytical works and empirical studies continue to underscore the goal of full productive and remunerative employment as the centre-piece of an inclusive growth strategy.[50] With the universal commitment now to the campaign on realising the 2030 Agenda, there is a renewed emphasis to give effect to the goal of full, productive employment and decent work (SDG 8).

2.6 Goals and Priorities of Inclusive Growth

In the backdrop of the discussions above, it appears that inclusive growth as a paradigm needs to be further reviewed, especially since the manifesto and goals of the 2030 Agenda are being increasingly incorporated in the development agenda across the world. In general, the present study contends that inclusive growth must continue

[48] World Bank (2012, p. 29, ff.).

[49] See the ILO Convention No. 122, calling on all countries to pursue the goal of full employment.

[50] In a recent contribution, Bhaduri (2019, p. 235) contends that the "foremost requirement of inclusiveness in development is rapid expansion of employment and livelihood opportunities in situations of huge surplus labour and mass unemployment." Also see Nayyar (2014), Islam and Islam (2015), Felipe (2012).

to adopt pro-poor strategies; focus on the distributional aspects of the *benefit-sharing* (to reduce inequality); design effective processes for greater participation, especially those who are underprivileged and face disadvantages and discrimination.[51] Based on existing literature on inclusive growth, one may identify a set of broad goals and policies towards attainment of inclusive growth in a country.[52]

The above discussion implies that inclusive growth carries a large and pervasive agenda, and the policy elements and their relative weights will vary according to individual country situation. As the World Bank Growth Commission Report, in the context of designing a growth strategy, emphasised there cannot be a single recipe relevant for all countries.[53] Even in the context of an individual country it would be impossible to give fair weights to all the goals, and associated indicators, of inclusive growth (such as the 17 goals and 169 indicators of the SDG Agenda). Priorities have to be chosen. In the section above, the study has set out a case for an inclusive growth strategy focused on the goal of full employment. Here, seven key goals are chosen,[54] which are inherently linked to employment.

Enhancing growth and structural transformation. In the recent literature on inclusive growth, *high, sustainable growth* is almost universally accepted as a necessary condition for addressing various other goals. In fact, in the 2030 Agenda framework,[55] it is contended that developing countries in particular, would need to grow at an average of at least 7 per cent per year over the next decade and a half in order to reach such other targets as moving closer to the goal of full employment, and eradication of extreme poverty. This is a tall order, since given historical trends, only a handful of countries are likely to achieve such growth rates. One may recall, World Bank (2008) identified only 13 countries as having achieved that for a sustained period. Nevertheless, a high growth is necessary and in the post-GFC period several developing countries, e.g. in South Asia, have shown that such a growth-path is not unfeasible.

For sustained growth, an economy needs to undergo significant *structural transformation.* In the process of economic growth there takes place a structural shift in the value-added composition away from the primary sector towards the secondary or industrial sector (Kuznets 1955; Kaldor 1957). Historically all the countries that remained poor failed to achieve structural transformation as they were unsuccessful to diversify away from primary goods, mainly agriculture, into modern activities, including manufacturing. Lewis (1954) argues that in the process of capitalist growth, low-wage and low-productivity labour would move to high productivity industrial sector. A manifestation of the structural change is thus the gradual increase in the employment share of the latter sector. In the recent past, many developing countries

[51] Also see Bhalla (2007), Ianchovichina and Lundstrom (2009), Klasen (2010) op. cit.

[52] Also see Islam and Islam (2015) op. cit.; Felipe (2012) op. cit.

[53] The formulation of a growth strategy is best done through "a dedicated team of policy makers and economists, working on a single economy over time" (World Bank 2008, p. 31).

[54] In the following Chap. 3, the progress of Bangladesh towards inclusive growth has been examined based on these seven goals and selected indicators of the respective goals.

[55] UN (2015).

have attained rapid growth, but without perceptible structural transformation (also see Chaps. 3 and 6). Thus, the pace and pattern of growth are crucial starting points in an inclusive growth strategy.

Reducing poverty and inequality. There is almost a universal acceptance, among academics and practitioners, that reducing poverty and inequality should be a central pillar of inclusive growth. In fact, several analysts have shown that reducing inequality could act as an instrument of reducing poverty. As cited above, Bourguignon (2004) and others have done simulation exercises to argue that growth can have a much bigger impact on poverty reduction if it were associated with a reduction in inequality.[56] As discussed above, the relationships are complex and less than straightforward. Whether there can be a *pattern* of growth that is egalitarian, and is not inhibited by growth–redistribution trade-offs, is an empirical question. Although there are limited instances where this has happened, e.g. in East Asian countries in the 1970s and 1980s, the factors that have rendered this possible need serious attention.

Generating productive employment. Generating and increasing productive employment, adequately discussed above, is a key pillar of social inclusion, especially if the aim is to embrace a full employment society. However, attaining the goal of full employment would require different time spans for different countries, depending on initial conditions, and the employment-intensity of their growth.

Currently, there are concerns that job-growth is slowing down across countries,[57] even where growth has been significant (India, for example, during its recent growth episodes). However, the goal, worthy as it is in economic and social terms, would enable a long-term planning of policy priorities and resource allocation (Bhaduri 2005; Felipe 2012). Hence, *productive employment generation to reduce full employment deficits*, for all the reasons cited earlier, would set an inclusionary agenda. This is a goal which has been accorded the highest importance in global fora.[58] Yet, at the national level, there has been scant systematic emphasis on its pursuit, beyond stating it as a national planning goal.

The present study has argued inclusive growth is not simply about generating the jobs, but also about providing access to these jobs, especially for the disadvantaged. For instance, jobs cannot be accessed without acquiring the right skills. There are specific groups in the labour market who are, and will continue to remain, at a disadvantage in getting access to jobs and training, in particular, the youth, the female workforce, and those physically challenged. In this regard, one particular challenge will be to target higher participation of women, and greater access of women to training and jobs, in order to reduce gender inequality.

Access to health, education/skills and public services. Achieving universal care and access to essential healthcare services is a significant goal of social inclusion.

---

[56] Bourguignon (2004) op. cit.

[57] See Islam and Islam (2015) op. cit.

[58] For example, see commitment 3 of the Copenhagen declaration, 1995; the MDG Target 1b; and now the SDG 8. The goal of full employment is enshrined in ILO Convention No. 122, which has been ratified by a large number of countries.

Besides, human capital accumulation is a critical source of growth; an expansion of, and access to, health services is instrumental in realising the potential of a nation's human capital.[59] It is argued that for developing economies there is a positive relation between health activities and growth, and that such economies might attain a double dividend from increased healthcare spending, i.e. a higher health level may be achievable for the population and a higher growth rate of income and consumption per head.

Similarly, access to education and skills development is a highly inclusionary measure. It is acknowledged as a significant step to enhancing participation in the world of work, and to increasing productivity in the economy. Based on a panel study of 100 countries observed between 1965–1995, on the effect of education on growth, Barro (2001) showed that growth has a positive relation with starting level of average years of school attainment of adult males at the secondary and higher levels. The result also accentuates the importance of knowledge spill over as educated workers would be complementary with recent technologies. Similarly, educational quality, measured by cognitive skills of the population, has a strong positive impact on individual earnings, on the distribution of income, and on economic growth.[60]

Access to a key element in public services, is that of infrastructure, which is not only critical to development and structural change, but also enhances participation by connecting people and businesses. In general, as Calderón and Servén (2004) observe, long-run economic growth is significantly influenced by volume of infrastructure stock. Moreover, larger infrastructure stocks as well as their improved quality arguably contribute considerably to the reduction of inequality. The fact that infrastructure both raises growth and lowers income inequality implies infrastructure development may be a key win–win ingredient for poverty reduction.

Again, as emphasised earlier, inclusive growth must emphasise not only on the expansion of the various public services as above, but also the mechanisms that would facilitate equal access for the underprivileged.

Extending social protection and safety nets. There is a vigorous consideration in countries across the development spectrum to extend and widen the coverage of social protection and social safety nets. There is in fact an increasing awareness to adopt a social protection floor (SPF), that ensures basic social security guarantees, i.e. that ensures that all in need can afford and have access to essential healthcare, and can have income security at least at a nationally defined minimum level.[61] This is not only to stem widespread poverty, but also to support the large bulk of the workforce who are in informal and vulnerable occupations. While these measures are central to social inclusion, the current coverage in developing countries is extremely small. The low social protection is crucially linked to low proportion of formal sector jobs, and hence the proportionately low support coming from the contributory schemes. Social safety nets funded largely by non-contributory transfers, exist in various forms

[59] See van Zon and Muysken (2003), among many others.

[60] For example, Hanushek and Wößmann (2007).

[61] This is being promoted and pursued through an ILO-UN initiative. Also note SDG 1.3.

and in varying scale and coverage. Although one appreciates the various constraints to their expansion, especially lack of fiscal space, there are nonetheless a burgeoning literature, drawn from country experiences, that, with political will and consensus, is feasible and affordable to provide critical income and social guarantees.

Promoting gender equality. The promotion of gender equality is essentially underscoring the promotion of human rights, especially in that women are largely deprived of the various rights that men enjoy. The campaign against non-discrimination, which is as much economic as social and political, is enshrined in national laws as well as international conventions which most countries have ratified. Nevertheless, despite the many policies and programmes that exist in every country, the gender gap is still unacceptably high in many countries. Engaging the female workforce in productive remunerative occupations is not only a critical part of social inclusion, it would enhance the wealth of nations and accelerate growth. Among others, Klasen (2000) found a substantial impact of gender inequality on economic growth. His results showed that gender disparity in education has an adverse effect on economic growth through lowering the quality of human capital. In addition, the study shows that gender inequality impedes improvement in reducing fertility and child mortality rates, and thereby inhibits progress in collective welfare in developing countries. While promoting gender equality would require purposive interventions, it is also integral to the promotion of the other goals of inclusive growth.

Strengthening governance and institutions. Governance and institutions are critical mechanisms not only in the process of development (Acemoglu and Robinson 2013), but also in the process of weaving social cohesion and enhancing inclusion.[62] The role of governance and institutions have been analysed and observed from multiple vantage points, with the focus largely on representation, rule of law, rights, and corruption. Attention is also drawn to rights at work and the governance of various indicators in the world of work. In the context of the process dimensions of inclusive growth, institutions and governance, are significant instruments to enable participation of weaker communities and to reduce discrimination.[63] Promoting and reforming institutions for an inclusive society is an important goal of the 2030 Agenda.

2.7 Inclusive Growth and the SDGs

Each of the above priority goals also correspond to one or the other of the SDGs and SDG targets.[64] Indeed, the 2030 Agenda for Sustainable Development of the UN is a call for countries around the world to make economic, social and environmental commitments to ensure sustainable, inclusive and holistic development. The concept

[62]Cf. Acemoglu and Robinson (2013).

[63]See Chap. 8 for further details.

[64]UN (2015) op. cit.

of inclusive growth is deeply embedded in the SDGs. The most direct manifestations of this are in SDGs 1, 8 and 10, which are respectively a call to end poverty in all its forms everywhere; promote sustained, inclusive and sustainable economic growth, full and productive employment and decent work for all; and reduce inequality within and among countries. These are equally central goals of the present study. More importantly, the overarching principle of the 17 SDGs to *leave no one behind* sheds a distinctive perspective on inclusive growth, especially that reductions in *average* poverty and inequality, would remain an inadequate yardstick of social inclusion (see Sects. 2.1 and 2.3).

The SDGs uphold the dignity of every human being and emphasise that the SDGs and their associated targets must be met for every person from every segment of society in every country (UN 2015). In order to operationalise the principle of leave no one behind, the SDGs emphasise that concrete measures are needed towards reducing global poverty and inequality, challenging injustice, and to improving the lives of those who are the farthest behind (UNDP 2018). However, as the present study has maintained, a systemic change towards inclusive growth also needs a restructuring of deep-rooted institutions, economic and political processes, government mechanisms and corporate models that tend to create and perpetuate unevenness in allocation of resources and in decision-making authority (CDP 2018). Furthermore, this is a realisation that trickle-down assumptions are impractical, and that clear and constructive efforts are required from the outset in order to ensure that growth is inclusive (Stuart and Samman 2017).

The articulation of the notion of inclusive growth in the SDGs equally implies that division and discrimination between various groups in society must be squarely addressed. The SDGs put the values of equity and non-discrimination at the core of the new agenda, with the objective of ensuring the inclusion of disenfranchised, disempowered and disadvantaged communities, and reducing inequality within and across countries. In order to give effect to such a commitment, what is required is to examine who is being left behind and why, empower those who are identified as left behind and enact policies that prioritise inclusive growth (UNDP 2018).

Of course, the SDGs, with 17 broad goals and 169 targets, are cast on a rather ambitious, and all-embracing platform, ostensibly to accommodate the concerns of individual and groups of countries as well as various global interest groups that are bound by an enveloping commitment to inclusive growth and sustainable development. This is rather a tall order, and though set to be realised by 2030, is likely to remain relevant far longer into the future. However, there is as yet no articulation of a strategy nor an approach on how best to move forward. Hence, while each goal and target are of great pertinence, the ambivalence on a strategy does not help in understanding how these are articulated.[65] At the risk of repetition, as argued previously, an inclusive growth strategy will require country-specific parameters and

[65]"It may be possible to have a smaller set of normative statements or imperatives that would sit alongside (or above, chapeau-like) the official goals, acting as a summary of their vision and clustering issue areas. Easy to communicate and therefore inspire, the imperatives could act as a glue that brings together the sprawling narrative" (Norton and Stuart 2014).

the individual country's perception of priorities. In this regard, the present study, given the postulations above, conforms to the SDG framework, and has chosen the goals that would likely ensure "every country enjoys sustained, inclusive growth and sustainable economic growth and decent work for all" (UN 2015, p. 5).

2.8 Designing a National Inclusive Growth Strategy

The design of an inclusive growth strategy is likely to be constrained not only by the need to address a large number of objectives and goals, but also because the latter are usually less than specific, and often empirically difficult to monitor. The impulses towards designing an inclusive growth strategy is thus mired in a complex constellation of development goals and priorities of an individual country and the policy choices it tries to adopt to realise these goals. While there are likely to be synergies in the process of reaching these goals (e.g. productive employment likely to be poverty-reducing), there are equally concerns of perceived trade-offs between goals (e.g. with regard to resource allocations).[66] Equally significant is the need to have a solid database at the national level to understand the underlying factors behind poverty and inequality, and their multidimensionality.

There are thus likely to be different stances on the relative importance attached to the goals (or pillars) as expounded above, and accordingly, there must exist country-specific variations in the design of an inclusive growth strategy. Nevertheless, the study maintains that the goals identified above provides the basis of consolidating a policy platform that would need to take into account a blend of economic, structural and institutional reforms.

Furthermore, as with the goals of the SDGs, there are always multiple indicators corresponding to each goal (see Annex Table 3.1). One must be mindful that while progress in the attainment of any one indicator may be desirable, it is unlikely to show palpable progress in the goal itself. The present study espouses a broad and simplified policy approach to addressing the major goals of inclusive growth, and prioritises full employment and decent work as the key catalyst and guide to this approach (Sect. 2.5). An employment-focused approach helps to simplify design of such a policy framework. While multiple measures are designed to attain the goals (and even each of the many indicators of a goal), the study subsumes these goals under three potential policy clusters, i.e. sub-strategies, which are closely interlinked. These interlinked sub-strategies, at the country level, can carry enormous variations in policy measures to attain the priority goals or selected indicators that planners deem to be immediately pertinent to their country. The policies within the sub-strategies would be intended to address, inter alia, the following:

Pace and pattern of growth. The significance of this policy cluster has already been mentioned in this study. Foremost, the policy cluster would be geared towards

[66]There may also be conflicting ideological positions among planners, e.g. with regard to relationship between growth and inequality (see Sect. 2.2).

attaining high, sustainable growth (a rising per capita GDP) and structural transformation. An employment-focused growth would enable to shift workers to higher productivity sectors; support reduction of *employment deficits* (and simultaneously achieve some of the indicators of SDG 8). Such a pattern of growth can provide specific attention to disadvantaged groups (e.g. youth unemployed, ethnic groups, etc.) and support reducing discrimination (e.g. gender disparities in labour force participation rate, wages, etc.). This would require a dedicated monitoring and a database with appropriate indicators. A pattern of growth, especially through expansion of job opportunities, can also lower regional inequalities.

Social inclusion interventions. There are innumerable varieties and country examples of social inclusion interventions. It is at the country level, that one can discern the priorities about inclusion of groups and regions and with what policy instruments. As argued earlier, interventions to facilitate greater access to economic/social opportunities are key to the process dimensions of inclusive growth, i.e. the ability to participate in the growth process itself. In particular, access to health, education, skills would certainly enhance prospects in the job market (or self-employment). In the case of loss of jobs or inadequacy of jobs availability, social protection and safety net measures are essential. In most countries, these measures are however, woefully inadequate, largely because informal workers constitute the bulk of the workforce.[67] The need for building up such a social system is being forcefully felt in the aftermath of the impact of the current pandemic. This sub-strategy would need to rethink the urgency of an effective social security strategy with a life-cycle approach as propounded by the ILO.[68]

Governance and institutions. This sub-strategy would contain policy measures that would, clearly provide support to, among other objectives, the realisation of the above sub-strategies. It assumes paramount importance to enhance participation and representation of underprivileged groups; in particular through (a) enhanced public financing of social inclusion interventions; (b) empowering the weaker population through strengthening/reforming institutions and governance structure (i.e. improving on the various governance indicators, such as representation and voice; (c) enhancing the bargaining power of the formal and informal workers for a better participation in an inclusive growth strategy (e.g. rights at work; and related indicators of decent work).

These sub-strategies with the appropriate policy measures are intended to provide the proximate factors to push an economy closer to the pillars. Promotion of non-discrimination and gender equality does not feature as a stand out goal, since this is assumed as a cross-cutting theme. This is shown schematically in the Diagram 2.2 .

The diagram is self-explanatory. However, doubts and debates are bound to arise when each of the sub-strategies are given policy content. The discourses on inclusive growth, significant as they are, still remain in the level of generalities, and the proposed strategy attempts to provide a pragmatic framework for designing an

---

[67] See Islam and Islam (2015) op. cit.

[68] See Chap. 7 of this book.

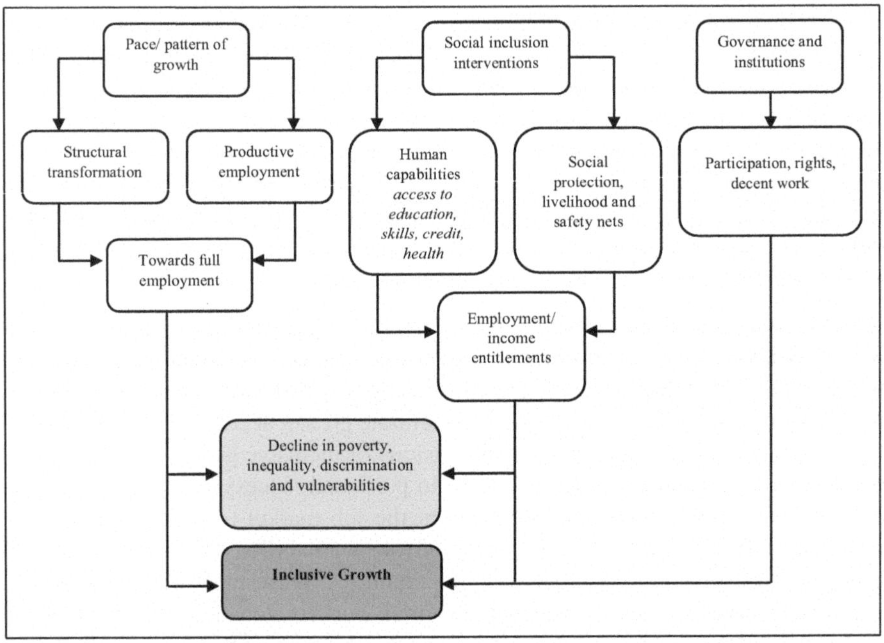

Diagram 2.2 Towards a strategy framework for inclusive growth. *Source* Authors

inclusive growth-path. Here too, in the diagram, the three broad policy clusters would require country-specific introspection in order to trace how each individual country designs its policy measures to attain the stated goals identified in a previous section.

The present study explores the *full employment and decent work* approach to inclusive growth, and hence the policy clusters are likely to carry that bias. A few remarks are in order on the full employment approach to inclusive growth, and how tentative planners have been in adopting such a strategy. Currently, in the global milieu of unemployment, workers' vulnerability and social distress, a strategy for more and better jobs is winning policy debates, but not necessarily the appropriate policy or budgetary attention. There is hardly a government that does not aspire to attain freely-chosen, productive employment for all its workforce. Commitments are often made through ratification of international conventions[69] and regional protocols,[70] but significantly through national laws and policies and strategies.[71] Yet examples are scarce on how these legislations, strategy formulations and their financing are followed through, and with what success.

[69]For example, various ILO Conventions which member countries have ratified.

[70]One example is The European Employment Strategy (now part of Europe 2020 Growth Strategy).

[71]These are many and take varied forms: The Full Employment and Balanced Growth Act, 1978 in the US; the Employment Equity Act, 1998 in South Africa; the Employment Promotion Law in China, etc.

The schematic framework as in Diagram 2.2 is purported to give effect to a commitment to the generation of full and productive employment and decent work as a critical means of alleviating poverty and inequity and ensuring social participation and cohesion,[72] through an appropriate choice of economic and social policies, as well as through the establishment of efficient institutions and the necessary legal framework. Growth, employment and the path to sustainable inclusive growth would require careful interaction of economic and social policies, and building the necessary rules and institutions towards a *virtuous* cycle of growth, equity and inclusion.[73] In as much as social gains are predicated on economic strides, economic growth too, in order to be sustainable, would require social legitimacy.

Each individual country would have to prioritise the indicators to achieve within each goal; hence policies would be emphasised accordingly. The present study will expand on *selected* policies of the sub-strategies, as well as highlight some of the critical debates and limitations of some of the current policy approaches to attaining the goals. This is carried out in the following essays through a selective investigation of the challenges of, and pathways to, inclusive growth in Bangladesh.

References

Acemoglu, D., & Robinson, J. A. (2013). *Why nations fail: The origins of power, prosperity and poverty*. London: Profile Books Ltd.

ADB. (2012). *Asian Development Outlook 2012: Confronting Rising Inequality in Asia*. Manila: Asian Development Bank (ADB).

Ali, I. (2007). *Pro-Poor to Inclusive Growth: Asian Prescriptions*. ERD Policy Brief No. 48 Manila: Economics and Research Department (ERD), Asian Development Bank (ADB).

Ali, I., & Son, H. H. (2007). Measuring inclusive growth. *Asian Development Review, 24*(1), 11–31.

Ali, I., & Zhuang, J. (2007). *Inclusive Growth toward a Prosperous Asia: Policy Implications*. ERD Working Paper No. 97. Manila: Economics and Research Department (ERD), Asian Development Bank (ADB).

Barro, R. J. (2001). Human capital and growth. *The American Economic Review, 91*(2), 12–17.

Berg, A. G., & Ostry, J. D. (2011). *Inequality and Unsustainable Growth: Two Sides of the Same Coin?* IMF Staff Discussion Note SDN 11/08. Washington, D.C.: International Monetary Fund (IMF).

Bhaduri, A. (2005). *Macroeconomic Policies for Higher Employment in the Era of Globalization*. Employment Strategy Paper 2005/11. Geneva: International Labour Organization (ILO).

Bhaduri, A. (2019). Macroeconomic perspective on development. In D. Nayyar (Ed.), *Asian transformations: An inquiry into the development of nations* (pp. 216–239). Oxford: Oxford University Press.

Bhalla, S. (2007). Inclusive growth? *Focus on employment. Social Scientist, 35*(7/8), 24–43.

Bourguignon, F. (2004, February 4). *The poverty-growth-inequality triangle*. Paper presented at the Indian Council for Research on International Economic Relations, New Delhi.

Calderón, C., & Servén, L. (2004). *The Effects of Infrastructure Development on Growth and Income Distribution*. Policy Research Working Paper 3400. Washington, D.C.: The World Bank.

[72]The ILO's pursuit of this goal, in its broad elements, is encapsulated in Decent Work, the Director-General's report to the International Labour Conference, Geneva, 1999.

[73]Also see WEF (2015).

CDP. (2018). *Leaving No One Behind*. Excerpt from CDP Report (ref. Economic and Social Council Supplement No. 13 (E/2018/33)). New York: Committee for Development Policy (CDP), United Nations (UN).

Cornia, G. A. (Ed.). (2004). *Inequality, growth, and poverty in an era of liberalization and globalization*. Oxford: Oxford University Press.

Cornia, G. A., Jolly, R., & Stewart, F. (1987). *Adjustment with a human face*. Oxford, UK: Clarendon Press.

Dabla-Norris, E., Kochhar, K., Suphaphiphat, N., Ricka, F., & Tsounta, E. (2015). *Causes and Consequences of Income Inequality: A Global Perspective*. IMF Staff Discussion Note SDN 15/13. Washington, D.C.: International Monetary Fund (IMF).

Dagdeviren, H., van der Hoeven, R., & Weeks, J. (2000). *Redistribution Matters: Growth for Poverty Reduction*. Employment Paper No. 2000/10. Geneva: International Labour Organization (ILO).

de Haan, A., & Thorat, S. (2013). *Inclusive Growth: More than Safety Nets*. SIG Working Paper 2013/1. Ottawa: International Development Research Centre (IDRC).

Dollar, D., & Kraay, A. (2002). Growth is good for the poor. *Journal of Economic Growth, 7*(September), 195–225.

Easterly, W. (2000). *The Middle Class Consensus and Economic Development*. Policy Research Working Paper 2346. Washington, D.C.: The World Bank.

FAO. (n.d.). *FAOStat*. Rome: Food and Agricultural Organization of the United Nations (FAO). http://www.fao.org/faostat/en/#home Retrieved: 11 July 2020.

Felipe, J. (2012). *Inclusive growth, full employment, and structural change: Implications and policies for developing Asia*. The Anthem—Asian Development Bank Series. London: Anthem Press.

Habito, C. F. (2009). *Patterns of Inclusive Growth in Asia: Insights from an Enhanced Growth-Poverty Elasticity Analysis*. ADBI Working Paper Series No. 145. Tokyo: Asian Development Bank Institute (ADBI).

Hanushek, E. A., & Wößmann, L. (2007). *The Role of Education Quality for Economic Growth*. Policy Research Working Paper 4122. Washington, D.C.: The World Bank.

Ianchovichina, E., & Lundstrom, S. (2009). *Inclusive Growth Analytics: Framework and Application*. Policy Research Working Paper 4851. Washington, D.C.: The World Bank.

ILO. (2009, June 19). *Recovering from the Crisis: A Global Jobs Pact*. Adopted by the International Labour Conference at its Ninety-eighth Session. Geneva: International Labour Organization (ILO).

ILO. (2010). *Recovering from the Crisis: A Global Jobs Pact*. Geneva: International Labour Organization (ILO).

ILO. (n.d.). *ILOSTAT*. Geneva: International Labour Organization (ILO). https://ilostat.ilo.org/ Retrieved 11 July 2020.

IMF. (2017, April). *World Economic Outlook—Gaining Momentum?* Washington, D.C.: International Monetary Fund (IMF).

Islam, R., & Islam, I. (2015). *Employment and inclusive development*. London: Routledge.

Kaldor, N. (1957). A model of economic growth. *The Economic Journal, 67*(268), 591–624.

Khan, A. R. (2001). *Employment Policies for Poverty Reduction*. Issues in Employment and Poverty, Discussion Paper 1. Geneva: Recovery and Reconstruction Department, International Labour Organization (ILO).

Khan, A. R. (2015). *The economy of Bangladesh: A quarter century of development*. Basingstoke: Palgrave Macmillan UK.

Khan, M. H. (2019). Institutions and development. In D. Nayyar (Ed.), *Asian transformations: An inquiry into the development of nations* (pp. 321–345). Oxford: Oxford University Press.

Klasen, S. (2000). *Does Gender Inequality Reduce Growth and Development? Evidence from Cross-Country Regressions*. Discussion Paper 212. Munich: Collaborative Research Center, Munich University.

Klasen, S. (2010). *Measuring and Monitoring Inclusive Growth: Multiple Definitions, Open Questions, and Some Constructive Proposals*. ADB Sustainable Development Working Paper No. 12. Manila: Asian Development Bank (ADB).
Kuznets, S. (1955). Economic growth and income inequality. *American Economic Review, 45*(1), 1–28.
Lewis, A. (1954). Economic development with unlimited supplies of labour. *Manchester School, 22*(2), 139–191.
McKinley, T. (2009). *Revisiting the Dynamics of Growth, Inequality and Poverty Reduction*. Discussion Paper 25/09. London: Centre for Development Policy and Research, School of Oriental and African Studies, University of London.
Milanovic, B. (2016). *Global inequality: A new approach for the age of globalization*. Cambridge, USA: Harvard University Press.
Nayyar, D. (2014). Why employment matters: Reviving growth and reducing inequality. *International Labour Review, 153*(3), 351–364.
Norton, A., & Stuart, E. (2014, November 26). SDGs: Why 17 goals and 19 indicators might not be such a bad thing. *The Guardian*.
Ostry, J. D., Berg, A., & Tsangarides, C. G. (2014). *Redistribution, Inequality and Growth*. IMF Staff Discussion Note SDN 14/02. Washington, D.C.: International Monetary Fund (IMF).
Piketty, T. (2006). The Kuznets curve: Yesterday and tomorrow. In A. V. Banerjee, R. Bénabou, & D. Mookherjee (Eds.), *Understanding poverty* (pp. 63–72). Oxford: Oxford University Press.
Piketty, T. (2014). *Capital in the twenty-first century*. Cambridge MA: The Belknap Press.
Ranieri, R., & Ramos, R. A. (2013). *Inclusive Growth: Building up a Concept*. IPC-IG Working Paper No. 104. Brasília: International Policy Centre for Inclusive Growth (IPC-IG).
Rauniyar, G., & Kanbur, R. (2010). *Inclusive Development: Two Papers on Conceptualization, Application, and the ADB Perspective*. Manila: Asian Development Bank (ADB).
Ravallion, M. (2001). Growth, inequality and poverty: Looking behind the averages. *World Development, 29*(11), 1803–1815.
Ravallion, M. (2005). *Inequality is Bad for the Poor*. Policy Research Working Paper 3677. Washington, D.C.: The World Bank.
Ravallion, M. (2009). *The Developing World's Bulging (but Vulnerable) "Middle Class"*. Policy Research Working Paper 4816. Washington, D.C.: The World Bank.
Sen, A. (1997). From income inequality to economic inequality. *Southern Economic Journal, 64*(2), 384–401.
Sen, A. K. (1999). *Development as freedom*. Oxford: Oxford University Press.
Sobhan, R. (2010). *Challenging the injustice of poverty: Agendas for inclusive development in South Asia*. New Delhi: Sage Publications India Pvt Ltd.
Stiglitz, J. E. (2016). Inequality and economic growth. In M. Jacobs & M. Mazzucato (Eds.), *Rethinking capitalism: Economics and policy for sustainable and inclusive growth* (pp. 134–155). New Jersey: Wiley-Blackwell.
Stuart, E., & Samman, E. (2017). *Defining 'leave no one behind'*. London: Overseas Development Institute (ODI).
UN. (2015). *Transforming Our World: The 2030 Agenda for Sustainable Development*. New York: United Nations (UN).
UNDP. (2018, August). *What does it mean to Leave No One Behind? A UNDP Discussion Paper and Framework for Implementation*. New York: United Nations Development Programme (UNDP).
van Zon, A., & Muysken, J. (2003). *Health as a Principal Determinant of Economic Growth*. Research Memorandum 024. Maastricht: Maastricht Economic Research Institute on Innovation and Technology (MERIT), Maastricht University.
Wan, G., & Wang, C. (2019). Poverty and inequality. In D. Nayyar (Ed.), *Asian transformations: An inquiry into the development of nations* (pp. 240–266). Oxford: Oxford University Press.
WEF. (2015). *The Inclusive Growth and Development Report 2015*. Geneva: World Economic Forum (WEF).

World Bank. (2005). *Pro-poor growth in the 1990s: Lessons and insights from 14 countries*. Washington, D.C.: The World Bank.

World Bank. (2008). *The Growth Report: Strategies for Sustained Growth and Inclusive Development*. Washington, D.C.: Commission on Growth and Development, The World Bank.

World Bank. (2012). *World Development Report 2013: Jobs*. Washington, D.C.: The World Bank.

World Bank. (n.d.a). *Poverty and Equity Database*. Washington, D.C.: The World Bank. https://datacatalog.worldbank.org/dataset/poverty-and-equity-database Retrieved 11 July 2020.

World Bank. (n.d.b). *World Development Indicator (WDI) database*. Washington, D.C.: The World Bank. https://databank.worldbank.org/data/home.aspx Retrieved 12 July 2020.

Chapter 3
Inclusive Growth in Bangladesh: Evidence and Issues

Towfiqul Islam Khan, Mostafa Amir Sabbih, and Muntaseer Kamal

Abstract Bangladesh has been able to achieve noteworthy progress in terms of sustained economic growth, poverty alleviation and several other social indicators. Despite these being no mean achievement, the extent of inclusiveness of the attained growth still requires closer inspection. To this end, the present chapter attempts to assess Bangladesh's progress over time in achieving inclusive growth through a set of indicators under seven broad pillars, viz. poverty and inequality, growth and structural transformation, employment, access to infrastructure and public services, health and education, gender equality, and governance and institutions. This exercise would help to assess and underscore the sources and foundations of inclusive growth, and to identify the binding constraints to future growth and its equitable sharing. Furthermore, this chapter provides a cross-country comparison with six other Asian countries to portray a comparative performance of Bangladesh. Finally, it presents a composite inclusive growth index that enables both cross-country and intertemporal assessment. Based on the findings, this paper has identified four priority areas to be acted upon for the attainment of inclusive growth in Bangladesh, i.e. employment; access to infrastructure and public services; access to education, health and social protection; and governance and institutions.

3.1 Introduction

Since its independence in 1971, the Bangladesh economy has been a subject of widespread interest and research among national and international academia and development practitioners. During the 1970s Bangladesh was seen as a *test case*

T. I. Khan (✉) · M. A. Sabbih · M. Kamal
Centre for Policy Dialogue (CPD), Dhaka, Bangladesh
e-mail: towfiq@cpd.org.bd

M. A. Sabbih
e-mail: sabbih@cpd.org.bd

M. Kamal
e-mail: muntaseer@cpd.org.bd

M. Muqtada (ed.), *Quest for Inclusive Growth in Bangladesh*,
South Asia Economic and Policy Studies,
https://doi.org/10.1007/978-981-15-7614-0_3

for development, with such challenges as, inter alia, tackling mass poverty (nearly four-fifths of the population was below poverty threshold) (Faaland and Parkinson 1976). Early efforts to grow a war-torn economy were handicapped by severe lack of resources, infrastructure and binding fiscal and balance of payments constraints. A quarter century later, at the back of sustained intensification of productivity of food agriculture, readymade garments (RMG)-based growth of industrialisation, and a steady flow of remittances from a rapidly rising number of migrant workers going abroad to seek an earning, Bangladesh managed to ease some of those binding constraints, and lay the foundations of stable growth, especially since the late 1990s (Rahman et al. 2014). It has since been a story of remarkably steady acceleration of economic growth with corresponding steady decline in poverty. Such overall robust economic performance has helped Bangladesh in graduating to a status of lower middle-income country (LMIC) according to World Bank income criteria in 2015 (Rahman and Bari 2016; ADB 2016). Understanding these achievements amid severe uphill conditions has equally given rise to varied research accounts on development planning in Bangladesh.

Furthermore, Bangladesh has attained substantial progress in a number of social indicators, and is often cited as the *development surprise* or *Bangladesh conundrum* for having leapfrogged on several social indicators, especially those under the Millennium Development Goals (MDGs), ahead of India and Pakistan, whose per capita incomes are relatively much higher (Mahmud et al. 2013; Asadullah et al. 2014). In particular, on counts of life expectancy, fertility rates, infant mortality, and girls' education, there has been significant progress within a short time. Population growth, within the dynamic of declining fertility and mortality rates and increasing enrolment of girls in primary and secondary education, has declined quite perceptibly; the demographic factor, often neglected in growth analysis, has played a significant role (World Bank 2012; Rahman et al. 2014). Per capita gross domestic product (GDP) growth has accelerated faster than overall GDP growth, thanks to a decline in population growth, moving from 1.5% during the 1980s to nearly 5% in the recent years, and to nearly 6% during the two most recent years. Together with this respectable per capita GDP growth, there has been the introduction and a rapid proliferation of various public expenditure and non-government organisation (NGO) programmes (especially microcredit), catering towards poverty alleviation, as well as elaborate safety nets and special employment and income programmes. These factors, along with changing demographic structure (resulting in a decline in dependency ratio), and increase in labour income, etc. have, within a span of two decades, nearly halved the incidence of poverty from its benchmark of nearly 57% in the early 1990s to attain an important MDG milestone (GED 2015a).

Despite this being a commendable feat, this chapter argues that the challenges in attaining an inclusive growth in Bangladesh are still formidable, one that would require a concerted and purposive strategy. Bangladesh's noteworthy economic and social progress over the last two decades—particularly in the case of poverty reduction and sustained economic growth was achieved in spite of major internal and external challenges, including natural calamities, the Global Financial Crisis

(GFC), and periods of major political instability. At the policy level, the importance of inclusive growth has also been recognised in Bangladesh. The Seventh Five Year Plan (7FYP) of Bangladesh aimed not only to adopt a set of strategies for fostering economic growth to a *seven-per-cent-plus* level, but also sought to implement complementary strategies and policies for making the growth-path inclusive (GED 2015b). The plan document, while defining inclusiveness, went beyond the income concept of welfare and included issues such as opportunity, productive employment and access to services for the marginalised and physically challenged people. Thus, the present policy framework of Bangladesh government aspires to attain an economic growth which is sustainable, broad-based in terms of employment opportunities, and one that would benefit the marginalised. The importance of governance-related issues was also acknowledged in the inclusive growth concept of 7FYP. The plan document emphasised that for development to be meaningful, its benefits must be widely shared by all the citizens of the country which would require strengthening of the key institutions, ultimately fostering inclusion (GED 2015b). Among the institutional aspects recognised by the 7FYP, pluralistic democracy is one. However, other institutional aspects concerning issues such as gender equality, access to education, health and social protection, employment opportunity, protection of labour rights to organise and strive for decent wages are also recognised as critical. These issues are particularly outlined in the 2030 Agenda for Sustainable Development, which Bangladesh has adopted as future guideline for its national development agenda. Having such a comprehensive development perspective has become more pertinent in view of the recent outbreak of COVID-19 when guarantee for healthcare, social protection and decent employment for all citizens has become critical for every nation.

How inclusive has growth been in Bangladesh? There may be multiple issues with regard to building an empirical base to assess a country's progress on inclusive growth. Nevertheless, the present chapter attempts to trace the progress of Bangladesh on the seven pillars involving seven development goals that the present book has identified (see Chap. 2), through trend analysis of various indicators under each pillar. The multiple indicators under each pillar are purported to provide a broad gauge of how Bangladesh is faring with regard to the respective development goals. Although inclusive growth has many qualitative dimensions as well, such empirical constructs nevertheless would help to assess and underscore the sources and foundations of such growth, and to identify the binding constraints to future growth and its equitable sharing in its outcomes and processes. To this end, this chapter tracks progress in the areas of the aforementioned seven goals related to inclusive growth in Bangladesh. Finally, it attempts to construct an inclusive growth index[1] for Bangladesh to evaluate broad progress of the country as well as its relative position vis-à-vis a select set of developing countries, drawn largely from South Asia (India, Nepal, Pakistan and Sri Lanka) and two from Association of Southeast Asian Nations (ASEAN) (Vietnam and Cambodia). This is simply indicative in nature, intending to portray

[1]See Box 3.1 in Sect. 3.10 for details on the construct of the index.

the comparative performance of Bangladesh. The proposed inclusive growth index also provides a benchmark assessment of Bangladesh's journey towards inclusive development during the recent period.

3.2 Sustainable Growth and Structural Transformation

During the past two decades, there has been, by and large, a marked increase in the rate of economic growth of Bangladesh. GDP growth has been fairly steady and rising; apart from the initial odd years since the mid-1990s, average annual growth rates have steadily increased from around 5% to around 7% (8.2% in 2018–19). Such a growth trend over a long period also showed remarkable resilience during the global financial and economic crisis of 2007–08 and has contributed significantly to a decline in the poverty incidence (Rahman et al. 2009, 2010; ADB 2016). The average growth rate of GDP per capita has increased by two and half times between 1991–1995 and 2011–2015 periods in Bangladesh. From among the selected countries, India had the highest average per capita GDP growth (5.5%) during 2011–2015, followed by Cambodia (5.5%), Sri Lanka (5.3%) and Bangladesh (5.1%) (Fig. 3.1). However, Bangladesh is the only country among them which could sustain and increase its average per capita GDP growth rate for a prolonged period. All the others have experienced volatility. Thus, growth has also been less volatile in Bangladesh, compared to the comparator countries. However, this growth trajectory may change in view of COVID-19. The global economy collectively is expected to experience the deepest recession in the recent decades (World Bank 2020), while GDP growth in Bangladesh is also anticipated to slow down in 2020. According to CPD (2020), GDP growth rate may not be more than 2.5% in 2019–20, which was originally programmed to be 8.2%.

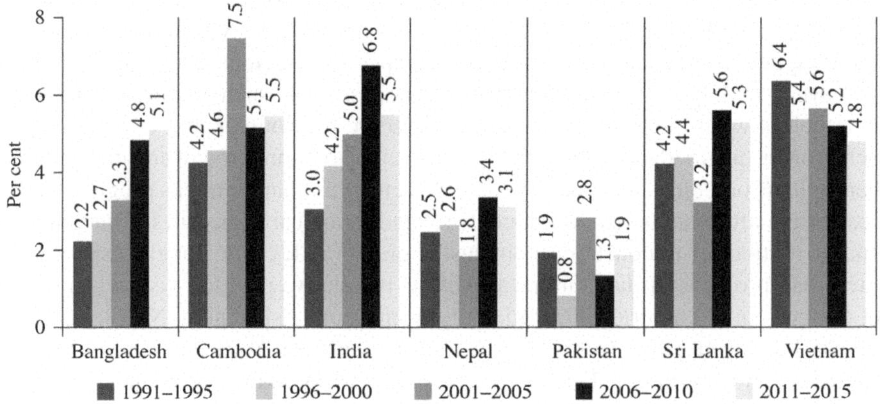

Fig. 3.1 GDP per capita growth (annual %, 5-year average) *Source* World Bank (n.d.a)

Table 3.1 Bangladesh's performance under selected indicators of growth and structural transformation

Indicator	1991	1995	2000	2005	2010	2015	2018
GDP per capita growth (annual %)[a]	N/A	2.3	2.7	3.3	4.8	5.1	6.3
Output per worker (GDP constant 2010 USD)	1,263	1,352	1,491	1,709	2,088	2,617	2,948
Manufacturing, value-added (% of GDP)	14.0	15.9	14.0	14.7	16.1	16.8	18.0
Gross value of agricultural production (current USD) per hectare	796	926	896	1,359	2,052	2,813	2,877[b]
Gross fixed capital formation, private sector (% of GDP)[a]	N/A	11.2	16.4	19.1	21.4	22.1	23.1
Export concentration index (HHI)	N/A	0.34	0.37	0.38	0.40	0.41	0.40

Source World Bank (n.d.a), ILO (n.d.), FAO (n.d.); UNCTAD (n.d.), and authors' calculations
Note HHI: Herfindahl-Hirschman Index
[a]The considered periods were 1991–1995, 1996–2000, 2001–2005, 2006–2010, 2011–2015, 2016–2018; [b]As of 2016; N/A implies not available

A decomposition of per capita GDP shows that around 71% of the growth in GDP per capita was attributed to increasing productivity, particularly in the industry sector (World Bank 2013). Labour productivity increased by more than two times to USD 2,948 in 2018 from USD 1,263 in 1991 (Table 3.1). However, the extraordinary growth levels of total factor productivity (TFP) that have been important drivers for Bangladesh's growth so far (Rahman et al. 2014; World Bank 2012) may not be sustainable. The contribution of capital stock to GDP growth has been minor in recent years, despite increases, albeit slow, in investment to GDP (ADB 2016).

Along with a steady GDP growth, Bangladesh's economy has been undergoing a moderate degree of structural transformation. There can be multiple dimensions and indicators of structural transformation, the more traditionally understood being the changing shares of the various sectors in national value-added, and in total employed labour force. In Bangladesh, the transformation is more evident in terms of the former than by the latter. In terms of value-added, the manufacturing sector has increasingly claimed a greater share in total GDP from 14% in 1991 to 18% in 2018 (Table 3.1). The role of services in the growth process is vital as it is the single largest contributor to the GDP (53% in 2018). This stable share of services and rising share of industry, particularly manufacturing, brought down the share of agriculture from about one-third of GDP in 1990 to 13.1% in 2018. While this shift has often been identified as a *poverty-reducing shift* and is necessary to sustain and improve the current growth rates (World Bank 2013), a more critical measure widely used to characterise structural transformation is the sectoral shares in employment, which have not correspondingly changed as markedly as the sectoral shares in value-added (ADB and ILO 2016). This is further discussed below.

There are indeed several other indicators that would support the extent and nature of the structural transformation in the economy. The present study has briefly looked at three such indicators. First, growth in agriculture and its productivity which is vital to an economy's transformation. Bangladesh has more than tripled its value of agricultural production from USD 796 per hectare in 1991 to USD 2,877 per hectare in 2016 (Table 3.1); however, this is still tangibly behind Vietnam, Nepal and Sri Lanka. One may note that agricultural productivity was far higher in East Asian economies during the 1960s and 1970s than those achieved by the countries under study. In Bangladesh, introduction of high-yielding variety (HYV) technology and higher cropping intensity have led to higher productivity from which farmers have certainly benefitted (Rahman and Khan 2015). The value of agricultural production per hectare grew at a faster rate (8.9%) in Bangladesh during 2001–2016 period compared to 1991–2000 period (1.3%). This pace of acceleration was much higher in Cambodia, Vietnam and Nepal during the corresponding period.

Second, the average share of private investment to GDP which has increased by more than 10 percentage points from 11.2% in 1991–1995 to 23.1% during 2016–2018 period. This is well below the observed levels (more than 30% of GDP) attained by the majority of the East and Southeast Asian countries during their early growth episodes. Furthermore, private investment in Bangladesh has been stagnated around 22% of GDP during most part of the last decade. Lack of adequate infrastructural facilities including supply of quality electricity and gas, relatively high rates of lending and lack of confidence among investors due to political uncertainties are some of the commonly cited reasons for stagnation in private investment in Bangladesh during this decade (CPD 2014, 2015).

Third, the export structure of Bangladesh, which reflects growth and maturity in the trade and industrialisation scenario of an economy, is yet to show perceptible diversification; instead, it is highly concentrated in some particular products. Based on the HHI or concentration index, export concentration in Bangladesh has increased in recent times and (with a value of 0.4) is the highest among the selected countries (Table 3.1). In point of fact, Bangladesh's export basket has continued to remain concentrated in only *one* product—apparels, and particularly in low-end items (Rahman 2014). In Bangladesh, the export growth was mainly concentrated in the garments sector (i.e. RMG) due to the advantage given to garments by Multi Fibre Arrangement (MFA) quotas before 2005 and preferential access to foreign markets (ILO 2013).

Bangladesh has been able to maintain a steady economic growth since the 1990s leading up to 2018. Nonetheless, stagnant private investment and high concentration of export to a single product will continue to pose challenges. Increased physical and human capital investment, coupled with the growth of TFP will be crucial towards graduating to upper middle-income country (UMIC) status as well as achieving a sustainable economic growth.

3.3 Poverty and Inequality

Bangladesh's sustained growth, complemented by a large number of long-standing public and NGO programmes that are focused on providing income and employment entitlements to the poor and vulnerable, have led to a significant fall in the incidence of poverty, and have contributed to meeting the MDG target of halving poverty incidence by 2015 (see Tables 3.2 and 3.3). There have equally been significant improvements in various other MDGs and social indicators (Jolliffe et al. 2014). As shown in Table 3.2, the poverty incidence declined from 56.6% in 1991–92 to 24.3% in 2016. The incidence of extreme poor denoted by the lower poverty threshold has

Table 3.2 Poverty trends in Bangladesh during 1991–92 to 2016 (%)

Year	National poverty line		USD 1.90 (2011 PPP)
	Upper	Lower	
1991–92	56.6	41.0	44.2
1995–96	50.1	35.6	35.7
2000	48.9	34.3	34.8
2005	40.0	25.1	25.7
2010	31.5	17.6	19.6
2016	24.3	12.9	14.8

Source Household Income and Expenditure Survey (HIES) (various issues), Bangladesh Bureau of Statistics (BBS); World Bank (n.d.a)
Note PPP: Purchasing Power Parity

Table 3.3 Income Gini coefficient in Bangladesh: 1973–2016

Year	National	Rural	Urban
1973–74	0.36	0.35	0.38
1981–82	0.39	0.36	0.41
1983–84	0.36	0.35	0.37
1985–86	0.38	0.36	0.37
1988–89	0.38	0.37	0.38
1991–92	0.39	0.36	0.40
1995–96	0.43	0.38	0.44
2000	0.45	0.39	0.50
2005	0.47	0.43	0.50
2010	0.46	0.43	0.45
2016	0.48	0.45	0.50

Source Statistical Yearbook of Bangladesh (various issues) and HIES (various issues), BBS

been even more significant, dropping from 41 to 12.9% during the same period. The rate of decline during this period outperformed a majority of countries (Giménez et al. 2014).

Nevertheless, Bangladesh's notable progress in reducing income poverty during the last two decades has been universally acclaimed by national and international experts as noteworthy, partially overcoming the challenges of being a *test case of development*. In fact, the rate of poverty reduction has been faster in the present decade compared to the previous ones (GED and UNDP n.d.). The incorporation of MDGs with national plans and policies, after their inception in 2000, powered the poverty reduction process of Bangladesh (Rahman et al. 2014). The steady growth of per capita income, growth of agricultural productivity and real wages, the spurt in RMG exports and remittances from migration have been significant explanatory factors (Rahman et al. 2014; ADB 2016). Empirical studies (Osmani et al. 2013; Osmani and Latif 2013) identified few other important factors that significantly contributed to rural poverty reduction, such as access to assets (both land and non-land), education, increasing number of household working members and greater connectivity. Furthermore, microfinance activities grew immeasurably during the 1980s and 1990s in terms of both scale and scope following the expansion of NGOs including Grameen Bank and BRAC. Khandker and Samad (2014) estimated that microcredit intervention contributed to more than 10% of extreme poverty reduction in rural Bangladesh during 2000–2010 period. Meanwhile, using a longitudinal household panel database, Razzaque (2010) estimated that the poverty headcount ratio of all the eligible non-participant households would fall by 7 percentage points, if they were brought under microfinance.

Nonetheless, despite this impressive achievement, there is little scope for complacency. Sobhan (2010) suggested that the persistence of widespread deprivation has been owing to the failure of policy regimes to address the root causes of poverty, i.e. in the inequitable distribution of economic and political resources. The incidence of poverty in Bangladesh is still one of the highest among the seven countries that are examined in this paper. Furthermore, the national poverty still encompasses a substantial portion of vulnerable population. Indeed, based on both national and comparative perspectives, deprivation still remains widespread in Bangladesh. A recent study by Bhattacharya et al. (2016) found that there exists regional disparity with regard to poverty reduction during the MDGs period. In view of COVID-19, poverty rate in Bangladesh may further increase—CPD (2020) estimated that COVID-19 may result in a rise of national poverty rate to 35% in 2020.

While poverty is on the decline, there is concern over steadily rising inequality, which could potentially inhibit the pace of growth and poverty reduction (Khan 2015). Bangladesh's income inequality has risen since the 1990s, commonly measured with Gini index, and as observed in Table 3.3. Osmani (2015) noted that from 2000 to 2010, Bangladesh experienced steady and strong GDP growth, averaging a rate of 5.8% per year, accompanied by rising income inequality. In fact, income inequality has been steadily increasing, and in view of COVID-19, income inequality may increase further to 0.52 in 2020 (CPD 2020).

Table 3.4 Performance of Bangladesh in selected indicators of poverty and inequality

Indicator	1990	1995	2000	2005	2010	2015	2018
Poverty headcount ratio at national poverty lines (% of population)	56.6[a]	50.1	48.9	40.0	31.5	24.3[b]	N/A
Poverty headcount ratio at USD 1.90 per day (2011 PPP) (% of population)	44.2[a]	35.7	34.8	25.7	19.6	14.8[b]	N/A
Median wealth per adult (USD)	N/A	N/A	452	544	1,069	2,152	2,673
Gini index (World Bank estimate)	27.6[a]	32.9	33.4	33.2	32.1	32.4[b]	N/A
Palma ratio	1.0[a]	1.3	1.3	1.3	1.3	1.3[b]	N/A
Expenditure on social protection (% of total government expenditure)	N/A	N/A	3.8[c]	2.5	7.5	6.5	6.3[b]

Source World Bank (n.d.a), IMF (n.d.), Credit Suisse (2019); and authors' calculations
Note [a]As of 1991; [b]As of 2016; [c]As of 2001; N/A implies not available

Inequality is tricky to measure, and various assumptions and perspectives provide different outcomes. Thus, as World Bank (2017) suggests, referring to consumption expenditure, inequality in Bangladesh has been steady and at an acceptable level. In terms of consumption expenditure, Bangladesh has had a relatively lower inequality among the selected countries. Though expenditure inequality was higher in post-2000 periods than it was in 1990s, it is relatively low by regional comparison and has remained fairly stable in recent years.

An alternative measure of inequality is the Palma ratio,[2] which is seen to be increasing consistently since the mid-1990s. The ratio increased from 1 in 1991 to 1.3 in 2016 (Table 3.4). However, Bangladesh appears to have a comparatively better ratio, while Vietnam, Sri Lanka and India showed more inequality with ratios of 2.1, 1.6 and 1.5, respectively. Income share held by the poorest 40% of population is regarded as a proxy for assessing the conditions of the vulnerable non-poor. In Bangladesh, these vulnerable groups include particularly those in self-employment, own account workers, unpaid family helpers and casual day workers (Islam 2014).

The above empirical observations tend to show fairly convincingly that income inequality in Bangladesh is much higher than consumption inequality (as observed from the respective Gini values), and that income inequality is constantly rising. As well-known, incomes of the rich are almost always underestimated, partly due to non-reporting and tax-avoidance. However, part of the explanation of rising income inequality may lie in the overall wealth distribution and other income-generating assets amongst the population. Bhattacharya et al. (forthcoming) attempted to estimate an approximate wealth distribution based on unit-level data from HIES 2005, 2010. Table 3.5, estimated under some assumptions, shows that wealth distribution is even more skewed than income, and that wealth inequality has increased (Gini ratio increased from 0.72 in 2005 to 0.74 in 2010). The aforesaid study demonstrated that income and wealth inequalities have increased in recent years which appear to be

[2]Palma ratio is the ratio of the richest 10% of the population's share of gross national income (GNI) divided by the share of the poorest 40%.

Table 3.5 Concentration of wealth at household level in Bangladesh: an approximation

Household position/indicator	National		Rural		Urban	
	2005	2010	2005	2010	2005	2010
Bottom 5%	0.06	0.04	0.01	0.08	0.02	0.02
Top 5%	47.99	51.32	35.24	35.75	51.67	53.64
Gini coefficient	0.72	0.74	0.63	0.62	0.78	0.79

Source Bhattacharya et al. (forthcoming)
Note Wealth is the sum of the value of agricultural assets, non-agricultural enterprises, owner-occupied houses, consumer durable goods, other land and properties, and other assets

greater in urban areas. In addition, there exists vast disparity between households with the highest and lowest wealth status. Meanwhile, median wealth per adult increased by 10.4% on average from USD 452 in 2000 to USD 2,673 in 2018 (Table 3.4), which is the third lowest among the comparator countries.

Social protection may contribute to different well-being dimensions to various degrees. Babajanian et al. (2014) identified reduced household health expenditure, increased food security and productive capacity, enhanced knowledge and social relations, and increased household consumption to be main contributions of social protection schemes based on their study on India, Bangladesh, Afghanistan and Nepal. Each of the aforementioned impacts has significant implication towards poverty reduction. For social protection, Bangladesh spent 6.3% of total government outlay in 2016 while the figure was 3.8% in 2000 (Table 3.4). In the regional context, Bangladesh is lagging behind India and Sri Lanka (see Sect. 3.6).

Reduction of poverty and equality and enhancing the living standards of the bulk of the population will continue to remain a major development challenge. It is in order to ameliorate the conditions of these vulnerable groups and million others, who constitute the socially excluded, that Bangladesh has embarked on an inclusive growth strategy (GED 2015b). Such a strategy would need to scrutinise why inequality is growing so persistently and ascertain whether this could potentially slow down the pace of poverty reduction. Results by Zaman et al. (2012) indicated towards a shift in the spatial distribution of poverty over the last three decades and suggested the need for policy adjustment to spur further reduction in regional poverty.

3.4 Employment

As contended in a previous chapter, productive employment generation is a central metric of inclusive growth, and will be an imperative policy challenge to absorb the growing labour force, to distribute the benefit of economic growth, and to reduce poverty in a sustainable way. Empirical evidence also showed that in many countries, including Bangladesh, economic growth has not transpired to desired rate of growth of productive employment (Islam and Islam 2015). According to recent Labour

Force Surveys (LFSs), labour force is growing at 3.51% annually, while employment is growing at around 3.36% (Islam 2014). Although the unemployment rate is officially stated as 4.2% (BBS 2017), which could apparently signal a condition of full employment, there are multiple indicators to show that there exists considerable slack in the labour market. Thus, the employment challenge would be to absorb not only the net additions to the workforce, but also the stock of unemployed and underemployed. Additionally, there are studies to suggest that the bulk of the labour force in Bangladesh is vulnerable. These include particularly those in self-employment, own account workers, unpaid family helpers and casual day workers (Islam 2014).

Table 3.6 provides some reflections on the progress Bangladesh has achieved with respect to employment and labour market outcomes. Labour income was the single most important contributor to poverty reduction in the period 2000–2010, with a share of 70% in total income (World Bank 2013). Bangladesh is characterised by its large labour force which provides the country with a comparative advantage in the production of labour-intensive goods (World Bank 2007). Around 59% of the population in Bangladesh participate in the labour force, which was not very different in the early 1990s (Table 3.6).

According to World Bank (2012), at the present rate of labour force growth (3.2%), approximately 21 million people will enter into the labour force over the next decade. This poses both a challenge and a window of opportunity of demographic dividend for Bangladesh. However, Bangladesh economy has absorbed just under 50% of the increase in the working age population into the economy in the period 2000–2010. World Bank (2012) illustrated that even a 7% GDP growth annually would add only

Table 3.6 Performance of Bangladesh in selected employment indicators

Indicator	1990	1995	2000	2005	2010	2015	2018
Labour force participation rate, total (% of total population aged 15+) (modelled ILO estimate)	57.8	57.8	57.7	57.5	56.9	56.6	59.0
Unemployment, total (% of total labour force) (modelled ILO estimate)	2.2[a]	2.5	3.3	4.3	3.4	4.4	4.3
Unemployment, youth total (% of total labour force aged 15–24) (modelled ILO estimate)	5.5[a]	6.3	9.7	8.9	6.4	10.8	12.1
Employment in industry (% of total employment)[b]	N/A	13.0	10.0	14.1	16.1	20.8	20.5
Employment in manufacturing (% of total employment)[b]	N/A	11.8	7.4	10.4	11.7	16.4	14.4
Share of own account and contributing family workers (%)	N/A	69.4[c]	68.9	63.6[d]	62.2	57.7[e]	55.8[f]

Source World Bank (n.d.a); ILO (n.d.)

Note ILO: International Labour Organization

[a]As of 1991; [b]The considered periods were 1991–1995, 1996–2000, 2001–2005, 2006–2010, 2011–2015, 2016–2018; [c]As of 1996; [d]As of 2006; [e]As of 2016; [f]As of 2017; N/A implies not available

1.5 million jobs if the employment elasticity of growth does not decline any further. Islam and Rahman (2017, p. 6) citing ADB and ILO (2016) noted that in order to fully utilise surplus labour within about 15 years, Bangladesh needs to grow 8% annually. Furthermore, except for in Nepal, youth unemployment is increasing gradually in all the selected countries in the recent years. About 12.1% of youth were unemployed in 2018 in Bangladesh, which is nearly thrice the national average unemployment rate. An analysis by Toufique (2014) showed an increasing rate of youth unemployment with each incremental level of education which indicates the low level of skills required by labour market, dominated by self-employment. Rahman (2014) stated that the assumption of youth entering the labour market smoothly through family employment contributed to the negligence towards youth labour force in the context of Bangladesh's labour market analysis. The author further stressed, since the youth receives education and aspires to get paid jobs and move to new occupations, this assumption may no longer be valid. Therefore, they require separate analysis as they face distinct demand and additional vulnerabilities due to their age (Rahman 2014).

Bangladesh is still dependent on the agriculture sector to engage its vast labour force which provides employment to nearly half of its workforce. Its share of employment in the industrial sector is still very low—only 20.5% in 2016–2018 period, below all the selected countries. Most of the labour force is being absorbed in the informal sector characterised by low skills and low earnings rather than in productive manufacturing sector (Ghani and Ahmed 2009). Employment in manufacturing sector was only 14.4% during 2016–2018 period (Table 3.6). It should also be noted that decline in real income in the industry sector that occurred during 2006–2010, more than offset the gains that took place during 2000–2005 (World Bank 2013). At the same time, the share of own account and contributing family workers in total employment declined from about 69.4% in 1996 to 63.6% in 2005 which further reduced to 55.8% in 2017 (Table 3.6).

Bangladesh is far from achieving a major structural transformation, especially when measured by the changes in the sectoral shares of employment. As Table 3.7 shows, the share of employed workforce in agriculture had remained somewhat constant over 1995–96 to 2016–17 period, although the sector's share in GDP had fallen sharply.

Thus, in order to attain a sustained growth-path toward a middle-income country (MIC), Bangladesh would require undergoing substantial *structural transformation* that would be commensurate with the foundations of a higher-income economy

Table 3.7 Sectoral composition of employment (%)

Sector	1995–96	1999–00	2005–06	2010	2015–16	2016–17
Agriculture	48.9	50.8	48.1	47.5	42.7	40.6
Manufacturing	10.1	9.5	10.9	12.4	14.4	14.4
Construction	2.9	2.8	3.2	4.8	5.6	5.6
Services	38.8	36.1	37.5	35.3	36.9	39.0

Source LFS (various issues), BBS

Table 3.8 Employment elasticity between 1999 to 2017: Selected sectors

Sector	Employment growth per annum (%)	GDP growth per annum (%)	Employment elasticity of GDP
Agriculture, forestry and fishing	1.31	3.86	0.27
Manufacturing, mining and quarrying	4.96	8.55	0.42
Construction	6.95	7.89	0.81
Wholesale and retail trade, repair of motor vehicles	2.55	6.59	0.27
Transportation and storage	4.52	7.35	0.48
Total	2.65	5.98	0.33

Source Authors' calculations based on the data from BBS

(ADB and ILO 2016). Such a transformation is commonly observed through shifts in the *sectoral shares in total employment*. In particular, this is associated with tangible increases in the modern sector's share in total employment. The latter simply characterises relatively rising labour productivity in the economy, with labour force shifting away from low-productivity agriculture to high-productivity manufacturing and services sectors which signifies the Lewisian turning point (Khan 2015). In order to boost productivity and structural transformation, measures would need to be put in place to upgrade skills and education, and infuse higher technology and innovation (World Bank 2012; ADB and ILO 2016). Thus, productive employment generation would need to be associated with growth of jobs in higher productivity sectors, and other conditions to facilitate labour movements between sectors, as well as between regions.

Table 3.8 provides some estimates of the employment growth in selected sectors of the economy during the period 1999–2017, alongside sectoral employment elasticities with respect to output. The relatively higher elasticity, i.e. employment potential, came from manufacturing and construction sectors. It is not clear how much of this employment is in informal form, and how productive and remunerative these are (see Chap. 6 for a further discussion).

The lack of, or slow growth in formal sector jobs during the past three decades is possibly among the greatest failures of development planning in Bangladesh. It is unclear from planning documents how a future development agenda would affect a process of structural transformation which, in turn, would lead to an increase in labour demand and shifts in labour demand to higher productivity sectors. The notion of sustained formal sector job growth (as part of an employment strategy) is, in the ultimate analysis, a significant cornerstone in the promotion of decent work.[3]

[3]It has institutional implications, including the potential to have a larger proportion of the workforce covered by some degree of social protection.

One must note that the employment question is not simply an issue in monitoring the number of jobs added. It is important to assess the quality of job creation, especially with regard to how productive and remunerative the jobs are. A World Bank study cited above contends that along with growth of jobs, the quality of employment has also improved. It provides evidence on this, through a number of indicators, e.g. the rise in wages of wage-workers, poverty decline among the self-employed, and a reduced risk of income uncertainty among the vulnerable groups. Several other studies however provide different perspectives on the quality of employment and contend that employment conditions continue to be poor. Real wages have risen, but has declined or remained stagnant in the recent past. Bulk of the employment continues to be in the informal sector, and that too in the low-end services sector. The incidence of the working poor is still unacceptably high, i.e. those who are working, often more than the standard working hours, but continues to remain below the poverty line (ADB and ILO 2016).

It is equally important to recognise that while the quantity matters in an employment-generating strategy, there must be a close understanding of the specific characteristics and functioning of the labour markets, and how job generation is affecting the various groups in the workforce. A detailed characterisation of the labour markets is beyond the scope of the present study. Apart from the less-than-satisfactory achievements in the quantity and quality of employment, the pattern of growth has also been one that cannot be described as inclusive. The phenomenon of rising inequality in Bangladesh can, in some sense, be found intriguing when bulk of the job generation appears to have occurred in labour intensive sectors, such as agriculture and RMG. On the other hand, rising inequality has its own dynamics where such factors as suppressed wages (i.e. lower than productivity growth), and low aggregate share of wages (in national income) could provide plausible explanations.

3.5 Access to Infrastructure and Public Services

The development of infrastructure is almost universally acknowledged to foster structural transformation, and if appropriately designed, to enhance job creation. In Bangladesh, access to infrastructure is a major bottleneck that, among other factors, inhibits private investment and acceleration of economic growth (CPD 2015, 2016; World Bank 2017). Nevertheless, Bangladesh has made some significant strides in expanding the access of its population to economic infrastructure, though still inadequate (World Bank 2012, 2017; ADB 2016). Investment in infrastructure, particularly in the quality of roads, ports, air transports and electricity supply, was cited in the Global Competitiveness Report as immediate policy priority for doing business in Bangladesh (WEF 2016). Let us examine the nature and extent of the development of infrastructure and public services in Bangladesh, with respect to selected indicators, and in relation to comparator countries.

While the access to electricity has more than doubled in the last two decades, nearly 15% of population still do not have access to electricity as of 2018 (Table 3.9),

Table 3.9 Bangladesh's performance in access to infrastructure and public services indicators

Indicator	1990	1995	2000	2005	2010	2015	2018
Access to electricity (% of population)	14.3[a]	19.7	32.0	44.2	55.3	73.1	85.2
Mobile cellular subscriptions (per 100 people)	0.0	0.0	0.2	6.5	46.0	84.1	100.2
Internet user (per 100 people)	0.0	N/A	0.1	0.2	3.7	14.4	15.0[b]
Improved water source (% of population with access)	68.1	72.1	76.0	79.8	83.5	86.9	N/A
Improved sanitation facilities (% of population with access)	34.4	40.0	45.4	50.7	55.8	60.6	N/A
Logistics Performance Index: Quality of trade- and transport-related infrastructure (1 = low to 5 = high)	N/A	N/A	N/A	2.3[c]	2.5	2.1[d]	2.4

Source World Bank (n.d.a)
Note [a]As of 1991; [b]As of 2017; [c]As of 2007; [d]As of 2017; N/A implies not available

which is the second lowest after Pakistan among the selected countries. Furthermore, Bangladesh has the worst ranking among Asian competitors with regard to power outages which has been a key reason for its low productivity in manufacturing sector (World Bank 2013). This has been hindering the potential for private investment and employment generation. In particular, the Bangladesh Enterprise Survey found that 78% of firms identified lack of access to electricity as a major constraint for businesses (USAID and DFID 2014).

The emergence of different private cellular network companies revolutionised mobile phone subscription in Bangladesh in the post-2000 period. In 2018, around 100 people out of every 100 persons had a subscription in Bangladesh. This was negligible in 2000 (Table 3.9). The extension of fibre optic lines by private operators across the country for the development of speedy internet facilities nationwide have also increased the number of internet users manifold over the last decade (GED 2015a). However, Bangladesh still has one of the lowest incidences of internet users among the selected countries. In 2017, only around 15 people per 100 persons had an internet subscription which was marginal in 2000.

Bangladesh has achieved marginal progress on the access of its population to either an improved water source or to an improved sanitation facility. In 1990, 68.1% of the population had access to improved water sources which increased to 86.9% in 2015, but still lagged behind other selected countries. However, access to safe water for all is an additional challenge here due to arsenic contamination and salinity intrusion which exacerbate the problem of availability of safe water especially for the poor (GED 2015a). ADB (2016) suggested that the probability of having access to clean water increases with the presence of a migrant worker in the family.

Bangladesh almost doubled its access to improved sanitation from 34.4% in 1990 to 60.6% in 2015 (Table 3.9), thanks to different government and non-government awareness programmes. However, more than 40% of population are still deprived of having improved sanitation facilities and the situation is worse in urban slum areas. In the slums, only 12% of the households use an improved sanitation facility in conformity with the government standard, with 15 or more people sharing one toilet due to lack of space (BBS 2014; GED 2015a). ADB (2005) in a study also found inadequate number of public toilets to be a serious problem in larger cities. By comparison, Sri Lanka, Vietnam and Pakistan have a far better access to improved sanitation. Furthermore, using the propensity matching technique, Begum et al. (2011) suggested that the combined access to improved water and sanitation can reduce incidence of diarrhoea which still persists as a major cause of infant mortality, morbidity and acute child malnutrition.

Quality trade and transport-related infrastructure is essential for a country's economic growth as well as national well-being (World Bank 2013). The Logistics Performance Index attempts to delineate said infrastructural quality of a country. In the aforementioned index, Bangladesh scored 2.4 in 2018 which was 2.3 in 2005 (Table 3.9). This situated Bangladesh in the fourth position in terms of infrastructure quality amongst the selected countries in 2018, while its position was fifth and third in 2005 and 2010, respectively.

3.6 Access to Education, Health and Social Protection

Bangladesh has achieved commendable success in some of the major social indicators, particularly in health and education, within a short period of time (Mahmud et al. 2013). Bangladesh was able to make notable improvement, e.g. in reducing hunger during last two decades (from a score of more than 50 in 1995 to 26.1 in 2018; Table 3.10) by successfully reducing the share of the undernourished population and the prevalence of stunting children by half and the under-five mortality rate

Table 3.10 Performance of Bangladesh in selected health and education indicators

Indicator	1995	2000	2005	2010	2015	2018
Global Hunger Index	50.3	36.1	30.7	30.3	27.3	26.1
Births attended by skilled health staff (% of total)[a]	9.5	10.1	12.8	22.3	39.1	49.8
Per capita government expenditure on health (PPP int. USD)	N/A	7.9	9.3	13.5	15.6	15.7[b]
Lower secondary completion rate, total (% of relevant age group)[a]	N/A	52.8	58.2	55.3	64.9	82.6
Pupil–teacher ratio in primary level	N/A	N/A	47.0	43.0	30.1[b]	30.1
Per capita government expenditure on education (PPP int. USD)	22.7[c]	28.3	31.4[d]	44.8[e]	59.1[f]	90.4

Source World Bank (n.d.a); IFPRI (n.d.); WHO (n.d.); and authors' calculations
Note [a]The considered periods were 1991–1995, 1996–2000, 2001–2005, 2006–2010, 2011–2015, 2016–2018; [b]As of 2017; [c]As of 1997; [d]As of 2004; [e]As of 2009; [f]As of 2016; N/A implies not available

by more than three times (IFPRI 2015). Bangladesh has tangibly reduced the hunger score, and has fared comparatively worse than most of the comparator countries, apart from Pakistan (32.6) and India (31.1) in 2018.

The successful programmes for immunisation, control of diarrhoeal disease, treatment of respiratory infections and supplementation of vitamin A are considered to be the most significant contributors in improving child nutrition status and the decline in child deaths (UNICEF 2014; GED 2015a). Klemm et al. (2008) found that supplementing newborns with vitamin A within days of being born significantly reduced mortality under 6 months of age by 15%. Also, the Expanded Programme of Immunization (EPI) has prevented an estimated 2 million deaths and disabilities of children since its inception and preventing estimated 200,000 deaths each year (Begum 2009). However, still 40 children per 1,000 live births aged below 5 years die every year, which is the third highest—after Pakistan and India—among the selected seven countries. These government interventions of Bangladesh have helped to nearly halve its underweight and stunting prevalence among its under-5 children (Bhattacharya et al. 2016). Indeed, National Nutrition Programme (NNP), launched in 2004, itself contributed to reducing prevalence of low birth-weight, moderate and severe malnutrition as well as improving exclusive breastfeeding practice, better than the national average (Chowdhury and Osmani 2010). The incidence, however, is still relatively high compared to other countries in the region. There are also rural–urban, regional and gender differences (Bhattacharya et al. 2016). Bangladesh has also achieved some progress as regards births attended by skilled health personnel. In Bangladesh, during 2016–2018, around 49.8% births were attended by skilled health personnel on an average, which was only 9.5% in the 1990s (Table 3.10). The incidence, which is the lowest among the selected countries, needs to be vastly improved to reduce further the incidence of child mortality.

Per capita government expenditure on health can be a useful lens to look into social protection efforts from the government. Bangladesh has long been an underperformer under this indicator. During 2000, the per capita government expenditure on health in international PPP was a mere USD 7.9, which became USD 15.7 in 2017 (Table 3.10). In the regional perspective, apart from 2000, Bangladesh has consistently been the poorest performer. In addition, still a large number of households, particularly the impoverished, are further burdened by out-of-pocket (OOP) expenditure for healthcare, which accounts for 64% of total health expenditure (MoHFW 2012; USAID 2016).

Although Bangladesh has made significant progress in raising its net enrolment in primary education, net enrolment in secondary education is only 66.5% mainly due to high dropout rate and low completion rate. Bangladesh had the third lowest secondary school completion rate among the selected seven countries, with 82.6% having completed secondary school education during 2016–2018 period. Poverty, through its interlinkage with other factors such as quality of education, parental attitude, etc. influences dropout rate of children (Ahmed et al. 2010). Poverty also has interlinkages with factors such as direct cost, indirect cost and opportunity cost of schooling, and pressure for early marriage (Sabates et al. 2010). Such dropout rates and the resulting low level of literacy and years of schooling in the early ages make skills acquisition challenging when they enter into the labour force.

Pupil–teacher ratio is a key indicator for assessing the quality of education since it provides a general indication of the average amount of time and attention a teacher is likely to give to its pupil. Bangladesh was successful in shrinking the pupil–teacher ratio in primary level over the last decade from 47 students per teacher in 2005 to 30.1 students per teacher in 2018 (Table 3.10). In a regional comparison, it is in the fourth position after Vietnam, Nepal and Sri Lanka. However, this is still not adequate to ensure effective learning of students (Rahman et al. 2016). Furthermore, around 80% of schools in Bangladesh run in double shifts which reduces the learning time in a school-year, which is currently about half of the international average of thousand years (CAMPE 2015). Effective learning is hampered by such systemic factors.

Similar to government expenditure on health, expenditure on education is also an important social protection instrument of the government. Despite education being one of the most priority sectors in national plan documents, Bangladesh is one of the lowest ranked countries in the world in terms of public expenditure for education, both as a share of GDP and total budget (Rahman et al. 2016). However, per capita expenditure on education, in PPP terms, has increased four times over the last two decades from a mere USD 22.7 in 1995 to USD 90.4 in 2018. Among the comparator countries, it was the lowest in 2018. Nevertheless, in a situation of lower domestic resource base, underutilisation of resources, delay in budget implementation, erosion of the real value of the primary and secondary school stipends, leakages in education-related social safety net programmes (SSNPs) are some of the commonly cited reasons that hamper the effectiveness of education spending from a social protection prism in Bangladesh (Rahman et al. 2016).

Social protection has numerous positive impacts on the socio-economic conditions of a country, especially from the perspective of inclusive development. Bangladesh has a long history of formal social safety net programmes. During the 1970s, vulnerable group feeding programmes received the highest focus. Disaster response and relief operations received the highest focus in 1980s, when introducing the component of development in addition to providing food accounted for a remarkable improvement. During the 1990s, programmes to support special groups, that included provision of conditional cash transfer, were widely introduced. In the 2000s, numerous programmes, often reinforced with graduation programmes, were introduced to support different types of risks and vulnerabilities. From 2015, Bangladesh adopted a strategic and comprehensive approach to social protection and developed the National Social Security Strategy (NSSS). The strategy followed a life-cycle approach. Nevertheless, the budgetary allocation for social safety net remained low compared to the size of the economy. According to the latest HIES data, only 32% poor households had access to social protection in 2016, while 19% of the non-poor households had this access. There is indeed room to increase coverage and improve the quality of targetting. The proportion of households in the bottom 40% receiving social protection transfers fell from 33.2% in 2010 to 29.6% in 2016. Indeed, according to the Social Protection Index of the Asian Development Bank (ADB), Bangladesh was also lagging behind Vietnam, Sri Lanka and Nepal (Table 3.11).

Table 3.11 Social Protection Index of various countries

Country	2005	2008	2009	2010
Bangladesh	0.050	0.040	0.040	0.050
Cambodia	0.020	0.020	0.020	0.020
India	0.110	0.010	0.050	0.001
Nepal	0.050	0.050	0.070	0.070
Pakistan	0.050	0.010	0.050	0.010
Sri Lanka	0.110	0.110	0.120	0.110
Vietnam	0.100	0.120	0.140	0.140

Source ADB (n.d.)

3.7 Gender Parity

Bangladesh has made notable progress in attaining gender parity on the educational front. For instance, Bangladesh has achieved gender parity in primary and secondary education in 2005 and 2000, respectively, and in youth literacy in 2010 (Table 3.12). The positive advancement occurred due to some specific public interventions which focused on girl students (UNDP 2015). Government interventions like Food for Education, Primary Education Stipend Program, and Reaching Out of School Children have been successful while considering the issue of gender parity (WFP 2015). Besides the government, NGOs have played a key role in achieving gender parity in Bangladesh. For example, the entry of BRAC schools significantly increased girls' enrolment, compared to boys (Sukontamarn 2005).

Table 3.12 Performance of Bangladesh under different gender equality indicators

Indicator	1990	1995	2000	2005	2010	2015	2018
Gross enrolment ratio, primary, GPI	0.8	N/A	N/A	1.0	1.1	1.1[a]	1.1
Gross enrolment ratio, secondary, GPI	0.5	N/A	1.0	1.1	1.1	1.1	1.2
Literacy rate, youth (aged 15–24), GPI, 10 years average[b]	0.6	0.7	0.7	0.9	1.1	1.1	1.0
Female labour force participation (%) (modelled ILO estimate)	24.7	25.7	27.0	27.9	29.9	32.4	36.1
Share of women in wage employment in the non-agricultural sector (% of total non-agricultural employment)	20.2[c]	26.7[d]	24.7	20.1	18.3	24.2	N/A
Women who were first married by age 18 (% of women aged 20–24)	N/A	73.3[e]	65.3	68.7[f]	64.9[g]	58.6[h]	N/A

Source World Bank (n.d.a)
Note GPI: Gender Parity Index
[a]As of 2017; [b]The considered periods were 1981–1990, 1986–1995, 1991–2000, 1996–2005, 2001–2010, 2006–2015, 2009–2018; [c]As of 1991; [d]As of 1996; [e]As of 1994; [f]As of 2004; [g]As of 2011; [h]As of 2014; N/A implies not available

However, women continue to be at a disadvantage in the labour market, earning much less than men in 2010 (BBS 2011). Regardless, labour force participation for women since 2000 has also improved. The increasing women workforce significantly benefitted from growth of the salaried manufacture-based jobs, as well as increased access to education (World Bank 2013; USAID and DFID 2014).

However, the share of women in wage employment in the non-agricultural sector, which is supposed to indicate their movement into higher quality employment, continued to decline since mid-2000s. Women in Bangladesh still have a very low share in wage employment in the non-agricultural sector, and the lowest amongst selected countries. In Bangladesh, 24.2% of women were engaged with wage employment in non-agricultural sector in 2015 which was 20.2% in 1991 (Table 3.12).

Furthermore, early marriages are still very widespread in Bangladesh; in fact, the highest in this region, followed by Nepal. In 2014, 58.6% women in Bangladesh aged 20–24, got married by the age of 18 which was 73.3% in 1995 (Table 3.12). Such marriages at early ages reduce the opportunity of women from getting empowered through participating in economic and political decision-making. Ahmed et al. (2010) found that due to the prevailing views about early marriage of girls, dropout rate is higher among girl students in rural Bangladesh. Pressure for early marriage is also present both from the religious point of view and security concern of girls, particularly in the rural areas (ICDDR 2007).

3.8 Governance and Institutions

The role of state governance and institutions is very crucial in fostering and sustaining inclusive growth. There is a large cross-country literature highlighting market-enhancing governance and institutions as an important ingredient of economic development (e.g. Acemoglu et al. 2001; Easterly and Levine 2003; Rodrik et al. 2004). The Worldwide Governance Indicators (WGI) report on six broad dimensions of governance for 215 countries over the period 1996–2015 (Kaufmann et al. 2010). The dimensions include: voice and accountability, political stability, government effectiveness, regulatory quality, rule of law and control of corruption.[4] The estimate

[4] *Voice and accountability* encapsulates perceptions regarding the degree to which citizens of a nation can take part in the government selection process, as well as freedom of expression, freedom of association and a free media; *Government effectiveness* delineates perceptions regarding public service quality, civil service quality and the extent of administrative liberty from political pressures; *Political stability* measures perceptions of the likelihood of political instability and/or politically-motivated violence, including terrorism; *Regulatory quality* captures opinions regarding the government's ability to create and maintain a sound policy environment that facilitates private sector development; *Rule of law* portrays perceptions of the degree of people's confidence in and willingness to follow the rules of society, and in particular, the quality of contract enforcement, property rights, the police, and the courts, as well as the likelihood of crime and violence; and *Control of corruption* captures assessment of the extent to which public power is misused for private gain, including both petty and grand forms of corruption, as well as capture of the state by elites and private interests.

Table 3.13 Bangladesh's performance under different indicators of governance and institutions

Indicator	1996	2000	2005	2010	2015	2018
Voice and accountability	−0.06	−0.23	−0.57	−0.27	−0.51	−0.73
Political stability and absence of violence and terrorism	−0.55	−0.72	−1.86	−1.43	−1.21	−1.03
Government effectiveness	−0.69	−0.58	−0.91	−0.74	−0.72	−0.75
Regulatory quality	−0.93	−0.84	−1.07	−0.85	−0.90	−0.83
Rule of law	−0.93	−0.91	−0.98	−0.80	−0.75	−0.64
Control of corruption	−0.97	−1.11	−1.39	−1.06	−0.81	−0.91

Source World Bank (n.d.b)
Note (−) 2.5 correspond to the lowest and (+) 2.5 correspond to the highest state of governance

gives the country's score on the aggregate indicator, in units of a standard normal distribution, i.e. ranging from approximately (−) 2.5 to (+) 2.5.

Bangladesh's strong growth and performance in social indicators contrasts with the relatively poor perceptions of governance in the country. Bangladesh scores poorly in all six indicators, and apart from regulatory quality and rule of law, the performance worsened in the remaining four indicators between 1996 and 2018 (Table 3.13). During 2018, Bangladesh fared worse than India and Sri Lanka in all the six indicators, than Nepal and Vietnam in five indicators, than Cambodia and Pakistan in three indicators. It seems looking at recent history (from the mid-1990s to 2018), the process of development has improved some dimensions of governance quality, at least in the sense that it is no longer abnormally low. Nonetheless, Bangladesh continues to have lower ratings in several indicators compared to other selected countries (see Chap. 8). Bangladesh Enterprise Survey found that 55% of firms identified corruption as a major constraint for businesses (USAID and DFID 2014). In addition, according to the evidence, it is unlikely that governance has contributed to any social development progress in Bangladesh (Asadullah et al. 2014).[5] To the contrary, despite substandard governance quality, social outcomes have improved in Bangladesh compared to its less corrupt neighbours (e.g. India), providing evidence in support of the idea of a development surprise (Asadullah, et al. 2014). However, the effectiveness of social spending may have been undermined by poor governance (Gupta et al. 2002; McGuire 2006).

3.9 Inclusive Growth in Bangladesh: A Recapitulation

This section details out Bangladesh's performance on the basis of the pillars of inclusive growth amongst selected peer countries. Taking cue from that, it also provides an aggregate-level analysis of cross-country performance in attaining inclusive growth.

[5]These issues on the comparative performance of Bangladesh regarding governance and institutions, and their impact on growth and inclusion have been treated at length in Chap. 8.

3.9.1 Poverty and Inequality Pillar

Bangladesh has performed reasonably well in this pillar. However, success in reducing poverty was somewhat offset by increasing inequality. Also, pace of progress in poverty alleviation is relatively slow compared to the peer countries. Lower share of expenditure on social protection as well as low level of median wealth per adult adversely influenced Bangladesh's performance on this pillar. Cambodia showed remarkable progress over the taken timeframe. Pakistan and Sri Lanka showed gradual progress up to 2010 on this pillar, but both declined in 2015. Meanwhile, India, Nepal and Vietnam showed mixed trends (Table 3.14).

3.9.2 Growth and Structural Transformation Pillar

India, Sri Lanka and Vietnam have performed consistently well in this premise. Over the selected timeline, Bangladesh's performance on this pillar has been moderate; however, on a welcome note, an upward trend can be observed (Table 3.14). The recent performance of Bangladesh in terms of economic growth depicts a similar story. However, it has reasons to be concerned about export concentration and labour productivity.

3.9.3 Employment Pillar

On the employment parameter Bangladesh's performance was average. Bangladesh's decline of employment score in 2015 can be attributed to a multitude of waning factors—declining labour force participation rate, stagnated unemployment rate, high level of youth unemployment, relatively lower share of employment in industry, and persisting high share of own account and contributing family workers—against drastic improvement of comparator countries. Unemployment rate, particularly youth unemployment rate, must be checked if Bangladesh wishes to reap the benefits of the demographic dividend. Increase of employment in industry or manufacturing can propel Bangladesh into a higher trajectory within this dimension. Cambodia, Sri Lanka and Vietnam consistently outperformed Bangladesh in this pillar (Table 3.14).

3.9.4 Access to Infrastructure and Public Services Pillar

The crying need for bigger and better infrastructure in Bangladesh is evident from the analysis of this pillar. Despite the success in indicators like improved water

Table 3.14 Pillar-wise scorecard

Year	Bangladesh	Cambodia	India	Nepal	Pakistan	Sri Lanka	Vietnam	Bangladesh rank
1. Poverty and inequality								
2000	4.51	2.42	4.25	2.01	5.85	5.77	5.11	4
2005	5.56	5.48	3.36	1.52	6.55	7.09	5.94	4
2010	5.63	5.97	4.29	5.40	6.69	7.29	4.36	4
2015	4.50	7.72	1.56	1.62	6.44	6.57	6.93	5
2. Growth and structural transformation								
2000	4.13	3.77	6.90	3.14	4.12	8.59	6.42	4
2005	4.51	4.23	7.06	4.14	4.49	8.02	6.47	4
2010	4.90	3.72	7.61	4.60	3.41	8.17	7.31	4
2015	5.97	4.85	7.87	4.79	3.54	8.62	7.35	4
3. Employment								
2000	4.67	5.04	4.85	6.31	4.47	5.76	6.16	6
2005	4.18	5.37	5.10	7.29	4.73	5.68	6.32	7
2010	4.79	7.82	4.61	4.61	4.75	5.84	6.90	4
2015	3.44	8.52	4.73	7.60	2.44	5.84	4.57	6
4. Access to infrastructure and public services								
2000	3.73	1.82	5.55	3.26	5.05	9.23	6.56	5
2005	4.40	2.38	5.81	2.92	6.47	7.12	8.13	5
2010	4.42	1.80	5.79	3.53	5.45	6.68	8.96	5
2015	2.92	3.53	5.07	4.34	5.00	7.10	9.48	7
5. Access to education, health and social protection								
2000	2.71	1.49	4.46	3.21	4.13	10.00	7.12	6
2005	2.89	2.45	4.39	3.49	3.58	9.81	8.03	6
2010	2.21	3.31	4.14	3.57	2.51	8.89	9.38	7
2015	2.60	3.33	5.80	4.75	2.04	8.41	9.28	6
6. Gender parity								
2000	5.20	7.13	3.91	3.73	2.70	7.05	9.22	4
2005	5.53	6.90	4.52	4.53	2.46	7.58	8.85	4
2010	5.98	7.15	4.27	6.23	1.04	6.39	8.28	5
2015	5.49	7.76	5.34	7.15	2.41	5.42	7.98	4
7. Governance and institutions								
2000	3.82	2.79	7.82	5.73	3.19	7.38	5.14	5
2005	2.56	3.71	8.10	4.25	3.77	8.48	5.80	7
2010	3.22	3.56	8.91	4.20	3.65	8.09	6.02	7
2015	3.51	3.81	8.38	3.96	2.84	8.77	6.48	6

Source Authors' estimation

source and improved sanitation, lack of basic infrastructures like access to electricity and quality trade and transport facilities is holding Bangladesh back. Regardless of the proliferation of mobile phone usage in the recent years, limited access to internet is impeding Bangladesh from reaping the benefits of the information highway. Although gradual improvement in aggregate measure can be observed till 2010, it lacked momentum and fell significantly in 2015 (Table 3.14). This fall, once again, signifies Bangladesh's slower progress as opposed to the comparator countries. Sri Lanka and Vietnam had been stellar performers in this premise, while Cambodia always seems to be lacking. Pakistan is showing gradual decline.

3.9.5 Access to Education, Health and Social Protection Pillar

Apart from Sri Lanka and Vietnam, all the other selected countries exhibit poor performance on this pillar (Table 3.14). Vietnam is showing remarkable progress in this dimension, with Sri Lanka showing signs of decline from its initial high level. Bangladesh's performance in child nutrition, child birth facilities, and per capita government expenditure in health is worrisome. Moreover, key education-related indicators such as pupil–teacher ratio at the primary level and per capita expenditure on education has been below par. Overall, Bangladesh showed resilient performance on this pillar although at a very low level. Countries such as Cambodia and Nepal have shown gradual improvement, whereas Pakistan exhibited gradual decline.

3.9.6 Gender Parity Pillar

In the cross-country context, Bangladesh has been a strong performer in the field of gender equality. Bangladesh has accomplished outstanding progress in women's education. Despite that, women's lack of involvement in wage employment in the non-agriculture sectors and early marriage are major concerns for Bangladesh in achieving further gender equality. Pakistan consistently underperformed on this pillar, while Nepal showed accelerated improvement in its performance. Cambodia, Sri Lanka and Vietnam showed great performance throughout the considered time period (Table 3.14).

3.9.7 *Governance and Institutions Pillar*

A clear necessity for improved governance in Bangladesh is perceptible. Bangladesh displayed mixed performance in various constituent indicators of this pillar. Particularly, enhancing regulatory quality, imposing rule of law and controlling pervasive corruption should become Bangladesh's foremost priority. Overall, Bangladesh showed improving performance before declining in 2015. India, Sri Lanka and Vietnam displayed better performances on this pillar (Table 3.14). In order to ensure the growth process being inclusive, better governance system and effective institutions are critical.

3.10 An Inclusive Growth Index

Based on the methodology given in Box 3.1 and information on the above pillars (representing the broad goals of inclusive growth) for each of the selected countries, the study has estimated a scorecard for each of the pillars, as well as a composite index. The scorecard for each of the pillar takes on a value between 1 to 10, i.e. a higher value is indicative of a better performance, whether seen comparatively or as a trend. One thing that must be taken into cognisance is that this scorecard and the aggregate index are *relative* in nature, i.e. these measure improvements or deteriorations from a set of reference points taken from the selected sample. This implies that even if a country makes progress in absolute terms, the index value might still decline given the comparators progress at a faster pace.

"Box [Constructing an inclusive growth index] starts"

Box 3.1 Constructing an inclusive growth index The proposed inclusive growth index took cognisance of pros and cons associated with several other composite indices (e.g. Human Development Index (HDI), Multidimensional Poverty Index (MPI), etc.). The design and approach of this study's inclusive growth index was profoundly influenced by the contributions of Samans et al. (2015) and McKinley (2010). However, indices from the aforesaid two studies do not bring forth an overall aggregate ranking or league table of countries. Also, different weights to the pillars and sub-pillars were not considered given the multifarious policy and institutional requirements by particular countries in the pursuit of inclusive growth.

Choice of pillars and indicators

In order to construct the inclusive growth index, seven pillars, viz. poverty and inequality; growth and structural transformation; employment; access to infrastructure and public services; access to education, health and social protection; gender parity; and governance and institution were selected. The selection process of the pillars was based on the developed theoretical framework and interrelation among different pillars of inclusive growth alongside available global research contributions. Each pillar consists of six selected indicators (see Annex Table 3.1). The indicators under each pillar were selected keeping the developing country context and the recent list of Sustainable Development Goals (SDGs) indicators under purview.

Construction of the index

In order to reach a composite index, indicators of various types and dimensions were needed to be normalised first so that aggregation becomes possible. The indicators were transformed into a 1–10 scale (worst to best) using a linear min–max transformation technique adopted from Samans et al. (2015). Subsequently, this method used simple arithmetic mean of the normalised component indicator scores to reach to the pillar score. This can be presented as:

$$\text{indicator score} = 9 \times \frac{(indicat\,or\;value - sample\;minimum)}{(sample\;maximum - sample\;minimum)} + 1$$

This transformation takes the following form for indicators which exhibit worse outcomes with higher values:

$$indicator\;score = -9 \times \frac{(indicator\;value - sample\;minimum)}{(sample\;maximum - sample\;minimum)} + 10$$

The composite index is basically a weighted average of the pillar scores. The weights were assigned based on the pillars' perceived relative significance on the process of attaining inclusive growth. Similar method can be found in McKinley (2010) which involves implicit value judgment. In this process, poverty and inequality, growth and structural transformation, and employment received 20% weight each, while access to infrastructure and public services, health and education, gender equality, and governance and institutions received 10% weight each. In the aggregate inclusive growth index, 1 represents the worst outcome while 10 represents the best.

Limitations of the index

The construction of the inclusive growth index was severely hindered due to limited availability of relevant data which dictated the choice of indicators to some extent. Some relevant indicators could not be incorporated due to poor availability/absence of data for the selected countries. Moreover, consistent time series data was rarely available. In order to find the missing data points for the selected years, data for the nearest available period was used. Additionally, to solve the problem of volatility in some indicators as well as to generate data points, 5- or 10-years moving average was taken. Still the problem of missing values could not be solved entirely. This concern was addressed accordingly while carrying out the aggregation process by adjusting the weighting scheme.

"Box [Constructing an inclusive growth index] ends"

3.10.1 Inclusive Growth Index

In the cross-country context, Bangladesh has not performed adequately in the attainment of inclusive growth. While the average performance could be termed on par with Nepal and Pakistan, Bangladesh is still lagging behind India, Sri Lanka, and Vietnam—with Cambodia and Nepal gradually overtaking. Moreover, Bangladesh's performance gradually improved during 2000–2010, but deteriorated in 2015 (Table 3.15). Over the timeframe, Bangladesh has performed moderately well in growth performance, and in achieving gender equality. These were complemented by modest performance in the dimensions of poverty and inequality, and employment. Conversely, Bangladesh's accomplishment in health and education, governance and institutions, and access to infrastructure and public services has been unconvincing in the cross-country context.

Amongst the seven selected countries, Bangladesh was ranked fifth in 2000, while its position was sixth for each of the review periods of 2005, 2010 and 2015. The key reason behind this apparent inertia is the rapid progress achieved by Nepal and Cambodia compared to the somewhat plateaued performance by Bangladesh. Cambodia displayed remarkable progress in poverty and inequality, employment, and health and education parameters with a prevailing high level of gender equality; although with limited access to infrastructure and constrained governance and institutions. At the same time, Nepal attained laudable success in growth and structural transformation, health and education parameters, gender equality alongside an

Table 3.15 Inclusive growth index

Year	Bangladesh	Cambodia	India	Nepal	Pakistan	Sri Lanka	Vietnam	Bangladesh rank
2000	4.21	3.57	5.37	3.89	4.39	7.39	6.34	5
2005	4.39	4.56	5.39	4.11	4.78	7.46	6.83	6
2010	4.65	5.08	5.61	4.68	4.23	7.26	6.98	6
2015	4.23	6.06	5.29	4.82	3.71	7.18	7.09	6

Source Authors' estimation

already strong employment dimension. Nepal's recent socio-economic achievements were acknowledged globally as the country was found eligible for graduation from the least developed country (LDC) category in 2015. However, Nepal is exhibiting gradual decline in governance and institution pillar.

Sri Lanka and Vietnam have been the stellar performers in the attainment of inclusive growth among the selected countries. These two countries boast impressive performance in almost all the pillars considered. Amongst them, Sri Lanka displays exceptional figures in growth and structural transformation, access to infrastructure and public services, and governance and institutions with near-perfect score in health and education. However, employment parameter for Sri Lanka seems to be stagnating. Meanwhile, Vietnam exhibits increasingly strong performance in growth and structural transformation, access to infrastructure and public services, health and education, and gender equality. However, rising inequality is undermining Vietnam's otherwise commendable performance.

Even though India's growth performance is improving and the governance and institutions scenario is amongst the very best, its aggregate performance is plateauing. This can be explained as a combination of deteriorating and fluctuating parameters, viz. poverty and inequality, employment, access to infrastructure and public services, and health and education. Pakistan, on the other hand, is a frontrunner in terms of poverty and inequality, and access to infrastructure. Despite that, poor performance in health and education, gender equality, and governance and institutions are retaining Pakistan's overall performance at an unconvincing level.

3.11 Concluding Remarks

This chapter has made an attempt to track progress of Bangladesh towards attainment of inclusive growth both over time and vis-à-vis other comparable Asian countries based on a select set of indicators. As emphasised at the beginning, estimates for several of the indicators under respective pillars are indicative and relative in nature, since data have not been always available as a consistent series over the period considered. Equally, there are many qualitative dimensions of the inclusive growth pillars which have not been considered in the present study. Given the above caveat, the empirical inquiry in this chapter brings out that Bangladesh had a mixed performance in the inclusive growth indicators as identified in the present study. Although Bangladesh did not perform exceedingly well on any dimension of inclusive growth, it registered strong performance in the areas of poverty and inequality, growth and structural transformation, and gender parity.

Bangladesh has been particularly lauded for its persistent economic growth performance over the last decade. On many counts, the country has shown resilient performance in terms of several socio-economic indicators. However, our analysis on inclusive growth of Bangladesh in a cross-country comparison shows that the country could not improve its position against the select set of countries of South and Southeast Asia. Since 2000, Bangladesh's performance in terms of the inclusive growth index value has improved, except for the period between 2010 and 2015. However, at the same time, both Cambodia and Nepal have shown drastic improvement in performance, while Pakistan slipped. It is curious to note that Bangladesh attained better score in the economic growth and structural transformation pillar compared to Cambodia and Nepal. Regrettably, the country did not attain the similar feat in three of the seven pillars, viz. employment, access to infrastructure and public services, and access to education, health and social protection. Governance and institutions is the other pillar where the country performed low, which dragged its overall performance among the bottom countries. In all these areas, Bangladesh attained less than 4 points (on a scale of 7). These areas will need to receive the highest attention when the country plans for its inclusive growth trajectory.

The policy discourse in Bangladesh often puts too much emphasis on economic growth outcome, undermining the importance of an inclusive growth concept. In the era of SDGs, it is critical to have a balance among the development objectives. In view of the COVID-19 pandemic, when the country will seek for a recovery path, the seven pillars as propagated in this chapter may provide a guideline for the future development strategy of Bangladesh.

3.12 Annex

See the Table 3.16.

Table 3.16 Inclusive growth index: Pillars and indicators

Pillar	Indicators
1. Poverty and Inequality	• The proportion of the population living below nationally determined poverty lines • The proportion of the population living below the USD 1.90 per day per person international poverty line (2011 PPP) • Median wealth per adult (USD) • Gini index • Palma ratio • Expenditure on social protection (% of total government expenditure)
2. Growth and Structural Transformation	• Real rate of growth of gross domestic product per capita • Share of manufacturing in total value-added • Value of agricultural production per hectare • Private investment as share of GDP • Export concentration index • Value-added per worker

(continued)

Table 3.16 (continued)

Pillar	Indicators
3. Employment	• Labour force participation rate • Unemployment rate • Youth (15–24) unemployment rate • Share of the employed in industry • Share of the employed in manufacturing • Share of own account and contributing family workers
4. Access to Infrastructure and Public Services	• Proportion of the population with access to electricity • Number of mobile phone subscribers per 100 people • Number of internet users per 100 people • Proportion of the population with access to safe water • Proportion of the population with access to adequate sanitation • Logistics performance index: Quality of trade and transport-related infrastructure
5. Health and Education	• Global Hunger Index • Percentage of births attended by skilled health staff • Per capita government expenditure on health (PPP international USD) • Pupil–teacher ratio in the primary level • Per capita government expenditure on education (PPP international USD) • Completion rate (lower secondary)
6. Gender Equality	• Ratio of young literate females to young literate males (aged 15–24 years) • Female–male enrolment ratio in primary schools • Female–male enrolment ratio in secondary schools • Share of women in wage employment in the non-agricultural sector • Female labour force participation rate • Early marriage: Women who were first married by age 18 (% of women aged 20–24)
7. Governance and Institutions	• Voice and accountability • Political stability and absence of violence/terrorism • Government effectiveness • Regulatory quality • Rule of law • Control of corruption

Source Authors' compilation

References

Acemoglu, D., Johnson, S., & Robinson, J. A. (2001). The colonial origins of comparative development: An empirical investigation. *The American Economic Review, 91*(5), 1369–1401.

ADB. (2005). *Country Strategy and Program: Bangladesh, 2006–2010*. Manila: Asian Development Bank (ADB).

ADB. (2016). *Bangladesh Country Diagnostic Study: Consolidating Export-led Growth*. Manila: Asian Development Bank (ADB).

ADB. (n.d.). *Social Protection Indicator (SPI) database*. Manila: Asian Development Bank (ADB). https://spi.adb.org/spidmz/ Retrieved: 20 June 2020.

ADB & ILO. (2016). *Bangladesh Employment Diagnostic Study: Looking Beyond Garments*. Manila: Asian Development Bank (ADB) and Geneva: International Labour Organization (ILO).

Ahmed, S. G., Rahman, M. M., & Pal, M. (2010). *Dropout rate in secondary level education in Bangladesh: A study of VAB schools*. Dhaka: The University Press Limited (UPL).

Asadullah, M. N., Savoia, A., & Mahmud, W. (2014). Paths to development: Is there a Bangladesh surprise? *World Development, 62*(October), 138–154.

Babajanian, B., Hagen-Zanker, J., & Holmes, R. (2014). *How do Social Protection and Labour Programmes Contribute to Social Inclusion? Evidence from Afghanistan, Bangladesh, India and Nepal*. London: Overseas Development Institute (ODI).

BBS. (2011). *Report on Labour Force Survey 2010*. Dhaka: Bangladesh Bureau of Statistics (BBS), Government of Bangladesh (GoB).

BBS. (2014). *Preliminary Report on Census of Slum Areas and Floating Population*. Dhaka: Bangladesh Bureau of Statistics (BBS), Government of Bangladesh (GoB).

BBS. (2017). *Quarterly Labour Force Survey: Bangladesh 2015–2016*. Dhaka: Bangladesh Bureau of Statistics (BBS), Government of Bangladesh (GoB).

Begum, T. (2009). Millennium Development Goal and child survival: Bangladesh perspective. *Journal of Shaheed Suhrawardy Medical College, 1*(1), 18–21.

Begum, S., Ahmed, M., & Sen, B. (2011). Do water and sanitation interventions reduce childhood diarrhoea? New evidence from Bangladesh. *Bangladesh Development Studies, 34*(3), 1–30.

Bhattacharya, D., Khan, T. I., & Sabbih, M. A. (2016). *Delivering on the Promise: Ensuring the Successful Implementation of the Post-2015 Agenda in Bangladesh*. Dhaka: Save the Children Bangladesh.

Bhattacharya, D., Khan, T. I., Khan S. S., Sinha, M. M., Fuad, S. M., Biswas, S., & Muzib, A. (forthcoming). *Quest for Inclusive Transformation of Bangladesh: Who Not to Be Left Behind*. Report prepared by the Centre for Policy Dialogue (CPD) and the Citizen's Platform for SDGs, Bangladesh.

CAMPE. (2015). *Quality Education: Teacher for the Next Generation*. Dhaka: Campaign for Popular Education (CAMPE).

Chowdhury, O. H., & Osmani, S. R. (2010). Towards achieving the right to health: The case of Bangladesh. *Bangladesh Development Studies, 33*(1&2), 205–273.

CPD. (2014). *Bangladesh economy in FY2013–14: Third interim review of macroeconomic performance*. Dhaka: Centre for Policy Dialogue (CPD).

CPD. (2015). *Bangladesh economy in FY2014–15: Third interim review of macroeconomic performance*. Dhaka: Centre for Policy Dialogue (CPD).

CPD. (2016, January 3). *State of the Bangladesh Economy in FY2015–16: First Reading*. Issue paper prepared for a media briefing, organised by the Centre for Policy Dialogue (CPD), Dhaka, Bangladesh.

CPD. (2020, June 7). *Challenges of Policymaking in Times of Pandemics: State of the Bangladesh Economy in FY2020*. Issue paper prepared for a virtual media briefing, organised by the Centre for Policy Dialogue (CPD), Dhaka, Bangladesh.

Credit Suisse. (2019). *Global Wealth Databook 2019*. Zurich: Credit Suisse. https://www.credit-suisse.com/media/assets/corporate/docs/about-us/research/publications/global-wealth-databook-2019.pdf Retrieved: 20 June 2020.

Easterly, W., & Levine, R. (2003). Tropics, germs, and crops: How endowments influence economic development. *Journal of Monetary Economics, 50*(1), 3–39.

Faaland, J., & Parkinson, J. R. (1976). Bangladesh: The test case for development. London: C. Hurst & Co.

FAO. (n.d.). *FAOSTAT Data*. Rome: Food and Agriculture Organization of the United Nations (FAO). http://www.fao.org/faostat/en/#data [Retrieved: 20 June 2020].

GED. (2015a). *Millennium Development Goals: Bangladesh Progress Report 2015*. Dhaka: General Economics Division (GED), Planning Commission, Government of Bangladesh (GoB).

GED. (2015b). *Seventh Five Year Plan FY2016—FY2020: Accelerating Growth, Empowering Citizens*. Dhaka: General Economics Division (GED), Planning Commission, Government of Bangladesh (GoB).

GED & UNDP. (n.d.). *A Situation Analysis Report on Poverty and Hunger (different MDGs) Bangladesh: A Baseline for Needs Assessment and Costing*. Dhaka: General Economics Division (GED), Planning Commission, Government of Bangladesh (GoB) and United Nations Development Programme (UNDP).

Ghani, E., & Ahmed, S. (2009). *Accelerating growth and job creation in South Asia*. New Delhi: Oxford University Press.

Giménez, L., Jolliffe, D., & Sharif, I. (2014). Bangladesh, a middle income country by 2021: What will it take in terms of poverty reduction? *Bangladesh Development Studies, 37*(1&2), 1–19.

Gupta, S., Verhoeven, M., & Tiongson, E. (2002). The effectiveness of government spending on education and health care in developing and transition economies. *European Journal of Political Economy, 18*(4), 717–737.

ICDDR, B. (2007). Consequences of early marriage on female schooling in rural Bangladesh. *Health and Science Bulletin, 5*(4), 13–18.

IFPRI. (2015). *Global Hunger Index: Armed conflict and the challenge of hunger*. Washington, D.C.: International Food Policy Research Institute (IFPRI).

IFPRI. (n.d.). *Global Hunger Index* (various issues). Washington, D.C.: International Food Policy Research Institute (IFPRI). https://www.globalhungerindex.org/results.html Retrieved: 20 June 2020.

ILO. (2013). *Bangladesh: Seeking Better Employment Conditions for Better Socioeconomic Outcomes*. Studies on Growth with Equity. Geneva: International Labour Organization (ILO).

ILO. (n.d.). *ILOSTAT database*. Geneva: International Labour Organization (ILO). https://ilostat.ilo.org/data/ Retrieved: 20 June 2020.

IMF. (n.d.). *Government Finance Statistics*. Washington, D.C.: International Monetary Fund (IMF). https://data.imf.org/?sk=a0867067-d23c-4ebc-ad23-d3b015045405 Retrieved: 20 June 2020.

Islam, R. (2014, April 28–29). Expanding employment opportunities: Policy challenges for the post-2015 development agenda. Paper presented at the *International Symposium on Human Development in Global South: Emerging Perspectives in the Era of Post-Millennium Development Goals*, organised by the Institute of Human Development, New Delhi, India.

Islam, R., & Islam, I. (2015). *Employment and inclusive development*. London: Routledge.

Islam, R., & Rahman, R. I. (2017). *Bangladesh Employment and Labour Market Watch 2017*. Dhaka: Centre for Development and Employment Research.

Jolliffe, D., Mujeri, M. K., & Sharif, I. (2014). A decade of progress in reducing poverty: An introduction to the special issue. *Bangladesh Development Studies, 37*(1&2), v–vii.

Kaufmann, D., Kraay, A., & Mastruzzi, M. (2010). *The Worldwide Governance Indicators: Methodology and Analytical Issues*. World Bank Policy Research Working Paper 5430. Washington, D.C.: The World Bank.

Khan, A. R. (2015). *The economy of Bangladesh: A quarter century of development*. Basingstoke: Palgrave Macmillan UK.

Khandker, S. R., & Samad, H. A. (2014). Microfinance growth and poverty reduction in Bangladesh: What does the longitudinal data say? *Bangladesh Development Studies, 37*(1&2), 127–157.

Klemm, R. D. W., Labrique, A. B., Christian, P., Rashid, M., Shamim, A. A., Katz, J., et al. (2008). Newborn vitamin A supplementation reduced infant mortality in rural Bangladesh. *Pediatrics, 122*(1), 242–250.

Mahmud, W., Asadullah, M. N., & Savoia, A. (2013). Bangladesh's achievements in social development indicators: Explaining the puzzle. *Economic & Political Weekly, 48*(44), 26–28.

McGuire, J. W. (2006). Basic health care provision and under-5 mortality: A cross-national study of developing countries. *World Development, 34*(3), 405–425.

McKinley, T. (2010). *Inclusive Growth Criteria and Indicators: An Inclusive Growth Index for Diagnosis of Country Progress*. ADB Sustainable Development Working Paper No. 14. Manila: Asian Development Bank (ADB).

MoHFW. (2012). *Expanding Social Protection for Health: Towards Universal Coverage Health Care Financing Strategy 2012–2032*. Dhaka: Ministry of Health and Family Welfare (MoHFW), Government of Bangladesh (GoB).

Osmani, S. R. (2015). *Linking Equity and Growth in Bangladesh*. Background paper prepared for the Seventh Five Year Plan of the Government of Bangladesh. Dhaka: Planning Commission, Government of Bangladesh.

Osmani, S. R., & Latif, M. A. (2013). The pattern and determinants of poverty in rural Bangladesh: 2000–2010. *Bangladesh Development Studies, 36*(2), 1–41.

Osmani, S. R., Latif, M. A., Sen, B., Rahman, R. I., Ahmed, M., Khan, T. F., & Islam, R. (2013). *Dynamics of Poverty in Rural Bangladesh: Report of the Benchmark Survey*. Dhaka: Institute of Microfinance (InM).

Rahman, M. (2014). *Trade Benefits for Least Developed Countries: The Bangladesh Case*. CDP Background Paper No 10. New York: Committee for Development Policy (CDP), United Nations Department of Economic and Social Affairs (UNDESA).

Rahman, R. I. (2014). *Demographic Dividend and Youth Labour Force Participation in Bangladesh*. Research Report No. 187. Dhaka: Bangladesh Institute of Development Studies (BIDS).

Rahman, M. & Bari, E. (2016). *The Political Economy of Change—Escaping the Middle-income Trap: Perspectives from Bangladesh*. Dhaka: Friedrich-Ebert-Stiftung and Centre for Policy Dialogue (CPD).

Rahman, M. & Khan, T. I. (2015). *Ensuring Food Security in Bangladesh: Beyond Production, And Next Challenges*. Paper prepared for UN-ESCAP South and South-West Asia Office. Dhaka: Centre for Policy Dialogue (CPD).

Rahman, M., Bhattacharya, D., Iqbal, M. A., Khan, T. I., & Paul, T. K. (2009). *Paper 1: Bangladesh*. Global Financial Crisis Discussion Series. London: Overseas Development Institute (ODI).

Rahman, M., Iqbal, M. A., Khan, T. I., & Dasgupta, S. (2010). *Paper 12: Bangladesh Phase 2*. Global Financial Crisis Discussion Series. London: Overseas Development Institute (ODI) and Dhaka: Centre for Policy Dialogue (CPD).

Rahman, M., Khan, T. I., & Amin, M. A. (2014). *The Economy of Tomorrow—How to Produce Socially Just, Sustainable and Green Dynamic Growth for a Good Society: Case Study of Bangladesh*. Dhaka: Friedrich Ebert Stiftung (FES) Bangladesh Office.

Rahman, M., Khan, T. I., & Sadique, Z. (2014). *Public Expenditure Trends in Low-income Countries in the Post-MDG Context*. Background Paper prepared for the European Report on Development (ERD) 2015. Brussels: ECDPM.

Rahman, M., Khan, T. I., & Sabbih, M. A. (2016). *Education Budget in Bangladesh: An Analysis of Trends, Gaps and Priorities*. Dhaka: Campaign for Popular Education (CAMPE) and Centre for Policy Dialogue (CPD).

Razzaque, M. A. (2010). Microfinance and Poverty Reduction: Evidence from a longitudinal household panel database. *Bangladesh Development Studies, 33*(3), 47–68.

Rodrik, D., Subramanian, A., & Trebbi, F. (2004). Institutions rule: The primacy of institutions over geography and integration in economic development. *Journal of Economic Growth, 9*(2), 131–165.

Sabates, R., Hossain, A., & Lewin, K. M. (2010). *School Drop Out in Bangladesh: New Insights from Longitudinal Evidence*. Research Monograph No. 49. Dhaka: Institute of Educational Development, BRAC University.

Samans, R., Blanke, J., Corrigan, G., & Drzeniek, M. (2015). *The Inclusive Growth and Development Report 2015*. Geneva: World Economic Forum (WEF).

Sobhan, R. (2010). *Challenging the injustice of poverty: Agendas for inclusive development in South Asia*. New Delhi: Sage Publications Ltd.

Sukontamarn, P. (2005). *The Entry of NGO Schools and Girls' Educational Outcomes in Bangladesh*. LSE STICERD Research Paper No. PEPP10. London: London School of Economics and Political Science.

Toufique, K. A. (2014). *Labour Market Transition of Young Women and Men in Bangladesh*. Work4Youth Publication Series No. 13. Geneva: International Labour Organization (ILO).

UNCTAD. (n.d.). *UNCTADSTAT*. Geneva: United Nations Conference on Trade and Development (UNCTAD). https://unctadstat.unctad.org/wds/ReportFolders/reportFolders.aspx?sCS_ChosenLang=en [Retrieved: 20 June 2020].

UNDP. (2015). *Promote Gender Equality and Empower Women: Where are We?* Dhaka: United Nations Development Programme (UNDP) Bangladesh Country Office.

UNICEF. (2014). *Vitamin A Supplementation Programme in Bangladesh*. Dhaka: United Nations Children's Find (UNICEF) Bangladesh Country Office.

USAID. (2016). *Universal Health Coverage and Health Financing in Bangladesh: Situational Assessment and Way Forward*. Dhaka: United States Agency for International Development (USAID).

USAID & DFID. (2014). *Bangladesh: Inclusive Growth Diagnostic*. Washington, D.C.: U.S. Agency for International Development (USAID) & London: Department for International Development (DFID).

WEF. (2016). *The Global Competitiveness Report 2016–2017*. Geneva: World Economic Forum (WEF).

WFP. (2015). *What are the Current Issues in Bangladesh?* Rome: United Nations World Food Programme (WFP).

WHO. (n.d.). *Global Health Observatory data repository*. Geneva: World Health Organization (WHO). https://apps.who.int/gho/data/node.home [Retrieved: 20 June 2020].

World Bank. (2007). *Bangladesh: Strategy for Sustained Growth*. Bangladesh Development Series No. 18. Dhaka: The World Bank Office, Bangladesh.

World Bank. (2012). *Bangladesh: Towards Accelerated, Inclusive and Sustainable Growth—Opportunities and Challenges*. Dhaka: The World Bank Office, Bangladesh.

World Bank. (2013). *Bangladesh Poverty Assessment: Assessing a Decade of Progress in Reducing Poverty, 2000–2010*. Bangladesh Development Series No. 31. Dhaka: The World Bank Office, Bangladesh.

World Bank. (2017). Bangladesh Development Update. Dhaka: The World Bank Office, Bangladesh.

World Bank. (2020). *Global Economic Prospects (June 2020)*. Washington, D.C.: The World Bank. https://openknowledge.worldbank.org/bitstream/handle/10986/33748/9781464815539.pdf Retrieved: 22 June 2020.

World Bank. (n.d.a). *World Development Indicators DataBank*. Washington, D.C.: The World Bank. https://databank.worldbank.org/source/world-development-indicators/preview/on [Retrieved: 20 June 2020].

World Bank. (n.d.b). *Worldwide Governance Indicators DataBank*. Washington, D.C.: The World Bank. https://databank.worldbank.org/source/worldwide-governance-indicators Retrieved: 20 June 2020.

Zaman, H., Narayan, A., & Kotikula, A. (2012). Are Bangladesh's recent gains in poverty reduction different from the past? *Bangladesh Development Studies, 35*(1), 1–26.

Chapter 4
Macroeconomic Policy, Price Stability and Inclusive Growth

Muhammed Muqtada

Abstract During the past two decades, the economy of Bangladesh experienced a fairly sustained macroeconomic stability, and was able to achieve substantial growth in gross domestic product (GDP). However, there is evidence that suggests this growth has neither been inclusive, nor has it been able to bring about structural changes needed to sustain higher growth. The chapter contends that the macroeconomic policy-making would require a rethink in order to meet the above challenges. It notes that the current COVID-19 pandemic and the sharp economic downturn, requiring extraordinary stimulus measures to protect lives and livelihoods, are likely to bring the above challenges into sharper focus. The chapter reviews the current macroeconomic policy framework of Bangladesh, and underscores the need for balancing its usual emphasis on stability, with the need for structural change and social inclusion. This, in turn, would require an expansionary macroeconomic policy, albeit prudent, that focuses robustly on stepped-up investment, job growth, and reduction of inequality and vulnerability. To this end, the chapter explores the critical role of monetary, fiscal, external and financial inclusion policies, and how far these could be reoriented to address said challenges.

4.1 Introduction

While macroeconomic policies are designed to pursue the fundamental macroeconomic goals set by planners, there are often serious controversies with regard to what these goals are, as well as with the policy instruments that are at disposal to achieve

This chapter draws from a working paper by the author, Muqtada (2018), published by the CPD; content re-used with permission.

M. Muqtada (✉)
Development Economist; Formerly a Director in the Employment Sector of the International Labour Organization (ILO), Geneva, and a Visiting Fellow, Centre for Policy Dialogue, Dhaka, Bangladesh
e-mail: muqtada1@gmail.com

M. Muqtada (ed.), *Quest for Inclusive Growth in Bangladesh*, South Asia Economic and Policy Studies,
https://doi.org/10.1007/978-981-15-7614-0_4

these goals. There have been intense debates, both amongst academicians and practitioners, on the precise role and objectives of macroeconomic policies.[1] These debates are often ideologically charged, concentrating, at the core, on whether macroeconomic policies ought to be defined largely by supply-side and price stability considerations, or whether these should also influence demand-management in the economy. In practice though, the debates do not strictly compartmentalise the macroeconomic goals and policies. Nevertheless, the relative weights of the policies that these ideological positions entail have political overtones and define political agendas, such as the relative roles of the government and market economy. Although the practices of macroeconomics in current times recognise and engage both the government and private sector, there are still stiff conflicts in articulating the dominant policy instruments in macroeconomic management.

As well-known, since the 1980s, macroeconomic policy in both the developed and developing countries, has been predominantly driven by considerations of price stability (i.e. getting prices right), based on the so-called Washington Consensus. In the context of the economic and political imperatives of the period that followed, inflation-control became the overriding objective to induce stability and growth. In the process, the importance of employment as a central objective of macroeconomic policy, and hence also implicitly the associated role of demand-side policies, such as the size of public investment and expenditures, which were the usual hallmarks of macroeconomic planning during the 1950s till the early 1970s, were relegated.[2]

Bangladesh undertook major macroeconomic reforms during the 1980s, and more vigorously during the 1990s, largely within the framework of the stabilisation and structural adjustment programmes that were shaped by the loan facility agreements with the Bretton Woods institutions. The following sections of the present chapter describe how Bangladesh, within a relatively short period of time, managed to curtail its debts and deficits substantially, in order to attain macroeconomic stability and accelerated growth. It can be noted that various other factors, including fortuitous circumstances, facilitated both stability and growth. This has greatly supported Bangladesh to *graduate*, i.e. move out of the United Nations (UN)-defined category of a *least developed country* (LDC). Although the economy has been fairly stable and its GDP has grown, there is widespread evidence and analysis that this growth has hardly been inclusive.[3] Income and asset inequality has been persistently increasing, and growth so far has not been able to ensure any significant structural transformation. While Bangladesh is committed to attaining the Sustainable Development Goals (SDGs), and equally to the goal of achieving the status of an upper middle-income

---

[1]See Stiglitz (2010) and Krugman (1999) on one hand, and Mauro (2011) on the other, for a discussion from different standpoints, on themes that have gained increasing prominence in recent times.

[2]See for example, Bhaduri (2019), Epstein (2007), Nayyar (2015) and Pollin (2008) for a vigorous emphasis on the employment objective of macroeconomic policy.

[3]See Khan (2015), CPD (2017a).

country (UMIC), such targets and expectations are likely to confront major macroeconomic challenges.[4] A relatively inadequate private investment to GDP ratio, an unacceptably low revenue–GDP ratio vis-à-vis expanding expenditures on social and physical expenditures, and shaky foundations of export growth and diversification among others, are some of the significant challenges ahead. The current COVID-19 pandemic and the severe contractions in growth are likely to aggravate the macroeconomic indicators, although the government is expressing optimism, not shared by analysts, of a V-shaped recovery in FY2020-21.[5]

The present study, largely due to fluidity of the database, abstracts from the volatility created by the current recessionary tendencies, and confines to the review of the general macroeconomic policy framework, which has been (arguably) following a conservative stance to meet its de facto targets of debts and deficits. The study through an examination of the policy instruments (chiefly monetary and fiscal) argues in favour of, and calls for, a relatively more expansionary macroeconomic policy to be able to meet the economic and social challenges of inclusive growth. Section 4.2 of this chapter provides a brief account of the macroeconomic reforms undertaken in Bangladesh, and their broad impact on growth and stability. Section 4.3 provides some insights on the problems of promoting inclusive growth in Bangladesh, and how far these are likely to challenge the current status quo of macroeconomic policy-making. In Sect. 4.4, the study examines critically the role and limitations of the monetary policy, and its ability to pursue its stated dual objectives of price stability and inclusive growth. Bangladesh, under the current trends in price stability and low inflation volatility, is well-positioned to focus on its other mandate, i.e. facilitating investment and inclusive growth, which would require a more aggressive monetary stance. Given the limitations of the financial sector infrastructure and the need for vigorous mobilisation of financial resources and broad-based credit utilisation, Sect. 4.5 scrutinises the role of financial inclusion and its potential impact on inclusive growth. Section 4.6 takes a partial look at the role of the fiscal policy in Bangladesh; the limitations posed by the low revenue–GDP ratio, and posits some alternatives towards creating fiscal space for employment and social safety nets. The important role of external stability in promoting stability and import competitiveness is examined in Sect. 4.7. Finally, in Sect. 4.8, major conclusions are drawn and policy recommendations are made, based on the learning outcomes of the present study.

4.2 Macroeconomic Reforms, Stability and Growth

During the 1980s, Bangladesh faced an acute crisis of resource imbalances. In an incipient economy, there were huge burdens on public expenditure relative to the insignificant revenue base, which caused unsustainable fiscal deficits. The large number of loss-making state enterprises in the then largely nationalised economy

[4] See IMF (2017) for a brief assessment of these challenges.

[5] See MoF (2020). Also see CPD (2020) on factors that may affect GDP growth in the current year.

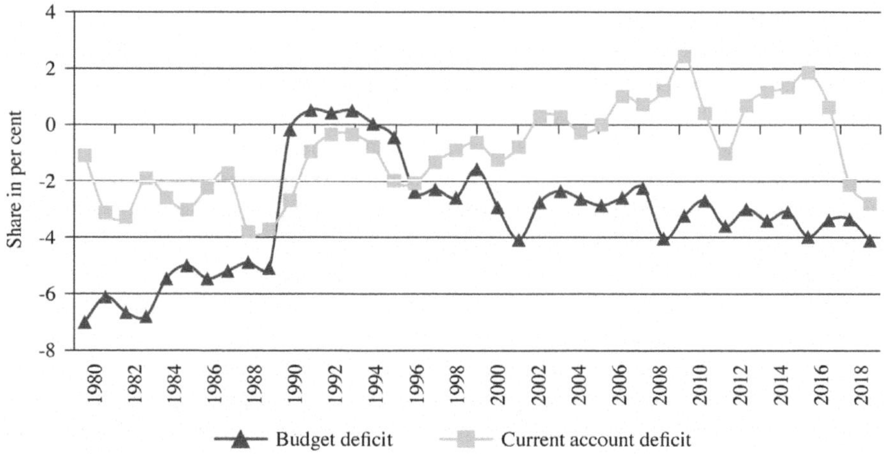

Fig. 4.1 Budget deficit and current account deficit of Bangladesh as share of GDP. *Source* IMF (n.d.)

added to the resource burden, and the country's development expenditures were hugely met through donor resources. Monetisation of government deficits and adverse movements in terms of trade, especially in the aftermath of the second oil-price shock, contributed to a sharp deterioration in macroeconomic imbalances. These led to significant fiscal and current account deficits and an increase in the inflation rate during the mid-1980s.[6] Fiscal deficit stood at nearly 10% of GDP, while inflation went up to around 12% during the first half of the 1980s. Stabilisation reforms were predominantly focused on restraining fiscal and current account deficits, and lowering the inflation rates. These were accompanied by various liberalisation measures (related to trade and finance) and structural adjustment programmes (e.g. privatisation, rationalisation of sectoral loans and subsidies, among others). While many analysts questioned the pace and sequencing of these programmes, as well as the initial (social) costs and impact on the economy, the reforms had helped the Bangladesh macroeconomic framework gain a stronger footing (Mahmud 2004; Osmani 2008; Ahmed and Mahmud 2006). By the widely accepted indicators of stabilisation, Bangladesh, since the turn of this century, has witnessed a comfortable stretch of macroeconomic stability. Figure 4.1 shows that budget deficits, since the mid-1990s, have been well below the widely accepted yardstick of 5%. The current account has been in surplus during most of this period, except in the very recent past.

The above evidence, together with the fact that growth started to pick up especially since mid-1990s, would tend to suggest that stabilisation measures were largely satisfactory. Bangladesh, in due course, avoided following the strict conditionalities of the Washington Consensus. However, there are debates and unresolved questions on whether, and how far, stabilisation can be achieved through approaches

---

[6]For an account of the state of the Bangladesh economy during this early period, see Khan (1995) and Bhattacharya and Titumir (2001).

that are more flexible than the guidelines and targets set by the lending agencies. While an unconditional acceptance of the so-called Washington Consensus is now much less observed, the experience of Bangladesh to some extent shows alternative paths, especially with regard to sequencing and pacing of stabilisation. High inflation is undesirable, so are severe debts. But those countries which could attain better debt sustainability have been able to avoid the conditional path, Bangladesh being a prime example which prudently managed to cut down its dependence on conditional borrowing.[7] Bangladesh could regain a fair rate of growth and price stability without facing a constricted fiscal and import space, and was able to divert resources to development expenditures and targetted poverty programmes. Thus, despite the initial shocks and adverse social and economic effects of stabilisation and structural adjustment reforms, macroeconomic policy-making in Bangladesh has been relatively prudent, through which it attained stability during the post-reforms period of the 1990s. In particular, it is noteworthy that, Bangladesh refrained from fiscal profligacy to drive growth. The economy managed to reduce its debt–GDP ratio to below 35%, and external debt servicing to around 4% of export earnings.

One needs to point out that, there were several fortuitous conditions that cushioned the growth effects of the subsequent reforms. The global boom of 2002–2007, the falling fuel and commodity prices, and the growing significance of remittances (as per cent of GDP) were vital to sustaining stability and growth. Remittance and net exports, in particular, have been significant factors for Bangladesh in the growth of national savings and foreign exchange reserves—in reducing the current account deficit and strengthening the import capacity.

4.3 An Inclusive Growth for Bangladesh: Macroeconomic Policy Challenges

The current macroeconomic policy framework, which has been instrumental in attaining an inflation rate of below 6%, a budget deficit below 5%, and an overall debt–GDP ratio of 35%, has been widely acclaimed by analysts as well as donor agencies (IMF 2017). However, while such stability has facilitated a relatively high and sustained GDP growth rate, inequality has been increasing continuously, and employment generation has been declining. In order to pursue an inclusive growth strategy as envisioned in the Seventh Five Year Plan (7FYP) of Bangladesh, the macroeconomic policy framework was expected to confront several challenges.

First, Bangladesh, in its Vision 2021, had projected an ambitious pathway for GDP growth, with the country aiming to reach an annual rate of 10% (GED 2012). This has, however, been moderated in the 7FYP,[8] with a projection of nearly 8%

---

[7]See Easterly (2001) and Muqtada (2014) on how conditional borrowing was linked to undertaking of strict macroeconomic reforms during the 1980s. In many African countries such reforms led to a compression syndrome, and a reduction in aggregate demand.

[8]The plan adopted for the period FY2015-16 to FY2019-20.

during the planned period. Experts do not consider this to be unachievable, but a tall order nonetheless. According to various projections, the average growth rate over the planned period is more likely to be around 7%[9]; in fact, the hard statistics show that the long-term average GDP growth rate had been 5.7% during FY1993-94 to FY2016-17, and had reached 8.15% in FY2018-19, according to the Bangladesh Bureau of Statistics (BBS). Although the COVID-19 pandemic has caused output contractions, and preliminary growth rate for FY2019-20 is estimated at 5.2%, the government, amidst a lot of scepticism, is projecting a V-shaped recovery to 8.2% during FY2020-21.[10] While others have estimated and/or predicted lower figures (e.g. International Monetary Fund (IMF) and The World Bank), the government is predicting higher growth rates, largely based on the anticipated economic activities that would arise on the completion of several mega infrastructural projects.[11] Nevertheless, Bangladesh is currently among the fastest growing countries in the world and the crucial challenge is to assess the *drivers* of growth and how their relative weights might need to change to ensure sustainability. Currently, more than 70% of GDP is accounted for by private consumption expenditure.[12] Any further planned growth would have to be intrinsically linked to the growth of private sector investment to GDP ratio, which has remained relatively low at around 23% (FY2017-18). According to the Planning Commission of Bangladesh, a planned growth rate of 8% would require an increase in the investment–GDP ratio to 32.5% or more (assuming that the existing incremental capital–output ratios (ICORs) remain the same).[13]

The above warrants a critical role of public investment, which has been gradually increasing in the recent years, from less than 5% in FY2007-08 to around 8% in FY2017-18 (Fig. 4.2).

During the past few years, the government has increased its public investment programmes, not only to enhance overall investment–GDP ratio, but also to crowd in private investment through intensifying the development of physical (roads, ports, information technology (IT), communications) and social (skills, education, health) infrastructures. Substantial rise in public investment has been so far been unable to crowd in private investment. Numerous factors have been forwarded to explain the recent slowdown in the pace of private investment, such as infrastructure bottlenecks, energy crisis, skilled manpower and high bank-lending rates. Analysts are equally

[9]For various growth projections for Bangladesh, see IMF (2017), ADB (2017) and World Bank (2017a).

[10]CPD (2020).

[11]For example, the under-construction flagship project, the Padma Multipurpose Bridge, which is expected to expand connectivity and economic activities in a major way.

[12]In FY2017-18, GDP expenditure shares were: private consumption (70.8%), private investment (23.3%), government consumption and investment (14.3%) and net exports (−8.7%).

[13]For alternative growth–investment scenarios for Bangladesh, see Mujeri (2014).

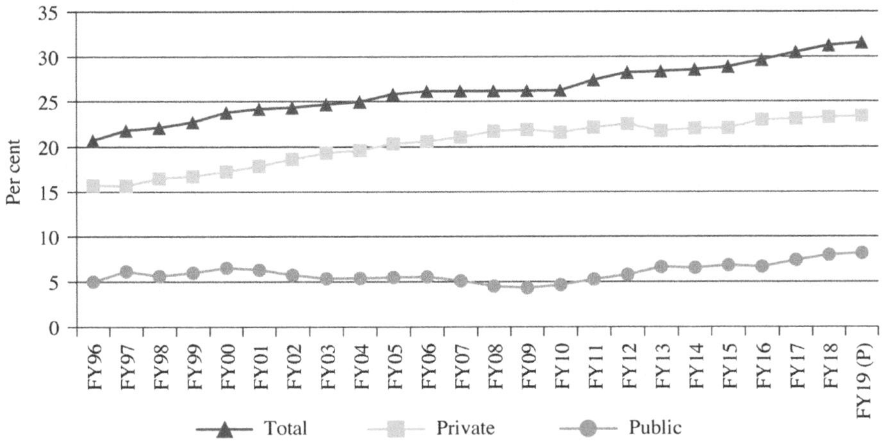

Fig. 4.2 Investment as share of GDP. *Source* Author's calculations from the BBS data. *Note* P denotes provisional estimate

concerned with other broader issues of institutional weaknesses and poor governance, especially corruption, policy instability and inefficient government bureaucracy which tend to impede domestic and foreign investment[14] (see Chap. 8 for an elaboration).

Second, a critical challenge that the macroeconomic regime in Bangladesh faces is how to preserve and/or sustain price stability while ensuring a sustained high growth momentum, and accommodating its commitment to inclusive growth. It has been noted above that, various reforms (especially financial reforms, fiscal restraints) and various developments, whether policy-induced and/or owing to fortuitous circumstances, have so far helped in maintaining such a balance. As explained later in this chapter (in Sect. 4.4), Bangladesh has been attaining an average growth rate of 6% and above during the past decade, with the inflation rate ranging from 6 to 8%. However, current GDP forecasts of 8% or more, as perceived by the Planning Commission, will require a review of how a faster growth of aggregate demand and its implications for the economy's fiscal, current accounts and the exchange rate, will be accommodated within the current targets of debts and deficits.

Third, a large proportion of the labour force in Bangladesh is the working poor and/or the vulnerable. These include particularly those in self-employment, own account workers, unpaid family helpers and casual day-workers (Islam 2014a). Despite major achievements in the reduction of poverty, the incidence of extreme poor as well as the absolute number of people under poverty remains unacceptably high. Furthermore, addressing the disconcerting rise in inequality and introducing measures to enhance the living standards of the bulk of the population will constitute a major development challenge. In order to pursue the central pledge of *leave no one*

[14]See for example, WEF (2017).

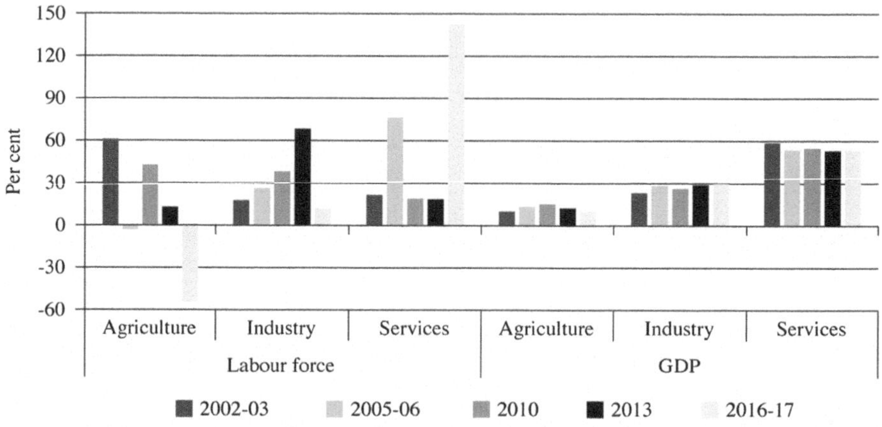

Fig. 4.3 Incremental contribution of employment and GDP by broad economic sectors. *Source* Author's estimations from BBS (2004, 2008, 2011, 2015, 2018)

behind in the 2030 Agenda for Sustainable Development (UN 2015), and to ameliorate the conditions of the majority of these vulnerable groups and millions of others who constitute the socially excluded, Bangladesh has embarked on the challenges of inclusive growth strategy. As argued in Chap. 2, the centre-piece of such a strategy would lie in achieving the goal of full, productive, remunerative employment (SDG 8) (UN 2015). Macroeconomic policy would need to embody an employment strategy, and an overall pattern of growth, that is inequality-averse (Khan 2015), as had been the experience of the East Asian countries in the early periods of their growth.

Fourth, in order to attain a sustained growth towards a middle-income country (MIC), Bangladesh would need to undergo substantial structural transformation that would be commensurate with the foundations of growth associated with a higher-income economy. Such a transformation is observed not just in terms of sectoral changes in GDP, but also in terms of the shifts in the sectoral shares in total employment. In particular, this is associated with tangible increases in the modern sector's share in total employment.[15] Although employed workforce in agriculture is declining, and manufacturing employment is growing, the changes are slow. It may be noted that a relatively higher level of growth in employment in the industrial sector in most periods (between 4 and 8%), compared to that in agriculture (−0.1 to 4%) and services sectors (between 1 and 5%), has contributed to mild changes in the structure of employment in the economy (BBS 2004, 2008, 2011, 2015, 2018). The incremental contribution of employment by the industrial sector which had gradually increased over time during 2002–03 and 2013, has considerably slowed down in the more recent period (Fig. 4.3). Nevertheless, these changes in sectoral employment trends are too volatile and inadequate to characterise a structural transformation.

[15]This signifies a characterisation of an economy moving towards the Lewisian turning point. For further reflections on this, see Islam (2014b); also see Chap. 6 in this volume.

Among the several other indicators of structural change is the growth of formal sector employment, of which, the waged-and-salaried workers constitute an important proportion. Again, the progress is observed to be unsatisfactory.[16]

In order to boost productivity and structural transformation, measures would need to be put in place to upgrade skills and education, and infuse higher technology and innovation. Thus, productive employment generation would need to be associated with the growth of jobs in higher productivity sectors, and other conditions that facilitate labour movements between sectors, as well as between regions.

In Bangladesh, the pattern of growth generated through the macroeconomic stance has been short on inclusion and job generation (see Chap. 3). The macroeconomic framework needs a closer review to foster a truly inclusive growth in Bangladesh. It will need to accommodate policies that would generate jobs, for example, through incorporating a productive, remunerative employment strategy.[17] It will also have to undertake budgetary and public investment measures (provision of public goods and income entitlements) to address the millions of unprotected and vulnerable population.

In the light of the country's planned objectives to consolidate an ambitious growth and structural transformation programme to reach the UMIC status by 2031, and towards the provision of jobs for all working-age men and women—the scope of the current macroeconomic policy framework will need to be considerably expanded. In the context of the present study, this would imply a closer evaluation of the macroeconomic policies that currently exist. Indeed, the imperatives for "upgrading the macroeconomic policy-making practices and institutions" (IMF 2017, p. 16) to be able to attain the ambitious growth targets, as well as many other pursuits under a strategy of inclusive growth, have also been emphasised elsewhere.

The following sections provide critical insights on the current practices of macroeconomic policy and argue that a more flexible and expansionary use of the macroeconomic instruments would be necessary to address the objectives of price stability and inclusive growth. Given the scope of the study, only some salient features are highlighted, mainly with regard to monetary and fiscal policy instruments.

4.4 Monetary Policy, Price Stability and Inclusive Growth[18]

Maintaining price stability is a predominant and critical objective of Bangladesh's macroeconomic policy framework. However, while adjusting to targets within the broad fiscal and monetary goals that have provided stability to the economy, Bangladesh has refrained from the conservative stance of inflation targetting

---

[16]See Chaps. 3 and 6 of this volume.

[17]In point of fact, a clearly articulated and comprehensive employment strategy does not exist in Bangladesh planning.

[18]For further details on the issues of price stability, growth and inclusion in Bangladesh, see Muqtada (2015).

(Hammond 2012), which, during the past two decades, has been widely adopted both in the developed and developing countries.[19] In fact, while the Bangladesh Bank's primary objective is to achieve its inflation target, it also has "sufficient space in its monetary programme for lending to activities which support broad-based investment and inclusive growth objectives" (Bangladesh Bank 2014, p. 12). Apparently, the recent practice of monetary policy is predominantly focused on price stability, and is relatively muted on how the monetary policy framework ought to contribute to investment and inclusion. This stance has however been violently shaken by the severe economic crisis caused by the present pandemic, that has prompted the government to undertake massive stimulus measures. The Bangladesh Bank is at the centre of intermediation for a large number of measures, including injecting liquidity, subsidised lending, and various refinancing schemes to support most affected groups and sectors.[20] The ongoing crisis would be a litmus test for the monetary policy of Bangladesh Bank on how it attempts to ensure a balance between inflation control and inclusive growth.

The price stability challenge in Bangladesh, as in other developing countries, is complex; it requires a careful review of what constitutes a realistic short-run inflation target, how low it should be, and whether it is calibrated through potential estimates of inflation–growth trade-offs. It is equally important to trace the multiple causes of inflation, and the varied policy instruments that are traditionally applied to contain inflation. There are very few empirical studies of inflation–growth trade-offs in Bangladesh, let alone a continuous monitoring of such trade-offs.[21] In fact, except for an odd year or two, Bangladesh hardly had double-digit inflation over this entire period. Usually, the volatility in inflation rates comes from factors affecting both non-food prices (e.g. commodity) and food prices, which contribute a large share to headline inflation. Food price inflation in Bangladesh occurs owing to various factors—supply disruptions due to floods and other natural disasters (as happened pervasively in 2017), price distortions by market intermediaries, and a rise in food import prices, among others. Clearly, controlling inflation in Bangladesh requires various other interventions to complement the monetary instruments. Long-term public investments and other measures would be needed to address structural factors and food price volatility. One may note that, over the last two decades, the rate of inflation in Bangladesh has fluctuated, and the level of fluctuation which was much higher in the 1990s decelerated in the 2000s. The volatility in the inflation rate was 44.3% during 1996–2014 (Fig. 4.4). A comparison of Bangladesh and Vietnam shows that, though inflation volatility in Vietnam was much higher, GDP growth volatility and average GDP growth was almost similar for both the countries. Hence, volatility of inflation in Bangladesh has not been a major concern during the past two decades.

[19]Conservative proponents of inflation targètting propose an inflation rate of 3% or less.

[20]The crisis effects and the stimulus measures are still in a fluid state; for an interim evaluation see CPD (2020).

[21]See Farashuddin (2008), Younus (2012), Anwar and Islam (2013). These tend to suggest trade-offs at around 7–8% inflation rates, except Biswas et al. (2016), where the threshold is estimated at 6.25%. Sample size, the period concerned and methodological differences account for these variations.

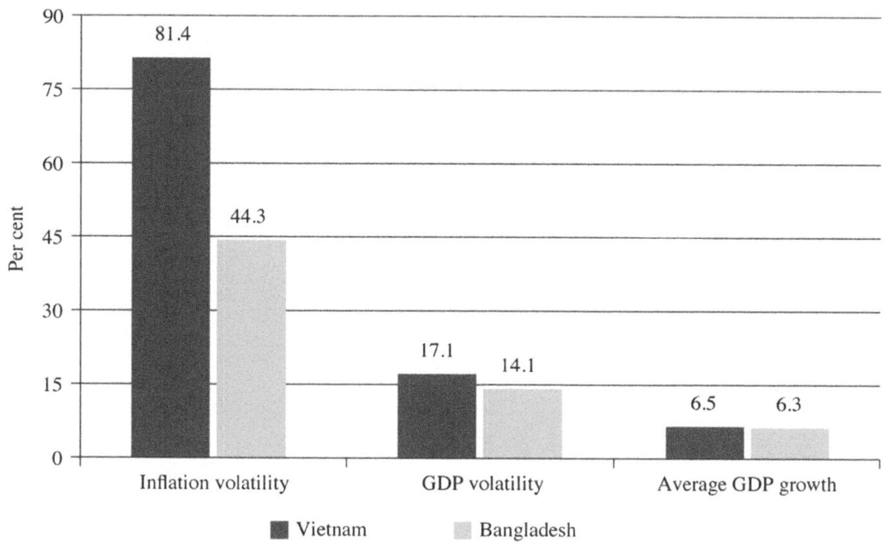

Fig. 4.4 Inflation volatility and GDP growth volatility in Vietnam and Bangladesh: 1996–2014. *Source* Author's calculations from the World Bank (n.d.)

Bangladesh has thus far experienced a relatively low and stable inflation largely through a conservative monetary policy as well as other non-monetary factors. Nevertheless, some risk factors exist, noted below, that can spark inflationary tendencies as well. It appears that the instruments at disposal may not be adequate to respond to inflationary tendencies (Muqtada 2015). The Bank rate (viz. the policy rate) has been held nearly constant almost since FY2003-04 (Bangladesh Bank uses the repo rate as a proxy policy rate); instead, it addresses price stability largely through the credit/deposit channel, often by maintaining a closely monitored relationship between broad money (M2) and reserve money (RM).[22] The use of control over money aggregates (credit channel) provides a pseudo-control over the credit flow to the private sector.[23] There are, however, several other factors that would explain constraints to the flow of credit to the private sector, including those that explain investment constraints in general.

The credit channel does have its limitations, and can frequently miss the inflation targets. On the other hand, the policy rate channel, widely in vogue where money and financial market are well-developed, cannot be fully applied since the transmission mechanisms are very weak, and financial infrastructure is underdeveloped. The ongoing reforms for greater market competition in the sector are likely to place increasing responsibility on the Bank's policy rate, the effectiveness of which will

[22]This implies a careful calibration of inflation rate tracking and potential output growth, weighted by a money demand multiplier; this is often a sum up of projected inflation, GDP growth, plus a multiplier factor.

[23]See details in Muqtada (2015).

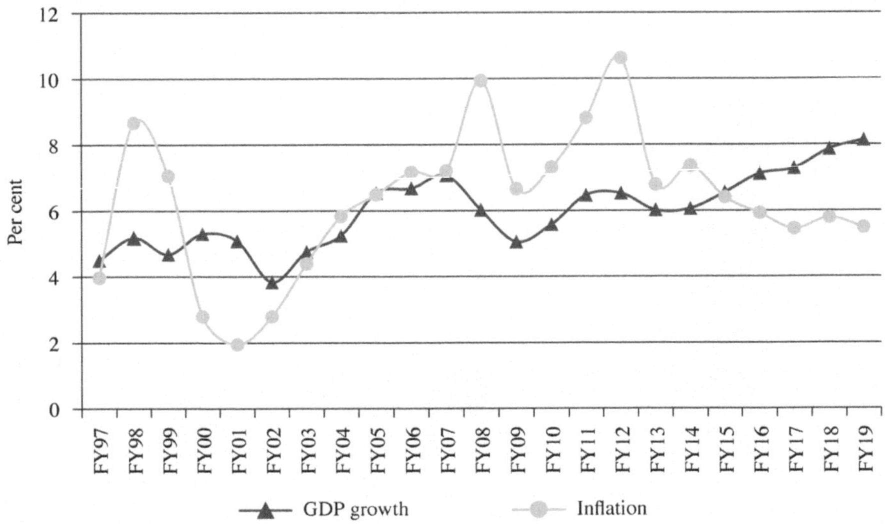

Fig. 4.5 GDP growth and inflation. *Source* Author's compilation from the BBS data

depend on, among others, a much greater financial deepening, strengthening of credit and debit markets and interbank transactions and integration—all within an efficient regulatory and accountable framework.[24]

As noted earlier, the overall trend relationship between GDP growth and inflation over the past two decades has been relatively stable, i.e. growth has not been overly threatened by the observed fluctuations in the price levels, nor is inflation seen as among the major constraints to investment (Fig. 4.5).

In fact, Fig. 4.5 does show a positive relationship between growth and a mild inflation over a prolonged period. It does not, however, shed light on how much lower the inflation rate should be, and most importantly, how to attain that level without affecting output levels.

Nevertheless, there remains an apprehension regarding the efficiency of the existing monetary and financial system, in their ability to control inflation and exchange rate stability in the future, particularly when the economy is poised for a higher growth-pathway,[25] one which may require greater external interaction. There are various other potential threats to price stability that can trigger inflation uncertainties. Foremost among these, is the potential fiscal dominance. Bangladesh at its current and projected pace of growth would require much higher public expenditure to meet various infrastructural and social needs (Mansur 2014). If revenue growth fails to finance such expenditure, an increased borrowing, especially from

[24]Muqtada (2015).

[25]Bangladesh, despite the ongoing pandemic, projects a growth rate of 8.2% during FY2020-21.

the banking sector, is likely to cause price instability.[26] A second potential is the exchange rate volatility. During the recent past, the real effective exchange rate (REER) has been stable. Although, in principle, Bangladesh maintains a market-based, free-floating exchange rate regime, Bangladesh Bank intervenes occasionally to buy/sell foreign currency to smoothen volatility and to support international competitiveness of Bangladesh exports. In a growing economy, much will depend, ceteris paribus, on the growth of export capacity to meet the import surge, and the future steadiness of remittance flows. Third, risks can equally come from non-price factors affecting inflation (supply shocks) or non-economic factors (e.g. political instability).

During the ongoing pandemic, some of the above risks are already surfacing. The dramatic fall in export earnings[27] and remittances are threatening to affect current account deficit and the exchange rate. Further, the fairly bold economic growth rates that policymakers in Bangladesh are projecting over the next Five-Year Plan (8FYP) would require careful articulation of policies to avoid trade-offs between growth and inflation.

However, currently, with inflation rates being within a comfortable band over the past several years, it would be critical to review how the monetary policy could influence savings and investment; and hence, aggregate demand. Since savings appear to be relatively more responsive to income growth than policy rates,[28] the more significant constraint would lie with investment growth. Private investment has been nearly stagnant for a prolonged period, with a slight increase in the two recent years. One has to see how far this has been due to the recent declining trend in lending rates which are still in double-digits.[29]

Bangladesh has been undertaking various banking and financial sector reforms, with the expectation of enhancing greater competition in the sector, and to strengthen the regulatory framework. These have led to some specific positive developments. However, many failings and anomalies still remain, which are reflected in the persistently unacceptable non-performing loans (NPLs) and capital adequacy ratios (CARs). A careful strategy is needed to bring about a further reduction in—high NPLs, excess liquidity, high interest rate spreads and the huge proportion of classified loans, especially in the state-owned commercial banks (SCBs). For instance, as Table 4.1 shows, despite Bangladesh Bank's attempt to reinforce compliance with Basel II framework, and its subsequent efforts toward the implementation of Basel III framework,[30] there still remains a huge variation in CARs and the NPLs amongst the

---

[26] In the recent past, Bangladesh has been meeting its borrowing needs increasingly through National Savings Certificates (NSCs). See Sect. 6.2 on the relative importance of the sources of public borrowing in Bangladesh.

[27] CPD (2020) mentions a 61% decline in month-on-month export earnings during May 2020.

[28] See Farashuddin (2008).

[29] Bangladesh Bank has recently issued instructions to commercial banks to place a cap on deposit (6%) and lending rates (9%). It is still unclear how this decree will work, while at the same time ensuring market competitiveness.

[30] Since the introduction of the Basel II framework in 2009, there has been greater accountability and risk-resilience capacity in the sector; but there is still need for closer enforcement to curb

Table 4.1 Selected indicators of the banking sector in Bangladesh (%)

Bank type	FY2005			FY2015			FY2018		
	CAR	Gross NPL ratio	Interest rate spread (overall)	CAR	Gross NPL ratio	Interest rate spread (overall)	CAR	Gross NPL ratio	Interest rate spread (overall)
State-owned	−0.8	24.4	5.1	4.9	21.9	3.7	2.0	28.2	3.6
Foreign	24.6	1.5	7.9	24.1	5.7	7.7	23.0	6.7	7.1
Private	9.5	7.8	5.3	11.8	8.3	5.1	12.2	6.0	4.3
All	7.1	15.8	5.3	10.3	9.7	4.9	10.0	10.4	4.5

Source Author's compilation from the Bangladesh Bank data

various groups of commercial banks. The interest rate spread has declined somewhat, but is still high, and is often attributed to loan defaults (and scams), but also to alleged collusion and oligopolistic practices in the fixing of lending rates.[31] Some of these factors are linked to political and vested interests and serious governance deficits, which negate the initiatives to bring financial institutions towards best-practice standards.[32] Currently, the turmoil in the banking and financial sector, unless quickly brought under control, could potentially increase exposure to investment risks.

Despite the caveats above, the monetary policy of Bangladesh, under the current trends in price stability and low inflation volatility, is well-positioned to focus on its other mandate, i.e. facilitating investment and inclusive growth, with a focus on employment. There are sufficient reasons to argue in favour of pursuing, albeit with caution, an expansionary policy, in a milieu of substantial slack in the labour market that would tend to boost aggregate demand and job generation, such as through tailored credit extension to SMEs and micro-enterprises. This will be all the more pressing during the current challenges to overcome the COVID-19 pandemic-related economic downturn which has disproportionately affected the informal sector enterprises.

4.5 Financial Sector Development and Financial Inclusion

A strong financial system and an appropriate financial infrastructure are essential to sustain price stability, encourage savings and investment, and foster growth and job creation. In the past two decades, despite the drawbacks as mentioned, the financial sector has managed to cope with the needs of a growing economy, such as through mobilisation of savings and credit growth to the private sector. Similarly, one observes a substantial growth in M2, especially during the past decade, which is higher than many countries with similar per capita GDP. Table 4.2 provides a trend picture of the key indicators of financial sector deepening in Bangladesh.

While the pace of financial sector deepening has to be stepped up for financial resource mobilisation and credit utilisation by the private sector, there are several other issues that the financial system needs to address in order to promote growth and social inclusion. The financial system is rather fragmented and consists of formal and informal entities, the latter being outside the regulatory framework. The formal sector financial system includes the banks, the non-bank financial institutions, the insurance companies, and extends to the regulation of the money and capital markets. There are

loan defaults and government interferences that impairs the risk management culture. Capital adequacy is still below BASEL III requirements for some banks, and the prospects of full BASEL III implementation by 2019 seem bleak.

[31] See Islam (2012).

[32] See Habib et al. (2017); in the recent past, the financial and banking sector has been jolted by a series of scams and fraudulent practices.

Table 4.2 Growth of financial sector deepening indicators (%)

Indicator	FY 05	FY 06	FY 07	FY 08	FY 09	FY 10	FY 11	FY 12	FY 13	FY 14	FY 15	FY 16	FY 17	FY 18
M2	16.7	19.3	17.1	17.6	19.2	22.4	21.3	17.4	16.7	16.1	12.4	16.3	10.9	9.2
Private sector credit	16.8	18.1	15.0	24.9	14.6	24.2	25.8	19.7	10.8	12.3	13.2	16.8	15.7	16.9
Domestic credit	17.4	19.9	14.4	21.0	16.1	17.8	27.5	19.5	11.0	11.6	10.0	14.2	11.2	14.7

Source Author's calculations from the Bangladesh Bank data

Table 4.3 Microfinance sector of Bangladesh

Particular	Jun-10	Jun-11	Jun-12	Jun-13	Jun-14	Jun-15	Jun-16	Jun-17
Number of licensed NGO-MFIs	516	576	590	649	742 (cancelled 45)	753 (cancelled 56)	758 (cancelled 78)	783 (cancelled 84)
Number of clients (million)	25.3	26.1	24.6	24.6	25.1	26.0	27.8	29.9
Total borrowers (million)	19.2	20.7	19.3	19.3	19.4	20.4	23.3	24.9
Amount of outstanding loans (billion BDT)	145.0	173.8	211.3	257.0	282.2	352.4	459.4	583.6
Amount of savings (billion BDT)	51.4	63.3	75.3	94.0	107.0	135.4	171.2	216.7

Source MRA (2014, 2018)
Note NGO: Non-government organisation; BDT: Bangladeshi Taka

a few so-called semi-formal financial institutions, such as the Palli Karma-Sahayak Foundation (PKSF), Grameen Bank and the cooperatives.

The formal sector which also includes a large number of licensed microfinance institutions (MFIs), has a rather skewed credit distribution structure. Too much credit is devoted to only a few large clients, and credit is concentrated in a few selected sectors, e.g. readymade garments (RMG) and textiles, and in the corporate sector. A significant dimension in the development of the financial structures toward greater inclusion and participation would be the broadening of the lending base, and diversification of credit allocation. Within the formal financial structure, the MFIs play an important role in the extension of microcredit to the poor and underserved. It may be noted that, Bangladesh has played a pioneering role in advancing the role of microcredit-lending and the processes of financial inclusion.[33]

While these financial inclusion institutions and initiatives have played a significant role in Bangladesh, especially during the peak of poverty incidence of the 1970s and 1980s, there has been criticism in the recent years on their performance (Table 4.3) as well as on the growing disconnect, between *social inclusion* objectives and interests

[33]Grameen Bank, BRAC and Proshika in Bangladesh, have been globally recognised as prominent and effective initiatives of financial inclusion, that support poorer people, through access to resources/opportunities and financial choices, to strengthen their efforts for a better livelihood, and enhance individual capabilities. These models have been replicated in several other developing countries of the world.

of the lending institutions. Nevertheless, the MFIs have spread and deepened the concept of financial inclusion.

The renewed financial inclusion drive, under the supervision of the Bangladesh Bank and conducted both through existing formal banking network as well as new forms of micro-lending and mobile lending, is poised to attain several objectives: (i) financial institutions can be a significant contributor to the objective of inclusive growth (by extending credit and financial services to the underserved populations and regions of the country); (ii) financial institutions are likely to develop and deepen the financial sector by strengthening and extending institutions to non-traditional sectors and regions, especially in the rural areas; (iii) these institutions, especially through directed lending to agricultural production, would tend to ease supply constraints, which would support measures to curb food inflation and sustain price stability. In the above scenario, the financial inclusion initiatives intend to go beyond the simple social profitability context of MFIs, and are defined as being under supervision of official authorities.[34] The intended objectives are to ensure greater access to finance for the underserved population that would invest in productive activities and diversification, and help to extend the structures of financial services that would potentially allow greater mobilisation of savings. Among the more recent financial inclusion initiatives, the following are noteworthy:

- Agriculture sector credit policy, including *directed lending* by encouraging all commercial banks to extend lending to the sector with subsidies support from Bangladesh Bank's refinancing schemes;
- A credit programme for share-croppers, enabling more than half a million of this vulnerable group, to receive credit through a special finance facility;
- *Ten Taka account* for farmers, which is a novel initiative to facilitate the opening of bank accounts for hitherto unbanked poor farmers, wage labourers and other vulnerable groups (with as small a deposit as BDT 10), and which can be used by the accountholders as savings and payments medium, as well as to receive various input subsidies and social safety net payments from the government;
- Stepped up lending to small and medium-sized enterprises (SMEs), by the commercial banks and financial institutions, through refinancing incentives, especially to support small businesses, women entrepreneurs and backward regions;
- Mobile banking, which under a surge in demand for mobile financial services, has led to the extension of mobile banking licenses to several banks, e.g. BRAC Bank's subsidiary, bKash. These are rapidly expanding their services throughout the country.

The above financial inclusion initiatives, through greater reach and depth, are likely to strengthen the foundations of the banking and the financial system as a whole, if pursued within a common framework of prudential regulations. Unlike the microcredit campaign of the MFIs, the current financial inclusion initiatives are likely

---

[34]For example, banks and financial institutions are supervised by the Bangladesh Bank; MFIs are supervised by the Microcredit Regulatory Authority (MRA); so on and so forth.

to impart impulses to the growth of productivity and structural changes, through its multipronged credit advances to productive sectors and economic diversification.[35]

Financial inclusion, in Bangladesh, is emerging as a crucial cornerstone of inclusive growth. It has the potential not only to reach the most vulnerable and poor in the financial system, but also to engage them in productive activities, and thereby helping them to work out of poverty.[36] There are studies to suggest that financial inclusion also helps in an economy's effort to reduce inequality.[37] The financial inclusion initiatives, as observed above, have been increasingly supporting the expansion of financial services to the poor and vulnerable, largely in the rural areas.

While the formal financial structure purports to foster growth, structural diversification and job creation, and thus contributes to inclusion, the formal institutions would also need to step up the development of an inclusive financial system. Such a system needs to be thoroughly reviewed and have alternatives explored, on how the formal financial system could extend and interact services that are being enabled by financial institutions and other non-formal credit institutions. This would then reinforce a widened lending base, further expand access to credit and other financial services (such as deposit and savings, insurance and payments), to less banked regions, groups (women, marginal farmers), and serve to pursue the 2030 Agenda.

There are other considerations too. With too many banks competing for too few sectors/clients in urban areas, the *rural connect* is emerging as a significant avenue to diversify their lending portfolios. The critical issues for normal banking would relate to how to minimise operational and credit risks, and reduce delivery costs. In this regard, the private commercial banks (PCBs) are engaged in evolving strategies that would advance the rural connect to extend normal banking approaches—particularly to support the smaller businesses and the missing-middle—and thereby address the existing credit market imperfections.

It would be interesting to see how the government, in a broader monetary policy framework, develops appropriate institutional and regulatory framework to provide new intermediation initiatives between bank profitability and financial inclusion.

4.6 Fiscal Policy, Employment and Social Inclusion

4.6.1 Bangladesh's Fiscal Position: Selected Issues

Balancing the budget and keeping deficit low as a principle is always a critical consideration in maintaining price stability. Severe and unsustainable government debts can often lead to monetary policy interventions, raise interest rates, and cause

[35] Akter (2016) on the need to extend coverage of the microcredit finance market.

[36] The critical role of financial inclusion in poverty alleviation and inclusive growth is now widely recognised (UN 2006).

[37] See for example, Beck and Demirgüç-Kunt (2008).

market uncertainties. On one hand, such a fiscal dominance situation is as undesirable as extreme forms of fiscal consolidation; on the other, a country may resort to this order to return rapidly to low fiscal deficits.[38] Fiscal deficit and overall debt–GDP ratio, of course, vary in size from country to country, and the burden of fiscal responsibility[39] would depend on how well an individual country copes with its debt sustainability. In this context, it may be noted that, there are combinations of policy choices and policy instruments that can be used in attaining fiscal balances, but which can have different secondary economic and social outcomes.

Bangladesh is not among the 96 countries where the fiscal rules are currently in vogue.[40] Instead, the country has been establishing its fiscal and public spending accountability through various processes, such as greater transparencies and better oversight in the public expenditure reviews and budget formulation.[41] Given that Bangladesh has maintained a relatively low budget deficit for a prolonged period, Bangladesh has not yet confronted the urgency of introducing fiscal rules and related statutory compulsions. During the last several years, the deficit has hardly crossed 4%, except in FY2007-08, when the economy resorted to selected stimulus measures to cope with the impact of the Global Financial Crisis (GFC) (Fig. 4.6), and now in fighting the current pandemic crisis.[42]

In FY2017-18, the deficit as share of GDP had once again risen close to 5%. The deficit had increased due to a decline in revenue collection and enhanced current expenditure, largely on increases in pay and allowances, and in subsidies.[43] Such year-on-year fluctuation in fiscal deficit are not a cause of alarm, unless there is a trend in rise in price and/or debt–GDP ratio, which is stable and well-below the widely accepted standard of 40%. The deficit is likely to be higher during FY2020-21 due to the pandemic, and one has to see how it affects debt sustainability. Thus far, the foreign reserves (currently equivalent to more than six months of imports) and a current account surplus provide a comfortable cushion.

Nevertheless, in general, Bangladesh's fiscal situation is in some ways at a crossroads; it has a controlled fiscal deficit position, but within a low revenue-expenditure equilibrium. Fiscal deficit is deemed to be low and stable, thereby supporting the

---

[38]The debate on fiscal consolidation has ruled over much of the past two decades, especially in the European Union (EU), and intensified, as debt–GDP ratio continued to increase in a milieu of slow growth and rising unemployment.

[39]In this regard, one may note that, a large number of countries, both in developed and developing countries, have adopted fiscal rules with specified numerical thresholds related to revenues, expenditures, budget balance and debts. The rules are often statutory, and some countries have established Fiscal Responsibility Councils to monitor compliance with statutes. It is interesting to review the Consultation IV Reports of the IMF for these countries. See IMF (2017).

[40]Varied fiscal rules exist in India, Pakistan and Sri Lanka, see IMF (2017).

[41]See World Bank (2015).

[42]See for instance, Rahman et al. (2010) for a brief account of the impact of the GFC in Bangladesh, and some of the stimulus measures undertaken by the government. Also see CPD (2020) for an early account of the likely adverse impact of ongoing economic downturn and stimulus measures on budget deficit and public finances.

[43]See World Bank (2017b).

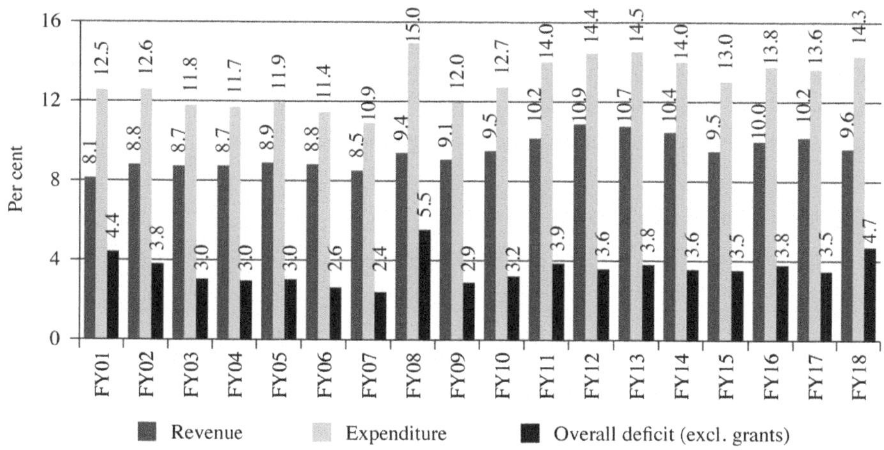

Fig. 4.6 Key components of fiscal framework as share of GDP. *Source* Author's calculations from the Ministry of Finance (MoF) data

overall macroeconomic stability of the economy. In contrast, as Bangladesh moves towards its desired middle-income status by 2021, such a comfortable status quo of revenue and expenditure levels is unlikely to cope with the surge of development needs, especially with further anticipated pandemic-induced stimulus measures, and demand for substantial infrastructure, public services and imports. A commonly observed binding constraint facing Bangladesh is its relatively low tax-base, and consequently a low revenue–GDP ratio that restricts the scope for expansionary expenditure policies (see Box 4.1). Besides, there are also several sticky expenditures, e.g. wages, salaries and interest payments of the government that constitute a substantial part of the budget. It is likely that the burden of a continued consolidation or conservative fiscal regime will be borne through restraints in social and capital expenditures, which are likely to increase substantially during the ongoing crisis of aggregate demand.

"Box [GDP growth and revenue mobilisation] starts"

Box 4.1 GDP growth and revenue mobilisation A striking feature of the macroeconomic scenario in Bangladesh is the incongruence between the growth of GDP and that of revenue mobilisation. In terms of revenue mobilisation, Bangladesh, despite having high growth of GDP, is lagging behind not only compared to that of developing countries, but also to its own development aspirations. Since FY2008-09, there has been no major breakthrough in trends of revenue mobilisation, with revenue–GDP ratio decelerating since FY2011-12. In fact, in FY2017-18, revenue–GDP ratio in Bangladesh was only 9.6% with the tax–GDP ratio being 8.6%. Average tax–GDP ratio in developing countries is about 15%. Given the current trends, the target to reach a revenue–GDP ratio of 16.1% and a tax–GDP ratio of 14.1% by FY2019-20, as aspired in the 7FYP, appears to be rather remote. Furthermore, the current economic crisis will adversely affect revenue earnings in FY2019-20.[44]

Revenue as share of GDP (%)

Source	FY 09	FY 10	FY 11	FY 12	FY 13	FY 14	FY 15	FY 16	FY 17	FY 18
a. Total revenue	9.2	9.5	10.1	10.9	10.7	10.4	9.6	10.0	10.2	9.6
a.1 Tax revenue	7.5	7.8	8.7	9.0	9.0	8.6	8.5	8.8	9.0	8.6
a.1.1 NBR Tax	7.1	7.5	8.3	8.7	8.6	8.3	8.2	8.4	8.7	8.3
a.1.2 Non-NBR Tax	0.4	0.3	0.4	0.3	0.3	0.3	0.3	0.3	0.3	0.3
a.2 Non-tax revenue	1.7	1.7	1.5	1.8	1.7	1.8	1.1	1.2	1.2	1.0

Source Author's calculations based on the MoF and BBS data
Note NBR: National Board of Revenue

The gap between target of revenue mobilisation and the actual attainment, i.e. the revenue shortfall, has been a recurring phenomenon with drastic increases in recent years. In a recent study, Khan (2018) observed that 68% of the eligible taxpayers in Bangladesh did not pay income tax in 2017, and that more than one-third of the highest earners did not pay taxes.

Inability to collect income tax as targetted has plainly been one of the major reasons of revenue shortfall. Government's increased reliance on value added tax (VAT) for revenue generation and lower than targetted VAT collection has further added to rising concern. To this end, it must be mentioned that the government aspires to finance 33.5% of the additional funds required to attain the SDGs in Bangladesh from public sources during the FY2016-17 to FY2029-30 timeframe. Given this substantial resource requirement, and also taking into account Bangladesh's dual transition (i.e. promotion to World Bank's lower middle-income lending category and the impending graduation from LDC status), the imperatives of revenue mobilisation call for a serious rethink of current measures and policy reforms.

"Box [GDP growth and revenue mobilisation] ends"

[44]See CPD (2020), which projects a major shortfall in revenue earnings during FY2019-20.

Structural transformation and its association with shifts to higher income status, is not only manifest in changing sectoral shares of value-added and employment, but also in several other indicators. One such is the transformation in budget structures, especially in public expenditure patterns. The latter, as per cent of GDP, are above 40% in major advanced economies and nearly 30% in emerging economies, compared to about 14% (FY2014-15) in Bangladesh. Even Sub-Saharan African (SSA) countries, on an average, have an expenditure–GDP ratio of more than 20%.

In Bangladesh, public expenditure to GDP ratio is not only remarkably low, but it had also generally declined between FY2012-13 and FY2016-17. However, it exhibited a sudden spike in FY2017-18, which has largely been due to a substantial rise in Annual Development Programme (ADP) expenditure between FY2016-17 and FY2017-18. Nevertheless, public expenditure to GDP ratio is still well-behind the 7FYP target of reaching 21.1% by FY2019-20. Among the constituents of non-development expenditure, two components, namely pay and allowances and interest payments, account for nearly half of the total during the considered timeframe. The recent increases in salaries and benefits for government employees have resulted in the upward trend of pay and allowances. Interest payments as share of GDP has been hovering around the two per cent mark. Given the government's dependence on National Savings Directorate (NSD) certificate sales, interest payments may continue to increase in the near future.

4.6.2 Seeking an Expansion in Fiscal Space

In order to move towards the envisioned middle-income country status, and subsequently to become a UMIC by 2030, as well as to enhance social inclusion, in line with its commitment of resources to achieve the SDGs, Bangladesh would inevitably require inter alia, an expanded fiscal space and budget flexibility:

- Since a prime objective of the fiscal policy is to ensure the stability of an economy, it is necessary to create a fiscal space to cushion impacts of cyclical downturns on aggregate demand. This has become all the more challenging during the current downturn caused by the pandemic.
- The substantial growth of GDP and incomes over the past two decades, and even higher projected growth (e.g. of 8.2% for current FY2020-21), would put a high demand on infrastructure and public goods and services.[45]
- Towards social inclusion, a fiscal space and a proactive budget is required to pursue a strategic and robust public investment and expenditure policy to address market failures. These are also needed to support a range of employment-intensive sectors, various employment interventions (e.g. self-employment through micro-credit lending), social safety net programmes (SSNPs) to support the massive proportion of vulnerable people in the rural areas, and other active labour market

[45]See for example, Mansur (2014).

policies (ALMPs) to enhance skills and employability of the workforce. There is vigorous contention, from academics and policy researchers, that a more proactive fiscal policy would be necessary to yield better employment outcomes.[46]

Although a greater fiscal space is desirable for a dedicated strategy of inclusive growth, many of the basic social inclusion programmes can be accorded priority even without necessarily seeking big expansions in the budget. Such measures, according to Keynesians, may be necessary when an economy has to address high levels of unemployment and/or collapse in household incomes through fiscal stimulus, as Bangladesh resorted to in the aftermath of the GFC, during 2008–2009, and is doing so during the current pandemic 2020.

A fiscal space is as much about raising revenues and budget reallocations as shifting policy choices. Conservative macroeconomic reforms not only severely restrict fiscal deficits and the budget size, but also in many ways, influence the pattern of expenditures, both of which may adversely affect job growth and social welfare. The affected sectors in a restrictive framework are usually agriculture and social services, the very sectors that should provide the impetus and the human capital required for an inclusive growth. An overemphasis on fiscal deficits and a disregard for aligning fiscal instruments to the structural and social imperatives of the economy can lead to missing the potential influence of built-in tools of fiscal policy. In Bangladesh, which has a relatively strong fiscal position, and commitment to inclusive growth and structural diversification, the implications of pursuing a so-called *credible* fiscal regime needs to be revisited.[47]

In view of the above, what are the likely fiscal options for Bangladesh's agenda for future inclusive growth, employment and structural transformation? While there is generally a growing consensus on, and advocacy of, the need for greater fiscal space and structural reforms, there is scarcely any review or assessment of: (i) the extent of the fiscal space that is needed; (ii) how such a space has to be created; (iii) an identification of the priority areas for which the fiscal space is required; or (iv) the nature of the structural reforms that would support future development, inclusion and employment goals. This would warrant a full review of the country's fiscal stance vis-à-vis its commitment to attaining the UMIC status, as well as the 2030 Agenda.

It is beyond the scope of the present study to assess the growth of the various components of revenue sources that would create a higher revenue–GDP ratio, or their differential impacts on various income-groups. Nevertheless, based on current data and policy analysis, a few points are in order on seeking an expanded fiscal space.

First, the paradox, as stated earlier, of low debt levels coexisting with relatively low revenue expenditure levels would need to be firmly addressed, largely through raising revenue earnings. While there have been increasing contributions from income tax and VAT during the past decade and a half, the overall increase in revenue from these

[46]See Krugman (2005), Chowdhury and Islam (2012); on Bangladesh, see CPD (2017a, b).

[47]See IMF (2017) on the exhortations for improving budget practices in Bangladesh.

two sources, as per cent of GDP, is still very low (see Box 4.1). The average revenue–GDP ratio for UMIC, which Bangladesh is expecting to attain by 2030, is 21.4% (10.4% in FY2013-14). Recently, there have been a number of measures and a major drive to boost revenue mobilisation. NBR expects to raise its revenue earnings both through better coverage of the tax net, as well as through continuous reforms and consolidation of both the income tax and VAT systems.[48] Both the sources have the potential to produce much greater yields, if subjected to further reforms and better tax administration. In terms of income tax and VAT yields, Bangladesh ranks among the lowest in South Asia (World Bank 2012).

Second, the revenue raising process, and the instruments and legislations to do so, have differential impacts on efficiency and equity. Although tax revenues have, since FY2000-01, increased at appreciable rates (though from a low base), there are several studies that suggest that the current returns are far lower than the potential/predicted values.[49] There are many well-known factors that account for this. Effectively, there are the structural factors (large proportion of agriculture and informal sector population that characterise the small tax-base), with less than 1% of the country's population contributing to tax revenues.[50] The economy, and incomes of various groups have grown, but the tax-base has not grown concomitantly. Moreover, there are many sources of income, especially held by the rich, on which taxes are low or exempted, while there are other concealed sources (e.g. widespread black money) that are often a root cause of corruption and rent-seeking. The corporate sector is relentlessly influencing the government to reduce corporate tax rates, to appropriate exemptions and subsidies, and to recapitalise bankrupt banks with taxpayers' money. On the other hand, the poorer and the salaried middle-income classes, who are likely to be disproportionately burdened with income taxes and VAT, do not have a similar lobby.

Third, much more needs to be accomplished on establishing a far more efficient tax administration, and enforcement of reforms that enhance efficiency and transparency. Many of these issues are often an outcome of poor governance—which is characterised by deliberate leakages, lack of administrative capacity for tax collection, and fairly widespread rents earned through collusion and complicity. The current tax system accommodates exemptions and subsidies to various industries and/or groups (such as to the RMG and other export-oriented industries). While many of these could be worthy and can stand on merit for various considerations, these can equally lead to arbitrariness and biases. Legislations, policies and enforcement must be articulated to reflect transparency, uniformity and equity.

Fourth, while revenue mobilisation remains the key instrument in creating greater fiscal space, there are some elements on the expenditure side, whose relevance could be reviewed periodically, without political or administrative prejudices, and downsized if priorities were to shift. Such periodic reviews could release resources through switching expenditure priorities. Nevertheless, for several reasons cited above, total

[48] Over the past several years, there has been a consistent shortfall of revenue earnings from the government's projected targets (CPD 2017b).

[49] Also see for example, CPD (2017b) and Ahmed (2015).

[50] There is reportedly a recent rise in the number of taxpayers, from about 1.5 million to 3.3 million.

public expenditure in Bangladesh will need to expand to match the imperatives of higher growth, infrastructure development and social inclusion initiatives, e.g. the National Social Security System (NSSS).[51] In this context, a serious lacuna lies with budget implementation itself, which has consistently fallen below targets, as has been observed with the ADP; this occurs despite downward revision of expenditure targets caused inevitably by revenue shortfalls. The size of budget has been increasing in every successive year, while the rate of implementation has fallen constantly below targets. Realisation rates for both components of public expenditure, i.e. non-development and development expenditure have exhibited a downward trend between FY2012-13 and FY2017-18—a reversal of trend from the earlier half of the past decade. In FY2017-18, implementation rate of total public expenditure was 80.4%, while the corresponding rate for development expenditure was 76.8%.

Fifth, the other common options in creating a fiscal space besides via *additional resource mobilisation and switching expenditure priorities are official development assistances (ODA) and public borrowings* (all these sources together are often encapsulated as the fiscal diamond). These options, which are available in different measure to the individual country, have their own costs and benefits, and need to be cautiously exercised.[52] The present study has reviewed the first two options above. ODAs have been low in general, and although foreign borrowing has recently started increasing, its relative share in total borrowing has declined (see Table 4.4). Foreign borrowing currently constitutes nearly a quarter of total debt financing.

Public investment (currently at 7.5%) will need to complement a flailing private investment to reach the ambitious growth targets of the Eighth Five Year Plan (8FYP), to achieve the proposed high growth-path to UMIC by 2030, as well as to realise multiple SDGs. This would likely imply continued higher public borrowing. Table 4.4 points to some features of financing the budget deficit in Bangladesh: share of domestic borrowing has gone up to 75.5% in FY2017-18 from 72.4% in FY2009-10; of this, the non-bank borrowing constitutes nearly 64% of total domestic borrowing. In Bangladesh, public borrowing especially from the banks and financial institutions has remained fairly restrained. As was observed earlier, banking contributes approximately a third of domestic financing, the rest accruing largely from sale of government's NSCs. The recent increase of domestic financing of deficit via sale of high-interest-bearing NSCs has given rise to various concerns,[53] especially that it could potentially threaten the interest rates and liquidity position of the economy. Owing to the current pandemic and economic crisis for which huge stimulus packages are being rolled out,[54] Bangladesh will need to reassess the growth of borrowing, domestic or foreign, through bank or non-bank sources, and recalibrate its deficits and debt sustainability.

---

[51] See Chap. 7 of this volume.

[52] See Harasty et al. (forthcoming).

[53] For example, the IMF (2017) estimates that the cost of budget borrowing has increased by between a quarter to half per cent of GDP.

[54] At the time of writing, several stimulus packages have been announced, the amount equal to 3.7% of the national budget (CPD 2020).

Table 4.4 Financing of budget deficit (crore BDT)

Description	FY10	Share (%) FY10	FY18	Share (%) FY18	Average annual growth (%) FY18 over FY10
Foreign borrowing (net)	6,036	27.6	25,620	24.5	19.8
Foreign borrowing	11,004	50.3	33,132	31.7	14.8
Amortisation	−4,968	−22.7	−7,512	−7.2	
Domestic borrowing	15,819	72.4	79,004	75.5	22.3
Borrowing from banking system (net)	−2,093	−9.6	11,731	11.2	
Long-term debt (net)	5,769	26.4	6,171	5.9	0.8
Short-term debt (net)	−7,861	−36.0	5,560	5.3	
Non-bank borrowing (net)	17,912	82.0	67,273	64.3	18.0
National savings schemes (net)	11,699	53.5	46,289	44.2	18.8
Others	6,213	28.4	20,984	20.1	16.4
Total—Financing	21,855	100.0	104,624	100.0	21.6

Source Author's calculations based on MoF (2011, 2019)

A noticeable shift in the pattern of ADP financing is evident during the FY2008-09 to FY2017-18 timeframe. Between FY2008-09 and FY2013-14, the key source of ADP financing was bank borrowing followed by foreign aid and grants. However, since FY2014-15, sale of NSD certificates has emerged as the main source of ADP financing. In this connection, it must be noted that the budgetary planning still regard bank borrowing and grants as the major sources of financing. Not only there is a discrepancy between planning and reality, but also there is the apprehension that dependence on such high-cost borrowing might aggravate the debt sustainability scenario.

It is not certain whether the pace at which such a fiscal space will be augmented could match the speed of expenditure and financing needs of a rapidly growing economy (IMF 2017). In case higher public borrowing becomes necessary, much will depend on how these resources are raised, and how far these can be switched to capital expenditure, after accommodating rising current account expenditures.[55] Other options are being explored by Bangladesh to raise capital funds such as

[55]Krugman (2005).

the sovereign wealth fund,[56] to accelerate structural transformation and aggregate demand. Since inflation and debts/deficits have been relatively low and stable over the past two decades, a measured fiscal expansion could be accommodated without exerting excessive pressure on the current debt discipline.[57]

4.6.3 A Budget for Social Inclusion

A progress towards social inclusion does not happen automatically via trickle down. A country's budget is among the key instruments that can lead and encourage such a progress. The present study does not make any attempt to design such a budget; rather, it indicates broad directions and priorities of an inclusionary budget. The budget is an outcome of multiple policy choices that effectively define an individual country's fiscal and public policy stance. The priorities in these choices and the programme measures that are adopted would determine the size and composition of the budget. There exist powerful advocacies on the role of fiscal policy and empirical observations on the multiple ways by which fiscal measures can influence employment and social inclusion outcomes:

(i) growth support, especially when there is underspending from non-government sectors (e.g. through increases in public investment), to generate growth and jobs;
(ii) redistributive support (e.g. special employment schemes[58]);
(iii) wage/employment subsidies;
(iv) SSNPs and other allocations for supporting ALMPs via automatic stabilisers and discretionary fiscal measures);
(v) public provisions (e.g. on health, education and skills development), among others.

The need for a fiscal space, and measures to enhance it would require closer scrutiny of not only the revenue-expenditure programme, but also greater efforts in linking budget allocations to priorities of inclusive growth. Existing allocation structure may not be consistent with the priorities of inclusive growth. This would require articulation in budget planning and design of the social inclusion expenditure framework.[59]

Foremost, sectoral expenditure prioritisation is significant. In particular, as mentioned previously, support to boost job generation would be a crucial fiscal

---

[56] See previous discussion; also Ahmed (2015) and IMF (2017).

[57] It may be pertinent to recall the Keynesian contention that if financed by borrowing, an increase in autonomous government expenditure—whether investment or consumption—would cause output to expand through a multiplier process, particularly when there are unemployed resources.

[58] See Bhaduri (2005) for a persuasive case of integrating employment-based programmes in budget planning.

[59] The current sectoral allocations show that defence and public order and safety together capture more budget resources (11.4%) than either physical or social infrastructure expenditures.

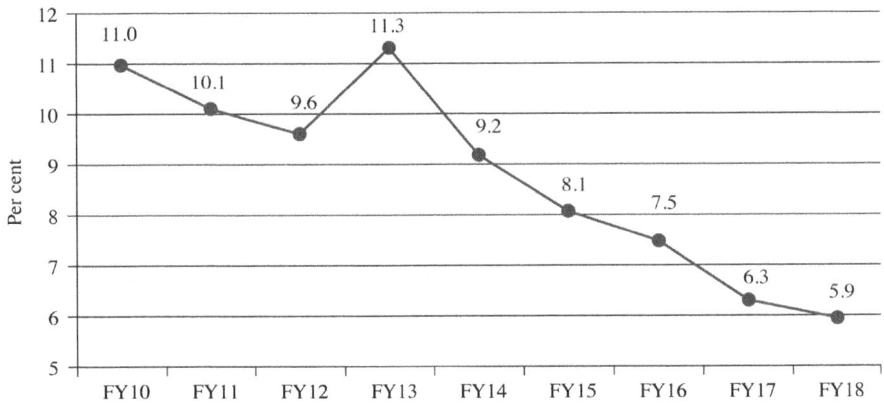

Fig. 4.7 Share of agriculture and allied sectors (other than subsidy) in total budget. *Source* Author's compilation from budget documents (various years), MoF, Government of Bangladesh (GoB)

prerogative. Allocations to employment-friendly sectors are one such consideration. Among the many ways that fiscal instruments in Bangladesh have been used to promote inclusive growth, mention must be made of some sectoral measures; for example, those introduced to promote labour-intensive, export-oriented industrialisation (see Chap. 5).

A comparison between FY2009-10 and FY2019-20 shows that allocations in health, local government and rural development, social security and welfare, and agriculture have declined. In particular, a continuous decline in allocations to agriculture (Fig. 4.7) is a matter of concern. In fact, allocation to agriculture is now lower than that in the defence sector. Major allocations are needed in agriculture in order to improve technology, skills and input levels, which will ultimately contribute in the much-needed productivity enhancement of the sector. This would potentially raise the incomes of the vast majority of the households through both agricultural activities, as well as rural non-farm (RNF) enterprises (see Chap. 6). Boosting jobs, wages/incomes and productivity in the agriculture sector through purposive fiscal interventions is likely to be a significant impulse towards reducing poverty and inequality.

The budget on social sectors too, would need a reassessment to move *beyond a status quo budget*.[60] Figure 4.8 provides a context of such a review.

Expenditure as a percentage of GDP on education and health has been less than encouraging and slower than the planned increase for the respective years of the 7FYP. One may note that while the 7FYP had a planned increase in the two sectors, the real per capita expenditure is tangibly lower than the nominal increase (CPD 2017a). In fact, allocation to health has remained significantly lower than 1% of GDP throughout the past several years, which is unlikely to pace up the much-needed public provisions on health and the development of a national health system—the fragility of which has

[60] See CPD (2017a).

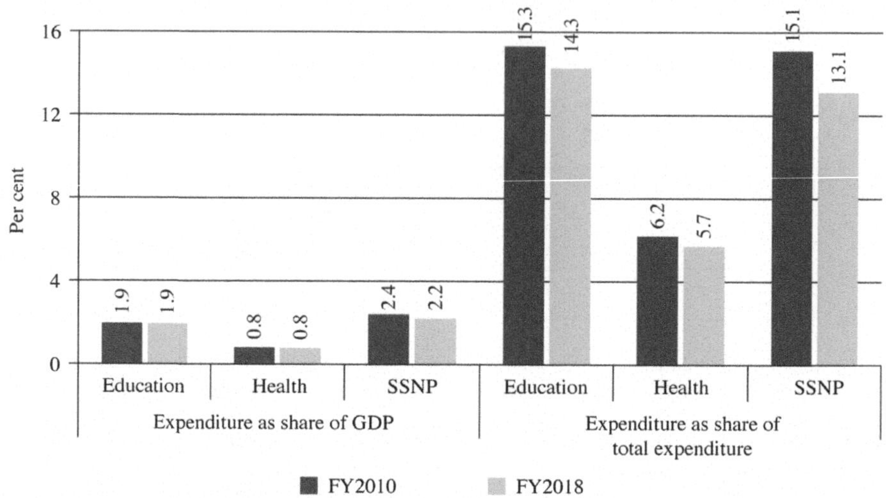

Fig. 4.8 Education, health and SSNP expenditure/allocation as share of GDP and total budget. *Source* Author's calculations from the MoF data

been exposed by the current pandemic. The core programme of the sector, Health, Population and Nutrition Sector Development Programme (HPNSDP) 2011–2016, which had several targets, under 40 indicators, to be achieved by the terminal year, is far behind target.[61] Similarly, allocation for SSNPs, which is a crucial element in the gradual consolidation of NSSS of the government, is a mere 2% of GDP, much lower than that are observed in many Asian countries. The current budget FY2020-21 has pledged higher allocations on SSNPs to help mitigate growing vulnerability caused by the pandemic. While allocations to education and health have marginally increased, one has to note that, this increase in per capita terms (given the massive population base that needs coverage) can be paltry. In other words, the simple average per capita allocations do not reflect to what extent actual benefits impact at the household level (Mahmud 2002). Despite high priority pledged to job generation, education, social protection and other social sectors, budgetary allocations and follow-up measures do not reflect the commitments convincingly.[62]

[61]Compare this to allocation to defence, which has been more than 1% of GDP throughout the past decade.

[62]For instance, with respect to budgets in Bangladesh, it appears that allocations for six ministries concerning social welfare and security have gone through a generally declining trend, both as percentage of GDP and total budget (CPD 2017b).

4.6.4 Thinking Alternatively

A budget for inclusive growth would need to go beyond simply social spending, and include an appropriate and accountable expenditure framework (perhaps in the same manner as the government is planning to achieve the SDG targets) that addresses various goals of inclusive growth. There are, of course, many indicators and goals where the progress may be less perceptible, e.g. the reduction of income inequality, which has been increasing persistently over the past decade. Some of the social spending towards health, education, pensions and other transfers is intended to provide some palliatives, but would require vigorous initiatives to create more and better income-earning opportunities for the *bottom deciles* of the population.

Analysts quite rightly point out that the expansion of efforts to mobilise resources, especially revenues, would be the *cornerstone* of any pro-poor fiscal strategy.[63] In other words, a greater fiscal space has to be generated to address pro-poor programmes and targets. In the 7FYP, the government, for the first time, recognised the need for a specific review of these issues to create fiscal space to address aspects of social inclusion, and incorporated some budget reform measures (taking a combination of the revenue raising and reallocations route), especially to address an important component of inclusive growth, viz. the continuously rising inequality in the economy. The reforms include measures to increase allocations to education, health, social protection, and more importantly, to rural infrastructure. These allocations would help support programmes, if designed and implemented well, to increase jobs and income opportunities, especially in the rural areas. These would also significantly contribute to productivity and growth. The reallocations would come about from resources raised from ambitious targets of personal income taxes (additional 2.5% of GDP), VAT (additional 1.8% of GDP), local government revenues, and further, from a 1% reduction in energy subsidies (Table 4.5). The 7FYP has come to an end without much happening on reprioritising expenditures. Further analysis and policy efforts are required to explore such expenditure switching in the future Plans to address priorities and concerns of inclusionary and equitable growth. As mentioned above, a fiscal space is essentially an exercise in policy choices. While raising additional resources will remain a distinct advantage, there are a number of empirical studies which show that such choices can be pursued prudently through budgetary reallocations on priorities.[64]

In Bangladesh, the focus of the fiscal regime appears to be overwhelmingly on raising revenues and restraining fiscal expenditure in an accounting bind. There is hardly much consideration of the possibilities of mobilisation of resources on a broader front, such as through impacts on the real economy. One such effect can be through enhancing employment and wages, eventually to create a greater fiscal

---

[63] See for example, Mahmud et al. (2008) and IMF (2017).

[64] Hoy and Sumner (2016), for example, carry out a detailed simulation exercise to show how large reductions in poverty (at different threshold levels) can be realised simply through reducing allocations on defence spending and subsidies to fossil fuels. The authors refer to these as *public bads*. They also advocate a prudent taxing of the rich, to generate additional fiscal space.

Table 4.5 Reducing income inequality—fiscal proposals in 7FYP (% of GDP)

Reform measure	Base-year values FY2015	Increase over 5 years	End-year values FY2020
Increase spending on education	2.2	0.8	3.0
Increase spending on health	0.8	0.4	1.2
Increase spending on social protection	2.0	0.3	2.3
Increase spending on rural infrastructure	2.0	1.0	3.0
Total increase in social spending	2.5		
Financed by			
Cutback on energy subsidy	2.0	−1.0	1.0
Increase in personal income tax	1.0	2.5	3.5
Increase in VAT	4.2	1.8	6.0
Increase in local government revenues	0.2	0.5	0.7
Total financing	5.8		

Source Author's calculations from the 7FYP data

space (Diagram 4.1). The prudent use of existing fiscal space can itself generate a greater fiscal space. The spending on employment generation and on physical and social infrastructures (e.g. skills) is part of the structural reforms that would help boost private sector investment. The expansion of output and employment that is likely to be induced, can potentially trigger a virtuous cycle of higher fiscal space (via higher taxes and private consumption) and further rounds of structural reforms.

4.7 External Stability, Growth and Jobs

While external stability is crucial to sustaining domestic price stability, it is equally significant in promoting export competitiveness, export diversification and employment generation. These, in turn, are strongly related to, and are important considerations in, the trade and industrialisation policy of Bangladesh. This section highlights the significance of external stability, within the macroeconomic policy framework, for promoting growth, export competitiveness and employment.

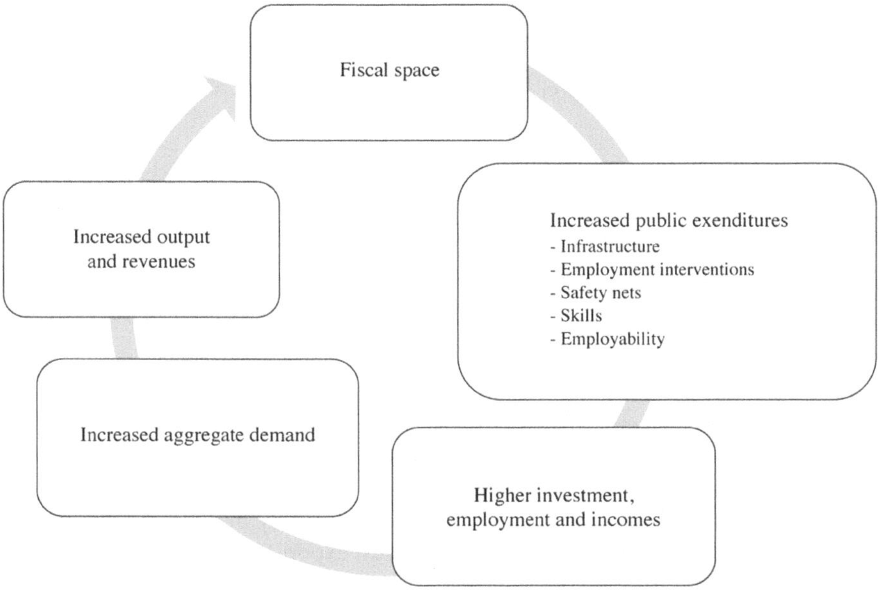

Diagram 4.1 Generating fiscal space through real economy effects. *Source* Prepared by the author. *Note* In order to pursue *inclusive growth* and the SDGs, especially in the milieu of renewed vow to pursue the goal of full employment and decent work (SDG 8), public expenditures and public investment will need to be immensely stepped up. This would require, as argued above, moving out of the current low revenue-expenditure syndrome to pursue a well-calibrated fiscal expansion that would significantly boost the real economy through higher investment, employment and incomes

4.7.1 External Stability: Potential Threats and Challenges

Along with achieving remarkable stability in inflation rates and budget deficits, Bangladesh has also experienced an overall balance of payments (BoP) surplus during the past decade. It has had a current account surplus and a stable REER for most of the post-GFC period, except in the recent years. Since FY2010-11, Bangladesh's overall BoP registered a negative value for the first time in FY2017-18. At the end of FY2017-18, overall BoP balance was to the tune of negative (−) USD 0.88 billion—indicating a decline of about USD 4 billion since FY2016-17 (see Table 4.6). Such a development may not be uncommon in a growing economy, but one that needs to be taken into account in designing and undertaking measures to ensure resilience of external stability. This is particularly important given the emerging risk factors and disquieting trends that include, inter alia, a surge in the trade gap, accumulation of external debt, depletion of forex reserves, depreciation of BDT, ongoing global trade war, and the high probability of global economic slowdown due to the pandemic.

Table 4.6 exhibits how the overall balance scenario has gone through considerable volatility during the last decade or so, with varying movements in current, capital and financial accounts.

Table 4.6 Trends in elements of the overall balance (USD million)

Year	Current account	Capital account	Financial account	Overall balance
FY2009	2,416	451	−825	2,058
FY2011	−1,686	642	651	−656
FY2013	2,388	629	2,863	5,128
FY2016	4,262	464	944	5,036
FY2017	−1,331	400	4,247	3,169
FY2018	−9,780	292	9,076	−885

Source Author's compilation from Bangladesh Bank data

The substantial decline in the overall balance in FY2017-18 was largely associated with the deficit in current account. As can be observed from Table 4.6, deficit in current account balance recorded a considerable rise in a single year, from (−) USD 1.33 billion in FY2016-17 to (−) USD 9.78 billion in FY2017-18. The spike in current account deficit in FY2017-18 was mostly accounted for by the rise in trade deficit. The increasing trade deficit was driven by a modest export growth (5.8%) as opposed to the robust import growth (25.2%) in FY2017-18.[65] Despite remittance income growing respectably between FY2016-17 and FY2017-18, the overall surplus in the non-trade component (which includes remittance income) of the current account balance could not compensate for the high level of trade deficit.

The balance situation was somewhat alleviated by a significant increase in financial account balance—which rose from USD 4.25 billion in FY2016-17 to USD 9.08 billion in FY2017-18. This substantial rise between FY2016-17 and FY2017-18 is largely due to flow of medium- to long-term (MLT) loans coupled with other short-term loans (net). However, the other two components of the financial account, i.e. (net) foreign direct investment (FDI) flows and (net) portfolio investment, recorded a decline during this period.

These recent developments in current account deficit, rising financial account surplus and depreciating overall balance signal towards a number of stress points in the macroeconomic management of Bangladesh which could put pressure on debt sustainability. The increasing demand for forex in the backdrop of the BoP situation has resulted in a depreciation of the BDT. In order to prevent further depreciation of BDT, Bangladesh Bank engaged in large-scale sale of foreign currency. This, in combination with other factors, has resulted in some depletion of the forex reserves (from an equivalent of 6.3 months' import to 5.5 months' import payment, between FY2016-17 and FY2017-18). While the depreciation of BDT may have helped exporters and remittance-earners, the implications for import prices and debt servicing have been unfavourable. It must be noted though that forex reserves have gone up during the recent months of the on-going pandemic for a number of factors, including increased remittances, loans and grants, falling imports, etc.

[65]The sudden surge in growth of imports may have been due to import requirements of an array of mega projects in infrastructure and energy sectors that have been launched in the recent period.

It must also be mentioned that a substantial part of the imports by the government is not underwritten by overseas loans. Hence, a considerable part of the pressure on domestic foreign currency market is originating from the government. Moreover, debt repayment liabilities of private sector borrowers (who are increasingly borrowing from foreign sources and will need to repay from proceeds accruing from the domestic market) are expected to rise with consequent pressure on the local forex market. Bangladesh's impending graduation from LDC status is likely to add further challenges to sustaining external stability.

Although the above challenges to stability may not be considered unusual in an economy which is growing, and which also faces frequent internal shocks (such as significant losses to agriculture/rural sector due to floods in 2016), these point to the need for a rethink of the long-term foundations of such stability and its interlinkages with domestic investment and structural transformation. Short-term measures, such as the Bangladesh Bank's frequent interventions in the exchange market (under its *managed* free-floating regime) may not always be adequate in smoothening exchange rate volatility and sustaining a steady REER. Much will depend on the extent of, and exposure to, risks that could potentially lead to major disruptions and a longer period of instability. In particular, there needs to be a robust foundation for major increases in export earnings (on trade account) to enhance capacity to meet the country's growing import needs as well as measures to step up FDIs and net portfolio investment. On both these accounts, Bangladesh's performance is rather lukewarm, compared to, for instance, with that of Vietnam, which through appropriate policy and institutional reforms, has registered a relatively much higher growth of exports and FDIs during the past decade.

4.7.2 External Stability, Exports and Jobs Growth

There are several potential challenges and risks to external stability and growth of exports (also see Chap. 5). The following paragraphs point to one significant among these, i.e. the overwhelming dependence on RMG as the dominant source of export earnings. A steady REER has been maintained to allow a conducive support to the growth of RMG exports, which account for the bulk of the country's export earnings. Normally, a steady and competitive REER would, as observed in many countries, support trade expansion, employment and export diversification (Epstein 2007). In Bangladesh, there has been a rapid rise in the RMG industry, which has also, until recently, led to a significant growth of manufacturing employment. However, there has been far too little export diversification. In fact, as Fig. 4.9 shows, RMG exports constitute more than four-fifths of export earnings, and its share has been continuously increasing.

Its growth bodes well for GDP growth, jobs and capacity to import; but this also implies a sharply growing export concentration, as shown in the trend in HHI in Fig. 4.9; and hence, potential vulnerability. While according to the government and the Bangladesh Garment Manufacturers and Exporters Association (BGMEA),

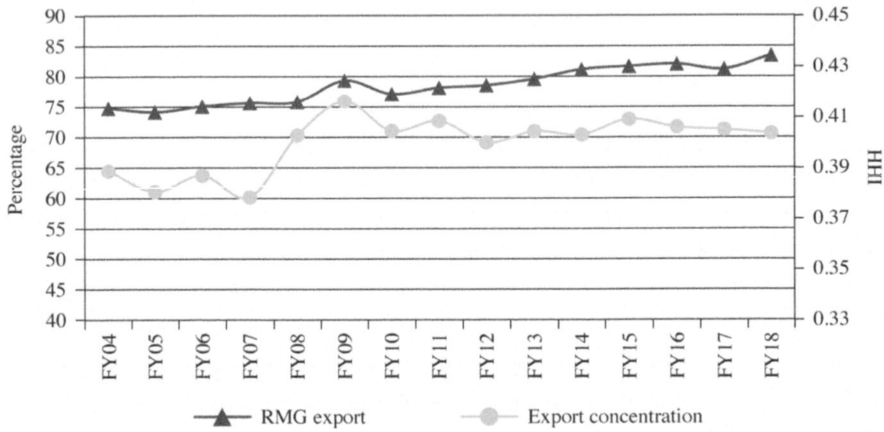

Fig. 4.9 RMG export as share of total export and export concentration (the Herfindahl-Hirschman Index (HHI)). *Source* Author's calculations based on data from the EPB (n.d.) and UNCTADSTAT (n.d.)

RMG is likely to maintain a growth momentum (13% on an average during the 7FYP period and beyond), the current global economic downturn is threatening to subvert such optimism. Besides, there are several issues that can affect such optimism:

(i) With per capita GDP increasing at more than 5%, real wages in the RMG sector are likely to rise, and erode the low labour cost factor as the dominant consideration in future growth projections of the sector. There is already a perceptible tendency towards use of labour-saving technologies by many RMG enterprises, to enhance productivity and reduce hiring costs. It may be noted that the rate of registered employment growth has been falling distinctly during the past few years.

(ii) Since the Rana Plaza tragedy, in which 1,132 RMG workers lost their lives, the industry as a whole has fiercely come under the global scanner, compelling firms to implement various compliance measures related to building and worker safety, and to broader working conditions, including rights at work.[66] These compliances, which are significant in promoting decent work, are likely to enhance costs considerably. These have affected, and continue to affect the smaller firms in particular.

(iii) Several other factors, such as the pace of global demand for RMGs and increasing competition from other countries (e.g. Cambodia, Vietnam, Ethiopia, India) to gain a greater share of the export market, can potentially slow down the growth of RMG exports from Bangladesh; and this could further reduce the growth and job-generating prospects of the sector.

The success in the rapid growth of the RMG sector over the past several decades, encouraged and supported by various policies, subsidies and incentives, have also

---

[66]See European Commission (2017).

created a near-complete dependence on the sector for the economy's export earnings. Several experts have emphasised that policy attention and incentives given to the sector have been highly biased, and have not been equally extended to other potential labour-intensive export-oriented industries.[67] Sustainability of the trade and external balance in the long-run would thus require a more diversified export structure. Currently, Bangladesh economy's export capacity to cope with the ever-growing import demands simply through the narrow RMG export base remains shaky and untenable.

As stated earlier, there are several other factors that can ease the challenges to external stability. Among these is the role of remittances and FDIs. Remittances which are currently about 37% of export earnings have grown significantly over the past decade, and have helped to build up the foreign exchange reserves of the Bangladesh Bank. However, remittance earnings have been declining during the recent past, and are expected to decline sharply due to current recessionary tendencies affecting labour-importing countries.

Further, FDIs, though rising, have not been as forthcoming into Bangladesh, as in some neighbouring countries, e.g. Cambodia or Vietnam. Although labour costs are still relatively low and attractive in Bangladesh, there have been less than satisfactory FDIs into the labour-intensive industries and other potential export sectors (for example, leather and leather-related industries received only 1.1% of total net FDI in 2016), nor has price and REER stability led to any substantial improvement in domestic investment. In other words, price stability and trade liberalisation measures have not been able to increase investment sufficiently. Such measures would need to be backed up by various structural measures. Bangladesh's competitiveness ranking has been improving recently—having moved up from 106 to 99 in the Global Competitiveness Index. However, its position was lower than Sri Lanka (85); and considerably lower than India (40) or Vietnam (55).[68] On a different development, in the recent past, access has been given to foreign borrowing by private firms on a limited scale, apparently to enhance growth of private sector credit, as well as to put downward pressure on domestic lending rates. The effects of this move would need to be monitored very closely, in relation to how the borrowing firms perform, and how exchange rate fluctuations could affect repayments and any potential drawdown on foreign reserves. It would be naive to ignore that Bangladesh will continue to face global shocks and uncertainties, for which the exchange rate regime exercises prudence over the management of its foreign reserves.[69]

Furthermore, with regard to stimulating domestic investment and raising FDI, greater competitiveness would be necessary, which will be determined as much by a stable REER and low labour costs as raising labour productivity. The latter

---

[67]There still remains anti-export biases and protection, which are restraining export potential of several industries. See Khan (2015), Ahmed (2015). Also see Chap. 5.

[68]See WEF (2017).

[69]The government has stalled its decision to give effect to the proposal to create a *sovereign wealth fund*, which would have had part of its foreign reserves directed to infrastructure development. While infrastructure development is critical to creating a basis for structural transformation, the use of the limited reserves would be risky unless the export-capacity-to-import is greatly stepped up.

would depend on a host of factors, including easing of investment and infrastructure constraints, and a major attention to restructuring the low skills profile of the workforce for a highly competitive external market. In order to foster structural transformation and job creation, macroeconomic and structural reforms would need to be supportive of, and consistent with, an integrated strategy of industrial and trade diversification. The following Chap. 5 takes up these issues in greater detail.

4.8 Conclusion

The broad objective of macroeconomic policy is to contribute to economic growth and social well-being in an equitable and sustainable manner. Bangladesh is committed to achieving the SDGs endorsed in the 2030 Agenda, which embody the pursuit of an equitable society through an inclusive growth strategy. A macroeconomic policy would need to spearhead such a strategy. In doing so, the study has argued that the overriding challenge of macroeconomic policy in Bangladesh would precisely be in giving effect to the dual mandate of achieving macroeconomic stability and inclusive growth. The current pandemic crisis and economic downturn have sharply exposed the need for a focused macroeconomic policy to pursue such a dual mandate in order to save lives and livelihoods.

At the risk of repetition, the first steps towards designing a macroeconomic policy framework for an inclusive growth would require, inter alia, a rethinking of a macroeconomic policy framework that goes beyond attaining targets of stability (which are essentially intermediate targets) and focuses robustly on growth, employment and income (Stiglitz et al. 2006; Bhaduri 2005). The challenges identified are—achieving a high and sustained growth and structural transformation to reach the UMIC status by 2031; a reduction in continuously rising inequality; measures to deal with weak employment performance; addressing unacceptably high incidence of vulnerable population, among others. This would require strategic planning, including a more aggressive fiscal and monetary stance.

This chapter has reviewed the usual macroeconomic policy instruments, and their current practices in Bangladesh. Regarding monetary policy, it has been observed that Bangladesh has maintained a comfortable stretch of price stability, and inflation has been relatively low. Monetary instruments which have an imprecise control over inflation targets have been complemented by low budget and current account deficits to help sustain low inflation.

One must note that, it would be difficult for Bangladesh to embark on the much-anticipated higher (double-digit) growth-path of achieving UMIC under the parameters that currently define existing stability conditions. This would involve, as the IMF suggests, *upgrading* of macroeconomic practices to cope with various challenges. In the monetary sector, one such practice is the use of the market-determined *policy rate* that would serve to enhance greater competitiveness and attract private investment. Despite various reforms undertaken to strengthen the banking and financial markets, the *policy rate* (as understood in a developed money/financial market), cannot be applied since the *transmission mechanisms* are very weak, and financial infrastructure is underdeveloped. This will require greater financial deepening, strengthening of credit and debit markets, and interbank transactions and integration.

Given the recent trends in price stability, the monetary policy needs to adjust its *inflation only* priority, and focus with equal force on its employment/inclusive growth mandate. This would entail stimulations and incentives to enhance domestic savings and investment, and boost aggregate demand. Private investment in Bangladesh is relatively low compared to its Asian comparators who have achieved higher growth and structural transformation. Financial markets are not only weak, but also fraught with anomalies, unacceptably high loan defaults and outright scams, especially in the PCBs and SCBs, which have shaken investors' confidence. This requires firm action to institute an efficient regulatory and accountable framework.[70]

Financial sector deepening needs to factor in an inclusive financial structure, whereby access to credit markets can be extended to unbanked and underbanked population and regions, the *rural connect* in particular. This would also help ease credit market imperfections and the skewed credit distribution, which currently exist. The financial inclusion initiatives would need to be stepped up within a strategic policy and regulatory framework. Such opportunities and access to credit for the disadvantaged poor, the small farms and enterprises, if appropriately designed and expanded through a comprehensive monetary policy and regulations, can by itself be an important redistributive measure, which could reduce the transfers and fiscal burdens of the government.

However, macroeconomic policies cannot, on their own, deliver desired employment and inclusion outcomes in the economy. Productive employment generation and state welfare are contingent on an integrated set of policies that would include various sectoral, labour market and institutional measures, which have to be incorporated in a dedicated budget. The present study has underscored the need for budget prioritisation, especially in a relatively low revenue–GDP ratio scenario, in order to yield greater fiscal space, and identified measures to pursue the government's stated goals of growth and equality. The chapter also underscores the need for a measured fiscal expansion, to step up public investment to complement the slow growth in private investment, as well as to meet the needs of UMIC growth-path through structural reforms and infrastructure development.

Fiscal policy is not only about financing development, but also a political statement of the government regarding its stance on the economic and social well-being of the people. Public policy and public expenditure will be critical for a more focused social inclusion, i.e. a budget for social inclusion through a closer review of priorities in both revenue and expenditure portfolios.

Closely linked to the above is the imperative of maintaining external stability. This is of paramount importance in not only maintaining low inflation, but also in enhancing competitiveness. Maintaining a steady REER is crucial to supporting

[70]See for example, CPD (2018) on the advocacy of setting up of an independent Commission to critically evaluate the existing regulations in the banking sector and their implementation, and to draw up reforms and strict measures toward a more competitive and efficient sector.

employment through growth of labour-intensive exports. Currently, the country is overwhelmingly dependent on RMGs for its export earnings. For a more resilient external stability, concerted measures are needed to broad-base the export structure, especially keeping in mind potential trade imbalances that are likely to rise with increasing import needs of a fast-growing economy.

References

ADB. (2017). *Asian Development Outlook 2017: Transcending the Middle-Income Challenge.* Manila: Asian Development Bank (ADB).

Ahmed, S. (2015). *Growth with equity: Contemporary development challenges in Bangladesh.* Dhaka: Bangladesh Institute for Bank Management (BIBM).

Ahmed, S., & Mahmud, W. (Eds.). (2006). *Growth and poverty: The development experience of Bangladesh.* Dhaka: The University Press Limited.

Akter, S. (2016). Overview of financial inclusion in Bangladesh. *The Journal of the Study of Modern Society and Culture, 63*(12), 225–255.

Anwar, S., & Islam, I. (2013). Should developing countries target low, single-digit inflation to promote growth and employment? In I. Islam & D. Kucera (Eds.), *Beyond macroeconomic stability: Structural transformation and inclusive development* (pp. 98–130). London: Palgrave MacMillan.

Bank, B. (2014). *Monetary Policy Statement (July–December 2014).* Dhaka: Chief Economist's Unit and Monetary Policy Department, Bangladesh Bank.

BBS. (2004). *Report on Labour Force Survey (LFS) 2002-2003.* Dhaka: Bangladesh Bureau of Statistics (BBS), Government of Bangladesh (GoB).

BBS. (2008). *Report on Labour Force Survey 2005-06.* Dhaka: Bangladesh Bureau of Statistics (BBS), Government of Bangladesh (GoB).

BBS. (2011). *Report on Labour Force Survey 2010.* Dhaka: Bangladesh Bureau of Statistics (BBS), Government of Bangladesh (GoB).

BBS. (2015). *Report on Labour Force Survey (LFS) Bangladesh 2013.* Dhaka: Bangladesh Bureau of Statistics (BBS), Government of Bangladesh (GoB).

BBS. (2018). *Report on Labour Force Survey (LFS) 2016-17.* Dhaka: Bangladesh Bureau of Statistics (BBS), Government of Bangladesh (GoB).

Beck, T., & Demirgüç-Kunt, A. (2008). Access to finance: An unfinished agenda. *The World Bank Economic Review, 22*(3), 383–396.

Bhaduri, A. (2005). *Macroeconomic Policies for Higher Employment in the Era of Globalization.* Employment Strategy Paper 2005/11. Geneva: International Labour Organization (ILO).

Bhaduri, A. (2019). Macroeconomic perspective on development. In D. Nayyar (Ed.), *Asian transformations: An inquiry into the development of nations* (pp. 216–239). Oxford: Oxford University Press.

Bhattacharya, D., & Titumir, R. A. M. (Eds.). (2001). *Stakeholders perceptions: Reforms and consequences.* Dhaka: Shraban Prakashani.

Biswas, B. P., Masuduzzaman, M., & Siddique, M. N. (2016). *Determining the Growth-maximizing Threshold Level of Inflation in Bangladesh.* Working Paper 1602. Dhaka: Bangladesh Bank.

Chowdhury, A., & Islam, I. (2012). The debate on expansionary fiscal consolidation: How robust is the evidence? *The Economic and Labour Relations Review, 23*(3), 13–38.

Commission, E. (2017). *Implementation of the Bangladesh Compact: Technical Status Report.* Brussels: European Commission.

CPD. (2017a, June 2). An analysis of the national budget for FY2017-18. Presented at the press briefing on *An Analysis of the National Budget for FY2017-18*, organised by the Centre for Policy Dialogue (CPD), Dhaka, Bangladesh.

CPD. (2017b, April 16). *State of the Bangladesh Economy in FY2016-17 (Second Reading): CPD's Budget Recommendations.* Issue paper prepared for the media briefing on "National Budget FY2017-18: CPD's Recommendations," organised by the Centre for Policy Dialogue (CPD), Dhaka, Bangladesh.

CPD. (2018). State of the Bangladesh economy in FY2017-18 (second reading): CPD's recommendations for the upcoming budget. In *Bangladesh economy in FY2017-18: Interim review of macroeconomic performance* (pp. 63–103). Dhaka: Centre for Policy Dialogue (CPD).

CPD. (2020, June 7). *Challenges of Policymaking in Times of Pandemics: State of the Bangladesh Economy in FY2020.* Issue paper prepared for a virtual media briefing, organised by the Centre for Policy Dialogue (CPD), Dhaka, Bangladesh.

Easterly, W. (2001). *The lost decades: Developing countries' stagnation in spite of policy reform 1980–1998.* Washington D.C.: The World Bank.

EPB. (n.d.). *All Statistics Data.* Dhaka: Export Promotion Bureau (EPB), Government of Bangladesh (GoB). https://epb.portal.gov.bd/site/files/835d1ce0-b985-4965-ae2b-dc5ccd5e4a62 Retrieved 6 August 2019.

Epstein, G. (2007). *Central Banks as Agents of Employment Creation.* DESA Working Paper 38. New York: United Nations Department of Economic and Social Affairs (UNDESA).

Farashuddin, M. (2008). Monetary policy and financial sector reforms. In S. R. Osmani (Ed.), *Emerging issues in Bangladesh economy: A review of Bangladesh's development 2005–06* (pp. 249–270). Dhaka: Centre for Policy Dialogue (CPD) and The University Press Limited (UPL).

GED. (2012). *Perspective Plan of Bangladesh 2010–2021: Making Vision 2021 A Reality.* Dhaka: General Economics Division (GED), Planning Commission, Government of Bangladesh (GoB).

Habib, S. M. A., Ahmed, N., Islam, N., Pandit, A. C., Nayn, Z., & Hossain, K. (2017). *Addressing Financial Crime in the Banking Sector of Bangladesh.* Banking Research Series 2016. Dhaka: Bangladesh Institute of Bank Management (BIBM).

Hammond, G. (2012). *State of the art of inflation targeting.* London: Centre for Central Banking Studies, Bank of England.

Harasty, C., D'Achon, E., & Muqtada, M. (Forthcoming). Towards a Pro-employment Budget. Submitted to the International Labour Organization (ILO).

Hoy, C., & Sumner, A. (2016). *Gasoline, Guns, and Giveaways: Is There New Capacity for Redistribution to End Three Quarters of Global Poverty?* Working Paper 433. Washington, D.C.: Center for Global Development (CGD).

IMF. (2017). *Bangladesh: 2017 Article IV Consultation – Press Release; Staff Report.* IMF Country Report 17/147. Washington, D.C.: International Monetary Fund (IMF).

IMF. (n.d.). *World Economic Outlook Database.* Washington, D.C.: International Monetary Fund (IMF). https://www.imf.org/external/pubs/ft/weo/2019/01/weodata/index.aspx Retrieved: 7 August 2019.

Islam, M. A. (2012). Financial sector reforms. *Bank Parikrama, 37*(3&4), 33–48.

Islam, R. (2014a, June 21). Human capital and inclusive growth: The challenges for Bangladesh. Paper presented at the *First BEF Conference on Vision 2030: Framework for Economic Policy Making and Strategy Formulation in Pluralistic Democracy*, organised by the Bangladesh Economists' Forum (BEF), Dhaka, Bangladesh.

Islam, R. (2014b). The employment challenge faced by Bangladesh: How far is the Lewis turning point? *Indian Journal of Labour Economics, 57*(2), 201–225.

Khan, A. R. (1995). A quarter century of economic development in Bangladesh: Successes and failures. *The Bangladesh Development Studies, 23*(3&4), 1–19.

Khan, A. R. (2015). *The economy of Bangladesh: A quarter century of development.* Basingstoke: Palgrave Macmillan UK.

Khan, T. I. (2018, November 8). Potential of personal income tax in Bangladesh: An examination of survey data. Presented at the dialogue on *Catalysing Development Finance for Bangladesh: Mobilisation and Utilisation Challenges*, organised by the Centre for Policy Dialogue (CPD), Dhaka, Bangladesh.

Krugman, P. (1999). *The return of depression economics*. New York: W.W. Norton and Company.
Krugman, P. (2005). Is fiscal policy poised for a comeback? *Oxford Review of Economic Policy, 21*(4), 515–523.
Mahmud, W. (2002). *National Budgets, Social Spending and Public Choice: The Case of Bangladesh*. IDS Working Paper 162. Brighton: Institute of Development Studies (IDS), University of Sussex.
Mahmud, W. (2004). Macroeconomic management: From stabilisation to growth? *Economic and Political Weekly, 39*(36), 4023–4032.
Mahmud, W., Ahmed, S., & Mahajan, S. (2008). Economic reforms, growth, and governance: The political economy aspects of Bangladesh's development surprise. In D. Brady & M. Spencer (Eds.), *Leadership and growth* (pp. 227–254). Washington, D.C.: The International Bank for Reconstruction and Development (IBRD)/The World Bank.
Mansur, A. H. (2014, June 22). Macro-fiscal management: Role of fiscal policy beyond 2030. Paper presented at the *First BEF Conference on Vision 2030: Framework for Economic Policy Making and Strategy Formulation in Pluralistic Democracy*, organised by the Bangladesh Economists' Forum (BEF), Dhaka, Bangladesh.
Mauro, P. (Ed.). (2011). *Chipping away at public debt: Sources of failure and keys to success in fiscal adjustment*. Washington, D.C.: International Monetary Fund (IMF).
MoF. (2011). *Monthly Report on Fiscal Position (May FY2010-11)*. Dhaka: Ministry of Finance (MoF), Government of Bangladesh (GoB).
MoF. (2019). *Monthly Report on Fiscal Position (December FY2018-19)*. Dhaka: Ministry of Finance (MoF), Government of Bangladesh (GoB).
MoF. (2020). *Economic Transition and Pathway to Progress: Budget Speech 2020-21*. Dhaka: Ministry of Finance (MoF), Government of Bangladesh (GoB).
MRA. (2014). *NGO-MFIs in Bangladesh (June 2013)*. Dhaka: Microcredit Regulatory Authority (MRA), Government of Bangladesh (GoB).
MRA. (2018). *NGO-MFIs in Bangladesh (June 2017)*. Dhaka: Microcredit Regulatory Authority (MRA), Government of Bangladesh (GoB).
Mujeri, M. K. (2014, June 21). Vision 2030: What lies ahead for Bangladesh in a post-MDGs world. Paper presented at the *First BEF Conference on Vision 2030: Framework for Economic Policy Making and Strategy Formulation in Pluralistic Democracy*, organised by the Bangladesh Economists' Forum (BEF), Dhaka, Bangladesh.
Muqtada, M. (2014). Toward employment-focused macroeconomic policies for Africa. In Wohlmuth, K., Gutowski, A., Kandil, M., Knedlik, T. & Uzor, O. O. (Eds.). *Macroeconomic policy formation in Africa—General issues* (pp. 27–62). Development Perspectives Yearbook, Vol. 16 (2012/13). Berlin: LIT Verlag.
Muqtada, M. (2015). *Challenges of Price Stability, Growth and Employment in Bangladesh: Role of the Bangladesh Bank*. Employment Working Paper 169. Geneva: International Labour Organization (ILO).
Muqtada, M. (2018). *Macroeconomic Policy, Price Stability and Inclusive Growth in Bangladesh*. CPD Working Paper 115. Dhaka: Centre for Policy Dialogue (CPD).
Nayyar, D. (2015). Globalization and democracy. *Brazilian Journal of Political Economy, 35*(3), 388–402.
Osmani, S. R. (2008). Achievements and challenges of the Bangladesh economy: An overview. In S. R. Osmani (Ed.), *Emerging issues in Bangladesh economy: A review of Bangladesh's development 2005-06* (pp. 1–24). Dhaka: Centre for Policy Dialogue (CPD) and The University Press Limited.
Pollin, R. (2008). *Is Full Employment Possible Under Globalization?* PERI Working Paper 141. Amherst: Political Economy Research Institute (PERI), University of Massachusetts.
Rahman, M., Iqbal, M. A., Khan, T. I., & Dasgupta, S. (2010). *Paper 12: Bangladesh Phase 2*. Global Financial Crisis Discussion Series. London: Overseas Development Institute (ODI).
Stiglitz, J. E. (2010). *The Stiglitz report: Reforming the international monetary and financial systems in the wake of the global crisis*. New York: The New Press.

Stiglitz, J. E., Ocampo, J. A., Spiegel, S., Ffrench-Davis, R., & Nayyar, D. (2006). *Stability with growth: Macroeconomics, liberalization, and development*. The Initiative for Policy Dialogue Series. New York: Oxford University Press.

UN. (2006). *Building inclusive financial sectors for development*. New York: United Nations (UN).

UN. (2015). *Transforming Our World: The 2030 Agenda for Sustainable Development*. New York: United Nations (UN).

UNCTAD. (n.d.). *UNCTADSTAT database*. Geneva: United Nations Conference on Trade and Development (UNCTAD). https://unctadstat.unctad.org/wds/TableViewer/tableView.aspx?ReportId=120 Retrieved 6 August 2019.

WEF. (2017). *The Global Competitiveness Report 2017–2018*. Geneva: World Economic Forum (WEF).

World Bank. (2012). *A review of economic developments in South Asian countries: Creating fiscal space through revenue mobilization*. South Asia Economic Focus, June 2012. Washington, D.C.: The World Bank.

World Bank. (2015). *Bangladesh Public Expenditure Review Update*. Dhaka: The World Bank Office, Bangladesh.

World Bank. (2017a). *Bangladesh Development Update*. Dhaka: The World Bank Office, Bangladesh.

World Bank. (2017b, September 27). *Bangladesh Development Update: More, Better, and Inclusive Jobs can Boost Growth*. Dhaka: The World Bank Office, Bangladesh.

World Bank. (n.d.). *World Development Indicator (WDI) database*. Washington, D.C.: The World Bank. https://databank.worldbank.org/data/home.aspx Retrieved: 3 February 2018.

Younus, S. (2012). *Estimating Growth-Inflation Trade-off Threshold in Bangladesh*. Working Paper 1204. Dhaka: Bangladesh Bank.

Chapter 5
Growth of Manufacturing Employment in the Changing Context of Trade and Trade-Related Policies

Khondaker Golam Moazzem and Md. Minhaz M. Reza

Abstract The growth of the manufacturing sector has been considered as one of the key policy tools for the structural transformation of the Bangladesh economy and as a major mean for achieving full employment. Following (Jenkins and Sen, Oxford Development Studies 34:299–322, 2006), this study has tried to distinguish the impact of trade on employment through three distinct effects—*size*, *composition* and *process*. The analysis tends to suggest that no single type of effect reveals any clear pattern of growth in manufacturing employment due to trade. At the same time, domestic-market-oriented industries have also been contributing to employment growth. In other words, trade-related policies and measures are likely to have a *partial* role in influencing the nexus of growth of production, exports and employment. However, the study shows that attempts to create *exports at any cost* or to overly protect domestic industries are likely to engender policy biases, rent-seeking and corruption. In the backdrop of different kinds of market failures and problems of governance, the choice of policies with regard to enhancing employment should be well-calibrated with policy priorities to increase productivity and export, with appropriate emphasis on both domestic- and export-oriented industries. In view of COVID-19, the above mentioned initiatives need to be customised and refocused.

This chapter draws from a working paper by the authors, Moazzem and Reza (2018), published by the CPD; content re-used with permission.

K. G. Moazzem (✉)
Centre for Policy Dialogue (CPD), Dhaka, Bangladesh
e-mail: moazzem@cpd.org.bd

Md. M. M. Reza
International Initiative for Impact Evaluation (3ie), New Delhi, India
e-mail: mminhax.reza@gmail.com

CPD-RMG Project, Centre for Policy Dialogue (CPD), Dhaka, Bangladesh

M. Muqtada (ed.), *Quest for Inclusive Growth in Bangladesh*,
South Asia Economic and Policy Studies,
https://doi.org/10.1007/978-981-15-7614-0_5

5.1 Introduction and Objectives

Industrialisation, in general, and the growth of the manufacturing sector, in particular, has formed the basis of the key policy tools employed by the successive governments in Bangladesh for the structural transformation of the economy, and is imperative for achieving full employment in the country. Achieving full employment is one of the major goals of inclusive growth in an economy (Felipe 2012; Ali and Son 2007).[1] Most developing economies are confronted with a high and persistent incidence of unemployment and underemployment. While orthodox economists tend to attribute this to lack of competitiveness in the labour market (or distortions/mismatch of skills, lack of human capital, labour regulations, among others), there are others who consider different factors and systemic failures (for instance, slow growth of private investment and rise in capital–labour pricing, impeding the economy from adequate and sustainable job creation). Full employment in an economy enables the opportunity to all members of the active labour force to be productive and earn a decent wage. Pursuing and designing a full employment strategy would essentially lie in articulating a combination of economic policies (including macroeconomic) and social policies which would fully engage the labour force in expanding productivity and developing a necessary institutional framework for achieving simultaneously freely chosen, productive employment, fundamental rights at work and adequate income from work.[2]

The present study focuses largely on the impact of the manufacturing sector on the generation of productive employment, and the support provided by the trade policies toward industrialisation and employment in the manufacturing sector (henceforth manufacturing employment) in Bangladesh. It is fairly evident from the trends in the growth of the manufacturing sector that in Bangladesh, the sector's gross domestic product (GDP) has grown steadily since the mid-1990s, though its share is still relatively low compared to many of the Asian countries, and lower than what was achieved by the East Asian countries during their early periods of industrial expansion. Furthermore, in the context of the latter countries, the share of manufacturing in total employment was nearly twice as that of Bangladesh's share of manufacturing employment (14.4% in 2016). In accordance with Kaldorian hypothesis and historical observance, the growth of manufacturing employment is the catalyst to structural transformation. In the High-Performing Asian Economies (HPAEs), manufacturing employment, productivity and wages grew in tandem. As Table 5.1 shows, while wages in Bangladesh's manufacturing sector grew to some extent, there was negative growth in employment. The share of manufacturing is not only inadequate, but

[1]According to Ali and Son (2007), full employment and productive employment are two primary factors that determine inclusive growth. Referring to the example of the Philippines, the paper indicates that a high level of structural transformation where workers shifted from low-productive to high-productive sectors, has contributed to economic growth and poverty reduction in the Philippines.

[2]See among others, Muqtada (2010).

Table 5.1 Manufacturing wage and employment growth

Component	2013	2016	2017	Average yearly changes between 2013 and 2017 (%)
Average monthly income (wage) in manufacturing (BDT)	11,703	12,380	12,068	0.78
Total employment in manufacturing (in thousand)	9,500	8,595	8,800	−1.84

Source BBS (2018)
Note In the previous surveys, average monthly income was not reported in similar patterns

has also been declining in the recent period. Between 2013 and 2016, it fell from 16.4 to 14.4%. The share had again increased slightly in 2017, but was still lower than that of 2013.

During the post-colonial period, most of the developing countries embarked on a process of industrialisation with objectives that ranged from consolidation of economic independence, enhancing productivity and generating productive jobs to absorb the high surplus labour observed in the agriculture sector. By and large, these economies pursued a path of import-substituting industrialisation (ISI) through preferential treatment to imported machinery, access to capital, overvalued exchange rate, high protection and quantitative restrictions. The ISI strategy, as subsequently documented, led to high capital intensity, low labour absorption and high social costs, and failed to deliver on the primary objective of generating adequate productive jobs.[3] While many South Asian countries continued to operate with inward-looking policies with some shift of policy emphasis toward small and less capital-intensive industries, the East Asian countries, in particular, swiftly shifted to outward policies, and adopted what came to be subsequently known as the *labour-intensive, export-oriented industrialisation (EOI) strategy*. Prices, policies and institutional mechanisms were set in place for domestic production and resource structure to take advantage of the trade boom of the period, and of the rising export opportunities for labour-intensive manufacturing goods.[4] The success of attaining full employment through a labour-intensive EOI strategy however, was dependent on several contingent factors, especially on the growth and patterns of global trade during the period, flow of foreign direct investment (FDI), and how individual countries, through easing of their respective supply constraints were poised to take advantage of these factors. Analysts have pointed out that fortuitous circumstances, trade liberalisation and greater export orientation alone will neither automatically ensure industrial *take-off*, nor will guarantee a state of full employment. Furthermore, the international environment for investment and industrialisation is fast changing, viz. trading environment, influence of trading blocs, technology, value chains and FDI patterns. While these

[3]For a detailed evaluation of ISI during that period, see Little et al. (1970), Bruton (1970).

[4]See for example, World Bank (1993), Khan (2007).

have influences on the domestic environment, both through resource and technology availability, as well as transaction costs, there are many other supply constraints that may inhibit such an industrialisation process.

While the East Asian (and some of Southeast Asian) countries and China have attained rapid structural transformation and full employment—most developing countries are yet to do so. Bangladesh is one of those countries requiring structural transformation and full employment. It may be noted that Bangladesh has undertaken significant trade liberalisation reforms starting from the mid-1980s, and has expanded export earnings quite significantly. Yet, as will be examined in detail below, the extent and pattern of industrial growth, and more importantly, the share of industrial/manufacturing employment is less than encouraging, especially compared to the HPAEs. EOI labour-intensive industrialisation is commendable, but this is a strategy for which a comprehensive trade and industrialisation strategy is required. While comparisons are not always useful, it may be instructive to look into the trade and industrialisation policies of Vietnam and Bangladesh. Starting from the mid-1990s till approximately 2019, export earnings of Vietnam and Bangladesh have increased at a disproportionate rate which reached USD 264 billion in Vietnam and USD 40.5 billion in Bangladesh during 2019; FDIs (registered) amounted to USD 38.2 billion in Vietnam and less than USD 3.2 billion in Bangladesh in 2019. On the other hand, while the share of industrial employment grew in Bangladesh from 10% in 1996 to 14.4% in 2010, it rose from 11 to 20.2% in Vietnam over the same period. Vietnam undertook various other policies that intermediated between trade reforms and helped the economy to diversify. The export concentration ratio for Vietnam declined from 0.2 in 1990 to about 0.14 in 2016; whereas during the same period, the ratio for Bangladesh increased from 0.34 to 0.4. Vietnam diversified vigorously towards technology, mobile phones and electrical machinery; whereas Bangladesh continued to depend overwhelmingly on readymade garments (RMG) and textiles. These are indicative of differential achievements with fairly similar liberalisation strategies. The examples tend to suggest that while trade liberalisation is significant in enhancing trade openness to facilitate industrial and job growth, there is no automaticity about it. Furthermore, while the expansion in exports is undoubtedly critical to industrial growth, the stance of *exports at any cost* that may often lead to policy biases, price distortions and rent-seeking, has come under serious scrutiny.[5]

As shall be observed later, while Bangladesh's manufacturing growth was initially related to labour-intensive export growth, it would be tendentious to suggest that Bangladesh had a prior strategy and structured policies to pursue an EOI labour-based industrialisation policy. There have been various fortuitous circumstances which have been subsequently supported by trade reforms and other public policies. Nevertheless, growth in the manufacturing sector in the past decades followed two distinct streams—growth of export-oriented industries and growth of domestic-market-oriented/import-competing industries. Major development policies emphasised on the growth of both streams of industries. However, their impact on growth of

[5]See Mazumdar (2008) for a general scrutiny of an unchallenging acceptance of the EOI strategy; Khan (2007) for a rise in policy biases in the trade regime of Bangladesh.

production, export and employment has been different for different industries. More specifically, trade policies and related measures influence the nature and growth of employment in different manufacturing industries in different ways. This chapter intends to examine, albeit in a limited scope, the nature of the growth–export–employment nexus in the manufacturing sector over the last few decades, and how that growth was influenced by trade-related policies and measures.

Based on the secondary data, the chapter presents some perspectives in the context of different sub-sectors of the manufacturing industry, such as: (a) categorising different sub-sectors in terms of their level of export orientation, viz. *highly export-oriented*, *moderately export-oriented* and *low export-oriented* industries; (b) conducting an in-depth analysis of the growth of production and export of different categories of industries and their implications on employment; and (c) undertaking an analysis of changes in employment with regard to level of labour- and capital-intensity in different sub-sectors. Based on these analyses, the study tries to appreciate the possible impact and implications of different policies (and trade-related policies in particular) on changes in employment in the manufacturing sector during the 2000s.

5.2 Practices of Trade-Related Policies in Different Categories of Manufacturing Industries

Bangladesh embarked on trade liberalisation reforms more than three decades ago, starting from the late 1980s. The various reforms which were consistent with the overall macroeconomic stabilisation policy framework supported the growth of exports and imports substantially, as observed in the expansion of the trade openness indicator. It increased from a low of 16.1% of GDP in 1987 prior to the reforms, to 38.2% in 2018. It is observed that trade policy appears to have a favourable impact on the growth of local industries (both domestic- and export-market-oriented) which were expected to have a positive impact on employment. As will be examined later, the results have been mixed, and it is difficult to identify a precise correlation between tariff reduction and employment outcomes in various sub-sectors of manufacturing, whether export-oriented or import-substituting. Within the manufacturing sector, some sub-sectors are more labour-intensive compared to others. One strategic approach towards promoting labour-intensive manufacturing growth is to implement sub-sector-based policies and measures. However, this sub-sector-specific approach towards policy analysis has to be viewed critically as various sub-sectors of the economy are integrated with one another, and one sub-sector might have competing interest with another.

5.2.1 Export-Oriented Industries

Nevertheless, successive governments took measures under the broader economic liberalisation initiative to induce the growth of the labour-intensive manufacturing sector. The main objective of the policies was to promote export-oriented industries by removing the anti-export bias in the economy. These policies had significant implications on exports and employment in one particular sub-sector, i.e. RMG. The policies included duty-free access to imported inputs, the reduction in tariff levels and a number of tariff rates, streamlining and simplification of import procedures, provision for financial assistance on traditional exports, tax rebates on export earnings and concessionary duties on imported capital, accelerated depreciation allowance and excise fund refund on domestic raw materials and inputs, and proportionate income tax rebates of at least 30% on export earnings.

During FY2004-05, the government took bold tariff measures for promoting the country's textile sector as the backward linkage industries of the RMG sector. It proposed a reduction in the existing rates of duty on most of the raw materials and essential machinery and spares needed by this industry. The number of Harmonized System (HS) 8 digit level items for the textile sector, which would enjoy duty-free and value added tax (VAT)-free import, was 34. Considering the importance of the textile industry as a backward linkage industry of the RMG sector, which was under tremendous pressure at the advent of the Multi Fibre Arrangement (MFA) phase out, the government proposed to reduce the income tax for the sector from 20 to 15%.

During FY2005-06, one positive move was that import of spare parts, dyes and chemicals for RMG had been zero-tariffed. An initiative had been taken to formulate a programme titled Post-MFA Action Program at the cost of USD 40 million, with assistance from development partners. In FY2004-05, the government allocated BDT 30 crore for retaining retrenched garment workers. As a token of proactive fiscal measure towards increasing employment opportunities, the budget proposed setting up a special fund of BDT 20 crore for retraining and creating employment opportunities for employees/labourers of the RMG industry.

In FY2006-07, the government again allocated an additional BDT 30 crore for retraining retrenched garment workers in continuation of the previous year. Considering the huge demand for workers in the RMG sector, such funds for retrenchment were not necessary. During FY2007-08, the government provided support to the textile sector by withdrawing import duty on textile machinery along with other items.

In FY2009-10, the government extended the tax holiday facility, in a staggered manner, for new industries to be set up between July 2008 and June 2011, which include textiles and RMG enterprises. Also, the government earlier announced a special package of BDT 3,424 crore for FY2008-09 targetting industries affected by the Global Financial Crisis (GFC). A second package was announced at the time of the budget for FY2009-10 with an allocation of BDT 5,000 crore. In 2011, it became apparent that the textiles and apparels had been among the most adversely affected sectors due to the GFC, particularly in FY2009-10. The government allocated BDT 2,000 crore under the second stimulus package as part of providing support to encourage export diversification (5% additional cash incentive in FY2008-09, 4% for FY2010-11 and 2% for FY2011-12); 5% additional cash incentive for small and medium-sized enterprises (SMEs) against their apparels export in FY2008-09; and 10% cash incentives on electricity bill for FY2009-10 for SMEs which did not have captive generator facility.

In FY2011-12, the budget proposed the increase of supplementary duty (SD) on the import of all kinds of fabrics and RMG articles from 20 to 45%. This enhanced the protection available for domestic-market-oriented apparel industries. At the same time, the proposed measure to continue with 5% regulatory duty (RD) on the import of finished products (along with 25% import duty) was also likely to help protect the local industry.

5.2.2 Domestic-Market-Oriented Industries

Besides the textile and RMG sector, the government provided support to domestic-market-oriented industries—it proposed to impose VAT on processed, and primarily agricultural products like fruit, pulp and paste, packed spices in powdered form, flavoured milk and yoghurt, etc. In order to give a further boost to the dairy and poultry industry of the country, the government proposed to withdraw customs duty (CD) and VAT on 87 capital machineries needed for this sector. The government continued the allocation in the Equity Entrepreneurship Fund (EEF) in FY2004-05. This fund was reserved for providing equity support to computer software, food processing and agro-based industries. It is to be mentioned that the system and framework of EEF was restructured.

The agro-based industry and paper industry received priority in FY2006-07. An analysis shows that the proposed budget increased allocation for credit support under the agro-based industries programme from BDT 100 crore in the previous budget, to BDT 150 crore. Budgetary allocation under the Equity Development Fund (EDF) was increased from BDT 100 crore in the revised budget of FY2005-06, to BDT 200 crore in FY2006-07. The government extended the benefit of tax exemption and rebate to agro-processing, jute and textile industries up to 30 June 2008 which was a positive measure for the promotion of agro-based industries. In the budget for FY2006-07, SD of 15% was imposed on the import of advertising materials, commercial catalogues, etc. This would support domestic paper industries. The domestic tiles industry was actively promoted by the government, which is complementary to the booming construction sector. For this, the government decided to reduce SD on locally manufactured tiles from 20–5%.

The FY2009-10 budget proposed changes (reduction/increase) in CD, SD and VAT for various imported raw materials, intermediate products and finished products, which were likely to raise the effective rate of protection (ERP) for domestic industries. According to CPD (2010), these would not substantially affect total tax incidence (TTI); CPD estimated a decrease by (−) 1.5%. Increasing SD for various imported materials was also suggested, which was expected to aid import-substituting industries.[6]

Apropos CPD (2011), various fiscal measures favourable to import-substituting industries were proposed, especially those involved with manufacturing electronic items and vehicles. These fiscal measures, particularly the time-bound ones, were positive for the investment climate in the domestic electronics industry. As indicated in the budget, this initiative was aimed at protecting the interest of domestic industries by enhancing the ERP for import-substituting industries, and discouraging import of those commodities. For the same purpose, 5% RD had been imposed on 43 items (at 8 digit level) that are eligible for paying 10% CD, but not treated as intermediate goods. On the other hand, RD had been exempted for eight items (at 8 digit level) which were to pay 25% CD. However, these items are treated mainly as intermediate goods. Different sectors were benefitted from the revised duty structures of the national budget of FY2013-14. SD on import of milk powder and ceramic bathroom fittings had been made zero. The domestic ceramics industry was a promising one and reducing import duties could hurt the industry.

In order to ameliorate the competitiveness of emerging local products in the domestic market (such as glass and ceramics) against imported ones, the national budget for FY2013-14 proposed to increase SD (such as on the import of float glass in the glass industry) to render imported products (e.g. glass) more expensive in the domestic market (CPD 2014).

There is scant analytical comparative assessment of the relative influences (*biases*) of the liberalisation and tariff strategy on the growth of domestic-market- and export-oriented industries. From among the latter, it is evident that the RMG in particular has received various forms of policy and fiscal support. It has grown substantially, and has dominated the export share of manufacturing exports. Notably, RMG exports as percentage of total exports was 3.9% in 1983–84; it was 83.9% in 2019.

Despite the rapid achievements of the RMG sector, Bangladesh has not quite succeeded in establishing an EOI labour-intensive industrialisation strategy that would significantly absorb the 2 million net additions to the workforce and move the economy towards full employment similar to the HPAEs. For various reasons, no other sub-sector has been able to follow the RMG trail, an issue that requires closer scrutiny. Whether it is the alleged anti-export biases and/or the protection structure towards import-substituting industries, the employment outcomes appear to be inadequate.

[6]For details, see CPD (2010).

5.3 Full Employment Through Implementing Trade Policies: A Review

The foreign and domestic trade environments not only affect the demand for labour in the economy, but also the skill composition and workers' wages of the existing labour force, as higher industrialisation is expected to result in more skilled jobs. Policies towards foreign trade, as many experts have pointed out, are among the most important factors for promoting economic growth and development (Fischer, 2000). These policies also shape the structure and growth of employment. According to Puyana (2011), trade liberalisation would increase the elasticity of employment. However, such a relationship could be constrained if there is low labour absorption in the industrial sector owing to increasing incentives towards capital intensity and undue protection under cover of import substitution policies (Nassar 2010). Trade policies, including export and import policies, focusing on export diversification have an impact on economic growth and employment. International competitiveness also plays an important role for the smaller economies as their higher level of economic growth is dependent, among others, on international trade and investment.

There are various empirical studies that document the interlinkages between trade liberalisation, exports and their impact on employment, skills and wages. Trade and market openness can have a positive effect not only on boosting economic growth, but also on the total employment in an economy (OECD 2012). In the OECD study, the 14 main multi-country econometric studies show that trade plays an independent and positive role in raising incomes. The higher wages attract a higher number of workers in the formal and more productive sectors, leading to an overall increase in employment.[7] Orbeta (2002) shows that an increase in the propensity to export shifts the demand for labour upward. In terms of the employment structure, the impact of openness on the proportion of women workers is not significant at the aggregate level, but is a boon for them at the manufacturing sub-industries level. An increase in export propensity also leads to an increase in the proportion of low-skilled production workers both at the aggregate and manufacturing sub-industries level.

Feliciano (2001) using micro-level data, analyses the impact of trade reform on Mexican wages and employment. Industries that had greater reductions in protection levels had a larger percentage of low-skill workers. On the other hand, wage dispersion increased in both the non-tradable sector, and to a much greater degree, in the tradable sector. This pattern suggests that trade reform increased wage inequality. The decline in import license coverage led to a reduction in the relative wages of workers in reformed industries by 2%, but did not affect the relative level of employment. Reductions in tariffs had no statistically significant effect on relative wages or relative employment. In general, while studies show that increased competition through trade liberalisation actually contribute towards the goal of full employment as the economies experience higher labour productivity (Krugman 1981; Melitz 2003), the above trade impacts are difficult to generalise.

[7] According to the study, in order to increase productivity, employment and economic growth, it is important to protect the workers' rights rather than promote protectionist policies to protect jobs.

On the other hand, Rodrik (2008) stressed on the importance of *effective industrial policy* to correct the market failures pertaining to the markets for labour, credit, products and knowledge. The study argues that industrial policy allows the government to target where the industry is failing in an effort to make a correction and create more indirect demand for labour in both the domestic and foreign markets. The chapter further posits that interventions through industrial policies are necessary to overcome market failures and allow the countries to catch up with the other economies in terms of industrial development and export competitiveness. Lall (2004) found that the differences in industrial competitiveness are among the main causes of disparities in income in the Asian economies. Trade liberalisation may result in skills acquired (by both men and women workers) and gender sensitivity among all workers. However, trade openness of an economy is not necessarily able to address the market failures, particularly with regard to labour, credit, products and knowledge. Hence, government intervention through effective industrial policy could attempt to address those market failures, especially the one concerning job generation. Of course, for the latter, various other policies must come into play. Macroeconomic stability, particularly through price stability, is considered to be pivotal for addressing the full employment issue.

Examining the various issues raised above is a tall order, and beyond the scope and space of the present chapter. According to Jenkins and Sen (2006), trade affects manufacturing employment in three ways: (a) impact on output of the manufacturing sector, and thereby positively impacting employment (called *scale effect*); (b) rise in output of exportables by replacing output of importables, and thereby positively contributing to employment (called *composition effect*); and (c) changes in labour coefficients within industries, and thereby positively impacting employment (called *process effect*). Using both aggregate and sub-industry-level manufacturing data, the study provides some insights, on these various effects and their implications for policy design. Diagram 5.1 presents a schematic relationship between trade and employment in the manufacturing sector.

5.4 Overview of Manufacturing Employment: Structure, Composition and Growth

5.4.1 Overall Employment Structure in Bangladesh Economy

The Bangladesh economy has experienced a major change in the structure and composition of employment over the last decades. Although the rate of labour force participation did not change much (around 58%), the level of employment has considerably increased—from 39 million in 2000 to 60.8 million in 2017 (Table 5.2). However, both overall and sectoral growth of employment have slowed down over the years. A relatively higher level of employment growth was observed in case of manufacturing and services sectors; in contrast, employment growth in the

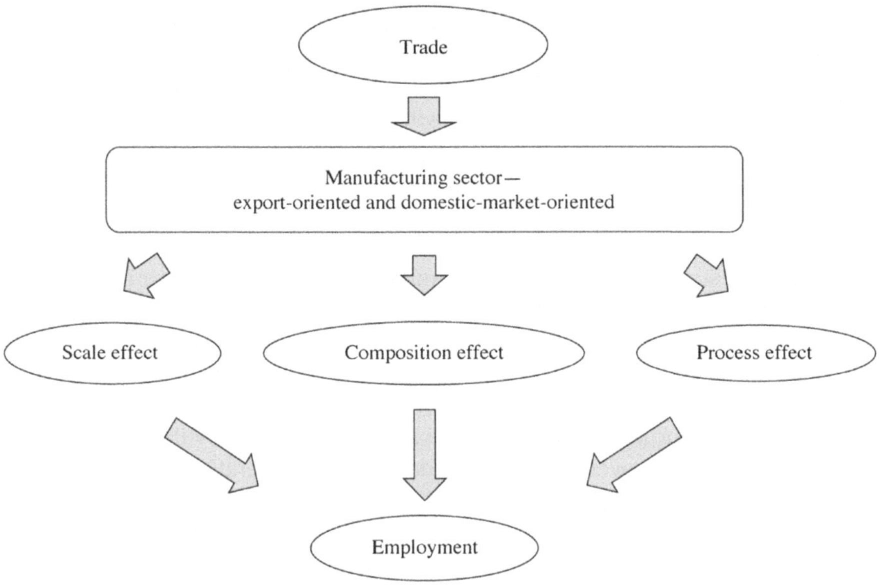

Diagram 5.1 Relationship between trade and employment in the manufacturing sector. *Source* Prepared by authors based on Jenkins and Sen (2006)

Table 5.2 Employment by broad economic sectors

Sector	2000	2006	2010	2013	2015–16	2016–17
Employed by broad economic sectors (million)						
Agriculture	24.2	22.8	25.7	26.2	25.4	24.7
Industry	4.0	6.9	9.6	12.1	12.2	12.4
Services	9.2	17.7	19.1	19.8	22.0	23.7
Total	39.0	47.4	54.1	58.1	59.5	60.8
Composition by broad economic sectors (%)						
Agriculture	62.1	48.1	47.6	45.1	42.7	40.6
Industry	10.3	14.5	17.7	23.0	20.5	20.4
Services	23.5	37.4	25.5	32.0	36.9	39.0
Total	100.0	100.0	100.0	100.0	100.0	100.0
Year-on-year percentage change (%)						
Agriculture	-	−0.9	3.2	0.6	−1.0	−2.8
Industry	-	12.1	9.8	8.7	0.3	1.6
Services	-	15.4	1.9	1.2	3.7	7.7
Total	-	3.6	3.5	2.5	0.8	2.2

Source Authors' calculations based on BBS (2018)

agriculture sector had slowed down and ultimately reached negative terrain in recent years. Overall, the structure of employment has changed and shifted from agriculture to non-agriculture sectors, particularly in the manufacturing and services sectors. Despite the slowdown of employment growth in agriculture, it still accounts for the largest share of employment.

These changes in the structure and composition of employment denote: (a) a higher level of economic growth over the years could not ensure a similar level of growth in employment, rather employment growth has stagnated over the years; (b) the gap between sectoral GDP growth and employment growth is higher in case of the manufacturing sector; and (c) shifting employment from agriculture is still slow due to limited scope of employment generation in the non-agriculture sector. Hence, it is important to explore the strengths and weaknesses in the manufacturing sector with regard to scope of employment generation in order to ensure inclusive development.

Rise in manufacturing employment has largely been driven by the robust growth of the RMG sub-sector over the last three decades. The overall employment in the manufacturing sector was about 8.8 million in 2016–17 which was only 3.7 million in 1999–00; in other words, manufacturing employment has increased by 137% within 17 years, or on average 8.1%, annually. This is mainly attributed to the gradual rise of the RMG sector which constituted over 40% of total manufacturing employment. In 2017, the share of employment of RMG workers was about 45.4% of total employment. Such an overwhelming contribution of the RMG sector makes the dynamics and changes in manufacturing employment dependent on the performance of a single sector. A robust growth of employment in the manufacturing sector requires the growth of numerous labour-intensive *RMG-like* sectors with an export capacity of over USD 5–10 billion which could help to diversify the employment base in the manufacturing sector.

5.4.2 Structure of the Manufacturing Sector

The change in manufacturing employment is directly linked with its structure, composition and growth of the sector. The manufacturing sector comprises of sub-sectors which are either export-oriented or domestic-market-oriented. The majority of enterprises in different sectors are domestic-market-oriented (Fig. 5.1); industries which are fully domestic-market-oriented include coke and refined petroleum, machinery and equipment, motor vehicles and trainers, installation of machinery and recycling, etc. Industries which are exposed more to export market include RMG (95% of total production), transport equipment (82%), leather and leather goods (74%) and textiles products (57%). A part of enterprises of other sub-sectors is also exposed to export markets, such as paper and paper products, computer, electronic and optical products and electrical equipment, etc.[8]

[8]Lack of exposure to the export market is likely to happen due to limited capacity of these sub-sectors to participate in the export market.

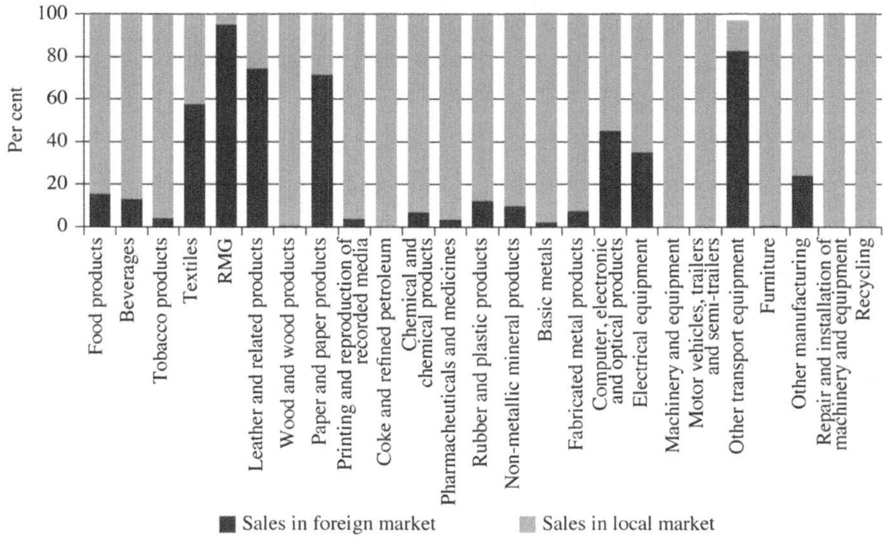

Fig. 5.1 Ratio of market exposure of different manufacturing industries. *Source* Authors' calculations based on BBS (2010, 2013)

The structure and composition of the manufacturing sector is still overwhelmingly dominated by the RMG and textiles industries, which accounted for 33.7 and 13.3% of total value-added of the manufacturing sector in 2012 for RMG and textiles, respectively. However, RMG has lost its market share over time (from 38.5% in 2000 to 33.7% in 2012). In fact, other traditional manufacturing industries have also lost their shares, such as food processing (from 18.2 to 11.3%), tobacco products (8 to 2%), chemical products (from 5.5 to 1.6%) and pharmaceuticals (from 4 to 2%). In contrast, a number of non-traditional industries have been growing in the country which include basic metals (0.01 to 16.8%), non-metallic products (from 4.1 to 6.5%), rubber and plastic products (from 0.4 to 0.9%) and computer, electronics and optical products (from 0 to 0.7%), etc. Most of the other industries are either stuck at the same level or have declined in terms of market share; these include beverages, leather, paper products, fabricated metal products and transport equipment. Overall, the manufacturing sector has experienced compositional changes both in case of traditional and non-traditional industries, and these are likely to have impacts on employment as well.

The present study divides the manufacturing sector into three categories: (a) highly export-oriented industries (herein after HEIs); (b) moderately export-oriented industries (MEIs); and (c) low export-oriented/domestic-market-oriented industries (LEIs).[9] Table 5.3 presents the list of industries under these categories. The contribu-

[9]HEIs—if the share of sales of a particular industry in the foreign market equals or exceeds 40% of total market sale in 2012; MEIs—if the share of sales of a particular industry in the foreign market

Table 5.3 Share of total manufacturing outputs (%)

Category of industry	Share of total manufacturing outputs		
	2000	2005	2012
Highly export-oriented	*44.4*	*56.4*	*50.9*
RMG	37.8	38.0	33.7
Leather	2.1	1.5	1.4
Other transport equipment	2.9	1.2	0.7
Paper products	0.9	0.8	1.1
Textiles	0.7	14.9	13.3
Computer, electronic and optical products	0.0	0.0	0.7
Moderately export-oriented	*26.1*	*16.2*	*16.1*
Electrical equipment	5.7	0.6	2.7
Other manufacturing	0.0	0.1	0.2
Food	18.2	13.2	11.3
Beverages	1.8	0.2	1.0
Rubber and plastic products	0.4	2.1	0.9
Low export-oriented	*29.6*	*27.3*	*32.9*
Non-metallic mineral products	4.1	8.5	6.5
Fabricated metal	2.1	0.6	1.3
Chemical products	5.5	1.8	2.6
Tobacco products	8.2	5.9	1.6
Recorded media	3.9	2.1	0.2
Pharmaceuticals, medicinal chemical and botanical products	4.0	6.2	2.1
Basic metals	0.0	0.6	16.8
Furniture	0.7	1.4	0.7
Wood and cork	0.3	0.0	0.1
Petroleum products	0.3	0.1	0.1
Machinery and equipment	0.0	0.0	0.2
Motor vehicles, trailers and semi-trailers	0.5	0.1	0.7

Source Authors' calculations based on BBS (2010, 2013)

tion to manufacturing GDP is highest for HEIs, followed by LEIs and MEIs. Interestingly, the contribution of export-oriented industries to the GDP has weakened, while that of domestic-market-oriented industries has increased over time. During 2012, the share of HEIs was 50.9%, which was mainly driven by the production of RMG and textiles. The contribution made by the LEIs had progressed significantly—their share to manufacturing GDP had increased from 6.6% in 2001 to 24.4% in 2012.

equals or exceeds 10%, but is less than 40% of total market sale in 2012; LEIs—if the share of sales of a particular industry in the foreign market is less than 10% of total market sale in 2012.

These LEIs are largely domestic-market-oriented industries, such as basic metals, non-metallic mineral, chemical, pharmaceuticals and tobacco products. Hence, the dynamics and changes in the structure of manufacturing employment need to be explained both through the sectors' orientation to export, as well as their orientation to domestic market.

5.4.3 *Export of Manufacturing Goods*

The export of manufacturing goods is still highly concentrated in a limited number of products; for example, woven and knit garment products account for 81.6% of total exports (Table 5.4). However, an intra-RMG compositional change is discerned with the share of woven products declining (from 49.8% in 2003 to 41.9% in 2017) vis-à-vis a rising share of knit products (from 25.3% in 2003 to 39.7% in 2017). In case of non-RMG products, the share of leather and leather goods has increased (from 2.9 to 3.6%), while the share of other export products, such as jute goods, footwear and handicrafts, has declined. The structure of export is measured by the

Table 5.4 Export of different manufacturing industries

Export item	Share of total export					
	2002–03	2004–05	2009–10	2014–15	2015–16	2016–17
Export of manufacturing goods (million USD)	6,086	8,006	15,517	29,922	21,318	22,009
Share of manufacturing goods (%)	100.0	100.0	100.0	100.0	100.0	100.0
Woven garments	49.8	41.6	37.1	41.9	43.2	41.9
Knitwear	25.3	32.6	40.0	39.8	39.0	39.7
Leather	2.9	2.6	1.4	2.1	3.4	3.6
Jute goods	3.4	3.6	4.9	2.9	2.2	2.3
Chemical products	1.5	2.3	0.6	0.4	0.4	0.4
Footwear	0.7	1.0	1.3	2.3	0.6	0.7
Ceramic products	0.3	0.3	0.2	0.2	0.1	0.1
Handicrafts	0.1	0.1	0.0	0.0	0.0	0.0
Others	16.1	16.1	14.5	10.4	11.1	11.3

Source EPB (n.d.)

Export Concentration Index (ECI).[10] The ECI value or the Herfindahl–Hirschman Index (HHI)[11] of Bangladesh is rather high (0.6), which is largely influenced by the high export share of RMG products; however, it has changed very little over the last several years. Between 2004 and 2014 Bangladesh's ECI had increased by 7.6%, but the rise has slowed down in recent years.

Different categories of industries have experienced different levels of export growth during 2001–2012 (Table 5.5). The average yearly export growth in case of MEIs was found to be higher (111%) compared to that of HEIs (32.8%) and LEIs (79.7%). Relatively high export growth in case of MEIs and LEIs is partly owing to their low export-base compared to that of HEIs. Among the HEIs, export growth is higher for industries such as textiles, paper products and transport equipment; on the other hand, among MEIs, high growth is found in case of beverages, plastic and electrical equipment; among LEIs, they are non-metallic minerals, fabricated metals, pharmaceuticals and petroleum products. In other words, export orientation alone may not sufficiently explain changes in employment in different manufacturing industries.

5.5 Production, Export and Employment in Different Manufacturing Industries

5.5.1 Exploring the 'Size Effect' of Trade on Employment

This section highlights the impact of trade on manufacturing production and its linkages with employment—how changes in production and export in different manufacturing sub-sectors impacted employment. The manufacturing sector accounted for about 5 million workers in 2012 which increased to about 8.6 million in 2016. Likewise, employment distribution is highly concentrated in a few sub-sectors.[12] The top five manufacturing sub-sectors which accounted for 81.6% of manufacturing GDP comprised about 88.6% of total manufacturing employment (Table 5.6). However, the nexus between the share of manufacturing production and share of manufacturing employment in the top five sectors are not necessarily at the same level over the years. While the share of manufacturing GDP had significantly increased between 2000 and 2012 for the top five sectors (from 60.7 to 81.6%), the share of employment

[10]The ECI portraits the degree of concentration of a country's export in a small number of products or a small region. The perfect concentrated index must hold the value of 1, implying the country is concentrated only on a single product.

[11]The sectoral HHI is defined as the square root of the sum of the squared shares of exports of each industry in total exports; takes a value between 0 and 1. Higher values indicate that exports are concentrated in fewer sectors.

[12]The RMG industry is accounted for about 55% of total manufacturing employment, followed by textiles (16.1%), non-metallic products (8.9%) and beverages (5.6%).

Table 5.5 Average yearly manufacturing export growth: 2001–2012 (%)

Category of industry	Average yearly export growth
Highly export-oriented	*32.8*
RMG (HS 61 and 62)	34.3
Leather (HS 41)	3.5
Other transport equipment (HS 87)	183.3
Paper products (HS 48)	876.2
Textiles (HS 59)	3522.7
Computer, electronic & optical products (HS 90)	18.4
Moderately export-oriented	*111.0*
Electrical equipment (HS 85)	96.7
Other manufacturing (HS 96)	42.4
Food (HS 16)	-
Beverages (HS 22)	546.3
Rubber and plastic products (HS 39 and 40)	129.7
Low export-oriented	*79.7*
Non-metallic mineral products (HS 25)	410.2
Fabricated metal (HS 72, 72, 74, 75, 76, 78, 79 80, 81, 82 and 83)	265.1
Chemical products (HS 28 and 29)	12.0
Tobacco products (HS 24)	78.4
Recorded media (HS 92)	−4.0
Pharmaceuticals, medicinal chemical and botanical products (HS 30)	106.8
Basic metals (HS 71)	-
Manufacture of furniture (HS 94)	762.7
Wood and cork (HS 44 and 45)	−7.7
Petroleum products (HS 27)	474.3
Machinery and equipment n.e.c. (HS 84)	17.8
Motor vehicles, trailers and semi-trailers (HS 8716)	-
Repair and installation of machinery and equipment (HS 82)	48.2
Recycling	-

Source Authors' calculations based on World Bank (n.d.)
Note n.e.c.: Nowhere else classified

had marginally increased during this period (from 86.6 to 88.6%). At the disaggregated level, the relationship between changes in shares of manufacturing GDP and manufacturing employment is found to be mixed—GDP and employment changes in a *positive* direction are discerned in the case of basic metals and partly of non-metallic industries; while both GDP and employment changes towards a *negative* direction are observed in case of food processing; and GDP and employment changes are in

Table 5.6 Relation between share in manufacturing outputs and manufacturing employment

Manufacturing industry	Share of manufacturing outputs (%)			Share of manufacturing employment (%)		
	1999–00	2005–06	2012	1999–00	2005–06	2012
Top 5 industries	60.7	75.2	81.6	86.6	86.5	88.6
Food	18.2	13.2	11.3	8.8	6.5	5.6
Textile	0.7	14.9	13.3	25.4	21.0	16.1
RMG	37.8	38.0	33.7	41.8	49.1	55.1
Non-metallic mineral products	4.1	8.5	6.5	9.9	8.9	9.4
Basic metals	0.0	0.6	16.8	0.7	1.0	2.4
Other manufacturing industries	39.3	24.8	18.4	13.4	13.5	11.4
Total	*100.0*	*100.0*	*100.0*	*100.0*	*100.0*	*100.0*

Source Authors' calculations based on the data from Bangladesh Bureau of Statistics (BBS) and Bangladesh Economic Review

opposite direction in RMG and textiles sub-sector. Hence, the *size effect* in major manufacturing sub-sectors provides a mixed signal with regard to impact and implications of production on employment. Other than the top five sectors, a rise in the share of manufacturing employment, owing either to a rise in the share of production or decline in the share of production, is observed only in cases of leather and wood-cork sub-sectors. On the other hand, a number of sectors have experienced declining employment during a rise/decline in products such as beverages, tobacco products, paper products, petroleum products, chemical products, pharmaceuticals, rubber and plastic, fabricated metal, computer and electronics, electrical equipment and motor vehicles, etc. Overall, sub-sectors other than the top five have lost their shares over the years both in terms of manufacturing outputs and employment.

In case of the export of manufacturing industries, growth in employment was not always commensurate with growth in export, as observed during the last decade (Fig. 5.2). While the MEIs have experienced the highest level of growth in export during 2000–2012, these industries have registered the lowest level of growth in employment generation. In contrast, the HEIs have registered the lowest level of growth compared to the other two categories, but have experienced the highest level of growth in employment.[13]

[13]One must note the caveat that *size* in the above analysis refers to the percentage share in value-added, and not to the size of enterprises.

Fig. 5.2 Export–employment nexus. *Source* Authors' estimations

5.5.2 *Exploring the 'Composition Effect' of Trade on Employment*

This section highlights the *composition effect* of trade on employment—how more production for export shifts more employment from domestic-market-oriented/import-competing industries towards export-oriented industries. Traditionally, both share of production and share of employment are the highest in case of HEIs (Table 5.7). On the other hand, share of employment is higher in case of LEIs, even though their share is lower in manufacturing GDP. Over the years, no major compositional change has been observed in either manufacturing production or employment. However, some changes in shares of manufacturing GDP and employment are discerned in all three categories of industries. The composition effect is relatively strong in case of HEIs—as share of employment has increased consistently against moderate rise in manufacturing production. In contrast, composition effect is either

Table 5.7 Summary of output–export–employment nexus

Category of industry	Share of manufacturing output			Share of manufacturing employment		
	2000	2005	2012	2000	2005	2012
Highly export-oriented	44.4	56.4	50.9	68.9	71.6	74.2
Moderately export-oriented	26.1	16.2	16.1	10.9	8.7	7.9
Low export-oriented	29.6	27.3	32.9	20.1	19.7	17.8

Source Authors' estimations

weak or negative in case of MEIs and LEIs. Three categories of industries have experienced three different levels of growth in employment between 2000 and 2012. Overall, the composition effect of trade on employment is rather low.

5.5.3 Exploring the 'Process Effect' of Trade on Employment

The *process effect* assesses the impact of changes in coefficients in terms of labour and capital in a particular industry and their likely impact on employment. The composition of capital and labour in different manufacturing sub-sectors, as measured by capital–labour ratio, widely varied; even within the same categories of industries, the composition is found to be different for different sub-sectors. This study defines labour- and capital-intensive industries based on the capital–labour ratio in the production process of different industries.[14] While most of the manufacturing industries in Bangladesh are labour-intensive, a few industries are capital-intensive, such as textiles, transport equipment, electrical equipment, beverages, chemical products, pharmaceutical products, basic metals and petroleum products (Table 5.8). Major labour-intensive industries are RMG, recycling, non-metallic products, tobacco, furniture and recorded media. It has been found that, in general, employment growth in the labour-intensive industries is relatively higher compared to that in capital-intensive industries. During 2012, employment growth in both categories of industries was high; but the growth of employment in labour-intensive industries was almost twice as that of capital-intensive industries. It is important to examine whether such growth in employment in labour-intensive industries is induced by international trade.

At the disaggregated sub-sector level, employment growth in both categories of industries was rather mixed. With the labour-intensive industries, significant positive growth in employment between 2006 and 2012 was observed in case of RMG, leather, fabricated metal, wood and cork and other manufacturing and recycling. Meanwhile, negative growth in employment was discerned in case of furniture, tobacco and recorded media. The sub-sectors under the capital-intensive industries which portray higher growth in employment include petroleum, chemicals, basic metals, electrical equipment and transport equipment.

Reviewing the growth of employment in capital- and labour-intensive industries through the lens of their export orientation, it is found that export orientation of enterprises registers a major contribution to employment growth (Table 5.9). HEIs comprise both labour- and capital-intensive industries, and the current evidence shows that growth in employment in both categories of industries is relatively high. In case of MEIs, growth in employment is mostly low, except in electrical equipment

[14] We have considered the 70th (equal or more than that) percentile of capital–labour ratio for manufacturing industries as capital-intensive, and below that considered as labour-intensive. And the given result is more congruent to the common scenario. Capital-intensive industries—if the value of capital–labour ratio of a particular industry is equal to or exceeds 400. Labour-intensive industries—if the value of capital–labour ratio of a particular industry is less than 400.

Table 5.8 Capital–labour intensity in the manufacturing sector and employment growth (%)

Category of industry	Yearly average employment growth		
	1996–2000	2000–2006	2006–2012
More capital-intensive			
Petroleum products	2.4	−10.8	61.5
Beverages	25.0	10.4	6.0
Chemical products	−15.8	−2.9	68.4
Pharmaceuticals, medicinal chemical and botanical products	7.8	28.4	−4.1
Basic metals	−4.2	13.8	51.7
Electrical equipment	−1.3	−8.0	23.8
Other transport equipment	−12.9	−8.7	29.8
Textiles	4.5	0.6	4.1
Average	2.44	1.65	6.40
More labour-intensive			
Rubber and plastic products	−6.6	47.3	6.2
Machinery and equipment n.e.c	−25.0	-	-
Paper products	10.6	1.3	22.7
Motor vehicles, trailers and semi-trailers	−14.4	−5.9	17.2
Computer, electronic and optical products	-	-	-
Food	6.2	−1.3	6.7
Leather	−21.2	14.5	42.5
Fabricated metal	4.4	−11.4	51.5
Wood and cork	−1.0	−15.1	89.4
Other manufacturing	2.4	72.2	44.8
Tobacco products	−4.5	−1.3	−2.7
Repair and installation of machinery and equipment	-	-	-
Non-metallic mineral products	16.0	2.1	12.0
Furniture	5.8	62.4	−1.9
Recycling	-	-	27.0
RMG	10.0	7.8	13.9
Recorded media	20.1	8.4	−11.3
Average	*7.00*	*5.32*	*12.06*

Source Authors' estimations

Table 5.9 Capital–labour intensity and employment growth under different types of export-oriented industries

Category of industry	Type of intensity	Capital–labour ratio	Yearly average employment growth		
			1996–2000	2000–2006	2006–2012
Highly export-oriented		-	*5.7*	*5.0*	*11.4*
RMG	Labour-intensive	91.9	10.0	7.8	13.9
Leather	Labour-intensive	302.9	−21.2	14.5	42.5
Other transport equipment	Capital-intensive	438.6	−12.9	−8.7	29.8
Paper products	Labour-intensive	313.7	10.6	1.3	22.7
Textiles	Capital-intensive	425.3	4.5	0.6	4.1
Computer, electronic and optical products	Labour-intensive	310.9	-	-	-
Moderately export-oriented		-	*4.7*	*−0.2*	*8.1*
Electrical equipment	Capital-intensive	446.4	−1.3	−8.0	23.8
Other manufacturing	Labour-intensive	196.9	2.4	72.2	44.8
Food	Labour-intensive	304.4	6.2	−1.3	6.7
Beverages (HS 22)	Capital-intensive	1354.6	25.0	10.4	6.0
Rubber and plastic products	Labour-intensive	340.4	−6.6	47.3	6.2
Low export-oriented		-	*5.0*	*3.9*	*8.0*
Non-metallic mineral products	Labour-intensive	179.0	16.0	2.1	12.0
Fabricated metal	Labour-intensive	270.9	4.4	−11.4	51.5
Chemical products	Capital-intensive	879.0	−15.8	−2.9	68.4
Tobacco products	Labour-intensive	186.0	−4.5	−1.3	−2.7
Recorded media	Labour-intensive	87.9	20.1	8.4	−11.3
Pharmaceuticals, medicinal chemical and botanical products	Capital-intensive	844.7	7.8	28.4	−4.1
Basic metals	Capital-intensive	736.6	−4.2	13.8	51.7
Furniture	Labour-intensive	135.6	5.8	62.4	−1.9

(continued)

Table 5.9 (continued)

Category of industry	Type of intensity	Capital–labour ratio	Yearly average employment growth		
			1996–2000	2000–2006	2006–2012
Wood and cork	Labour-intensive	244.8	−1.0	−15.1	89.4
Petroleum products	Capital-intensive	1399.9	2.4	−10.8	61.5
Machinery and equipment n.e.c	Labour-intensive	331.0	−25.0	-	-
Motor vehicles, trailers and semi-trailers	Labour-intensive	313.0	−14.4	−5.9	17.2
Repair and installation of machinery and equipment	Labour-intensive	185.9	-	-	-
Recycling	Labour-intensive	97.2	-	-	27.0

Source Authors' estimations

and other manufacturing equipment, which are capital-intensive and labour-intensive industries, respectively. In contrast, the employment performance in different labour and capital-intensive industries under low export-oriented industries is mixed. High growth is observed in case of fabricated metal, basic metal, chemicals, wood and cork and petroleum products, while negative employment growth is observed in case of furniture, media, pharmaceuticals, tobacco, etc. Overall, trade (i.e. export orientation) influences employment in both labour- and capital-intensive industries. In other words, the *process effect* is not unidirectional. More importantly, there is a combined effect of *size*, *composition* and *process* related to trade. Multiple factors besides export orientation also affect employment; the impact of non-trade-related issues on growth in employment, particularly in few domestic-market-oriented industries, needs further analysis.

High import penetration was not found to be a contributing factor for growth of employment in any manufacturing sub-sector. However, the nature and extent of linkages between import penetration and level of employment in different sub-sectors are not the same. On one hand, industries with high import penetration ratio such as textiles, wearing apparels and leather experienced considerable growth of employment. Contrarily, industries with moderate import penetration ratio such as chemical industry experienced negative growth. While the rise of the shares of textiles, wearing apparels and leather in total industrial output have contributed to a rise of employment opportunities in these sectors, the shrinkage in the share of chemical and chemical products in total industrial output, perhaps is indicative of the creation of lower levels of employment opportunities in these sectors.

5.5.4 Employment Elasticity of Manufacturing Industries

The overall employment elasticity[15] in the manufacturing sector is not very encouraging[16] (0.28) (Table 5.10). However, HEIs are more elastic compared to that of the MEIs and LEIs. The scenario essentially depicts that the country's employment growth and its relative concentration is strongly associated with the growth and gravity of different export-oriented industries.

Leading industries such as RMG has an employment elasticity higher than the average (0.42). The highest level of employment elasticity was found in case of leather (0.97), media (1.18) and chemical products (0.89), while low or even negative employment elasticity was found in case of tobacco products (−0.34), food (0.13), textiles (0.04), wood (−0.29), electrical equipment (0.14) and motor vehicles (0.09). Thus, from the employment generation point of view, RMG is still ahead of other industries which equally contribute to production, export and employment. A number of domestic-market-oriented industries with moderate employment elasticity are contributing to production and employment (e.g. chemical products and plastic products). Besides, a number of manufacturing industries have experienced a negative employment elasticity which include tobacco and wood and cork, which indicate a negative relationship between growth in production and employment.

5.6 Trade Impulses to Growth of Manufacturing Sector in Bangladesh: Constraints

5.6.1 Policies for Labour-Based and Export-Oriented Industrialisation

Analysis reveals that successive policies have focused on the trade-led growth of the manufacturing sector, which will contribute to employment generation. The five-year plans, industrial policy, export policy and import policy order and SME policy, among others, have more or less common objectives in terms of labour-intensive and export-oriented industrialisation. Several sectors have been specified as priority sectors in key development policies having fiscal and budgetary support. During the early stage of development in the 1980s, the RMG sector was hugely benefitted through a number of fiscal measures which include duty draw back facility, bonded warehouse facility, subsidised credit facility and zero-duty import facility of machineries, raw

[15]Employment elasticity is defined here as percentage change in manufacturing employment over percentage change in manufacturing GDP over a period.

[16]Islam (2001) showed that employment elasticity in manufacturing declined from 0.76 during 1981–1985 to 0.66 during 1986–1992 while using ILO-EMP/RECON database on employment; on the other hand, Islam (2004) calculated employment elasticity of the manufacturing sector as 0.39 based on the regression result in respect with poverty incidence and annual GDP growth.

Table 5.10 Employment elasticity of manufacturing industries during 2000–2012

Category of industry	Employment elasticity
Highly export-oriented	*0.42*
RMG	0.42
Leather	0.97
Other transport equipment	0.32
Paper products	0.35
Textiles	0.04
Computer, electronic and optical products	-
Moderately export-oriented	*0.36*
Manufacture of electrical equipment	0.14
Other manufacturing	0.60
Food	0.13
Beverages	0.44
Rubber and plastic products	0.49
Low export-oriented	*0.34*
Non-metallic mineral products	0.21
Fabricated metal	0.13
Chemical products	0.89
Tobacco products	−0.34
Recorded media	1.18
Pharmaceuticals, medicinal chemical and botanical products	0.40
Manufacture of furniture	0.58
Wood and cork	−0.29
Petroleum products	0.57
Machinery and equipment n.e.c	-
Motor vehicles, trailers and semi-trailers	0.09
Repair and installation of machinery and equipment	-
Recycling	-
Total	*0.28*

Source Authors' estimations based on the data from Survey of Manufacturing Industries (SMI)

materials and intermediate products. Interestingly, such facilities were allowed for other industries as well, but the growth of non-RMG export sectors remained modest.

In recent years, the government's budgetary measures have emphasised issues and concerns raised by the business bodies of the RMG sector. During the last decade, multiple issues related to the RMG sector got priority in the government's fiscal measures, including the reduction of corporate tax, advance income tax (AIT), reduction of import duties on different industrial items and providing cash incentives for export in non-traditional markets. These changes have been undertaken in accordance with demand from the business bodies of the RMG sector. On the other hand, the support provided to non-RMG enterprises was scant and sporadic. Considering the level of contribution made by different industries on employment such as non-RMG export-oriented as well as domestic-market-oriented industries, government policies should pay more attention towards those industries. A major criticism of government policy support is that selected products under different sub-sectors, whether it is domestic-market-oriented or export-oriented, is largely influenced by different pressure groups which raise the efficacy of support mechanism. In other words, given the limited scope for revenue expenditure, such kinds of biased support deprive various important sub-sectors which might have higher potential to contribute to export and employment. The Ministry of Finance (MoF), which is the authority to provide the fiscal benefits, did not have any mechanism to assess the impact of these benefits to the industry. Hence, an irrational, pressure-group-influenced and un-assessed incentive mechanisms have been continued.

5.6.2 *Tariff Regime and Implications on Growth of the Manufacturing Sector*

Production of manufacturing industries in Bangladesh is heavily influenced by tariff, para-tariff and other technical requirements at import stage on various kinds of raw materials, intermediate goods, capital machineries and finished goods. Thus tariff regime has direct and indirect impact on production of export-oriented and import-competing industries, thereby contributing to *size*, *composition* and *process* effects on employment. With a view to examining the impact and implications of the tariff regime over the last one and a half decades, a total of 17 sectors have been identified on which necessary analysis has been carried out. The study measures relative burden of tariff and para-tariff by estimating the simple averages of tariff in different categories of industries (HEIs, MEIs and LEIs).[17] The selected products are known as the top importable products (top five products in each category at 6 digit level) in 2012 and 2016.

[17]The data having zero (0) figures and blanks in all export and import dataset have been replaced by 0.01 value. The justification for this kind of minor addition is that it would provide a better dataset without having any mathematical errors. On the other hand, the data having zero (0) figures in tariff data set has also been replaced by 0.01 value, and leaving all the blanks unchanged.

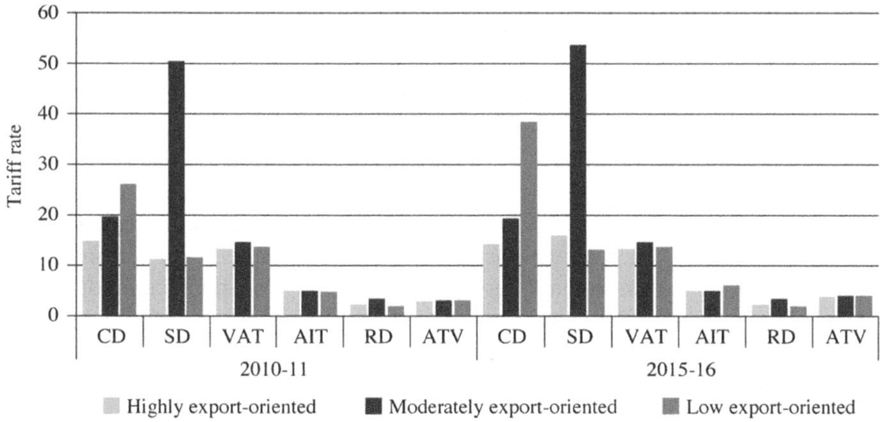

Fig. 5.3 Industry-wise tariff and para-tariff. *Note* ATV: Advance trade VAT *Source* Authors' calculations.

A mixed trend has been observed in case of tariffs and para-tariffs on the import of different categories of products (Fig. 5.3). The HEIs have enjoyed relatively less burden in all types of tariffs and para-tariffs compared to that of MEIs and LEIs. This possibly happened owing to the government's policy to protect domestic-market-oriented industries through tariffs and para-tariffs, which are relatively large in number under MEIs and LEIs.

During 2012–2016, though CD in HEIs and MEIs has declined at different levels, the duty has increased in the case of LEIs. In case of different types of para-tariffs, including SD, VAT, AIT, RD and ATV—these have either mostly increased or remained unchanged for all categories of industries. More specifically, para-tariffs are relatively high in case of MEIs and LEIs. Overall, these are indicative of the government's policy to support and protect domestic industries. Rahman et al. (2011) identified a number of consequences on employment due to changes in tariff. There is significant positive impact of restrictive CD, found in case of direct employment. However, when trade variables are used alone, significant negative coefficients are found on demand for labour.

Analysis on tariffs and para-tariffs on different categories of export-oriented industries imposed between 2010–11 and 2015–16 indicates that tariffs and para-tariffs were not necessarily high in LEIs/domestic-market-oriented industries. These indicate that protection/support is not necessarily always about job creation, unless more support is provided to small and medium industries. Hence, recalibration of tariff regime to remove anti-export bias could not protect industries with high employment and/or their productivity prospects. The most important issue is to remove rent-seeking and corruption.

5.6.3 Effect of REER on Export and Import

Among many, exchange rate is considered as one of the major policy variables which could influence the country's external trade. The empirical results from different studies corroborate the fact of having a significant relationship between exchange rate volatility and export and import. Hassan et al. (2016), Younus and Chowdhury (2014) and Aziz (2012) evinced that an appreciation (depreciation) in real effective exchange rate (REER) decelerates (accelerates) the domestic export earnings, and therefore, experienced a resultant effect on trade balance. An appreciation of REER makes import more affordable and export more expensive, driving off the potential demand for exportable products in the reported countries. Studies on selected Asian developing countries generally corroborate the above. Sharma (2003) and Veeramani (2008) showed that the demand for Indian exports increases when its export prices fall in relation to world prices; and also deteriorates when export prices increase in relation to world prices. The Indian non-financial sector firms also experienced a downturn in export during 2000–2010 due to a real appreciation of rupee against the partner countries' currency (Cheung and Sengupta 2013). The firms having a smaller share of total export are found to be more affected by an adverse effect of exchange rate. Dhasmana (2012) found India's trade balance to have a positive long-run association between real exchange rate depreciation, with its key trading partners. Volatility of REER also exhibits a negative long-term relationship. It is found in the case of Pakistan that REER has a positive impact on export performance only in the presence of trade openness (Zulfiqar and Kausar 2012). The same analysis also revealed that Pakistan experienced a negative association with export growth during 1981–2010, which actually oppugns the case of India (Sharma 2003).

Over the last 15 years (i.e. 2001–2016), the REER index of Bangladesh has more or less had a tendency to appreciate, and it reached at some 137.95 during 2015–16 (Fig. 5.4). On the other hand, since an appreciation of REER makes import cheaper, import growth is likely to be influenced positively. The results essentially illustrate that due to an appreciation in REER, export earnings for the country get reduced and import gets encouraged substantially. According to Aziz (2012), during the period of 1976–2009, the devaluation of REER made a positive contribution to the country's external trade.

5.7 Impact and Implications of COVID-19 on Production, Export and Employment in the Manufacturing Sector

The outbreak of COVID-19 worldwide is the latest example of *act of nature*, which has caused a considerable level of disorder in domestic and global supply chains. The risks associated with such global systemic concerns have multiple dimensions, which are related to the process, control, supply and demand, business environment, and thereby related to industries' survival and ensuring employment. Bangladesh

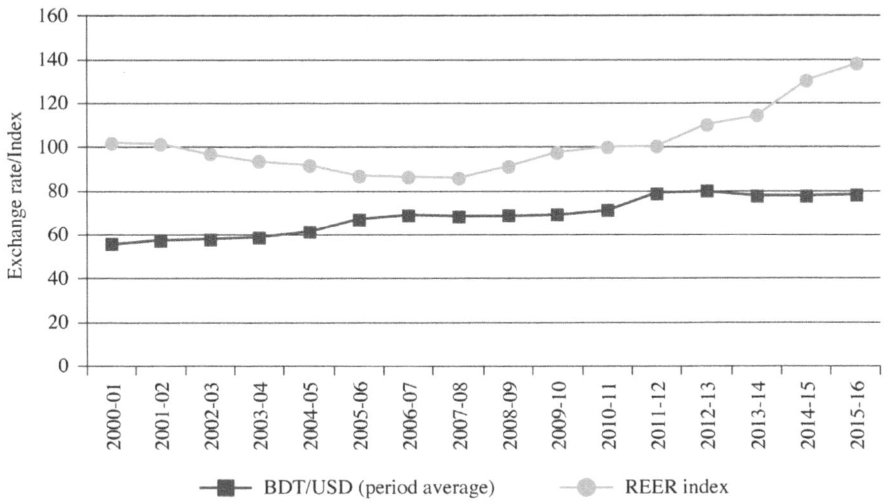

Fig. 5.4 National exchange rate versus REER. *Source* Bangladesh Bank

economy, like elsewhere, has become exposed to a number of these risks due to the snowballing nature of the adverse impact of this crisis. A number of international and local organisations have estimated the possible damages caused by COVID-19 on Bangladesh economy in terms of production, sales, export, employment and unemployment, level of poverty, inequality and overall size of the GDP. According to ADB (2020), Bangladesh's GDP may get shrunk by 0.01%—this is collectively reflected through a reduction in agriculture production (−0.68% of GDP); squeezed activities of business, trade, personal services (−1.66% of GDP); and reduction of activities in light/heavy manufacturing, utilities and construction (−1.2% of GDP). However, this estimate was carried out in April 2020, when Bangladesh was exposed to coronavirus in a limited scale. A possible reestimation of the impact on the economy based on the significant impact of the virus in following months (the peak of the spread of the virus is yet to be predicted) would illustrate a worsening picture. In recent estimates, GDP growth has been gauged to be at a much lower level in FY2019-20—within the ranges of 1.6% (World Bank 2020), 2.5% (CPD 2020a) and 3.8% (IMF 2020). The official estimate of GDP growth for FY2019-20 is, however, indicated to be 5.2%.

A sectoral decomposition of losses in terms of production and employment indicates that extent of impact varies widely between different sectors in terms of the amount of losses, share in GDP, loss of employment and their share in sectoral employment (Table 5.11). According to ADB (2020), manufacturing sector would experience a loss of about USD 3.2 million, which is about 1.2% of GDP and 4.2% of the sectoral share of GDP. Transport sector, which is an important support service of the manufacturing sector, would have a loss of USD 1.1 billion, which is about 4.6% of the sectoral share of GDP. Different businesses and personal services would have a collective loss of about USD 4.6 billion, which is 4.6% of the sectoral share

Table 5.11 Estimates of loss in Bangladesh economy due to COVID-19 pandemic

Sector	Loss as % of total GDP	Loss (million USD)	Loss in employment (in'000)	Loss as % of sectoral GDP	Loss as % of sectoral employment
Agriculture, mining and quarrying	−0.68	1,870	1,254	−4.36	−4.32
Business, trade, personal and public services	−1.66	4,558	784	−4.55	−4.66
Hotels, restaurants and other personal services	−0.50	1,374	140	−4.58	−4.55
Light/heavy manufacturing, utilities and construction	−1.20	3,279	650	−4.22	−3.92
Transport services	−0.39	1,058	213	−4.57	−4.57
All	−4.43	12,138	3,041	−4.43	−4.33

Source ADB (2020)
Note Additional impact is assumed for all sectors under longer containment and larger demand shock

of GDP. Overall, the manufacturing sector and associated service sectors have been severely affected, which have weakened the conclusions made in earlier sections on the issue of full employment in the manufacturing sector.

The prolonged cessation of economic activities caused a significant adverse impact on both domestic-market- and export-oriented industries. Major manufacturing industries and their related activities reportedly impacted by the pandemic, include—leather and finished leather products, live and chilled food and jute spinning (in export of goods); garments accessories and packaging, plastic, pharmaceuticals, cosmetics and toiletries (in import of goods and raw materials); woven and knit products (in import of intermediate products); and computer and accessories, medical instruments and hospital equipment, eyeglass and electronics (in import of goods). A large section of SMEs operating in domestic-market-oriented industries, which are reported less, faced many challenges for their survival. According to IMF (2020), both exports and imports will experience negative growth rates during FY2019-20 (−17.9 and −8.8%, respectively) (Table 5.12). Although the level of adversity would reduce in FY2020-21, the country's trade may not return to a normal state in FY2020-21, particularly that of export.

Domestic SMEs were particularly hard-hit in view of the corona pandemic. The businesses of these enterprises are overwhelmingly dependent on a few important religious and cultural events. In that context, cancellation of the *Pohela Baishakh*

Table 5.12 Changes in the external sector (%)

Component	FY2017	FY2018	FY2019	Pre-COVID		New projection	
				FY2020	FY2021	FY2020	FY2021
Export of goods	1.7	6.7	10.1	−1.5	7.0	−17.9	−0.8
Import of goods	9.0	25.2	1.8	1.0	10.0	−8.8	4.8
Remittances	−14.5	17.3	9.6	18.0	7.0	1.4	−7.1

Source IMF (2020)

(New Year of Bangla calendar) festival as part of the government's COVID-19-related restrictive measures has resulted in significant losses for these SMEs. These losses are expected to rise further with the duration of the public holiday having been extended till 15 May 2020 which significantly affected businesses that profit from Ramadan and Eid-ul-Fitr.

A significant negative impact is observed in the world of work as well, pertaining to employment, decent wages, occupational safety and health-related issues. Job security in Bangladesh is very weak in most of the economic establishments since the major portion of employment is in the informal sector. According to the Labour Force Survey (LFS) 2017, 82.6% of employment in Bangladesh is in the informal sector (BBS 2018), under which workers do not get legal protection for retaining jobs, benefits in case of leave and termination along with other entitled dues. Hence, taking special measures to protect these workers has become crucial. According to Policy Research Institute of Bangladesh (PRI), a think tank in Bangladesh, about 1–1.5 crore people working in different sectors have lost their jobs, and the majority of them are in the informal sector.[18] According to ADB (2020) estimates, about 3.04 million workers are likely to be unemployed. Manufacturing sector would experience a loss in employment of 0.65 million workers under different categories of light/heavy manufacturing industries.

Workers in different sectors have been working at a wage rate lower than their stipulated wages during the pre-COVID period. Workers in the RMG sector received wages at the level of 60–65% of their gross wages. CPD (2020b) identified that a considerable number of workers (about 30%) did not even get that wage. In fact, this amount of wage is usually provided to workers when they are laid-off. However, lowering the wages could not ensure the job of a large section of workers in the RMG sector. According to the Industrial Police, as many as 19,919 workers have been officially terminated from 115 RMG factories. Besides, a considerable number of workers from the RMG sector had to undergo an informal termination of their jobs as they were either laid-off or retrenched or forced to resign from different factories. The situation in the domestic-market-oriented manufacturing industries was much worse because of a lack of monitoring and enforcement of labour laws and rules.

[18]See details on The Business Standard (2020).

It is evident that the manufacturing sector had almost no shock-absorption capacity in order to address the risks caused by the COVID-19 pandemic. Most of the enterprises have no contingency plan to manage the risks in the short-term and to gradually move towards recovery. This is reflected both in case of export-oriented industries, especially RMG industry, as well as in domestic-market-oriented industries in terms of scaling down production and employment, lower level of payment to workers and in large part, domestic-market-oriented industries shutting down their operations with or without paying the workers. In this situation, the government has announced a number of stimulus packages for the export-oriented and domestic-market-oriented industries mainly to pay workers' wages and to initiate businesses with working capital. A large part of these facilities is targetted towards export-oriented industries, mainly RMG industry, in the form of deferment of payment of bank loans, utility bills, import payment and export receipts, deferred payment facility of VAT and AIT, etc. In the national budget for FY2020-21, various fiscal measures for the export-oriented industries, particularly for the RMG sector, have been kept unchanged without making any upward revision (withholding tax rate retained at 10–12% level for another year) and offering tax-holiday facility for diversified garment products. A large part of these package facilities has been availed by RMG factories, particularly those which are member factories of two associations. Non-member factories, particularly those of sub-contracting factories, buying houses, garment-accessory-related factories, could not avail those benefits. In the case of domestic-market-oriented industries, the package is limited, and are allowed for those based on bank–client relationship. It is apprehended that a large section of cottage, micro, small and medium enterprises (CMSMEs) which have limited or no banking transactions would be deprived of getting the benefit. According to CPD (2020b), only 6–7% of SMEs would avail that facility. Overall, the fiscal, monetary and sectoral measures undertaken by the government would make a limited contribution in addressing the risks faced by a large segment of manufacturing enterprises. In such a situation, if the pandemic prolongs over an extensive period (as it seems to be), a large segment of these enterprises would not survive without broad-based support. The likely impact on the world of work would be much worse in the future. Hence, the hypothesis of creating full employment by promoting domestic- and export-oriented manufacturing industries would be more difficult in the coming days.

5.8 Conclusion

The study has observed that owing to trade reforms and several other factors, including fortuitous circumstances, Bangladesh over the past three decades appeared to have embarked on trade liberalisation and labour-intensive industrialisation, which could potentially generate productive jobs and reach a state of full employment. This has been the characterisation of export and employment growth in the HPAEs during the early phases of their development. The growth of the RMG sector and its share in manufacturing value-added, exports and employment has been quite striking. However, unlike in HPAEs, it has not evolved into an EOI *strategy*, where exports have diversified and graduated into a broad-based export structure. While RMG has spearheaded the growth of formal, paid jobs, especially for women, its share in total employment is static or declining. Hence, while the share of manufacturing employment is steadily increasing, it is still far too low to ensure any structural transformation.

Meanwhile, Bangladesh has stepped up its protection and other support to domestic import-substituting industries. While domestic industries too should create jobs,[19] if properly planned, many experts believe that an anti-export bias has been created.[20] The latter would imply that export diversification is likely to be adversely affected. Whether the lack of adequate diversification is due to trade regimes or to various constraints to growth of manufacturing industries per se, is unclear.[21] Given the relatively low levels of FDI flows, in a milieu of rising imports in a fast-growth country, export growth would need to be boosted both for job growth as well as to ease potential foreign exchange constraints. The above discussion leads to a number of issues which need to be thoroughly investigated in order to calibrate policies and interventions that would, seriatim, minimise distortions towards the objectives of higher employment growth and export growth. This would, in turn, be contingent on an appropriate design of a comprehensive trade and industrialisation policy. The objectives of such a policy need to be clear and pragmatic, not only to include export expansion, but also for employment generation. The present study, within a limited framework, tends to argue that the two are not automatic. Further, attempts to create *exports at any cost* or to overly protect domestic industries are likely to engender policy biases, rent-seeking and corruption. Bangladesh would need to explore its own *golden mean*.[22]

The manufacturing sector of Bangladesh has experienced growth in employment over the years; however, growth in employment has slowed down in the more recent period. The present study shows that employment growth has been variable and highly concentrated on a limited number of sub-sectors. This chapter analyses how employment growth in the manufacturing sector has been influenced by trade. Following Jenkins and Sen (2006), it has tried to distinguish the impact of trade on employment through three distinct effects—*size*, *composition* and *process*. The analysis tends to suggest that no single type of effect reveals any clear pattern of growth in manufacturing employment due to trade; rather, such growth is found to be a combined effect of all—*size*, *composition* and *process*. While a large share of changes in employment has taken place in HEIs, changes in employment are also observed in case of MEIs and LEIs. Moreover, both the labour- and capital-intensive industries under *different export categories of industries*, experienced growth in employment.

---

[19]Note that non-traded sector plays a significant role in employment generation.

[20]See Ahmed (2015), Khan (2007).

[21]Private investment is still relatively low.

[22]Mazumdar (2008).

However, higher growth in employment in both labour- and capital-intensive industries is revealed in HEIs. In contrast, a few LEIs have experienced negative growth in employment. While the employment content of export-oriented industries is heavily influenced by RMG, which is labour-intensive, not all export-oriented sub-sectors can be relied upon to generate employment. Similarly, domestic-market-oriented industries have also been contributing to employment growth through *size*, *composition* and *process* effects. These observations require further scrutiny, especially through per unit/enterprise-level data, and comparison of trade effects on both employment and productivity, to ensure which sub-sectors are best supported.

The growth of the manufacturing sector has been constrained by various factors which have adverse effects on employment. According to the World Economic Forum (WEF), major problematic factors for enhancing competitiveness in Bangladesh includes some 16 different constraints. Among the five major constraints, *corruption* has ranked number one for six times since 2006, implying that it has become a *core chronic curse* to the potential and existing health of the economy. *Inadequate supply of infrastructure* came second in the ranking in 2017 as one of the major impediments for doing business in Bangladesh. It is evident that infrastructural backwardness deters the potential foreign investments in Bangladesh since the constraint is unable to attract both foreign and domestic investments. These constraints, coupled with *inefficient government bureaucracy* have added to the uninviting business environment extensively. Furthermore, *policy instability* and *inadequately educated labour force* and *poor work ethic in the national labour force* became the newly perceived constraints in 2017, and are currently considered to be the top impediments for doing business in Bangladesh. While there are some constraints which have improved significantly in the ranking (e.g. tax rates, tax regulations, crime and theft, foreign currency regulations), the business environment overall has been worsened by these emerging issues.

Poor technological readiness is a prime weakness restraining the manufacturing sector of Bangladesh. Bangladesh is specialised in bulk-scale low value-added products, where skill requirement is low. Apart from RMG, few other sectors have the potential to absorb such a large volume of workers. For such volume-led employment, the manufacturing base is rather limited in other potential sectors, such as leather and footwear, pharmaceuticals and food processing. Given the poor educational background and inadequate qualifications of the pool of labour force, it is difficult to develop industries which require more advanced skills.

While the current policies are largely supportive of export-oriented industries through various trade and budgetary measures, low export-based and/or domestic-market-oriented industries have also been partly supported by fiscal measures. The recent shifts in the tariff regime cater to domestic-market-oriented industries which are low export-oriented and import-competing industries. Although such policy support partially contributed to a degree of rising in export and domestic production of both categories of industries, the impact on employment is not evident, except in a few sub-sectors. In other words, trade-related policies and measures are likely to play a *partial* role in influencing the growth in production and exports, and thereby on growth in employment. However, there are a number of other factors which also influence the performance of industries both in the domestic and export markets. Hence, it is difficult to conclude that the export orientation of industries or labour-intensive nature of industries alone could contribute to a rise in employment in a labour-abundant economy like Bangladesh. Against the backdrop of different kinds of market failures and problems of governance, the choice of policies with regard to enhancing employment should be well-calibrated with policy priorities to increase productivity and export with appropriate emphasis on both domestic-market- and export-oriented industries.

The hypothesis that this study intends to prove through discussion on trade and other public policies and domestic business environment would be difficult to establish if one or more of the critical assumptions changes. The assumption of having no major shocks to take place at local and global levels has been questioned with the COVID-19 pandemic worldwide and its adverse impact on the Bangladesh economy. As discussed, the manufacturing sector has been severely affected due to the pandemic which forced the businesses to scale down their operations particularly in case of export-oriented industries; or even to shut down business, particularly those of the domestic-market-oriented industries. The employment both in export-oriented and domestic-market-oriented industries have been badly affected. The limited shock-absorption capacity due to the absence of contingency plans forced these businesses to seek support from the government. However, the limited fiscal and financial capacity of the government and banking sector would make small-scale contribution to addressing the risks. However, if the pandemic prolongs (as it currently seems it may), the sector would confront a major crisis in terms of survival and ensuring employment. In that context, the conclusions drawn regarding full employment hypothesis would be weakened.

References

ADB. (2020). *COVID-19 economic impact assessment template*. Manila: Asian Development Bank (ADB). Retrieved April 3, 2020, from https://data.adb.org/dataset/covid-19-economic-impact-assessment-template.

Ahmed, A. (2015). Relationship between foreign direct investment and company taxation: Case of Bangladesh. *American Journal of Trade and Policy, 2*(2), 125–129.

Ali, I., & Son, H. H. (2007). *Defining and measuring inclusive growth: application to the Philippines*. ERD Working Paper Series 98. Manila: Asian Development Bank (ADB).

Aziz, N. (2012). Does a real devaluation improve the balance of trade? Empirics from Bangladesh economy. *The Journal of Developing Areas, 46*(2), 19–41.

BBS. (2010). *Survey of manufacturing industries 2005–2006*. Dhaka: Bangladesh Bureau of Statistics (BBS), Government of Bangladesh (GoB).

BBS. (2013). *Survey of manufacturing industries 2011–2012*. Dhaka: Bangladesh Bureau of Statistics (BBS), Government of Bangladesh (GoB).

BBS. (2018). *Labour force survey 2016–2017*. Dhaka: Bangladesh Bureau of Statistics (BBS), Government of Bangladesh (GoB).

Bruton, H. J. (1970). The import-substitution strategy of economic development: A survey. *The Pakistan Development Review, 10*(2), 123–146.

Cheung, Y., & Sengupta, R. (2013). Impact of exchange rate movements on exports: An analysis of Indian non-financial sector firms. *Journal of International Money and Finance, 39*(C), 231–245.

CPD. (2010). Analysis of the national budget for FY2009–10. In *State of the Bangladesh economy in FY2008–09 and outlook for FY2009–10* (pp. 61–100). Dhaka: Centre for Policy Dialogue (CPD).

CPD. (2011). Analysis of the national budget for FY2010–11. In *State of the Bangladesh economy in FY2009–10 and outlook for FY2010–11* (pp. 63–97). Dhaka: Centre for Policy Dialogue (CPD).

CPD. (2014). Analysis of the national budget for FY2013–14. In *State of the Bangladesh economy in FY2012–13 and outlook for FY2013–14* (pp. 23–59). Dhaka: Centre for Policy Dialogue (CPD).

CPD. (2020a, June 7). *Challenges of policymaking in times of pandemics: State of the Bangladesh economy in FY2020.* Issue paper prepared for a virtual media briefing organised by the Centre for Policy Dialogue (CPD), Dhaka, Bangladesh.

CPD. (2020b, June 9). *Responding to COVID-19—A rapid assessment of stimulus packages and relief measures: Will the target groups get the benefits?* Issue paper prepared for a virtual dialogue organised by the Centre for Policy Dialogue (CPD), Dhaka, Bangladesh.

Dhasmana, A. (2012). *India's real exchange rate and trade balance: Fresh empirical evidence.* Working Paper 373. Bangalore: Indian Institute of Management.

EPB. (n.d.). *Export data.* Dhaka: Export Promotion Bureau (EPB), Government of Bangladesh (GoB). Retrieved January 10, 2018, from https://epb.gov.bd/site/view/epb_export_data/.

Feliciano, Z. M. (2001). Workers and trade liberalisation: The impact of trade reforms in Mexico on wages and employment. *ILR Review, 55*(1), 95–115.

Felipe, J. (2012). *Inclusive growth, full employment, and structural change: Implications and policies for developing Asia* (2nd Ed.). Manila: Asian Development Bank (ADB).

Fischer, S. (2000). *Lunch address given at the conference on Promoting Dialogue: Global Challenges and Global Institutions.* Washington, D.C.: American University.

Hassan, R., Chakraborty, S., Sultana, S., & Rahman, M. M. (2016). *The impact of the real effective exchange rate on real export earnings in Bangladesh.* Working Paper 1605. Dhaka: Monetary Policy and Research Department, Bangladesh Bank.

IMF. (2020, June 3). *Bangladesh: Requests for disbursement under the rapid credit facility and purchase under the rapid financing instrument-press release; staff report; and statement by the executive director for Bangladesh.* Washington, D.C.: Asia and Pacific Dept., International Monetary Fund (IMF).

Islam, R. (2001, February 5–9). Poverty alleviation, employment and labour market: Lessons from the Asian experience and policies. Paper presented at the *Asia and Pacific Forum on Poverty*, organised by the Asian Development Bank (ADB), Manila, Philippines.

Islam, R. (2004). *The nexus of economic growth, employment and poverty reduction: An empirical analysis.* Geneva: International Labour Organization (ILO).

Jenkins, R., & Sen, K. (2006). International trade and manufacturing employment in the South: Four country case studies. *Oxford Development Studies, 34*(3), 299–322.

Khan, A. R. (2007). *Growth, employment and poverty: An analysis of the vital nexus based on some recent UNDP and ILO/SIDA studies.* DESA Working Paper 49. New York: United Nations Department of Economic and Social Affairs (UN DESA).

Krugman, P. R. (1981). Intra-industry specialization and the gains from trade. *Journal of Political Economy, 89*(5), 959–973.

Lall, S. (2004). Selective industrial and trade policies in developing countries: Theoretical and empirical issues. In C. C. Soludo, O. Ogbu, & H. Chang (Eds.), *The politics of trade and industrial policy in Africa: Forced consensus* (pp. 4–14). Ottawa: International Development Research Centre (IDRC).

Little, I., Scitovsky, T., & Scott, M. (1970). *Industry and trade in some developing countries: A comparative study.* London: Oxford University Press.

Mazumdar, S. (2008). *Crony capitalism and India: Before and after liberalization.* Working Paper 2008/04. New Delhi: Institute for Studies in Industrial Development.

Melitz, M. J. (2003). The impact of trade on intra-industry reallocations and aggregate industry productivity. *Econometrica, 71*(6), 1695–1725.
Moazzem, K. G., & Reza, M. M. M. (2018). *Growth of employment in the manufacturing sector: Impact of trade and trade-related policies*. CPD Working Paper 118. Dhaka: Centre for Policy Dialogue (CPD).
Muqtada, M. (2010). *The crisis of orthodox macroeconomic policy: The case for a renewed commitment to full employment*. Employment Working Paper 53. Geneva: International Labour Organization (ILO).
Nassar, H. (2010). *Growth, employment policies and economic linkages: Egypt*. Employment Working Paper 85. Geneva: International Labour Organization (ILO).
OECD. (2012). *OECD Employment outlook*. Paris: Organisation for Economic Co-operation and Development (OECD).
Orbeta, A. C. (2002). *Globalization and employment: The impact of trade on employment level and structure in the Philippines*. PIDS Discussion Paper Series 2002–2004. Makati City: Philippine Institute for Development Studies (PIDS).
Puyana, A. (2011). *Economic growth, employment and poverty reduction: A comparative analysis of Chile and Mexico*. Employment Working Paper 78. Geneva: International Labour Organization (ILO).
Rahman, M., Shadat, W. B., & Raihan, S. (2011). *Trade liberalisation, manufacturing growth and employment in Bangladesh*. New Delhi: Academic Foundation.
Rodrik, D. (2008). *Normalizing industrial policy*. Commission on Growth and Development, Working Paper 3. Washington, D.C.: The World Bank.
Sharma, K. (2003). Factors determining India's export performance. *Journal of Asian Economics, 14*(3), 435–446.
The Business Standard. (2020, April 1). Pandemic hits hard all business sectors of Bangladesh.
Veeramani, C. (2008). Impact of exchange rate appreciation on India's exports. *Economic and Political Weekly, 43*(22), 10–14.
World Bank. (1993). *The East Asian miracle: Economic growth and public policy*. World Bank Policy Research Report. New York: Oxford University Press.
World Bank. (2020). *Global Economic Perspective*. Washington, D.C.: The World Bank Group. Retrieved July 4, 2020, from https://www.worldbank.org/en/publication/global-economic-prospects.
World Bank. (n.d.). *World Integrated Trade Solution (WITS) database* (at 2 digit level). Washington, D.C.: The World Bank. Retrieved: January 12, 2020, from https://wits.worldbank.org.
Younus, S., & Chowdhury, M. M. I. (2014). *Real exchange rate and its impact on export, import and trade balance: Is there any J-curve effect in Bangladesh?* Working Paper 1408. Dhaka: Monetary Policy Department, Bangladesh Bank.
Zulfiqar, K., & Kausar, R. (2012). Trade liberalisation, exchange rate and export growth in Pakistan. *Far East Journal of Psychology and Business, 9*(2), 32–47.

Chapter 6
Alternative Approaches to Full Employment in Bangladesh: Role of the Rural Non-farm Sector

Muhammed Muqtada

Abstract The slow growth of employment in the modern manufacturing sector has raised scepticism on how far and how quickly Bangladesh economy could productively absorb its large pool of surplus labour and attain full employment. Following (Ranis and Stewart, J. Dev Econ 40:75–101, Ranis and Stewart, Journal of Development Economics 40:75–101, 1993), the present chapter reengages in and examines the potential role of rural non-farm activity (RNA) in wiping out rural unemployment and underemployment, as it did in the case of some East Asian countries. The chapter explores the extent and pattern of RNA growth in Bangladesh, its impact on jobs and incomes, as well as on labour market formations. It further contends that changes in rural labour market are often not reflected as structural change due to the presence of informality within the three traditional sectors, viz. agriculture, industry and services. It explores pathways in enhancing rural non-farm (RNF) employment and assesses the prospects of reaching rural full employment. Finally, the study stresses the need for a comprehensive policy framework and coordinated strategy for a vigorous growth of RNF enterprises, in order to increase the potential for higher productivity jobs and household incomes, and to enhance aggregate demand.

6.1 Introduction

A significant goal of the 2030 Agenda for Sustainable Development, which all countries, including Bangladesh, have committed themselves to, is the attainment of full productive employment and decent work (viz. Sustainable Development Goal (SDG)

This chapter draws from a working paper by the author, Muqtada (2018), published by the CPD; content re-used with permission.

M. Muqtada (✉)
Development Economist; Formerly a Director in the Employment Sector of the International Labour Organization (ILO) Geneva and a Visiting Fellow, Centre for Policy Dialogue, Dhaka, Bangladesh
e-mail: muqtada1@gmail.com

M. Muqtada (ed.), *Quest for Inclusive Growth in Bangladesh*,
South Asia Economic and Policy Studies,
https://doi.org/10.1007/978-981-15-7614-0_6

8). Since the 1950s, the developing countries have been relentlessly exploring alternative pathways for attaining higher economic growth, and thereby, employment for all. Among the many constructs of development strategies that influenced policy-making during this period in order to create jobs for the large surplus labour, the so-called *dual model*,[1] as pioneered by Arthur Lewis, has perhaps attained the widest currency. Based on the distinction between two sectors, which the author calls the *capitalist sector* (industry) and the *subsistence sector* (agriculture), it envisages that the former, with higher productivity and wages, will grow continuously until the surplus labour from the latter is fully absorbed. The role of industry in the process of structural transformation and growth has been widely stressed and documented (Clark 1940; Kuznets 1955; Rodrik 1997), as it has been historically found to play a crucial role in generating higher productivity employment, and in enhancing growth. In the process of economic growth, there takes place a structural shift in the value-added composition, away from the primary sector towards the secondary or industry sector. Kaldor (1967) provided a theoretical rationale for such patterns of structural change that characterised the growth of advanced countries. Since economic growth is historically associated with employment growth, the workforce structure is also seen to undergo a similar shift, with labour increasingly moving away from the primary sector towards industry.

This development stylisation, informed by the pattern of capitalist growth in advanced economies and arguably reinforced by the East Asian experience, has inspired policy-making among developing countries over the past several decades.[2] However, over this entire period, the growth of employment's share in industry/manufacturing, i.e. transfer of labour from agriculture to industry, has in most cases been disappointing. In fact, agriculture continues to be saddled with high surplus labour (largely in the form of underemployment), while it is the services sector which has grown the fastest, and in most cases, accounts for the bulk of the share of both employment and value-added. This is contrary to growth patterns predicted by Clark-Fisher hypothesis based on differential income elasticities of three traditional sectors; and also to the historical experience of the developed countries, where the tertiary sector expanded in relative terms only when development matured. The shift in the value-added and workforce composition in favour of the tertiary sector before industrialisation could mature, has resulted in sluggish employment growth, particularly for the unskilled and semi-skilled workforce in most developing countries. The labour market slack in Bangladesh continues to remain pervasive, and the nature of economic and labour market formations have tended to obscure the binary division of the economy as in Lewisian scheme, especially through the rapid growth of the services sector on the one hand, and of the informal and rural non-farm activities on

[1]The *dual model* (Lewis 1954) of economic development; the *investment criteria model* (Chenery 1953); the thesis of *critical minimum effort* (Leibenstein 1957); the theory of *Big Push* (Rosenstein-Rodan 1943); and the *tunnel effect* (Hirschman and Rothschild 1973) are major examples of such efforts.

[2]Nearly a century ago, in 1918, B. R. Ambedkar recognised the seriousness of the problem of *disguised labour* in agriculture, and stressed the need for industrialisation to absorb surplus labour (Krishnamurty 2008).

the other. There have been various postulations and debates regarding the possibilities of attaining the Lewisian turning point through one of these three sectors. Empirical validation has been scanty. Ranis and Stewart (1993), in their well-known paper, have contended that a dynamic RNA or the so-called Z-goods sector, under appropriate policy framework, can be a significant factor in accelerating growth of employment and incomes, and in nearly wiping out rural unemployment and underemployment.[3] In Bangladesh, given the rather slow growth in the employment share of the modern manufacturing sector, can RNA be an alternative catalyst, and an impetus to progress towards full employment?

The experience of Bangladesh, in respect of structural transformation, broadly resembles that of many developing countries as mentioned above.[4] The present chapter examines the potential of RNA in enhancing rural incomes and employment towards affecting structural change. In Bangladesh, share of employment in manufacturing, in relative terms, has remained low and sluggish, while there has been a rapid growth of RNA (see Hossain 2004; Raihan 2016). The present study will explore the extent and pattern of RNA growth in Bangladesh, and examine how far it carries the prospects, if at all, for Bangladesh to retrace the Lewisian turning point towards full employment. First, however, what is the status and level of unemployment in Bangladesh? How far is Bangladesh away from achieving full employment? According to the Bangladesh Bureau of Statistics (BBS), Bangladesh currently has an unemployment of 4.2% and underemployment of 3%. This is a highly improbable scenario, given that there exists pervasive slack in the labour market, especially in the rural and informal sectors.[5]

This chapter is organised as follows. Section 6.2 provides a cursory view of the issues and debates related to the role of RNF employment in effecting structural change and in moving the economy towards the goal of full employment. Examples are drawn from some of the East Asian countries. In Sect. 6.3, based on published data, the study assesses the trends in, and patterns of, non-farm employment in Bangladesh, and examines whether and to what extent the RNA can be perceived as a dynamic sector. Section 6.4 points to various conducive factors, such as, inter alia the growth of food-agriculture and better penetration of rural finance, which, in turn, have influenced the *push–pull* factors in individual household decisions. Section 6.5 probes further into the changes in labour market brought about by the rise in RNA, and assesses whether these reflect tangible structural change. The study contends, in Sect. 6.6, that various changes in rural labour market do not get appropriately reflected as structural change because of the vast and pervasive existence of the so-called informal sector in all the three traditional sectors. This is particularly due

---

[3]Citing analysis of the role of RNA in Taiwan, and contrasting the experience of the Philippines, Ranis and Stewart (1990, p. 38) demonstrates how growth of Z-goods sector in rural areas (i.e. rural non-agricultural goods such as textile, garments, processed food, etc.), along with a rapid growth food agriculture, can lead to a dynamic expansion of employment and incomes, "with a more egalitarian distribution of income and the elimination of rural underemployment." Also see Ranis and Stewart (1993).

[4]Also see details in Chap. 3 in this volume.

[5]See Islam (2014); also, discussion on unemployment in Chap. 3 of the present volume.

to the lack of any systematic evidence to assess the relative importance and role of informal activities and role of job, enterprise and productivity growth within the respective sectors. Section 6.7 examines the potential of RNA to bring about structural change and rural full employment. In this regard, it explores the potential pathways; in particular the future growth of agricultural productivity, the trends in RNA productivity and earnings, the rising household income and demand for RNA goods and services, and emerging role of remittances in rural Bangladesh. Section 6.8 provides some concluding remarks, especially in articulating a case for a more vigorous attention to growth of RNF enterprises, and the need for a comprehensive policy framework and coordinated strategy, in order to support and complement progress toward the goal of full employment in Bangladesh.

6.2 Emerging Role of RNF Employment: Issues and Debates

There can hardly be much contention that developing countries like Bangladesh must continue to expand the modern industry sector, especially manufacturing, in order to raise productivity, employment and incomes. In a planning perspective, major considerations need to be given to the relative weights and the incentives to various sectors vis-à-vis the overall strategy undertaken to enhance growth and employment. The prolonged slow growth of manufacturing employment in Bangladesh, the lack of diversification in the sector[6] are important considerations that need to be factored into the country's policy framework to attain structural transformation and inclusive growth. Besides, the pursuit of a strategy through which labour would seamlessly move to higher productivity modern sectors, is beset with various issues and constraints:

- In economies like Bangladesh, where the initial stock of surplus labour is high, it would be difficult in the short-run, to rely solely on the modern manufacturing sector in *moving the demand curve for labour outward* to absorb labour fast enough to raise the supply price of labour (Mazumdar 1999).
- A nascent, emerging modern industry sector can face its own *binding constraints* that could stall the unbridled growth of the sector (Rodrik 2006), and hence limit the mobility of labour.
- Surplus labour is not a given stock. That is to say, any *unlimited labour* theory should not rest on the premise of getting some of the workers out of agriculture without affecting production in a timeless analysis. Industrial development occurs over time and the real problem of employment necessitates the articulation of a

[6]See Chap. 5, on the overwhelmingly dominant share of readymade garments (RMG) in manufacturing output, employment and exports.

strategy of creating job opportunities through multiple avenues, and not only by diverting the unemployed and underemployed from agriculture.[7]

The above implies that alternative avenues and sources of (productive) employment growth need to be further explored. Industrialisation is critical for structural transformation; but to pursue it, at any cost, such as through an *urban bias* and rents and other privileges, which are likely to introduce distortions, takes attention away from other key sources of employment growth, such as through increased growth of agriculture and agricultural productivity, and non-farm activities and enterprises. As widely observed, agricultural growth is critical not only to address a potential *wage-goods constraint* (that could raise food prices and wages, and thereby slow down labour absorption in the modern sector), but also to enhance earnings in the sector itself. The latter, in turn, would likely enhance demand for non-farm goods and services.

Given the slow growth of industrial employment and limited opportunities of productive and remunerative employment in agriculture, employment has been growing fairly rapidly in the non-farm activities in Bangladesh, as we shall examine shortly.

It is noteworthy that the analytical and empirical literature on the role of RNF activities/enterprises is rather scanty, since much of the development paradigms were confined to exploring agriculture–industry resource and labour flows, and which were subsequently followed by the recognition of, and the burgeoning literature on, the catch-all informal sector.

The attention to the significance and dynamics of the role of RNA in accelerating growth and in supporting equity came from some forceful expositions on the East Asian economies (e.g. China, Taiwan-China, South Korea and Japan). While the *miracle* countries of East Asia are often seen to have pursued the traditional tenet of industrialisation as the main engine of growth (Grilli and Zanalda 1999), the significant role of RNA in those countries as *irrefutable agents* of change has often been underreported. The experience of the early development of East Asian countries, especially Japan, China, South Korea and Taiwan–China, offers formidable illustrations. The story of Japan's industrialisation, which is estimated to have taken half a century to reach the Lewisian turning point, brings out clearly how Japan relied heavily and cautiously on the small and rural enterprises. China, under a different economic set-up, and South Korea and Taiwan-China, under a different timeframe, also underscore similar experiences. In South Korea and Taiwan–China, in the early phase of their transition, there was a dominant non-factory proportion in manufacturing; and even when manufacturing started growing fast, there was a dominant proportion of small-scale enterprises although non-factory production declined substantially. In case of Japan, there are numerous examples to show how policies were carefully planned on ancillary activities, sub-contracts and rural location of industries to produce effective growth linkages between the small and the relatively

[7]For example, Adelman (1984) had contested the industry-first orthodoxy and advocated an agriculture-demand-led industrialisation.

large enterprises. This further illustrates how a country could plan undoing demand constraints that often inhibit the growth of the small RNF enterprises.

In the classic version of the dual model of Lewis (1954), the binary division of the economy, i.e. the subsistence (agriculture) and modern capitalist (industry) sectors, fails to recognise the existence and role of RNA. According to Lewis' postulation, the subsistence sector was seen as a provider of raw materials and wage-goods (marketable surplus), while the modern sector expanded continuously to absorb unlimited surplus labour from agriculture, until full employment equilibrium was reached. Nevertheless, historically speaking, irrespective of the economic level of the less developed economies, there always existed a varied spectrum of non-farm and RNA that produced variable proportions of self-provisioning as well as tradable goods. However, recognition of and support to RNA were confined to paltry budgetary allocations to support non-farm, small and cottage industries, that were largely to serve a *pro-poor* stance rather than integrating them in a *pro-growth* strategy.[8] There were exceptions. Countries, as those in East Asia, in their early stages of growth, according to many experts, viewed the role of RNA and rural industrialisation as pivotal to acceleration of growth (Saith 1987; Oshima 1988).

Apart from a handful of economies such as India, RNA failed to be acknowledged and analytically supported as part of a growth strategy. Hymer and Resnick (1969) was among the early authors to denote these as a catch-all sector, *Z*, to indicate the heterogeneity of activities that are characteristic of a peasant economy, although in their postulation, these were largely treated as homogenous activities. These RNAs, according to Hymer and Resnick, were essentially traits of the economy of the colonial period, and with growth of modern industries and trade in the post-colonial period, would tend to disappear. In their model, on the production side, labour shifted out of Z-goods to increasing cultivation of exportable cash crops; while on the consumption side, imported goods from the modern urban sector would tend to substitute the *self-provisioning* consumption items. All in all, Z-goods would tend to diminish.[9]

Ever since the International Labour Organization's (ILO) Kenya Employment Mission 1971 pointed out a strong pervasive presence of goods and services outside the so-called formal establishments (and coined these as *informal sector*), there has been a plethora of studies on the characterisation and relative role of the informal sector, both within the rural and urban sectors of an individual economy. The informal sector was observed to contain heterogeneous activities ranging from subsistence, artisanal products (*sponge activities*) to a more dynamic range of activities that were productive, profitable and remunerative (see Sect. 6.6) The proliferation of informal sector activities, and the surge in the growth of self-employment was apparently a negation of Hymer and Resnick's postulation.

---

[8]Among others, see Rosegrant and Hazell (2000), Haggblade et al. (2007).

[9]Evidently, the Hymer and Resnick model lacked empirical validation, and was also weak on the assumptions that were used. In particular, by assuming labour as the only input (for which the food and cash crops sectors would compete), the possibility of technology and coexistence of multiple activities, including RNA, is ignored.

Writing two decades later, Ranis and Stewart (1990), challenged the empirical basis and assumptions of the Hymer and Resnick (1969) model and forwarded their own to argue that RNA never perished, but often flourished, and had a positive and critical role to play in accelerating overall growth and job creation in labour surplus economies. They refuted Hymer and Resnick's assumption of a homogeneous Z-goods sector which tend to disappear as labour and land shift to production and exports of cash crops during the post-colonial period. Instead, they introduced two post-colonial scenarios for RNA: the unfavourable and the favourable archetypes. Drawing on the experience of the Philippines, they argue that in the unfavourable archetype, the existence of Z-goods is threatened, largely through the urban bias in policies (i.e. the creation of a modern U-sector) as well as through a neglect of the food producing agricultural sector (A_D), both of which resulted in weak rural linkages. In their post-colonial favourable archetype, exemplified by Taiwan-China, the growth of the A_D sector creates the conditions for a dynamic rural sector. In particular, increased productivity in this sector leads to greater resource availability for investment, and higher incomes for increased household consumption. This would generate greater demand for non-agricultural commodities, and hence increase RNA. Ranis and Stewart (1990) distinguished between those RNA that were traditional (Z_T) and those that were modern (Z_M).

The growth of RNA would critically depend on both favourable macroeconomic policies as well as those targetted to support RNA such as land reforms, infrastructure (e.g. roads, rural electrification), education, etc. In their postulation, Z_T would generally tend to shrink as Z_M flourished through the growth of small factories, modern technology and subsequently, through greater linkages to the urban and export sectors.[10] Thus Ranis and Stewart (1990) contended that not only did RNA continue its existence and flourish in the post-colonial period, but it created conditions that supported structural transformation and full employment in the rural economy. "Z_M gradually displaces Z_T and Z-goods sector retains a substantial, and likely growing, importance at least until the labour surplus has been eliminated" (Ranis and Stewart 1990, p. 10).[11]

A critical dimension of the Ranis and Stewart (1990) model is the introduction and role of a third *Z-goods* sector in the hitherto traditional binary approach to elimination of rural surplus labour.[12] In the backdrop of the above postulations on the alternative scenarios on the role of RNAs, the present study purports to examine, in the sections that follow, the growing importance of RNA and non-farm employment in Bangladesh. With appropriate support and policy interventions, can the RNA sector in Bangladesh evolve into the *favourable archetype* that could generate the potential to achieve a state of *rural full employment*, i.e. a tightening of rural labour

[10]The existence and growth of rural manufacturing goods in the informal sector was recognised by the ILO's Kenya Mission, 1971.

[11]Ranis and Stewart (1990) further argues that a dynamic Z-good sector would lead to a more egalitarian income distribution and the gradual elimination of rural underemployment.

[12]In this context, Ranis and Stewart (1990) specifically stressed the spatial dimension to economic growth.

markets, with increasing rural wages and household incomes? It must be reckoned that Ranis and Stewart (1990) confined their empiricism to rural employment, and did not integrate their RNA analysis in an economy-wide full employment model. Their analysis abstracted from issues of rural–urban migration, as well as resource flows. Nor did they specify at what point, and through what interventions, Z_M would evolve and replace Z_T. Their emphasis has been squarely on accelerating employment and incomes, and in tightening labour markets in rural economy via reducing underemployment. The following sections attempt to provide some insights, based on rather sparse data and existing studies, on the extent and patterns of growth in RNF economy in Bangladesh, and their potential in generating an impetus towards elimination of rural surplus labour.

6.3 Growth of RNF Employment in Bangladesh

During the post-colonial period, and since gaining independence in 1971, Bangladesh has struggled in the face of multiple constraints to recover from a poverty-stricken, food-deficient, low-income country to one that is now relatively robustly growing, and aspiring towards a structural transformation to attain a middle-income country (MIC) status.[13] A standard criterion used to capture this structural transformation in an economy is the extent of inter-sectoral shifts in employment of labour, largely from a low productivity (agriculture) sector to a higher productivity (industry) sector, and following Clarke-Fisher, to a more modern services sector. In Bangladesh, although there have been some important changes in the patterns of inter-sector labour mobility (Hossain et al. 2012), share of industry in total employment still remains relatively low; instead services sector employment has grown more predominantly, much of which include informal activities.[14] In fact, currently informal employment accounts for nearly 85% of the employed workforce.

As can be evinced, within the traditional three-sector framework, the agriculture sector's share in national value-added has declined considerably, but its share in total employment remains persistently high (nearly 41%). This implies, in general, that the sector is characterised by relatively low productivity, surplus labour. Manufacturing employment as percentage of total employed workforce has been increasing, but is still only around 15%, which is significantly lower than the shares achieved by most East and Southeast Asian countries (often 30% or more).[15] The share of services sector has grown in both value-added as well as employment. There is hardly any analysis of inter-sectoral employment to establish whether the current growth is associated with strong trends in labour movements, especially from low productivity agriculture to higher productivity manufacturing (and/or services sector).[16]

[13]See World Bank (2012); also, Gimenez et al. (2014).

[14]See BBS (2018) on recent trends in the growth of employment in the informal sector.

[15]Grilli and Zanalda (1999).

[16]Also see subsequent section on informal sector and structural change.

Table 6.1 Share of farm and non-farm in the rural employment (%)

Sector	1995	2000	2005	2010	2015–16 (LFS)	2016–17 (LFS)
Farm employment	60.36	63.12	56.76	55.16	54.10	51.70
Crop agriculture	54.63	55.19	52.90	49.24	–	–
Non-crop agriculture	5.73	7.93	3.86	5.92	–	–
Non-farm employment	39.64	36.88	43.24	44.84	45.90	48.30
Total	100.00	100.00	100.00	100.00	100.00	100.00

Source Various issues of HIES and LFS

Beyond the broad sectoral and industry-specific employment figures that are observed from the periodic Labour Force Survey (LFS) (which were 5-yearly until recently) and the Household Income and Expenditure Survey (HIES), it is difficult to gather a firm understanding of what has been happening to labour mobility and the factors explaining such shifts; in particular, from agriculture or farm sectors to non-agricultural rural activities (in goods and services). There are a few important survey-based studies, but these are not capable of producing a long-term trend analysis.

With regard to rural employment, an important structural shift concerns the changes in farm and non-farm employment. The LFS and HIES reports provide the following information. According to these sources, non-farm employment constituted more than 48% of all rural employment in 2016–17,[17] having increased from around 37% in 2000. Farm employment has correspondingly declined by nearly 10% points during 1995–2017 (Table 6.1).

Early studies have underscored the rising importance of employment in RNA in Bangladesh. According to Mahmud (1996, p. 6), estimates from 1991 showed that RNF sector accounted "for about one-fourth of the country's entire labour force, more than half of the non-agricultural labour force and about one-third of the rural labour force."[18] Despite the dominance of the RNA sector in the absorption of the rural labour force, the study contends that much of this was due to the expansion of low productivity self-employment in the RNA, which in turn, has constrained the growth of income levels of the sector. In other words, labour shifts appear to have been caused by a land-scarce, overcrowded agriculture. There were limited signs to show that these were due to any strong *pull* effect. The indicators that Mahmud (1996) uses in support of this contention are in respect of rural poverty, per capita rural income, and agricultural wages, all of which have remained virtually unchanged during the 1980s and early 1990s.

Such a contention has however been contested by other studies. In fact, early studies on RNA in Bangladesh had already started the debate on whether the RNF economy was truly a dynamic sector or a *sponge* for absorbing surplus labour (Islam 1987; Hossain et al. 1994; Hossain 2004). One such study, based on a survey of 62

[17]This is from the Preliminary LFS 2016–17.

[18]These shares increase significantly if the semi-urban areas within rural areas are included (Mahmud 1996).

villages, observed that nearly 57% of the households (both landless and land-owning) had at least one member engaged in some RNA. Using a smaller purposive survey of traders and transport workers, the study further finds that labour productivity in most of the activities was tangibly higher than the ruling agricultural wage rate.[19] Similarly, on the demand side, incremental household incomes led to substantial increases in the demand for non-food goods and services. This was particularly marked in the more agriculturally progressive villages. Based on the above and other related indicators, the study concluded that the RNA had the potential for enhancing productivity and household incomes, with agricultural wage labour shifting to self-employment in non-agriculture.[20]

The situation in the Bangladesh rural economy has vastly changed during the more recent decades. Using the same indicators as in Mahmud (1996) one observes that since the mid-1990s, rural poverty has declined and rural per capita income has increased considerably; agricultural real wages has been substantially on an upward trend[21] since 2003–04, although wage growth has stagnated or declined after 2012. A feature closely associated with these developments is the role played by RNA. While RNF activities and employment have always been a significant feature of the rural economy of Bangladesh, these have vastly increased in importance in the recent two decades. The increase in the share of non-farm employment from around 37% in 2000 to more than 48% during 2016–17 is particularly noteworthy.

More recent studies and evidence on the growth of RNA continue to support such a contention. Employment in non-farm which was growing at around 8% till the 1990s (Hossain et al. 1994), maintained its growth momentum during the subsequent decades. Employment in non-farm activities increased from 11.3 million in 2001–03 to 24.5 million in 2013, an increase of 117%. Between the two Economic Census periods, employment growth was nearly 7%; 8.1% in wage employment and 5% in non-wage employment.[22] RNF enterprises grew at nearly 8%, while RNF employment grew at 8.5% (see Table 6.2).[23] The broad and limited data on the relevant indicators suggest a fairly distinct upward trend in the growth of non-farm enterprises and employment.

While the above presents an aggregate perspective on the trends in growth of non-farm enterprises and employment, a more disaggregated picture would provide us with an understanding of which sub-sectors in the non-farm economy are growing relatively faster than others, as well as the proximate reasons for such differential growth. This is shown in Table 6.3, i.e. the growth rates between 2001–03 and 2013, beyond which the Economic Census survey reports are not available.

[19]The study, using the Rural Industry Study Project conducted by Bangladesh Institute of Development Studies (BIDS) during 1978–1981, finds that the average productivity in rural cottage and small industries was about 57% higher than agricultural wage rate.

[20]Hossain (2004).

[21]See GED (2015), Khan (2015).

[22]BBS (2015a).

[23]Various other statistical sources appear to confirm the trend increase in non-farm employment. The HIES also shows the share of employment in 2015–16 to be around 57% of total rural employment increasing from 37% in 2000.

Table 6.2 Growth of non-farm enterprises and non-farm employment in Bangladesh between 2001–03 and 2013

Location	Non-farm enterprises (million)		Growth (%)	Non-farm employment (million)		Growth (%)
	2001–03	2013		2001–03	2013	
Bangladesh	3.71	7.82	6.78	11.27	24.50	7.06
Urban	1.39	2.23	4.32	5.41	9.50	5.13
Rural	2.32	5.59	7.99	5.86	15.00	8.54

Source BBS (2015a)

Table 6.3 Average annual growth of non-farm enterprises and non-farm employment in Bangladesh between 2001–03 and 2013 (%)

Economic activity	Non-farm enterprise			Non-farm employment		
	Total	Urban	Rural	Total	Urban	Rural
Mining and quarrying	23.0	21.4	23.1	13.1	3.1	14.9
Manufacturing	5.6	4.8	5.9	7.6	6.3	8.8
Electricity, gas and water supply	12.2	12.4	12.0	7.6	7.9	7.1
Construction	7.3	4.6	12.1	2.1	0.7	8.1
Wholesale and retail trade	4.3	2.1	5.6	5.3	3.2	6.9
Hotels and restaurants	6.9	6.5	7.1	4.8	2.7	6.3
Transport, storage and communication	25.0	14.1	30.3	19.2	8.8	26.6
Bank, insurance and financial institutions	6.6	6.7	6.4	6.2	5.2	8.1
Real estate and renting	−15.6	−17.0	−13.2	−8.6	−9.2	−6.6
Public administration and defence	0.7	0.3	1.4	4.5	4.4	4.6
Education	2.0	4.9	1.3	4.7	6.1	4.2
Health and social work	2.1	1.0	2.9	5.1	4.8	5.6
Community, social and personal services	7.8	9.3	7.3	8.2	8.0	8.3

Source BBS (2007, 2015a).

According to Table 6.3, non-farm employment has grown commendably in several sub-sectors. In particular, rural employment in manufacturing, construction, bank, insurance and financial institution, and community, social and personal services has grown at more than 8%. Employment in transport, storage and communications has grown at more than 26%. The overall growth of the rural economy, along with infrastructure development, and spread of education in rural areas has enhanced growth of various economic activities and services. Further data and investigation would be required to assess the factors explaining these sub-sectoral growths of enterprises and employment in the RNF economy.

6.4 RNF Employment, Labour Mobility and Push–Pull Factors

There are multiple factors that have led to the overall expansion of RNF employment in Bangladesh. First, there have been major developments and interventions that have created a supportive environment for the growth of RNA. These interventions were not necessarily undertaken within a coordinated policy framework to foster the growth of RNA. Rather, various measures such as those to boost agricultural growth and labour-based public works programme, etc. had contributed to the growth of RNA in Bangladesh. Second, there are various micro-level factors that have influenced individual households to engage and participate in RNAs. However, owing to lack of appropriate data on RNA and RNF employment, there have been few (i.e. those that are based on household surveys and panel data) that have attempted to establish the relative importance of factors influencing RNF employment and the changing structure of the rural labour force (Hossain 2004). There cannot however be much dispute that the spurt of agricultural growth in Bangladesh opened up opportunities for major expansion of RNA activities, through product, consumption and labour market linkages. This is consistent with the Ranis-Stewart's *favourable archetype* of RNA expansion that is significantly influenced by increased productivity in food-agriculture. The impact of substantial increase in land and labour productivity has led to tangible increase in agricultural wages and rural household incomes. This is further examined in a following section.

There are, of course, many other notable factors that have made significant contribution to the expansion of RNA in Bangladesh. Mention may be made of the considerable expansion in rural infrastructure that has led to the expansion of markets and facilitation of non-agricultural job growth (self-employment, construction, transport and communication, wholesale and retail trade, etc.).[24] Similarly, there has been an increase in education and skill development which has supported access to higher paid jobs, especially in the services sector. A special mention may be made of the role of financial inclusion (FI) initiatives, both by the non-government organisations (NGOs) and public sector. In the near absence of financial services and lending from

[24]Hossain (2004).

the traditional banking and financial institutions, this movement gathered speed and space, largely through the reputed institutions such as Grameen Bank, BRAC, Palli Karma-Sahayak Foundation (PKSF), etc. Recently, there has been a major drive towards FI initiative to provide greater access to credit markets, and in supporting small-scale enterprises.[25] The objectives of these initiatives are being expanded from being purely poverty-reducing instruments to their wider application to various hitherto underserved and unbanked sectors, regions and population groups. An emphatic development has been the upsurge in entrepreneurship in rural areas (particularly women entrepreneurs). FIs are seen as a major avenue to develop financial structures and to deepen the financial sector by strengthening and extending institutions to non-traditional sectors.[26]

While the forces and factors described above have created the broad impulses and conditions conducive to the growth of RNA in Bangladesh, the underlying structural changes that may have occurred need to be assessed through an understanding of labour market mobility and the changing structure of the labour force.[27] Furthermore, whether these labour movements have been driven by so-called push or pull factors would certainly require a detailed mapping of household behaviour factors explaining such mobility.

Very few studies exist on the forces explaining whether and to what extent labour mobility is accounted for by push or pull factors. This is significant, since if it is the former, it would tend to denote an immiserizing growth of RNA, while the latter would tend to define a degree of dynamism in the sector. Studies indicate that it is not simply the landless, who due to lack of employment and earnings in agriculture, have engaged themselves in non-farm activities. A sizeable proportion of the landowning households are also observed to have significant non-farm engagements.[28]

Most of the early empirical evidence, from the 1980 and 1990s, with a few notable exceptions, tend to suggest that RNA expanded horizontally, soaking up surplus rural labour in marginal low-paying jobs. However, others offered an opposing contention. For instance, Hossain (2004) provides important insights, based on a relatively large

[25]See Chap. 4 in this volume for insights on the growth and influence of FIs, especially on the rural agriculture and rural self-employment initiatives.

[26]These are important initiatives, and are likely to generate an ethos of expanding credit extension, not only through corporate social responsibility (CSR)-induced programmes, but through normal banking channels as well. Some banks are already experimenting in mobile financial services (MFS). BRAC Bank launched (in 2011) its subsidiary, bKash, which is using the mobile banking platform to reach MFS to millions of unbanked populations.

[27]Such structural changes could be, for example, "from farm to nonfarm, from informal to formal, and from low to high skilled economic activities" (Shilpi and Emran 2016, p. 2). Also see Ranis and Stewart (1990).

[28]Apart from the size of landownership there are several other factors that tend to obscure the debate on household behaviour; e.g. whether the survey analysis refers to workers or labour time, to head of household or total members in household, to issues of principal or subsidiary occupations, varying extent of ownership of physical and human capital, or to whether households belong to agriculturally backward or progressive regions, etc. (Hossain 2004).

intertemporal village-level survey and panel data,[29] and attempts to distinguish some of the push–pull factors that tend to explain participation in RNA:

- In general, manual-work-centric activities, especially transport and construction, appear to be poverty-induced; whereas education and access to capital tends to explain greater participation in services and business activities. These are likely to offer higher earnings than in the farm sector.
- The study estimates that labour productivity in the services and business activities is 2–3.5 times higher than the agricultural wage rate. The panel data show that productivity increased across all categories of RNA, except cottage industries and rickshaw transport.
- Household income during the panel survey period (1987–2000) had increased tangibly, predominantly through earnings from RNA.
- Income elasticity of demand is positive for all RNA services, business and other non-farm activities.

Another panel study of rural households conducted over a three-year period (between 2010 and 2012) recorded a sizeable shift of the workforce from farm to non-farm activities. The study also conducted statistical tests to examine determinants of labour mobility. The findings broadly corroborated those in Hossain (2004) as noted above.[30]

While agricultural productivity and intensity of agricultural growth have unleashed the initial impulses of RNA growth,[31] there are several other factors that need to be closely examined regarding the relative influence of these push–pull factors. In particular, a flourish in the RNA sector will be characterised by, inter alia, a trend increase in demand for RNA goods and services, an increasing labour productivity in RNA sub-sectors, and an increasing differential between farm and non-farm wages (Oshima 1988). These characterisations are briefly examined in a subsequent section.

6.5 Changing Patterns in Rural Labour Markets: Recent Developments

Irrespective of the pull or push forces determining increasing participation in RNA, the sector has shown strong growth, especially during the past two decades. Table 6.2 rendered a snapshot of the growth of non-farm enterprises and employment, both in

[29]This is a BIDS-IRRI (International Rice Research Institute) survey of 1245 rural households from 62 villages in 57 districts, conducted in FY1987–88. This benchmark survey was followed by an IRRI survey of 1880 households from the same villages, and covered the households in the former survey. See Hossain (2004).

[30]See Pramanik et al. (2014).

[31]Such a process is historically observed in various other countries, see for example, Ranis and Stewart (1990) for Taiwan-China; Oshima (1988) for Taiwan-China and Japan; and Shilpi and Emran (2016) for Bangladesh.

rural and urban areas of Bangladesh during 2001–03 and 2013. Average employment size of a non-farm rural enterprise had increased from 2.5 to 2.7 persons per enterprise during the mentioned period. The Economic Census 2013 provides further insights on the growth rates and changing structure of rural establishments and employment (Table 6.4).

Establishments, dubbed as permanent, had grown at more than 4% during 2001–2013, and employment in these establishments had more than 7% growth. Economic households, i.e. households which engage a significant proportion of labour time in non-agricultural activities (shops, hawkers, cottage activities, etc.) had increased significantly (18%). These characteristics of the rural enterprise sector clearly show the trends towards increasing participation in RNA for additional household income.

The above trends are beginning to be reflected in the changing occupational structures and labour market formation in the rural areas, although it is too early to make any definitive conclusions. This is reflected in Tables 6.5 and 6.6 which draw on the most recent LFS available.

Table 6.4 Growth rates of rural establishments and employment between 2001–03 and 2013 (%)

Type	Establishment	Employment
Permanent	4.09	7.22
Temporary	6.86	8.05
Economic households[a]	18.26	13.90
Total (rural)	7.99	8.54

Source BBS (2015a).
Note [a]Those with non-agricultural economic activities (e.g. cottage activities, shops, hawkers, etc.)

Table 6.5 Changing structure of employed labour force by sector in rural Bangladesh

Sector	Employed workforce (as % of total employed)		
	2013	2015–16	2016–17
Agriculture, forestry, fishing	56.2	54.1	51.7
Manufacturing	13.9	11.3	11.3
Construction	3.4	5.2	5.3
Wholesale and retail trade	10.4	10.9	11.8
Transportation and storage	5.5	6.7	7.8
Admin and support services	0.5	0.4	0.4
Education	2.3	2.8	2.8
Other service activities	2.2	3.4	3.6
Accommodation and food services	1.2	1.4	1.5
Financial and insurance	0.4	0.3	0.3

Source BBS (2015b, 2017, 2018).

Table 6.6 Changing occupational structure in rural Bangladesh

Category	Share of employed labour force (%)											
	2005–06			2013			2015–16			2016–17		
	M	F	T	M	F	T	M	F	T	M	F	T
Employer	0.3	0.1	0.3	0.9	0.1	0.6	2.9	0.3	2.1	6.0	0.6	4.3
Own account worker[a]	51.5	11.6	42.0	55.9	11.5	42.7	51.1	36.8	46.7	49.4	44.0	47.6
Contributing family worker	10.9	71.8	25.5	5.7	59.0	21.3	5.3	44.9	17.6	4.6	34.2	14.1
Employee[b]	35.9	12.9	30.4	37.5	26.5	34.3	40.1	17.6	33.1	39.3	20.7	33.3
Others[c]	1.3	3.7	1.9	0.3	2.9	1.1	0.5	0.4	0.4	0.7	0.5	0.6
Total	100	100	100	100	100	100	100	100	100	100	100	100

Source Various issues of LFS

Note M, F and T implies male, female and total, respectively

[a]Self-employed in 2005–06

[b]Includes all paid regular, irregular and day labourers

[c]Includes domestic help/apprentices

According to the LFS surveys, over the past two decades, there has been a substantial decline in the proportion of rural employed labour force in agriculture and allied sectors. There has been a general increase in employment in most of professional, sales and services sector work. During the more recent five years 2013–2017, the proportion of those employed in agriculture and allied sectors had fallen markedly, from 56.2 to 51.7%, while the proportion of those engaged in most non-agricultural occupations had increased, notably in construction, wholesale/retail trades, transport/storage, education and other services, etc. (Table 6.5).

There are some distinctive changes in the occupational structure of the rural labour force. A noteworthy feature is the marked increase in the incidence of the *employer* category, from a negligible 0.3% in 2005–06 to 4.3% in 2016–17. Similarly, the incidence of *own account worker* also increased tangibly. More significantly, a striking feature of the changes in occupational structure was reflective of the changing patterns of women participation in the rural economy. During the decade 2005–06 to 2016–17, while the total incidence of own account workers was seen to have increased by 5%, the proportion of rural females under this category increased nearly four-fold, from 11.6 to 44%. This is a significant development since the participation of rural women has surged in various self-employment activities and microenterprises, thanks to the multitude initiatives by the government and non-government organisations to enhance women's productive participation in the economy. This appears to be consistent with the 18% growth rate in economic households, observed in Table 6.4. Further, the proportion of total contributing family workers declined substantially by 11% points, and for females, it declined even more sharply. The share of total employees (i.e. paid workers) had increased by about 3% during the 15-year period, by 8% for female workers. One also observes that there has been a decline in the incidence of domestic helps/apprentices. Although some of these shifts are not very large, there is, nevertheless, a trend in labour movement away from unpaid/family/domestic work towards paid wage employment and own account work (Table 6.6).

The incidence of workers working full-time in rural enterprises had grown at 8.3% from 53.9 million in 2001–03 to 61.7 million in 2013 (Table 6.7). During the same period unpaid family workers declined significantly from 11.2 million to 5.3 million. These are important trends in the changing workforce structures vis-à-vis the growth of RNA in Bangladesh.

Table 6.7 Percentage of employed persons (by working status) in establishments

Working status of employed person	2001–03 (million)	2013 (million)	Growth (%)
Working proprietor	31.11	30.01	6.76
Unpaid family worker	11.20	5.29	0.24
Full-time worker	53.90	61.71	8.29
Part-time worker	3.90	1.98	1.02
Casual worker	–	1.01	–
Total	100.00	100.00	7.06

Source BBS (2015a)

The labour market outcomes, as observed in Table 6.7, reflect perceptible movements of labour away from the unpaid non-wage sectors to wage and salaried RNA activities. Nevertheless, closer analysis and a significant database are required to assess methodologically the extent of these changes in the labour market structures, and to understand how far the pull factors are consolidating in the RNA sectors. The differentials in wages, productivity, skills in the various sub-sectors of RNA (both in goods and services) need to be monitored over time. In the absence of an adequate and appropriate database, it is difficult to assess how robust this labour mobility is, what factors are responsible, and whether such shifts in labour can continue at an adequate pace vis-à-vis the existing slack in the labour market to bring about a structural change which is sustainable.

6.6 Structural Change in a Milieu of Growing Informal Sector: A Rethink

6.6.1 Gaps in Assessment

A particular reason why in a country like Bangladesh, labour movements in a traditional three-sector analysis fail to show any robust structural change is the existence of informal activities and employment, in all the three sectors. Table 6.8 provides some insights from the three LFS between 2013 and LFS 2016–17 on the overwhelming presence of informal employment in agriculture, industry and services sectors.

According to the LFS 2016–17, informal employment represents nearly 96, 91, and 74% in the aforementioned sectors, respectively. The massive dominance of informal employment in all the three traditional sectors implies that when labour moves across sectors, there is a high probability that workers may be moving from one informal occupation to another.

The informal sector employment as registered in the LFS is a catch-all figure which captures unregistered (informal) workers working through informal arrangements, including in both registered or unregistered enterprises, as casual labour, as well as in

Table 6.8 Formal and informal employment in the traditional sectors (%)

Sector	2013		2015–16		2016–17	
	Formal	Informal	Formal	Informal	Formal	Informal
Agriculture	2.4	97.6	2.0	98.0	4.5	95.5
Industry	5.6	94.4	9.2	90.8	9.4	90.6
Services	22.9	77.1	27.8	72.2	25.7	74.3
Total	8.3	91.7	10.7	89.3	11.9	88.1

Source BBS (2015b, 2017, 2018)

personal household work (unpaid family or domestic work), or in self-employment.[32] Given the current LFS definition, in the rural areas, practically the entire labour force, barring a paltry 12%, belong to the informal sector through one or more of the above categories. This implies that within each of the three traditional sectors, i.e. agriculture, industry and services, despite the recent increases in formal employment, the large majority of employment is still in the so-called informal category.

A major gap in this regard is the lack of any systematic evidence to assess the *relative importance and role of informal activities and employment within the respective sectors* (ADB and BBS 2012). Apart from the one single national informal sector survey (ISS) (2010), there is neither any periodic national-level survey nor any trend analysis nor any database to *deconstruct* the informal sector in order to understand the structural changes and dynamism of the economic activities taking place within the sector. It is interesting to note that between the two LFS periods in Table 6.7, informal employment has declined (and formal employment increased) more tangibly in the services sector. While this is often contrary to the received wisdom that in developing countries it is the services sector which accounts for much of the expansion in informal employment, this must not necessarily imply that the services sector in Bangladesh is a *sponge* sector.

As mentioned above, much of the analytical attention is geared towards RNA (e.g. manufacturing, construction, services), which hitherto had been, and still are, subsumed under informal activities. Similarly, we also observe a steady growth in self-employment, which too needs to be unpacked to understand which activities/enterprises have been gaining pace and momentum, especially in creating a sustained demand for labour. The self-employed workforce has increased from 19.8 million in 2003 to around 27 million in 2016–17.[33]

A more searching analysis is required to investigate the changes that are taking place in the patterns of rural employment and labour market structures *within the so-called informal sector*. Furthermore, owing to increasing modernisation/commercialisation, and use of technology, various activities/products, e.g. *dhekis* and manual handlooms are getting extinct. Thus, in Bangladesh, there is the existence of an overwhelming and growing informal sector, where there exists not only tremendous heterogeneity, but also exits of traditional activities along with the growth of new enterprises and activities. The catch-all informal sector, which contains more than four-fifths of the employed workforce, could not be dismissed as stagnant or dormant in a milieu of rapid and prolonged growth of gross domestic product (GDP). A recent study, ADB and BBS (2012), based on the first national survey, the ISS (2010) and Economic Census, underscores not only the growing significance of informal sector's contribution to Bangladesh's GDP, but also its growing efficiency, in terms of labour productivity (largely in non-capital-intensive sectors) as well as,

[32]Note, there have been definitional changes of informal employment in the LFS; LFS 2010 included not only those in informal unregistered enterprises, but also those informally employed in formal enterprises, as well as unpaid family, domestic work that were excluded previously; LFS 2013 additionally included enterprise criteria of no pension or no contribution to retirement fund (see Rahman et al., 2018).

[33]Various issues of LFS.

Table 6.9 Labour productivity by type of selected economic activity

Economic activity	Gross value-added per job (thousand BDT)		
	Formal	Informal	Total
Agriculture, hunting, forestry and fishery	39.1	49.0	47.2
Manufacturing	562.1	88.5	185.0
Construction	1,028.6	81.6	213.5
Wholesale and retail trade; repair of motor vehicles and motorcycles	149.7	135.7	140.1
Hotel, accommodation and food service activities	168.0	34.3	64.0
Transportation, storage and communication	592.7	60.1	182.2
Real estate and other business activities	1,116.6	330.5	697.7
Education	232.5	31.5	143.4

Source ADB and BBS (2012)

their organisation and working conditions (Table 6.9). This is broadly in conformity with the findings previously reported on productivity performance of the RNF activities and enterprises which are informal.

6.6.2 Formalising the Informal Sector

As noted in an earlier section, there have been sporadic studies, occasionally based on limited surveys, to show dualism in the informal sector, with some enterprises showing dynamism, and others dubbed as entities for survival. How is this dualism rationalised or reconciled with the *formal–informal dichotomy* as definitionally established in LFS? Should the so-called informal enterprises or entities (e.g. economic households as in Bangladesh Enterprise Survey 2013) be seen in terms of conventional (LFS) definition of having registration, pension fund contribution and formal contracts? Or in an orthodox development perspective where the differences in enterprises are seen in terms of investment, savings, technology, etc.? A recent study, Rahman et al. (2018) contends that one can discern the existence of a *formalisation spectrum* within the informal enterprises, and argues that the formal–informal dichotomy is often blurred.[34] Based on the ISS 2010 and using various criteria to establish the gradations of formalisation,[35] the study finds that productivity and

[34]For example, out of all registered enterprises, not all are registered for value added tax (VAT); and from among the latter, not all pay VAT.

[35]These included factors such as technology, financial tools, record keeping, legal dimensions, etc. See McKenzie (2010).

profitability, even after controlling for firm size and owner characteristics, increase substantially along the spectrum. Such a stance in some ways calls for a rethink of the traditional dichotomy, and queries what should be a standard formal enterprise or employment. This further implies that greater clarity is needed on designing policies that would be consistent with an appropriate strategy towards transitions to formality.[36] This is noteworthy, since there are policy campaigns to *formalise* the informal sector, usually accompanied by significant fiscal cover, as observed in many Latin American countries that concentrate on narrowing differences in regulatory frameworks governing the enterprises and the labour markets in the formal and informal sectors. On the other hand, from the findings above, though limited, there is an equally strong case to pursue the *formalisation spectrum*, i.e. for enterprises and employment to grow in their *gradations*, through strategic support to facilitate access to technology, credit markets, and to domestic and external demand. This is an arduous process which would require focused policy and resource support.[37] A careful calibration and sequencing of the two sets of policies would be needed for a smoother transition out of informality, as currently defined in Bangladesh. In other words, for informality to decline (i.e. conditions as defined by LFS 2013), an increase in registration, tax and other regulatory compliances among enterprises are pivotal, but a credible decline in unpaid family workers, domestic workers, etc., through policies and interventions to increase in productivity and income, is equally, if not more, significant.

Although there exist several studies on the informal sector, some based on limited, purposive surveys and others on rural industries and RNA, there is still a dearth of systematic knowledge and understanding of jobs and enterprise growth along the formal–informal dichotomy, especially trends in sub-sectoral productivity, employment and wages that could allow more convincing conclusions on the structural changes that may arguably be taking place.

6.7 Pathways to Rural 'Full Employment'

Bangladesh, like many of the contemporary developing countries, is yet to achieve a distinct structural change that could be dubbed as consistent with the Kaldorian pattern of economic transition. The agriculture sector has not been shedding labour at a fast-enough pace nor has the manufacturing sector employment been growing adequately enough to absorb the annual additions to the labour force and the existing stock of surplus labour. There is thus the need to look beyond a simple *industry fundamentalism*. The critical issue is that in order to ensure structural change, labour would need to shift to higher productivity sectors, irrespective of whether such productivity

---

[36]See Ghose (2017), who challenges the traditional formal–informal dichotomy, maintaining that such a view is an import from Western analysts on dualism in post-colonial developing countries. Also see Chen (2003).

[37]See Chandrasekhar and Ghosh (2018) on constraints to formalisation in the context of India.

lies in manufacturing, services or agriculture, and to higher productivity activities, whether these are in formal or informal enterprises and activities.[38]

Structural change primarily rests, among others, on increasing labour productivity, and hence, on investment and capital accumulation. In East Asian countries, not only was labour productivity high in agriculture and in modern sectors, but it was also more significant than in other Asian countries. While RNA was strongly facilitated by higher productivity in agriculture, there was, equally, a focused policy attention to rural development and RNA growth and its linkages to regional urban and international markets (Ranis and Stewart 1990; Saith 1987; Islam 1987; Haggblade et al. 2007). While there are several accounts now that have highlighted the role RNA has played in the process of growth and employment generation, Ranis and Stewart (1990), as noted above, emphasised its critical role in *wiping out* unemployment and bringing about a situation of *rural full employment*.[39]

As alluded to previously, one must be cautious about the claim by Ranis and Stewart (1990) in attaining *rural full employment* through RNA growth, since their study neither introduced the significance of inter-sectoral flows, nor rural–urban migration, with long-term implications for stability of such full employment. The indicators have rather been on establishing the process of tightening of rural labour markets, and corresponding rise in wages and household incomes. On migration flows in Bangladesh, recent net in-migration rates show that intra-sectoral (i.e. within rural and within urban) have been higher than inter-sectoral migration (see Annex Table 6.17). While rural–urban growth of net migration appeared to remain constant (at around 30 per 1000 population), rural–rural in-migration, has more than doubled during 2011–2018, from 15 to 33.7 (per 1,000 population). It would be interesting to understand the factors behind this rapid expansion in rural intra-sectoral movement, in particular, the pull–push factors. In East Asian economies, growth of the modern sector, especially through labour-intensive export-oriented industrialisation, facilitated a strong rural–urban migration.[40] Oshima (1988) has, in the context of East Asian economies, pointed out the significant role of RNA, especially in raising the rural household income and aggregate demand, which in turn, would reduce unemployment, underemployment and raise wages of farm and unskilled workers.[41] These are significant factors in pushing up overall aggregate demand in the economy.

For Bangladesh, from an aggregate policy perspective, there are at least three critical interrelated developments that, among others, need to be monitored, i.e. those which could enforce a dynamic role of the RNA in achieving acceleration in

[38]Lewis (1954), while proposing the primacy of the growth of the modern industrial sector also acknowledged the significance of improved labour productivity in agriculture in the process of structural change; a potential decline in food/wage goods production would cause a rise in prices and wages.

[39]Note, the text follows a qualified view of *full employment*.

[40]One may note that in South Korea during the early stages of industrialisation (1970s), nearly three quarters of the rural labour force that migrated to urban areas were in fact absorbed by the manufacturing sector. See Edgren and Muqtada (1990).

[41]Oshima (1988) further contended that reaching a state of rural full employment would facilitate capital labour substitution and help accelerate growth in the overall economy.

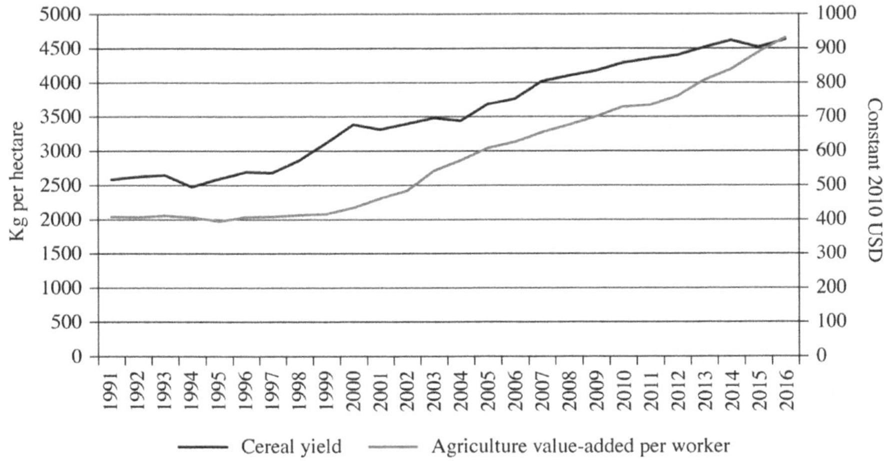

Fig. 6.1 Land and labour productivity trends in agriculture. *Source* World Bank (n.d.). *Note* Agriculture value-added per worker is shown in the right vertical axis

jobs/income growth, and a drastic reduction in slack in the labour market. These are: (i) rapid and sustained growth in agricultural productivity; (ii) growth in RNF productivity and earnings; and (iii) growth in rural household income and an increasing demand for non-farm products. There needs to be a virtuous cycle between increase in productivity and household incomes and the growth of RNA.[42]

6.7.1 Growth in Agricultural Productivity

Given the land and food scarcity that existed since its independence, Bangladesh pursued a concerted policy towards growth of food-agriculture. A progressive policy stance and a significant growth in food-agriculture are often critically related to growth and flourish in RNA (as observed in the East Asian countries during the early stages of their development).[43] In Bangladesh too, a rapid intensification in food-agriculture,[44] that was intermediated through various policy and pervasive intervention measures (e.g. inter alia input subsidies, irrigation programmes, price support and extension services), greatly supported attainment of near self-sufficiency in food production. This also resulted in a significantly increasing trend in both land and labour productivity (see Fig. 6.1).

Several analytical and empirical studies have weighed-in to point out the significance of agricultural productivity and growth in investible agriculture as a precursor

[42]See Oshima (1988).

[43]See Ranis and Stewart (1990), Rosegrant and Hazell (2000), Shilpi and Emran (2016).

[44]This was achieved through widespread introduction of high-yielding variety (HYV) technology, input subsidies, extension services, irrigation and mechanisation, etc.

Table 6.10 Growth rates (%) of land and labour productivity in agriculture (selected Asian countries)

Country	Value-added/agricultural worker 1980–2010	Cultivable area	Land productivity	Agricultural GDP
Bangladesh	2.10	−0.16	2.29	2.13
India	1.70	0.07	2.51	2.58
China	3.80	0.50	4.53	4.04
Indonesia		1.27	2.14	3.41
Malaysia	3.20	1.35	1.55	2.94
Pakistan	1.60	0.25	3.18	3.43
Thailand	2.00	0.82	2.17	2.99
Vietnam	2.10	1.70	2.00	3.70

Source Author's adaptation from Briones and Felipe (2013)

to the progressive growth of RNA.[45] Intensification and diversification of agriculture not only release resources for RNA, it also relaxes the wage-goods constraint. In Bangladesh, there has been an increase in labour productivity, largely owing to the intensification of food-agriculture. This is consistent with the Ranis and Stewart's (1990) condition for enhancing the favourable archetype of RNA. During the period 1980–2010, agricultural labour productivity in Bangladesh grew at a rate of 2.1% (Table 6.10), which compares favourably with several Asian countries (except China and Malaysia). The increase in the average productivity of labour in agriculture appears to be positively correlated with average productivity of land (e.g. yield per hectare).[46]

Given scarcity of land and declining trends in cultivable area (declining at − 0.16%), the growth in land productivity has supported the growth of labour productivity. Although land productivity has grown appreciably, output per hectare is still below that in some of the Asian neighbours, and far below what was attained by the East and Southeast Asian countries during their structural transformation.[47]

Bangladesh is, however, reaching a critical limit on how far it can depend on land productivity to enhance labour productivity, and potentially the supply price of labour. The recent increasing trends in land productivity have been achieved due to the overwhelming role of HYV rice and related technological developments and support structures; in particular, the spread of irrigation, input subsidies price support, extension services, etc. This has enabled Bangladesh to increase its total food production three-fold since the 1970s, and to achieve near food self-sufficiency. The predominant role of HYV rice is clear from Table 6.11.

[45]See Haggblade et al. (2007), Hossain (2004), Shilpi and Emran (2016).

[46]There are empirical studies to show that, assuming fixed input coefficients per unit of output, with increases in yield, there would be an implicit increase in the average productivity of labour, and a corresponding increase in the real agricultural wage rate (Bannerjee 2007).

[47]See Oshima (1988).

Table 6.11 Role of HYV rice in coping with food self-sufficiency

Year	Share of rice land under HYVs (%)	HYV output as share of total rice output (%)
1970–1975	11	29
1976–1980	14	29
1981–1985	24	41
1986–1990	34	51
1991–1995	48	65
1996–2000	57	74
2001–2005	66	80
2006–2010	79	89

Source Alam and Islam (2012)

However, HYV rice which has accounted for growth in yield per hectare, already occupies nearly four-fifths of the cultivable land for rice. In order to further enhance land productivity, which is still significantly lower than most East and Southeast Asian countries, a well-coordinated intensification and diversification of agriculture would be required. However, this will require careful evaluation and calibrated planning regarding available scarce land that would need to be allocated to food, non-food and non-farm activities.

6.7.2 Growth in RNF Productivity and Earnings

As labour productivity in agriculture (and intensification of cultivation) continues to increase, it has also generally led to increases in the supply price of labour (Mazumdar 1999).[48] This was the experience of the East Asian, and several other countries in the early stages of their development.[49] In Bangladesh, since FY2003-04, there has been a distinct upward trend in aggregate real wages in agriculture, although the growth rate has dipped somewhat during the past five years.[50] Nevertheless, real wages (male, BDT/day) in absolute terms have more than doubled since 2004.

As noted earlier, there are very few studies on the productivity growth of the various sub-sectors of the RNF economy in Bangladesh. Of these, Hossain (2004), based on the BIDS survey of rural industries, observed that RNA productivity was substantially larger than agricultural wages for almost all industries. This, and various other related indicators, show the necessary conditions for labour mobility from farm to non-farm sectors, which in turn is likely to boost earnings and productivity in the latter.

[48]"It is necessary to pursue the supplementary strategy of increasing the supply price of labour directly in the subsistence sector by increasing land productivity" (Mazumdar 1999, p. 6).

[49]See among others, Haggblade et al. (2007).

[50]Also see Khan (2015).

Wages and earnings are expected to increase simultaneously when the RNF economy is growing as a result of increased demand and increasing labour productivity. Various studies point out that productivity and earnings in several non-farm sub-sectors (construction, professional and services sector jobs) in rural areas appear to have increased faster than agricultural wages.[51] Table 6.12 shows that while wages in 2016–17 in manufacturing, wholesale and retail trade activities were more than 30% higher than in agriculture, they were significantly higher in services sector activities (education, health and social work).[52] All the indices had increased, though modestly in manufacturing, during 2013 and 2016–17. This is consistent with a *pull* scenario, where a growth in non-farm productivity has the *potential* to induce and absorb workers out of agriculture.

According to the study by Hossain (2004), share of non-farm income in total income increased during the 12-year period of the study for *all income groups*, especially those in the middle- and upper-income deciles (see Table 6.13). It is still premature to suggest whether such changing composition of household income truly reflects strong transition towards a structural change in output and labour markets.

At the aggregate level, HIES data tends to show that agriculture had declined in importance as a source of rural household income, from 35% in 2000 to 30% in 2010, partly supporting a period of transition. The study further corroborates that there has been an increase in household savings which has allowed the growth of various RNA activities.[53] It is interesting to note that while there has been a spurt in microcredit lending, the bulk of investments that the rural households make in RNA activities is met largely by household savings.

Income shares provide a more reasonable guide to the relative importance of different non-farm sectors, but this kind of data is hardly available on a representative scale. Among various other factors that have contributed to household incomes, a significant one is the spread of education. This is clearly observed from the increase in primary and secondary enrolment in rural areas. Education has enabled members of rural households to engage in outside farm activities and in several RNA activities such as in trade, transport, health, education, social work and other services sector occupations (see Table 6.12).

[51]For example, see Hossain (2004), Osmani et al. (2015).

[52]Table 6.12, which refers to salaried employees in various sectors.

[53]Hossain (2004, p. 23), based on HIES (2000), through his assessment of income elasticities of demand by rural households, argues that since "the non-farm income is now a major component of the rural income, and the rural income has been growing in spite of the sluggish performance of agriculture, the respectable growth in non-farm income itself with generate demand for non-farm goods and services."

Table 6.12 Rural employment and income scenario

Sector/industry	Employed person (thousand)				Growth (%)		Relative monthly income (agriculture = 100)	
	2000	2010	2013	2016–17	2000–2010	2010–2016–17	2013	2016–17
Agriculture, forestry and fisheries	18,357	22,745	23,570	22,689	23.9	−0.2	100	100
Manufacturing	2,266	4,193	5,813	4,959	85.0	18.3	121	131
Construction	735	1,800	1,415	2,326	144.9	29.2	106	110
Wholesale and retail trade, repair of motor vehicles	3,654	5,482	4,364	5,178	50.0	−5.5	130	131
Transportation and storage	1,376	2,804	2,316	3,423	103.8	22.1	121	127
Accommodation and food services activities	310	578	504	658	86.5	13.9	121	126
Public administration and defence	306	282	340	439	−7.8	55.6	151	235
Education	731	867	982	1,229	18.6	41.7	155	260
Human health and social work activities	176	283	287	219	60.8	−22.5	144	216
Activities of households as employers	–	610	532	439	–	−28.1	78	91

Source Author's compilation from various issues of LFS

Table 6.13 Pattern of distribution of income from non-farm sources: 1987 and 2000

Rank in per capita income scale	Share of household income (%)		Share of non-farm income (%)		Non-farm income (% of household income)	
	1987	2000	1987	2000	1987	2000
Bottom 40	17.1	14.1	12.5	10.7	30.6	40.8
Middle 40	37.1	34.8	32.3	34.1	36.3	53.2
Ninth decile	14.0	16.2	13.0	16.6	38.7	55.3
Top 10	31.8	35.0	42.2	38.5	55.5	59.2
Total	100.0	100.0	100.0	100.0	41.6	54.2

Source Hossain (2004)

6.7.3 Changing Structure of Household Income and Demand for RNF Goods and Services

Growth in agricultural productivity, as observed in various countries, has had a positive correlation with growth of employment and incomes in RNAs.[54] This appears to be the case in Bangladesh as well. These developments are registered in the increasing growth of rural household incomes. According to HIES 2010, rural per capita income in Bangladesh had increased by around 58%, nearly by as much as per capita urban income, during 2005 and 2010. This increase of income in the rural areas is further corroborated by various other studies, based on fairly large sample surveys. For instance, Hossain (2004) provides support to such a finding from a longitudinal survey of household income and expenditure patterns. According to this study, average per capita household income during the survey over two points in time (1987–2000) grew at nearly 2.8%. A more recent study by Osmani et al. (2015), based on a large sample survey, estimated a growth of 3.7% in rural income during the decade 2000–2010, which was encouragingly higher than the 2.8% growth observed during the preceding decade.[55] This has also led to significant improvements in related indicators, such as consumption expenditures on non-food and non-farm products and services (such as on education). Consumption expenditure, in nominal terms, increased from BDT 5,165 in 2005 to BDT 9,436 in 2010 and BDT 13,868 in 2016. The proportion of non-food expenditure increased from about 41% in 2005 to nearly 50% in 2016 (Table 6.14).

The increasing share of household income originating from the non-farm activities has been observed earlier. Figure 6.2 shows the significant changes in the relative shares of household incomes from various sources from 1995–96 to 2010. While the relative income share from agriculture had fallen, those from wage earnings and business and commerce had increased significantly. It can also be observed that, over the past two decades, remittances have been playing a dominant role in contributing

[54]See Rosegrant and Hazell (2000).

[55]See Osmani et al. (2015). The study is based on a survey of 6300 households.

Table 6.14 Household income and expenditure in Bangladesh (BDT)

Income and expenditure	2005			2010			2016		
	Total	Rural	Urban	Total	Rural	Urban	Total	Rural	Urban
Income	7,203	9,095	10,463	11,479	9,648	16,475	15,945	13,353	22,565
Total expenditure	6,134	5,319	8,533	11,200	9,612	15,531	15,715	14,156	19,697
Consumption expenditure	5,964	5,165	8,315	11,003	9,436	15,276	15,420	13,868	19,383
Food expenditure	3,209	3,023	3,756	6,031	5,543	7,362	7,355	7,002	8,255
Non-food expenditure (% of consumption expenditure)	46.2	41.5	54.8	45.2	41.3	51.8	52.3	49.5	57.4

Source Author's compilation from various issues of HIES.

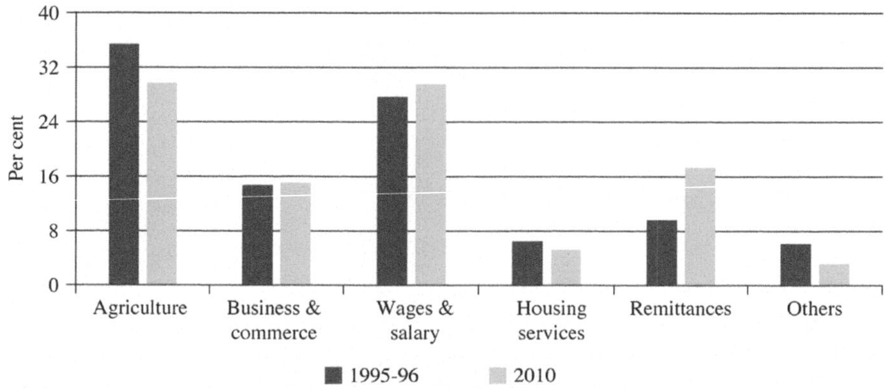

Fig. 6.2 Sources of rural household income: 1995–96 and 2010. *Source* BBS (1998, 2011)

to rural regeneration in general, and in raising average rural household incomes. The above, along with increasing housing and construction and other services sector, are expected to further boost rural incomes from RNA.

From the above discussions and available evidence, it can be noted that labour has been steadily flowing to RNF activities with earnings/salaries from most such activities being relatively higher than in agriculture. The general rise in household incomes, as well as the changing structure of income and expenditure is further reflected in the rising demand for non-farm goods and services. This lends further support to the *pull* dimension of labour mobility. The relative dynamism in the RNF sector is further underlined by the relatively high elasticity of demand for non-farm non-agricultural products, as shown in Table 6.15.

Table 6.15 has been constructed using the HIES 2010 *unit-level* data,[56] following methodology from Hazell and Roell (1983).[57]

One may note, as seen in Table 6.15, that the share of average rural household expenditure on food has declined even further to less than 50%. Table 6.15 clearly shows that for most RNA (rural manufacturing and services) elasticity is greater than or close to unity. It is 1.57 for education and health service sectors, and 1.96 for transport, recreation and others sectors. Previously, we have noted that Hossain (2004), based on HIES 2000, had found strong evidence for high-income elasticity

---

[56]Unit-level data were not available for the more recent HIES 2016–17.

[57]The expenditure pattern has been estimated by fitting the following log–log, double-log or log-linear models: $\ln E_i = \alpha + \beta \ln Y + u_i$, where E_i is the household expenditure on the ith consumption item, Y is the total household income, u_i is the disturbance term and α and β are the parameters of the function. This model is linear in the parameters α and β, linear in the logarithms of the variables E_i and Y, and can be estimated by simple Ordinary Least Squares (OLS) regression. In this exercise, the main target is to estimate the slope coefficient β which measures the elasticity of E_i with respect to Y, that is, the percentage change in E_i for one percentage change in Y. Following Hazell and Roell (1983), this exercise used total expenditure for each household as a proxy for income.

Table 6.15 Share of income and income elasticity of demand

Item	National average share of income (%)	Income elasticity	Rural average share of income (%)	Income elasticity	Urban average share of income (%)	Income elasticity
Food	53.33	0.78	57.23	0.83	46.75	0.72
Cereal	19.23	0.51	22.71	0.64	13.34	0.41
Non-cereal crops and fruits	14.96	0.77	16.03	0.81	13.16	0.71
Fish and livestock products	14.39	1.29	13.75	1.31	15.48	1.16
Other food products	4.76	0.84	4.75	0.86	4.77	0.71
Manufacturing products	10.29	0.98	10.82	1.04	9.40	0.91
Clothing	4.95	0.92	5.11	0.95	4.68	0.86
Other industrial products	5.34	1.02	5.71	1.10	4.72	0.94
Services	36.37	1.31	31.95	1.25	43.85	1.34
Housing and energy	15.53	0.97	13.27	0.82	19.35	1.05
Education and health	9.46	1.62	8.21	1.57	11.58	2.04
Transport, recreation and others	11.38	1.91	10.46	1.96	12.93	1.82

Source Author's estimation using BBS (2011) unit-level data

for most of the non-farm goods and services. The above underscores that the demand for non-food and non-farm products has been encouragingly high, over an extended period.[58]

6.7.4 *Remittances as a Game Changer*

Remittances from overseas employment have grown significantly, and have emerged as an important factor influencing average income and consumption patterns of rural

[58] While the income elasticity of demand for non-farm products is observed to be high, it would be difficult to ascertain the relative weights of consumption of RNF versus the urban and imported products (and hence, possible leakages). Nevertheless, there have been perceptible changes in labour markets and productivity gains in RNA to endorse tangible growth in the sector as a whole.

Table 6.16 Use of remittances as a means of expenditure investment and savings

Year	Area	% of remittance flow	Share of total remittance flow (%)			
			Food expenditure	Non-food expenditure	Investment	Savings
2013	Rural	93.83	27.03	17.65	27.41	13.04
	Urban	6.17	1.45	0.98	2.12	1.04
	Total	100.00	28.48	18.63	29.54	14.08
2016	Total		24.50	41.80	25.30	8.40

Source Author's estimation based on BBS (2014, 2016).

households. Its share in rural household income had increased from less than 1% in 1995 to more than 17% in 2010. The contribution of personal remittances to GDP had increased from 11.8% in 2009 to 12.2% in 2014. The large inflow of remittance into the country during the past decades, besides contributing significantly to maintaining current account surplus, has significantly changed the shape of the rural economy. Remittances have become a significant impetus in the overall rural development in Bangladesh, with nearly 94% (of USD 13.8 billion in 2013) of remittances flowing to the rural areas each year. This is a massive *injection* of resources to the rural economy, and in average terms, a significant boost to the income, consumption and savings of the remittance-receiving households (Table 6.16).[59]

The bulk of remittances sent by migrant workers are mostly used by their families for varied consumption- and investment-related purposes which are likely to impact employment and wages positively. At the household level, remittance has been contributing to raise income, consumption, savings and investment, sustain graduation from poverty, improvement of health and education entitlements and supporting asset and human capital accumulation.[60] Substantial remittance inflow is another driving force behind shifting employment from agriculture to other non-farm productive sectors, and holds a significant potential for investments and capital accumulation in the RNA sector. In this context, it may be noted that international migration itself has become an important source of employment in rural Bangladesh, and that between one-fifth to quarter of the annual additions to labour force are absorbed through overseas employment (see Annex Table 6.18). However, the ongoing pandemic and economic downturn in labour-importing countries, which are already shedding migrant workers, is likely to affect badly Bangladesh's overseas employment and remittance inflows. This is expected to affect adversely, at least in the short-run, not only the macroeconomic variables, but also employment and incomes of the rural households.

[59]See World Bank (2013). According to HIES (2010), annual remittances received per household, on average, was BDT 152 thousand.

[60]One must note, and as pointed out by several studies (e.g. Khan 2015), remittances have arguably been a disequalising force, at the household and regional levels. For instance, total migration during 2005–2018, from Cumilla and Chattogram had been 873 and 680 thousand, compared to paltry 36 and 28 thousand in Khulna and Rangpur, respectively.

6.8 Concluding Remarks

The discussions and empirical findings, reviewed from various secondary data sources and survey-based studies, underscore consensus on the increasing significance of RNA and RNF employment in Bangladesh. The evidence that is gathered from the above can be tentatively summarised as below:

- The employment share of RNF in total rural employment has significantly increased.
- Productivity in most RNA enterprises (goods and services) appears to be higher than in agriculture, implying a potential *pull* in labour mobility.
- Income elasticity of demand for most RNA goods and services is observed to be largely higher than or close to unity; labour productivity has grown, which has boosted growth of RNA and employment. Such labour productivity has been brought about, inter alia, by intensification of food-agriculture.
- Agricultural productivity (and diversification), together with non-farm employment, has helped raise real wages substantially in absolute terms[61] and rural household incomes.

Despite the dearth of systematic trend data on RNA, it is fairly evident that RNA has been establishing its growing importance in the rural economy of Bangladesh and that RNF employment has been rising quite rapidly. These have led to tangible changes in the labour market. The evidence, however, on the speed and volume of labour mobility and the precise determinants of such labour movements is rather limited. The data on labour force participation (including that of women workers) and occupational structure provide us perspectives on the sub-sectors that are growing, e.g. construction, transport, services, administration, etc. However, the database on RNA is still inadequate, and further systematic trend analysis would be required, both with regard to the relative pace of the growth of RNA sub-sectors, and the pace and determinants of labour mobility.

Given the above findings, how dynamic is the RNA sector in Bangladesh? Does it contain all the characteristics of *favourable archetype* of Z-goods, which according to Ranis and Stewart (1993), could potentially wipe out unemployment and underemployment (and achieve *rural full employment*)? Lessons from East Asian experiences, which significantly stress the importance of RNA, also warn us that much will depend on whether "higher levels of rural production and employment achieved may be said to be *secular and not transitional*" (Oshima 1986, p. 786, italics added).[62] Thus, while there are marked signs of growth and employment in RNA in Bangladesh, and as the *pathways* examined above tend to show, these signs, though encouragingly positive, need to evolve into more robust and secular trends to establish more visible

---

[61] As noted earlier, the growth rate of real wages had been stagnant in the recent period (between 2012 and 2017).

[62] While withdrawing surplus labour from agriculture would release some amount of wage-goods that could enhance wage employment in the RNA sub-sectors, it is unclear how far this will be sufficient to provide employment to all the potentially available labour force (Oshima 1986).

structural transformation. Such dynamism would of course require greater capitalisation and technology in RNA enterprises, and greater sectoral integration, possibly through supply chains, with urban and export sectors. Much will also depend on other factors influencing inter-sectoral labour flows. In the East Asian economies, the dynamism of the RNF was simultaneously reinforced by the above factors, especially the growth of labour-intensive, export-led industrialisation that helped achieve full employment in the economy overall.

At the risk of repetition, since job growth in the modern manufacturing sector has been unable to absorb labour adequately and productively, i.e. at the pace required to absorb surplus labour in agriculture, it appears that RNF has taken a crucial complementary job creation role. The caution that needs to be exercised is that policy and resource allocation need to be calibrated to: (i) encouraging further agricultural productivity growth, which provides the most significant boost to RNA; (ii) providing specific support to the growth of RNA through addressing various supply- and demand-side constraints.

During the early decades since independence, there was hardly any coordinated approach to envision and embrace the potential of the RNF sector in the *growth* strategy, one that could provide a platform for invigorated employment and income generation in rural sector.[63] In Bangladesh, as we observe from the policy stance of the Seventh Five Year Plan (7FYP), the RNF as a sector has hardly received much focus or coordinated attention. Whether and how far RNF trends could provide an alternative approach to tightening of the rural labour market would depend on a number of factors, viz. as implicit in pursuing the pathways reviewed above (Sect. 6.7). The policy framework towards expansion of the RNF sector would require coordinated support to ensure that the growing RNAs do not degenerate into inefficient *unfavourable archetypes*, but rather, unleash its full potential to productively pull labour from the slack sectors.[64]

6.9 Annex

See Tables 6.17 and 6.18.

[63]Most of these problems were identified in late 1950s when the First Five Year Plan of Pakistan (1955–60) was formulated, which were repeated almost religiously in successive development plans (Hossain et al. 1994).

[64]The utter neglect of the non-farm sector has been noted in various studies. Cf. Rosegrant and Hazell (2000).

Table 6.17 In-migration rates per 1,000 population by direction

Direction of in-migration	2011	2012	2013	2014	2015	2016	2017	2018
Total in-migrants	38.1	38.9	40.4	40.2	54.2	76.7	73.8	72.8
Rural in-migrants	22.1	21.6	31.7	29.4	30.7	39.5	37.8	38.5
Rural-to-rural	15.0	16.2	13.2	24.3	25.6	34.5	32.7	33.7
Urban-to-rural	5.3	5.3	18.5	5.1	5.1	5.0	5.0	4.9
Urban in-migrants	67.3	69.7	70.4	77.1	90.0	123.0	119.4	115.2
Rural-to-urban	23.7	26.2	12.1	28.2	29.5	30.3	30.3	30.6
Urban-to-urban	42.5	43.5	58.3	48.9	60.5	92.6	90.2	84.7

Source BBS (n.d.)

Table 6.18 Overseas migration as share of net annual addition to Bangladesh labour force (%)

Indicator	2001	2005	2009	2013	2017
Net annual addition to labour force (million)	1.9	1.1	1.8	1.3	1.4
Overseas migration (million)	0.2	0.3	0.5	0.4	1.0
Overseas migration as share of net annual addition to labour force	10.1	23.7	26.4	30.7	72.0

Source Author's calculation from the data of BBS and the Bureau of Manpower Employment and Training (BMET)

References

ADB & BBS. (2012). *The informal sector and informal employment in Bangladesh: Country Report 2010*. Manila: Asian Development Bank (ADB) and Dhaka: Bangladesh Bureau of Statistics (BBS), Government of Bangladesh (GoB).

Adelman, I. (1984). Beyond export-led growth. *World Development, 12*(9), 937–949.

Alam, M. S., & Islam, M. A. (2012). Long-term assessment of rice production scenario in Bangladesh: A macro dynamics. *Bangladesh Journal of Agricultural Research, 38*(2), 257–269.

Bannerjee, L. (2007). Flood disasters and agricultural wages in Bangladesh. *Development and Change, 38*(4), 641–664.

BBS. (1998). *Household Expenditure Survey, 1995–96*. Dhaka: Bangladesh Bureau of Statistics (BBS), Government of Bangladesh (GoB).

BBS. (2007). *Economic Census 2001 & 2003: National report*. Dhaka: Bangladesh Bureau of Statistics, Government of Bangladesh (GoB).

BBS. (2011). *Report of the Household Income and Expenditure Survey 2010*. Dhaka: Bangladesh Bureau of Statistics (BBS), Government of Bangladesh (GoB).

BBS. (2014). *Report on Survey on the Use of Remittance (SUR) 2013*. Dhaka: Bangladesh Bureau of Statistics (BBS), Government of Bangladesh (GoB).

BBS. (2015a). *Economic Census 2013*. Dhaka: Bangladesh Bureau of Statistics (BBS), Government of Bangladesh (GoB).

BBS. (2015b). *Report on Labour Force Survey (LFS) Bangladesh 2013*. Dhaka: Bangladesh Bureau of Statistics (BBS), Government of Bangladesh (GoB).

BBS. (2016). *Report of the Survey on Investment from Remittance (SIR) 2016*. Dhaka: Bangladesh Bureau of Statistics (BBS), Government of Bangladesh (GoB).

BBS. (2017). *Report on Quarterly Labour Force Survey (QLFS) 2015–16*. Dhaka: Bangladesh Bureau of Statistics (BBS), Government of Bangladesh (GoB).
BBS. (2018). *Labour Force Survey Bangladesh 2016–17*. Dhaka: Bangladesh Bureau of Statistics (BBS), Government of Bangladesh (GoB).
BBS. (n.d.). *Report on Bangladesh sample vital statistics* (various years). Dhaka: Bangladesh Bureau of Statistics (BBS), Government of Bangladesh (GoB).
Briones, R., & Felipe, J. (2013). *Agriculture and structural transformation in developing Asia: Review and outlook*. ADB Economics Working Paper 363. Manila: Asian Development Bank (ADB).
Chandrasekhar, C. P., & Ghosh, J. (2018, October 23). *Is "Formalisation" possible?* Retrieved December 8, 2018, from https://www.networkideas.org/news-analysis/2018/10/is-formalisation-possible/.
Chen, M. A. (2003, November). *Rethinking the informal economy*. Footloose Labour: A Symposium on Livelihood Struggles of the Informal Workforce, Seminar Issue 531. Retrieved December 10, 2018, from https://www.wiego.org/resources/footloose-labour-symposium-livelihood-struggles-informal-workforce.
Chenery, H. B. (1953). The application of investment criteria. *the Quarterly Journal of Economics, 67*(1), 76–96.
Clark, C. (1940). *The conditions of economic progress*. London: MacMillan.
Edgren, G., & Muqtada, M. (1990). Strategies for growth and employment in Asia: Learning from within. In *Employment challenges for the 1990s* (pp. 13–54). New Delhi: Asian Regional Team for Employment Promotion, International Labour Organization (ILO-ARTEP).
GED. (2015). *Seventh Five Year Plan FY2016–FY2020: Accelerating growth, empowering citizens*. Dhaka: General Economics Division (GED), Planning Commission, Government of Bangladesh (GoB).
Ghose, A. K. (2017). Informality and development. *the Indian Journal of Labour Economics, 60*(1), 1–16.
Gimenez, L., Jolliffe, D., & Sharif, I. (2014). *Bangladesh, a middle income country by 2021: What will it take in terms of poverty reduction?* Working Paper 87656. Washington, DC: The World Bank.
Grilli, E., & Zanalda, G. (1999). Growth and employment in developing countries: Where do we stand? In G. B. Navaretti, R. Faini, & G. Zanalda (Eds.), *Labor markets, poverty and development* (pp. 3–33). Oxford: Clarendon Press.
Haggblade, S., Hazell, P., & Reardon, T. (2007). *Transforming the rural non-farm economy*. Baltimore: Johns Hopkins Press.
Hazell, P. B. R., & Roell, A. (1983). *Rural growth linkages: Household expenditure patterns in Malaysia and Nigeria*. Research Report 41. Washington, DC: International Food Policy Research Institute (IFPRI).
Hirschman, A. O., & Rothschild, M. (1973). The changing tolerance for income inequality in the course of economic development: With a mathematical appendix. *The Quarterly Journal of Economics, 87*(4), 544–566.
Hossain, M. (2004). *Rural non-farm economy in Bangladesh: A view from household surveys*. CPD Occasional Paper 40. Dhaka: Centre for Policy Dialogue (CPD).
Hossain, M., Rahman, M., & Bayes, A. (1994). *Rural non-farm economy in Bangladesh: A dynamic sector or a sponge of absorbing surplus labour*. New Delhi: International Labour Organization (ILO)/South Asia Multidisciplinary Advisory Team (SAAT).
Hossain, M., Sen, B., & Sawada, Y. (2012). *Jobs, growth and development: Making of the "Other" Bangladesh*. Background Paper for the World Development Report 2013. Retrieved December 11, 2018, from https://siteresources.worldbank.org/EXTNWDR2013/Resources/8258024-1320950747192/82602931320956712276/82610911348683883703/WDR2013_bp_Jobs_Growth_and_Development.pdf.
Hymer, S., & Resnick, S. (1969). A model of an agrarian economy with non-agricultural activities. *American Economic Review, 59*(4), 493–506.

Islam, R. (Ed.). (1987). *Rural industrialization and employment in Asia.* Asian Regional Team for Employment Promotion, International Labour Organization (ILO-ARTEP): New Delhi.
Islam, R. (2014). The employment challenge faced by Bangladesh: How far is the Lewis turning point? *The Indian Journal of Labour Economics, 57*(2), 201–225.
Kaldor, N. (1967). *Strategic factors in economic development.* New York: New York State School of Industrial and Labor Relations, Cornell University.
Khan, A. R. (2015). *The economy of Bangladesh: A quarter century of development.* Basingstoke: Palgrave Macmillan UK.
Krishnamurty, J. (2008). Indian antecedents of disguised unemployment and surplus labour. *The Indian Journal of Labour Economics, 51*(1), 53–62.
Kuznets, S. (1955). Economic growth and income inequality. *American Economic Review, 45*(1), 1–28.
Leibenstein, H. (1957). *Economic backwardness and economic growth: Studies in the theory of economic development.* New York: Wiley .
Lewis, W. A. (1954). Economic development with unlimited supplies of labour. *Manchester School of Economic and Social Studies, 22*(2), 139–191.
Mahmud, W. (1996). Employment patterns and income formation in rural Bangladesh: The role of rural non-farm sector. *the Bangladesh Development Studies, 24*(3/4), 1–27.
Mazumdar, D. (1999). *Constraints to achieving full employment in Asia.* Employment and Training Paper 51. Geneva: International Labour Organization (ILO).
McKenzie, D. (2010). *Dimensions of informality in Bangladesh.* Washington, DC: The World Bank. Mimeo.
Muqtada, M. (2018). *Alternative approaches to full employment in Bangladesh: Role of the non-farm sector.* CPD Working Paper 116. Dhaka: Centre for Policy Dialogue (CPD).
Oshima, H. T. (1986). The transition from an agricultural to an industrial economy in East Asia. *Economic Development and Cultural Change, 34*(4), 783–809.
Oshima, H. T. (1988). Full-employment growth in Japan and Taiwan. *Philippine Review of Economics, 25*(1 & 2), 1–39.
Osmani, S. R., Ahmed, M., Latif, M. A., & Sen, B. (2015). *Poverty and vulnerability in rural Bangladesh.* Dhaka: The University Press Limited (UPL).
Pramanik, S., Deb, U., & Bantilan, C. (2014, October 15–17). Rural non-farm economy in Bangladesh: Nature, extent, trends, and determinants. Paper presented at the *8th Conference of the Asian Society of Agricultural Economists (ASAE)*, Savar, Bangladesh.
Rahman, M., Bhattacharya, D., & Al-Hasan, M. (2018). *The role of the informal sector in inclusive growth: A state of knowledge study from policy Perspectives.* Bangladesh Economic Dialogue on Inclusive Growth—Research Report 3. California: The Asia Foundation and London: Overseas Development Institute (ODI).
Raihan, S. (Ed.). (2016). *Structural change and dynamics of labor markets in Bangladesh: Studies on labor and employment.* Dhaka: SANEM Publications.
Ranis, G., & Stewart, F. (1990). *The dynamics of rural development: Theory and application.* Discussion Paper 608. Connecticut: Economic Growth Centre, Yale University.
Ranis, G., & Stewart, F. (1993). Rural nonagricultural activities in development: Theory and application. *Journal of Development Economics, 40*(1), 75–101.
Rodrik, D. (1997). *Has globalization gone too far?* Washington, DC: Peterson Institute for International Economics.
Rodrik, D. (2006). Goodbye Washington consensus, hello Washington confusion? A review of the World Bank's economic growth in the 1990s: Learning from a decade of reform. *Journal of Economic Literature, 44*(4), 973–987.
Rosegrant, M. W., & Hazell, P. B. R. (2000). *Transforming the rural Asian economy: The unfinished revolution.* New York: Oxford University Press.
Rosenstein-Rodan, P. N. (1943). Problems of industrialisation of Eastern and South-Eastern Europe. *the Economic Journal, 53*(210/211), 202–211.

Saith, A. (1987). Contrasting experiences in rural industrialisation: Are the East Asian successes transferable? In R. Islam (Ed.), *Rural industrialisation and employment in Asia* (pp. 241–303). New Delhi: Asian Regional Team for Employment Promotion, International Labour Organization (ILO-ARTEP).

Shilpi, F., & Emran, S. (2016). *Agricultural productivity and non-farm employment: Evidence from Bangladesh*. Policy Research Working Paper 7685. Washington, DC: The World Bank.

Poverty, 2000–2010. Working Paper 78559. Dhaka: The World Bank Office, Bangladesh.

World Bank. (2012). *Bangladesh—Towards accelerated, inclusive and sustainable growth: Opportunities and challenges* (Vol. 1). Washington, DC: The World Bank.

World Bank. (2013). Bangladesh Poverty Assessment: Assessing a Decade of Progress in Reducing Poverty, 2000–2010. Dhaka: World Bank.

World Bank. (n.d.). *World Development Indicator (WDI) database*. Washington, DC: The World Bank. Retrieved September 5, 2019, from https://databank.worldbank.org/data/home.aspx.

Chapter 7
Role of Social Protection in Ensuring Inclusive Growth in Bangladesh

Fahmida Khatun and Syed Yusuf Saadat

Abstract Bangladesh now stands at the crossroads of regaining its momentum of economic growth and dealing with rising inequality. Social protection measures can play an instrumental role in narrowing inequality through redistribution of some of the social entitlements among those who are left behind. The present chapter seeks to highlight the role of social protection in meeting the aspirations of Bangladesh to be an inclusive society. This chapter describes the characteristics of social protection in Bangladesh, and reviews the current state of social safety net programmes (SSNPs). It also sheds light on some of the limitations of these programmes, and budget allocations for various programmes, especially in light of the ongoing crisis caused due to COVID-19. Finally, this chapter assesses the National Social Security Strategy (NSSS) and makes recommendations for the way forward.

7.1 The Context

In promoting inclusive growth in an economy which is characterised by a high incidence of poverty, and a high proportion of vulnerable population and informal employment, social protection is likely to take a central place in development planning. During the period immediately after 1971, when Bangladesh was in the grip of mass poverty, deprivation and famine, there emerged a plethora of anti-poverty programmes and multi-pronged measures directed towards disaster rehabilitation and creating income and employment opportunities. The growth of these early measures,

---

This chapter draws from a working paper by the authors: Khatun, F. and Saadat, S. Y. (2018). Towards a social protection strategy for Bangladesh. CPD Working Paper 117. Dhaka: Centre for Policy Dialogue (CPD); content re-used with permission.

F. Khatun (✉) · S. Y. Saadat
Centre for Policy Dialogue (CPD), Dhaka, Bangladesh
e-mail: fahmida@cpd.org.bd

S. Y. Saadat
e-mail: saadat@cpd.org.bd

M. Muqtada (ed.), *Quest for Inclusive Growth in Bangladesh*,
South Asia Economic and Policy Studies,
https://doi.org/10.1007/978-981-15-7614-0_7

which were largely in the form of SSNPs, was considerably ad hoc and fostered through both government and non-government organisations (NGOs) initiatives. Since then, Bangladesh has come a long way in terms of attaining a fairly high per capita income growth, near food self-sufficiency, and a substantial reduction in poverty incidence. It has also developed elaborate and tested mechanisms to cope with natural disasters, which in the early periods had generated extreme vulnerability of the afflicted population. While these notable achievements have supported improvements in average welfare, the SSNP network continued to broaden to address the vulnerabilities of the poor and specific target groups.

Despite some degree of consolidation and coordination, SSNPs continue to grow sporadically at local, regional and national levels, which do not allow a full impact analysis or accountability of the resources that go into these programmes. New programmes and objectives have continued to come into play. There is, however, hardly any study or a public statement on whether this myriad of programmes and the associated resource allocations together conform to a public strategy on social protection or exposure on how the objectives are being achieved. Thus for better coordination and accountability of the numerous programmes of the various ministries and agencies, as well as those conducted by the large number of NGOs, what is patently missing is an objective and comprehensive review of the relevance and impact of the various programmes. After the advent of COVID-19 in Bangladesh, the need for effective SSNPs that protect the poor from shocks in the short-run, and promote inclusive growth in the long-run, has come to the forefront of public policy discussions.

In 2015, the Government of Bangladesh (GoB) announced an NSSS to ensure a more comprehensive social protection system for its population. The NSSS is currently the main social security strategy of the GoB, which falls under the umbrella of the Social Development Framework. The NSSS envisions a Bangladesh, where poverty and inequality are effectively tackled, growth and employment are efficiently accelerated, and the weak and vulnerable are adequately protected. The discussion on NSSS, which is yet to be fully detailed on its programmes and processes, resources, necessary institutions and legal framework that would be needed to implement the strategy, has been reviewed later in this chapter.

This chapter assesses some of the major initiatives focused on extending income and employment entitlements through SSNPs in Bangladesh. It also presents a critical analysis of these initiatives and calls for a thorough review, especially in the light of the recent crisis caused by COVID-19 in Bangladesh. It further provides a brief insight into the associated challenges to implement a social protection strategy that is commensurate with the vision of Bangladesh becoming an upper middle-income country (UMIC) and realising Sustainable Development Goal (SDG) Target 1.3 (implement nationally appropriate social protection systems and measures for all, including floors, and achieve substantial coverage of the poor and the vulnerable) by 2030. The estimated cost of providing universal social protection floors (SPFs) in Bangladesh is also included, which may be useful to gauge the necessary financial commitment of implementing universal social protection.

7.2 Definitional Issues

Social protection, in a broad sense, is concerned with preventing, managing and overcoming situations that adversely affect people's well-being (UNRISD 2010). Social protection is a broad concept that encompasses the notions embodied both in social safety net (Paitoonpong et al. 2008) and social security, and is conducted through a range of programmes that are often categorised as social assistance and social insurance. The former would tend to support the coping strategies of the poor and the vulnerable and minimise their economic and social risks, especially those associated with illness, old age, disability and unemployment. These programmes are largely in the form of non-contributory transfers and subsidies, and are funded out of public revenues. On the other hand, social security is understood to refer to some instruments of social insurance, which are contributory and largely funded by the employers and employees to cover old age or unemployment or other contingencies (US Social Security Administration 2017). Over time, these terminologies have become blurred. For instance, many who are under social security schemes and cannot contribute adequately to social insurance may require additional tax-supported assistance, such as through active and passive labour market policies. The International Labour Organization (ILO), for example, has used the term interchangeably.

According to the World Bank, social protection consists of "public interventions to assist individuals, households, and communities to better manage risk, and to provide support to the critically poor" (Holzmann and Jørgensen 2001, p. 530). On the other hand, the ILO defines social protection as "the set of public measures that a society provides for its members to protect them against economic and social distress that would be caused by the absence or a substantial reduction of income from work as a result of various contingencies (sickness, maternity, employment injury, unemployment, invalidity, old age, and death of the breadwinner); the provision of health care; and the provision of benefits for families with children" (García and Gruat 2003, pp. 13–14). Thus, the World Bank definition views social protection largely through humanitarian interventions, while the ILO definition perceives social protection as an instrument and public guarantee of social welfare.

In operational terms, it may be noted that there are large variations in country experiences pertaining to the development of social protection systems, both among the developed and developing countries (ILO 2017a). Accordingly, different approaches define an individual country's social protection framework. While Bangladesh will have to develop its own social protection system, based on its own vision and capacity, there are a few core principles that would have to guide such a strategy, as already foreseen in the NSSS. It is significant to recall here that Bangladesh is committed to the SDGs, of which Target 1.3 in particular calls for the realisation of "nationally appropriate social protection systems and measures for all, including floors, and by 2030 achieve substantial coverage of the poor and vulnerable" (UN n.d.). Such a commitment would naturally require a more comprehensive framework of social protection and the adoption of an SPF. ILO's *social protection floor* refers generally to basic social security guarantees that ensure universal access to essential healthcare and income security at least at a nationally defined minimum level (horizontal dimension),[1] and the gradual progression to higher levels of protection (vertical dimension) within a more mature and comprehensive social security system.[2] The World Bank too supports universal access to social protection, and considers it central to its goals of *ending poverty and boosting shared prosperity*.[3] Such universal access to social protection is meant to be achieved through a mix of traditionally understood social security measures as well as social assistance (largely tax-financed SSNPs, labour market programmes, e.g. public works programmes). The World Bank is, however, ambivalent on the issues of rights and guarantees as emphasised in ILO social floors. Hence, its pursuit of universality is subject to how programmes and operations are designed at the ground level. The International Monetary Fund (IMF), on the other hand, apparently resists the *guarantee* question and emphasises a targetting approach, i.e. for the most vulnerable groups (rather than either universality or guarantee) (IMF 2017). Thus, the current IMF position appears to fall short of the social inclusion goals, as envisioned in the SDGs which, inter alia, call for social protection for all. The above positions reflect the respective organisations' allegiance to their respective core bases, essentially distinguishing between *the growth to jobs to security* model versus the adoption of a welfare model of universal and basic guarantees.

The main considerations in the design of a strategy would ultimately be governed by an individual country's vision of social protection and by its capacity in realising it. Apart from multiple factors, there are at least three critical developments that are likely to influence the structure and evolution of the system. These are: (i) levels and trends of poverty and vulnerability (i.e. the *horizontal coverage*); (ii) fiscal restructure and debt sustainability that would broadly define the limits to tax-financed SSNPs; and (iii) labour market formations in the economy, as would evolve in the course of the country's progress towards full employment (SDG 8) and gradual and necessary growth in share of contributory funds (i.e. the *vertical coverage*).

7.3 Characteristics and Depth of Social Protection in Bangladesh

As is well-known, in Bangladesh, the level and coverage of social protection among the labour force are relatively very low. This is particularly striking given that the incidence of poverty, though falling, is still high with poverty headcount ratio of 14.8%

---

[1]This is in line with ILO's Social Protection Floors Recommendation, 2012 (No. 202) (see ILO 2012).

[2]This would be according to the Social Security (Minimum Standards) Convention, 1952 (No. 102).

[3]The World Bank's universal social protection coverage broadly consists of providing social assistance largely through cash transfers (means-tested), especially for children; benefits and support to working-age population in case of maternity, disability, work injury or unemployment; and old-age pension.

and 52.9%, at USD 1.90 and USD 3.20 per day, respectively, at 2011 Purchasing Power Parity (PPP) (World Bank n.d.).

According to the Quarterly Labour Force Survey (LFS) 2016–17, only 14.9% of employed people in Bangladesh were working in the formal sector (BBS 2018). The proportion of formal employment was larger for males than females. Formal employment was higher in urban areas with 22.7% than in rural areas with 11.9%. The services sector had the highest percentage of workers employed formally, with 28.2%, followed by 10.1% for the industry sector and 4.6% for the agriculture sector. There was a strong positive correlation between educational attainment and employment in the formal sector. Among the workers employed in the formal sector, 23.2% of services sector workers, 2.6% of industry sector workers, and 1.5% of agriculture sector workers were under the coverage of a pension or retirement fund.

A simple view of the current status of social protection in the country appears to be as follows: a total, systematic and coordinated approach to social security is yet to evolve—a primary reason being the extent to which fiscal space can be extended to accommodate a universal system of social security and a pension scheme. Equally, there exists the formidable challenge of extending social protection to the vast informal economy workers, which is likely to create dualism in the social protection system. The *formal* sector employment, which is normally associated with a degree of job protection and social security, is very small. Formal sector employment is largely confined to the public sector and large enterprises. While statutes and labour codes are governing social security benefits, for example, pension cover, employment injury, disability and maternity, etc., their implementations vary enormously across establishments. For the *informal* sector, there are various programmes, of varying scale and coverage, both within the framework of the government budget and NGO support. There exists a multitude of SSNPs that target the poor's income and employment entitlements. These are non-contributory schemes financed largely through public expenditure, although there are significant complementary contributions from NGOs, only a few of which have any pervasive presence. BRAC is a case in point. Examples of such SSNPs include: (i) cash and/or kind transfers to targetted poor, largely with conditionalities on education and health; (ii) wage-based labour-intensive public works programmes; (iii) vulnerable group feeding (VGF) and school feeding programmes, mother and child supplementary programmes; and (iv) price subsidies on food or energy, etc.

While there is a plethora of income or employment support, these are often ad hoc, with varying impact on variously defined target groups. Thus, we note that both for the formal and informal sector workforce, the process of effective social security coverage is of recent origin, and is rather limited. Nevertheless, the process of policy-making and institution-building has begun, and various factors such as continued commitment, resource allocation, implementation, and capacity building would need to play their part for a successful social protection strategy. The biggest challenge in any universal coverage will indeed come from the vast informal sector employees, whether in agriculture, industry, or service sector, pertaining to both rural and urban areas.

The GoB, along with many NGOs, has been undertaking several initiatives to create employment and income opportunities for the rural poor since the mid-1970s. Among these, the notable ones include the Food for Work Programme (FFW), Rural Maintenance Programme (RMP), Vulnerable Group Development (VGD) and Test Relief (TR). These food-waged employment programmes engage the landless and marginal rural population in activities such as rural road construction and maintenance, irrigation channels, flood control and embankments. Notwithstanding several limitations related to designing and implementation (Khatun et al. 2012; MSUK 2013), these programmes have, by and large, been playing a vital role in providing social protection to the vulnerable groups in Bangladesh.

7.4 Overview of SSNPs in Bangladesh

The SSNPs have largely emerged in response to various shocks and risks that the vulnerable groups frequently face in Bangladesh. Some of these programmes have been sustained over medium- and long-terms. The objective of these programmes is to protect the affected people from falling into extreme poverty (Rahman et al. 2011). However, objectives of SSNPs have evolved over time, and are now viewed from broad perspectives of income-poverty and human-poverty, although the distinction may be ambiguous. Several of the employment-generating programmes and direct transfers for the poor are used as a tool to address income-poverty. Programmes focusing on areas such as education, health, nutrition and water and sanitation are targetted to mitigate human-poverty. The SSNPs are considered as direct measures which are devised to address both income- and human-poverty. Examples of indirect or growth-oriented measures include mostly infrastructure development and rehabilitation programmes. However, some SSNPs are both direct and indirect. For example, direct measures like the FFW programme targetted towards the poor is used to construct infrastructure, which falls in the category of indirect measure likely to have multiplier effects on jobs and incomes.

In terms of modality, support under SSNPs can be in the form of: (i) direct cash transfer; and (ii) support through creating the opportunity for income. Direct support category includes programmes such as allowance for the widow, deserted and destitute women, old-age allowance, honorarium for insolvent freedom fighters, assistance to the mentally challenged, fund for mitigating risk due to natural disaster, fund for rehabilitation of the acid-burnt women and physically handicapped people, and maternity allowance for the poor lactating mother. There are also programmes for the seasonally unemployed poor which are carried out under the SSNPs. Some of these include Employment Generation Programme for the Poorest (EGPP), FFW, VGD, TR and Rural Employment and Road Maintenance Programme (RERMP).

There are various ways through which the SSNPs have been characterised and categorised (Rahman et al. 2011). However, the GoB currently categorises SSNPs into four types, and largely allocates resources into the national budget according to these categories: (i) cash transfer programmes; (ii) food security programmes; (iii) microcredit programmes; and (iv) development programmes.

Over the years, cash transfer programmes have expanded in terms of number, coverage and budget. Similar trend is observed in other South Asian and Latin American countries, where conditional cash transfer programmes are being aggressively promoted (Fiszbein and Schady 2009; Rahman et al. 2011). This could be because of the fact that cash transfers are found to be more cost-effective than food transfers in some selected areas of Bangladesh (Ahmed et al. 2016). Reduction in allocation for food security programmes in Bangladesh could be due to the achievement of food self-sufficiency and a relative decline in seasonal vulnerability.

Under cash transfers, the largest share is spent on pension for retired government employees and their families, followed by honorarium for freedom fighters. Among the food security programmes, Food Friendly Programme, EGPP, VGF, FFW, VGD, TR and open market sales (OMS) are the larger ones. Under the microcredit programmes and miscellaneous fund, two largest expenditures are block allocation for various programmes and social development foundation. The other programmes are for entrepreneurship support, various trust, fund and assistance, training and so on. The largest programmes in the development sector are for education and health.

As is well-known, during the early post-independence days, the only orthodox social protection programme in Bangladesh was the government service pension. In the aftermath of the 1974 famine, new social protection programmes were introduced to address the urgent humanitarian crisis. Most of these programmes involved food aid, and were financed by international donors. It was only in the 1980s that the social protection programmes in Bangladesh started to move away from a purely disaster response approach and towards adopting a poverty-alleviating and human capital development approach. As a result, various programmes related to education, healthcare, and life-cycle risks emerged gradually. The database on SSNPs is inadequate and there is no analytical framework to allow firm conclusions on the success of these initiatives, either individually or in respect of priorities. Nevertheless, there are descriptive accounts and evaluations to suggest that there have been perceptible positive impacts on underprivileged groups or regions. Understandably, the impact of these programmes would vary according to nature of objectives, resource adequacy and implementation capacity, and would be ideally assessed at the project or local levels. The limited space of this chapter precludes the scope of delving into these numerous programmes and sub-programmes that are served by the SSNPs that can be found in other studies (Rahman et al. 2011; Barkat-e-Khuda 2011; Osmani 2014; Ahmed 2015). Nevertheless, a few broad reflections on the overall conduct of SSNPs are given in the subsequent section.

7.5 Limitations of SSNPs: Broad Reflections

There are many programmes under the broad category of SSNPs in Bangladesh which are highly diverse in the size of allocations, the number of beneficiaries reached, and the key objectives and targets to be attained. Hence, an appropriate evaluation within a common framework is complex, and perhaps untenable. Although there exist various assessments of individual projects and programmes, especially of those run by the NGOs, there however, does not exist a consistent national-level database nor a comparative analysis of the relative performance and impact of these vast array of SSNPs (Osmani 2014). Nevertheless, various studies have pointed out a number of shortcomings. Among these, the most commonly observed are the inadequacy of allocation, weaknesses in targetting, leakages, lack of coordination among the implementing agencies, high administrative costs and inefficiencies, and absence of any impact evaluation framework (Khatun et al. 2012; MSUK 2013). It is beyond the scope of this chapter to delve into details of all the programmes that are listed in the budget. However, a few broad clusters of issues that are common to one or more of these programmes are cited below.

7.5.1 Coverage, Quantum of Support and Skewed Allocation

Although one observes 123 programmes under the SSNP budget, the majority of these are actually relatively very small. The latter may be serving a small group, but it is for a significant reason (e.g. destitute women, physically handicapped, ration for injured freedom fighters, etc.); or they exist because there are no built-in exit strategies in these programmes. Ahmed (2015) points out that among these programmes, 58% collectively account for a meagre 4% of the allocations, with more than half receiving an allocation of less than USD 6.3 million. Table 7.1, drawn from the Household Income Expenditure Survey (HIES) 2016 database, provides a cursory view of some of the significant programmes, with monthly amounts (averaged over the year) received under each, and the percentage distribution of beneficiary households under the schemes. The monthly disbursements vary enormously. However, some of these SSNPs where monthly amounts may be relatively small could cater to a large proportion of the beneficiaries (e.g. stipend for primary students, and stipend for secondary and higher secondary students) which account for the two largest beneficiary groups. Although the monthly amounts are relatively small, these SSNPs can have a strong catalytic effect (e.g. on female education enrolment).

On the other hand, some of the data have to be explored and endorsed at the project level. For instance, the monthly average amount (BDT 190) under the EGHP (which accounts for only 0.43% of beneficiaries) imply that target groups did not reach (or did not volunteer for) the 100-day goal. Most of these programmes and allocations are budgeted year to year, and are usually open-ended, except that each has a target number of beneficiaries to reach. There is no clear longitudinal assessment on how effective these have been, and if so, has the progress been marked in terms of the numbers who have graduated from the benchmark.

Thus, from the individual programmes and their allocations, it is difficult to ascertain whether the per capita beneficiary monthly receipts are adequate to improve the

Table 7.1 Average amount received during April 2016 to March 2017 from different SSNPs and recipient households

Type of programme	Monthly amount (BDT)	% of recipient households
Gratuitous Relief (GR)	50.5	5.88
VGF	56.6	7.38
General Relief Activities	67.1	1.03
Proshar Programme (ACDI VOCA)	83.3	0.01
Stipend for Primary Students	104.0	36.14
Housing Support	107.8	0.19
Stipend for Dropout Students	125.4	0.64
Stipend for Secondary and Higher Secondary Students	129.4	11.42
Ananda School (Reaching Out-of-School Children—ROSC)	132.8	2.13
Employment Generation for the Hardcore Poor (EGHP) for 100 days	190.9	0.43
TR	205.3	2.57
School Feeding Programme	223.5	4.44
Others	225.4	3.40
Allowances for Beneficiaries in Chittagong Hill Tracts Area	278.8	0.04
VGD	290.1	1.86
Old Age Allowance under the Ministry of Social Welfare	292.5	14.22
Widow, Deserted and Destitute Women Allowance	298.7	4.20
Maternal Health Voucher Allowance	329.2	0.03
Stipend for Disabled Students	354.2	0.48
Maternity Allowance Programme for the Poor Lactating Mother	385.8	0.18
Allowances for Financially Insolvent	395.0	1.40
Agriculture Rehabilitation under the Ministry of Agriculture	450.3	0.03
Char Livelihood	464.0	0.03
Food/Cash for Work (FFW/CFW)	525.5	0.32
Ration for Martyred Family and Injured Freedom Fighters	540.8	0.05
Urban Partnership for Poverty Reduction	583.1	0.03
Economic Empowerment for the Poor (Shiree)	613.9	0.04
Targeted Ultra Poor (TUP) (BRAC)	708.4	0.07

(continued)

Table 7.1 (continued)

Type of programme	Monthly amount (BDT)	% of recipient households
Allowances for Distressed Cultural Personnel	718.3	0.06
One Household One Farm	816.8	0.07
Shouhardo Programme	874.4	0.04
Nabojibon Programme (Save the Children)	903.8	0.02
Food Assistance in Chittagong Hill Tracts Area	1,062.6	0.20
Rural Employment and Road Maintenance for Protection of Public	2,066.5	0.03
Honorarium and Medical Allowances for Injured Freedom Fighters	2,614.6	0.44
Rural Employment Opportunity for Protection of Public	4,500.0	0.03
Honorarium for Insolvent Freedom Fighters	5,506.8	0.46

Source Authors' compilation based on the data from BBS (2017)

respective indicator of progress, or how many are recipients of more than one SSNP. Some studies show that, overall, the contribution of per capita amount received from SSNPs is a trivial proportion of average household consumption (Osmani 2014), although some of these, for example, stipends programmes, can have large long-term catalytic benefits.

7.5.2 Targetting and Adverse Selection

Beneficiary targetting (to bring in the right group of people) has been a major weakness of SSNPs. Even according to government estimates, of the 24.5% of the households who reportedly were benefitting from at least one of the 30 SSNPs covered in the HIES 2010, 82% of those beneficiaries belonged to the poor and vulnerable group, while some 18% of them were non-poor (GED 2015). The list of targetting criteria for the existing SSNPs are huge, obsolete and sometimes impractical (MSUK 2013). However, Khatun et al. (2010) found that beneficiary targetting was somewhat better in case of EGHP programme, but mistargetting was frequent in solvent areas such as Chattogram. The weak supervision of the SSNPs creates both targetting errors and leakages (MSUK 2013).

Although, in general, the SSNP beneficiary profile shows that nearly 77% are either extremely poor or poor, there are about 18% who are non-poor (GED 2015). It is not conspicuous how and when the so-called well-off get included in these safety net programmes. Reducing leakages and proper targetting can help release significant amount of resources that can serve the more vulnerable and deserving groups more effectively.

The 18% of non-poor population that gets into the SSNP coverage (BBS 2011), effectively account for nearly 47% of the total funds that accrue to SSNPs. Whether this is due to negligence of identification or a conscious pursuit of a universal targetting programme(s) is unclear. Nevertheless, this requires an appropriate assessment in order to provide greater transparency and legitimacy.

7.5.3 *Poverty and SSNPs: The Regional Question*

As noted earlier, the distribution of Employment Generation Programme (EGP) allocations follows a disaggregated poverty mapping in Bangladesh. Similarly, for total allocations under SSNPs, the HIES records the percentage of recipient households and the respective poverty incidence by sub-regions (Table 7.2).

Obviously, as is well-known and recorded, Rangpur has the highest incidence of poverty and commensurately registers among the highest number of SSNP-recipients. There are some apparent anomalies; Barishal, with average poverty incidence, has the highest number of beneficiaries, while Mymensingh, with a higher than average poverty incidence, has a much lower percentage of SSNP coverage. However, these are average numbers, and a lot will depend on the depth of poverty and vulnerability, and whether within every region the individual target household is identified well, and whether it receives adequate resource and other support as safety nets. Much will depend on the local-level administration and capacity for effective implementation and monitoring.

Table 7.2 Regional profile of poverty and SSNP recipients (%)

Division	Recipient household	People below	
		Lower poverty line	Upper poverty line
Barishal	56.2	14.5	26.5
Chattogram	17.6	8.7	18.4
Dhaka	12.4	7.2	16.0
Khulna	41.1	12.4	27.5
Mymensingh	24.9	17.6	32.8
Rajshahi	37.4	14.2	28.9
Rangpur	43.9	30.5	47.2
Sylhet	27.6	11.5	16.2
National	27.8	12.9	24.3

Source Authors' compilation based on the data from BBS (2017)

7.5.4 Lack of Clarity in Listing of Programmes

Given the large number of SSNPs in Bangladesh, the listing of programmes in the government documents is often very confusing. As observed earlier, SSNPs have been characterised in multiple ways. These involve transfers and subsidies, access to credit special employment schemes, empowering through education and health, etc. SSNPs can be direct or indirect; conditional or unconditional; in cash or kind; universal or targetted. It is hard to follow the trail of the programmes over a period, because these are often introduced and revised without following any transparent system.

7.5.5 A Summary of Evaluation

Not only has there been a proliferation of SSNPs, but these have also turned complex, especially, with their diversification and linkages to other dimensions of human development; some through means-tested conditional cash transfers (direct or indirect), others through universal access or targetting, for example, female education.

Most social protection programmes in Bangladesh were designed on an ad hoc basis, depending on the particular needs of the time. Thus, the programmes that we observe at present are rather disparate in nature. Many of these programmes do not have concrete targets or detailed exit strategies for beneficiaries. Tackling error, fraud and corruption in social protection programmes of Bangladesh is difficult since these terms are not clearly defined in the first place. Most government ministries do not have sufficient information or adequate capacity to perform an internal audit that will investigate the root causes of corruption in these programmes. Studies have shown that the greatest opportunity for error, fraud and corruption occurs at the stage of selection of beneficiaries (Van Stolk and Tesliuc 2010). In Bangladesh, it is common knowledge that social protection programme beneficiaries are not always properly selected. Due to limited monitoring and evaluation, such irregularities persist unabated. Inadequate assessment of the programmes means that there is no real mechanism in place for prioritising certain programmes over others.

7.6 Allocations and Priorities: Additional Remarks

7.6.1 Sectoral Programmes and SSNPs

In general, allocations have, in absolute amount, increased for cash transfer, food security and microcredit programmes. However, the percentage of cash transfers increased significantly, whilst the share of food security decreased. The cash transfer allocation has increased more than four-fold, which currently accounts for 70% of the budget allocation for SSNPs. This, as discussed later, has sharpened the already skewed distribution in the allocations. This study, and many others, have pointed out that the SSNPs have mushroomed enormously under various ministries and various banners (Rahman et al. 2011; Osmani 2014; Ahmed 2015). In the absence of a clear integrated mapping of these SSNPs, or their end objectives, or their relative costs and benefits, it is impossible to appreciate the significance of the relative allocations and discern why some SSNP allocations are increasing and others declining. While these SSNPs are administered largely in a top-down approach by the various ministries, it is unclear to what extent they complement or overlap with the sectoral allocations of the ministries. More significantly, given the changing economic and social landscape of Bangladesh, it is important that each ministry must evaluate the role and allocations of respective SSNPs in reinforcing the ministerial or sectoral goals, and determine how far these contribute to consolidating the foundations of the NSSS.

As pointed out previously, some of the largest programmes under the development sector are for education and health. Experts tend to argue as to whether development sector programmes ought to be classified under SSNPs, and whether they are central to the development of the SPF which usually encompasses state guarantees on access to basic health services and basic income security over various stages of life-cycle. Furthermore, Osmani (2014), based on an elaborate household survey conducted by the Institute of Microfinance (InM), tends to conclude that SSNP allocations in education are relatively biased in favour of well-off groups compared to the poor and extremely poor groups. Both owing to their dis-equalising effect as well as their development nature, there is a strong case made to remove the SSNPs that pertain to the education sector. However, SSNPs in general are a complex portfolio that has evolved over a scramble over limited resources by competing sectors and priorities. The pros and cons need to be transparent. A hasty judgement to retain or scrap some of these may jeopardise some of the priorities, e.g. the SSNPs that cater to promoting the right to basic education or to rectifying the gender ratio in school enrolment.

The above is one example of the need to rethink how allocations can be reprioritised. These issues need to be debated and rationalised both at individual sector levels as well as on a coordinated SSNP platform. With the introduction of the NSSS, and the changing economic and social development of Bangladesh, a full review is warranted on how the SSNP priorities and their allocations must be made.

7.6.2 Balancing Lop-Sidedness of Allocations

A particular note must be made of the pension budget in relation to the total SSNP allocations. The National Pay Scale 2015 Amendment, which almost doubled the salaries of government officials, had a strong distortionary effect on social security in Bangladesh. Following the change, the pensions for government officials were adjusted to be in line with the increment in salaries. This caused a substantial reallocation of resources from other social security programmes to pensions for

Table 7.3 Budget allocation for social protection and pension

Year	Social protection allocation		Social protection allocation excl. pension	
	As percentage of budget	As percentage of GDP	As percentage of budget	As percentage of GDP
FY2009	14.71	2.25	10.87	1.66
FY2010	15.12	2.42	11.71	1.87
FY2011	16.07	2.64	12.99	2.14
FY2012	13.63	2.40	10.50	1.85
FY2013	12.20	2.23	9.28	1.69
FY2014	12.33	2.26	9.17	1.68
FY2015	12.78	2.02	9.19	1.46
FY2016	13.60	2.08	9.39	1.44
FY2017	12.88	2.09	8.89	1.44
FY2018	13.06	2.17	10.37	1.72
FY2019	14.55	2.54	9.48	1.65
FY2020	16.32	2.92	11.73	2.10
FY2021	16.83	3.01	12.78	2.29

Source Authors' calculations based on the data from various issues of SSNP documents, Ministry of Finance (MoF), GoB

Note All values are revised budget numbers, except for the FY2020-21, which are budget figures

government officials. Total budget allocation for pension dwarfs the budget allocations for all other social security programmes. In FY2020-21, 24.07% of the budget for social protection was allocated for pension for retired government employees and their families, which is six times the allocation for the next largest social protection programme.

Social security budget has been hovering around 2% of the gross domestic product (GDP) since FY2008-09, as illustrated in Table 7.3. In FY2020-21, allocation for pension of government officials decreased by BDT 100 million. This is only the second time in the last 13 years that the allocation for pension of government officials has decreased in the budget. Social safety net budget excluding pension has also increased in FY2020-21, both as percentage of budget and as percentage of GDP (Table 7.3).

7.7 Social Protection During the Time of COVID-19

In order to deal with the emergent COVID-19 scenario, the government has moved to expand SSNPs that provide basic support to vulnerable groups. Since the government has committed to widen its social safety net coverage, it has become mandatory to prepare a list of the beneficiary households under the social safety net coverage of the government. This listing of the beneficiary must encompass both the rural and urban poor. Although there is already a list for the rural poor under the various SSNPs, there is no concrete list available for covering the urban poor. For the efficient utilisation of the support measures for the beneficiaries of the SSNPs, a strong commitment from NGOs and local bodies (upazila and union leaders) is also required to make the selection and distribution transparent.

Despite the directive of the government and a stern warning from the Honourable Prime Minister herself, members of the ruling party who were tasked with managing relief activities have been involved with misappropriating rice, soybean oil, sugar and other essential food items that were meant for distribution among the poor through safety net programmes such as VGF or OMS.

To ensure the transparency and inclusivity in the distribution of various SSNPs, political commitment is essential so that every needy household may get the necessary support. To prevent leakages in the SSNPs, it is mandatory to list those who are the current beneficiaries and who should be newly enrolled. Then breakdown of the allocation of resources should be made clear so that transparency and accountability can be ensured. Soon after preparing this updated list of the beneficiaries, it can be posted online in the concerned websites of the government (i.e. MoF, Ministry of Disaster Management and Relief, Ministry of Planning). Moreover, to ensure efficient utilisation, the money can be sent through mobile financial services (MFS) (or the bank account) of the respected beneficiaries. In the case of the relief distribution, cash support should also be encouraged for facilitating social distancing.

Allocation for social safety nets was increased from BDT 818.65 billion in the revised budget for FY2019-20 to BDT 955.74 billion in the budget for FY2020-21. This represents an increase of only 17% which is lower than the average rate of increase of 18% between FY2009-10 and FY2020-21. This indicates that the increment was business as usual, and no extraordinary budget allocation was being made for social safety nets, despite the fact that the poor are reeling from the shocks of COVID-19. Nevertheless, most of this increase has been allocated to COVID-19-related programmes, loans, interest payments and subsidies.

Table 7.4 shows the distribution of new additions to safety net budget in FY2020-21. The disaggregated numbers clearly show that a large portion of funds shown to be allocated under the safety net budget do not have any direct link with any safety net programmes. For example, BDT 66.25 billion or 31.28% of the new safety net budget allocation is for interest payment on National Savings Certificates (NSCs). However, NSCs are financial products and not a safety net mechanism per se. Interest subsidy for loans to cottage, micro, small and medium enterprise (CMSME) sector and interest subsidy to commercial banks together account for BDT 50 billion or 23.6% of the new safety net budget allocation. On the other hand, refinance scheme for the low-income professionals, farmers and marginalised businesses and credit for self-employment venture together also account for BDT 50 billion or 23.6% of the new safety net budget allocation. Interest subsidies on two liquidity support packages and interest-bearing loans which are conditional on stringent regulations can hardly be considered as appropriate SSNPs during the COVID-19 crisis since those who are the hardest-hit by the pandemic would either not be eligible for such loans or not be able to pay back the money.

Table 7.4 Distribution of new additions to safety net budget in FY2020-21

New additions to safety net budget allocation in FY2021	Billion BDT	Percentage
Interest payment on NSCs	66.250	31.28
Refinance scheme for the low-income professionals, farmers and marginalised businesses	30.000	14.16
Interest subsidy for loans to CMSME sector	30.000	14.16
Houses for the homeless	21.575	10.19
EGP through Palli Sanchay Bank, Karmasangsthan Bank, Probashi Kalyan Bank and PKSF	20.000	9.44
Interest subsidy to commercial banks	20.000	9.44
Agricultural subsidy	19.000	8.97
Distributing cash among the target-based communities	5.000	2.36
Total	211.825	100.00

Source Authors' compilation and calculations based on the data from MoF, GoB
Note PKSF: Palli Karma-Sahayak Foundation

The budget speech for FY2020-21 mentioned that direct cash transfers of BDT 2,500 would be provided per family for 5 million selected families nationwide. Unfortunately, the minimum cost of a small basket of essential food items for a family of four persons for one month based on prices in Dhaka city as of 11 June 2020 would be BDT 6,710 per month, assuming that each person consumes the national average amount of food per day. Alternatively, providing USD 1.90 per day, which is the current international poverty line, to a family of four persons for one month would require BDT 19,334 per month. Therefore, a direct cash transfer of BDT 2,500 is not enough based on local prices or the international poverty line. Moreover, assuming that each household consists of four individuals, provision of cash aid to 5 million poor households will still exclude 3.4 million poor households in Bangladesh, based on the latest poverty estimates by the Bangladesh Bureau of Statistics (BBS). It is cannot be ascertained whether the COVID-19 pandemic was not reason enough for the government to prioritise social protection or whether lack of fiscal space has limited the government's relief efforts. In any case, it is clear that SSNPs need more funding to reach those who are the farthest behind and have been the worst hit by the COVID-19 crisis.

7.8 Universal Social Protection Floors in Bangladesh

The ILO's Social Protection Floors Recommendation, 2012 (No. 202) (ILO 2012) asserts that social protection is a human right. It mentions that social protection is a necessity for development, a tool for reducing social exclusion, an investment in workers' empowerment and a mechanism that is conducive towards gradual formalisation of employment (ILO 2012). The Recommendation calls upon countries to establish and maintain SPFs, and progressively make the transition to higher levels of social security. In this regard, the ILO recommends that countries abide by 18 broad principles, which include, inter alia, universality, entitlement, adequacy, non-discrimination, transparency and tripartite participation (ILO 2012). Based on their national circumstances, countries are urged to guarantee income security and essential healthcare throughout the life cycle, so that everyone has a chance to live a dignified life, free from hardship. For this purpose, the ILO recommends that countries diversify their sources of finance to fund SPFs. It also suggests countries to take steps towards the reduction of fraud and tax evasion which tend to misappropriate valuable resources that may be otherwise utilised efficiently for the provision of social protection benefits.

Despite ILO's Social Protection Floors Recommendation, 2012 (No. 202), 55% of the global population, or around 4 billion people worldwide, did not have access to any form of social protection in 2017 (ILO 2017b). To make things worse, social protection coverage is lower in less developed regions of the world. In 2017, 61% people in the Asia and Pacific and 82% people in Africa did not have access to any social protection (ILO 2017b). Nonetheless, it appears that we are at the right juncture in history to expand the global reach of universal social protection, since many developing countries are currently as rich as some developed countries were, when they first introduced their social protection systems (Ortiz et al. 2017b).

It is easy to be deceived into thinking that providing non-contributory universal SPFs in developing countries with large numbers of vulnerable people is prohibitively expensive. However, it has been shown that for a sample of 101 developing countries, the average cost of providing universal SPFs is only 1.6% of the GDP (Ortiz et al. 2017b). Cost estimates for a smaller sample of 34 lower middle-income countries (LMICs) and 23 low-income countries (LICs) show that universal SPFs would cost only 2.1% of the combined GDP of those 57 countries, or only 0.23% of world GDP (Ortiz et al. 2017b). This is a rather meagre cost, considering that such universal SPFs would directly benefit 9.5% of the world's population, including 103 million severely disabled people, 153 million elderly and 364 million children (Ortiz et al. 2017b).

It has been estimated that if historical trends continue business as usual, then 60 million children of primary school age will remain outside the school and 167 million children will live in poverty in 2030 (UNICEF 2016). ILO's Social Protection Floors Recommendation, 2012 (No. 202), unambiguously acknowledges income security for children as a core component of a national SPF. Yet only 35% of children worldwide, 28% of children in Asia and 29.4% of children in Bangladesh were covered by social protection benefits in 2017 (ILO 2017b). The cost of providing universal cash benefits equivalent to 25% of the national poverty line to all children between 0 and 4 years old, in a sample of 57 developing countries, would be equal to only 1.4% of GDP (Ortiz et al. 2017b). Similar calculations for Bangladesh, using ILO's Social Protection Floors Cost Calculator, show that the cost of providing cash benefits equal to 25% of the national poverty line to all children less than 5 years old would be only 1.04% of GDP (Table 7.5). On the other hand, providing USD 1 per day at PPP to all children less than 5 years old in Bangladesh would cost 1.24% of GDP (Table 7.5).

Table 7.5 Cost of child benefits (as a percentage of GDP)

Type of programme	Universal				Directed to the poor (National poverty line)			
Age groups (in years)	0–4	5–9	10–14	0–14	0–4	5–9	10–14	0–14
Benefit level								
100% of national poverty line	4.17	4.26	4.46	12.90	3.48	3.56	3.73	10.79
75% of national poverty line	3.13	3.19	3.35	9.68	2.61	2.67	2.80	8.09
50% of national poverty line	2.08	2.13	2.23	6.45	1.74	1.78	1.86	5.40
25% of national poverty line	1.04	1.06	1.12	3.23	0.87	0.89	0.93	2.70
100% of minimum salary	7.98	8.15	8.54	24.70	6.67	6.81	7.14	20.65
75% of minimum salary	5.98	6.11	6.40	18.52	5.00	5.11	5.35	15.49
50% of minimum salary	3.99	4.08	4.27	12.35	3.33	3.41	3.57	10.33
25% of minimum salary	1.99	2.04	2.13	6.17	1.67	1.70	1.78	5.16
USD 2 per day at PPP	2.48	2.53	2.65	7.67	2.07	2.12	2.65	6.41
USD 1 per day at PPP	1.24	1.27	1.33	3.83	1.04	1.06	1.11	3.21

Source Authors' calculations based on ILO (n.d.)
Note (i) Calculations include only the cost of non-contributory social assistance benefits for the specified population—it does not include social insurance; (ii) Social insurance is financed by employers and workers contributions and delivers higher benefits; (iii) Child benefit consists of a cash transfer to families with children of the selected age groups; (iv) Administrative costs are included for all benefits and 3% administrative costs are assumed for all universal benefits; (v) Assuming that the total population is 158,512,570; GDP per capita is BDT 78,065; national poverty line is BDT 33,230; minimum salary is BDT 63,600; percentage of children in the population is 29.4%; percentage of orphans among children is 0.0% (rounded to first decimal place); percentage of older persons in the population is 5%; rate of disability is 3.24%; total fertility rate (TFR) is 2.4; and percentage of fertile age women is 2.1%

Research has shown that increase in job-protected paid maternity leave was associated with a significant decrease in infant mortality, although unpaid maternity leave was not (Human Rights Watch 2011). The 16-week maternity leave in Bangladesh is longer than those provided in Nepal, Pakistan and Sri Lanka, but shorter than the 26-week maternity leave that women in India are entitled to. In the absence of the income security provided by a paid maternity leave, women tend to work late into their pregnancy or return to work quickly after childbirth, thus exposing themselves to undue health risks that could have been easily avoided (ILO 2016).

ILO's Social Protection Floors Recommendation, 2012 (No. 202) urges countries to provide basic income security for women during maternity (ILO 2012). Regrettably, worldwide 41% of women with newborns received maternity benefits in 2017, while in Bangladesh, the share of women with newborns receiving maternity benefits was only 20.9% in 2017 (ILO 2017b). The cost of providing universal maternity benefits equivalent to 100% of the national poverty line to all mothers during four months around childbirth, in a sample of 57 developing countries, would be equal to only 0.43% of GDP (Ortiz et al. 2017b). Similar calculations for Bangladesh, using ILO's Social Protection Floors Cost Calculator, show that the cost of providing maternity cash benefits equal to 100% of the national poverty line to all mothers during four months around childbirth would be only 0.3% of GDP (Table 7.6).

The Maternity Allowance Programme in Bangladesh provides a one-time only payment of BDT 500 per month (approximately USD 6 per month or USD 0.20 per day) for a two-year period, to women above the age of 20 years old living in specifically targetted rural areas whose household income is less than BDT 1,500 per month and who were pregnant with their first or second child during the month of

Table 7.6 Cost of universal social benefits (as a percentage of GDP)

Type of benefit	Disability	Maternity	Orphans
Benefit level			
100% of national poverty line	0.93	0.30	0.01
75% of national poverty line	0.70	0.23	0.01
50% of national poverty line	0.47	0.15	0.00
25% of national poverty line	0.23	0.08	0.00
100% of minimum salary	1.78	0.58	0.01
75% of minimum salary	1.34	0.44	0.01
50% of minimum salary	0.89	0.29	0.01
25% of minimum salary	0.45	0.08	0.00
USD 2 per day at PPP	0.55	0.18	0.00
USD 1 per day at PPP	0.28	0.09	0.00

Source Authors' calculations based on ILO (n.d.)
Note (i) Calculations include only the cost of non-contributory social assistance benefits for the specified population—it does not include social insurance; (ii) Social insurance is financed by employers and workers contributions and delivers higher benefits; (iii) Disability benefit consists of a cash transfer to people with disabilities at active ages (15–64); (iv) Maternity benefit consists of a cash transfer to every pregnant woman for a period of four months (medical costs are not included); (v) Orphan benefit consists of a cash transfer to children under 15 years who have lost both parents; (vi) Administration costs are included for all benefits and 3% administrative costs are assumed for all universal benefits; (vii) All values shown up to second decimal place; (vii) Assuming that the total population is 158,512,570; GDP per capita is BDT 78,065; national poverty line is BDT 33,230; minimum salary is BDT 63,600; percentage of children in the population is 29.4%; percentage of orphans among children is 0.0% (rounded to first decimal place); percentage of older persons in the population is 5%; rate of disability is 3.24%; TFR is 2.4; and percentage of fertile age women is 2.1%

July (SPFMSP 2017). The Lactating Mother Allowance programme in Bangladesh also provides a one-time only payment of BDT 500 per month (approximately USD 6 per month or USD 0.2 per day) for a two-year period, to women above the age of 20 years old whose household income is less than BDT 8,000 per month (in case of formal employment) or less than BDT 5,000 per month (in case of informal employment) and who were pregnant with their first or second child during the month of July (SPFMSP 2017). It can be shown that increasing the maternity cash benefits to be equal to USD 1 per day at PPP to all mothers during four months around childbirth would cost only 0.09% of GDP in Bangladesh (Table 7.6).

Globally, there are around 785 million people who are 15 years or older and suffering from disability (ILO 2014). ILO's Social Protection Floors Recommendation, 2012 (No. 202) calls upon countries to provide basic income security and access to healthcare to persons with disabilities, in line with the specific needs of such persons (ILO 2012). Unfortunately, worldwide only 27.8% people with disabilities, and in Bangladesh only 18.5% of people with disabilities, were protected with benefits in 2017 (ILO 2017b). In the Asia and Pacific region, only 9.4% with disabilities were protected with benefits in 2017 (ILO 2017b). The cost of providing universal cash benefits equivalent to 100% of the national poverty line to all persons with severe disabilities, in a sample of 57 developing countries, would be equal to only 0.8% of GDP (Ortiz et al. 2017b). Similar calculations for Bangladesh, using ILO's Social Protection Floors Cost Calculator, show that the cost of providing cash benefits equal to 100% of the national poverty line to all persons with severe disabilities would be only 0.93% of GDP (Table 7.6). On the other hand, providing USD 2 per day at PPP to all persons with severe disabilities in Bangladesh would cost 0.55% of GDP (Table 7.6).

Income security is a crucial part of social protection for the elderly. ILO's Social Protection Floors Recommendation, 2012 (No. 202) mentions that basic income security and access to healthcare are essential for ensuring a secure and dignified life for the elderly (ILO 2012). Although pensions for the elderly are the most commonly provided form of social protection in the world, 32% of the elderly population worldwide and 66% of the elderly population in Bangladesh are still not covered with any social protection benefits (ILO 2017b). Bangladesh also has some of the most stringent legal requirements for obtaining old-age pensions in South Asia. The cost of providing universal cash benefits equivalent to 100% of the national poverty line to all persons aged 65 years and above, in a sample of 57 developing countries, would be equal to only 1.6% of GDP (Ortiz et al. 2017b). For Bangladesh, the cost of providing cash benefits equal to USD 1 per day at PPP to all persons aged 65 years and above would be equivalent to 0.65 of GDP, while providing cash benefits equal to USD 1 per day at PPP only to the poor who are aged 65 years and above would be equivalent to 0.5% of GDP (Table 7.7).

Using ILO's Social Protection Floors Cost Calculator, it can be shown that the cost of providing unemployment support, such as the 100-day EGP, equal to 100% of the national poverty line for 100 days per year for one person at working age

Table 7.7 Cost of pensions (as a percentage of GDP)

Type of programme	Universal	Directed to the poor (National poverty line)
Benefit level		
100% of national poverty line	2.18	1.69
75% of national poverty line	1.64	1.27
50% of national poverty line	1.09	0.85
25% of national poverty line	0.55	0.55
100% of minimum salary	4.17	3.24
75% of minimum salary	3.13	2.43
50% of minimum salary	2.09	1.62
25% of minimum salary	1.04	0.81
USD 2 per day at PPP	1.30	1.01
USD 1 per day at PPP	0.65	0.50

Source Authors' calculations based on ILO (n.d.)
Note (i) Calculations include only the cost of non-contributory social assistance benefits for the specified population—it does not include social insurance; (ii) Social insurance is financed by employers and workers contributions and delivers higher benefits; (iii) Pension is a cash transfer to people aged 65 or older; (iv) Administration costs are included for all benefits and 3% administrative costs are assumed for all universal benefits; (v) Assuming that the total population is 158,512,570; GDP per capita is BDT 78,065; national poverty line is BDT 33,230; minimum salary is BDT 63,600; percentage of children in the population is 29.4%; percentage of orphans among children is 0.0% (rounded to first decimal place); percentage of older persons in the population is 5%; rate of disability is 3.24%; TFR is 2.4; and percentage of fertile age women is 2.1%

per vulnerable household would be 2.14% of GDP (Table 7.8). On the other hand, providing USD 2 per day at PPP for 100 days per year for one person at working age per vulnerable household would cost 1.27% of GDP (Table 7.8).

7.9 The Broader Canvas: Social Protection and Inclusive Growth

There is growing evidence to contend that social sector expenditures, including expenditures on the development of social protection and safety net programmes, are not only a key element in inclusive growth, but also a significant factor in supporting aggregate demand and employment generation (Mathers and Slater 2014).

There is very scant information in Bangladesh on the precise impact of SSNPs on the various dimensions of inclusive growth, such as on growth and structural transformation, inequality and poverty. Mixed cross-country findings exist, but these are unremarkable since context and urgencies of programmes will vary. Institutions, implementation mechanisms and fiscal space, which are likely to determine the impacts, are also different.

Table 7.8 Cost of unemployment support (as a percentage of GDP)

Benefit duration	100 days	200 days	300 days	365 days
Benefit level				
100% of national poverty line	2.14	4.28	6.41	7.80
75% of national poverty line	1.60	3.21	4.81	5.85
50% of national poverty line	1.07	2.14	3.21	3.90
25% of national poverty line	0.53	1.07	1.60	1.95
100% of minimum salary	4.09	8.18	12.27	14.93
75% of minimum salary	3.07	6.14	9.21	11.20
50% of minimum salary	2.05	4.09	6.14	7.47
25% of minimum salary	1.02	2.05	3.07	3.73
USD 2 per day at PPP	1.27	2.54	3.81	4.64
USD 1 per day at PPP	0.64	1.27	1.91	2.32

Source Authors' calculations based on ILO (n.d.)
Note (i) Calculations include only the cost of non-contributory social assistance benefits for the specified population—it does not include social insurance; (ii) Social insurance is financed by employers and workers contributions and delivers higher benefits; (iii) Unemployment support consists of an employment guarantee for a set number of working days per year for one person at working age per vulnerable household; (iv) Administration costs are included for all benefits and 3% administrative costs are assumed for all universal benefits; (v) Assuming that the total population is 158,512,570; GDP per capita is BDT 78,065; national poverty line is BDT 33,230; minimum salary is BDT 63,600; percentage of children in the population is 29.4%; percentage of orphans among children is 0.0% (rounded to first decimal place); percentage of older persons in the population is 5%; rate of disability is 3.24%; TFR is 2.4; and percentage of fertile age women is 2.1%

7.9.1 Social Protection and Poverty

Social protection can affect the level of poverty either by preventing entry into poverty or by facilitating exit from poverty. In conventional neoclassical theory, social protection is believed to stabilise incomes, which enables households to take risks and graduate out of poverty. This line of reasoning, however, has been challenged by the contemporary behavioural economics perspective which advocates that merely reinforcing household productive capacities may not suffice in ensuring poverty exit.

In Bangladesh, there has been a rapid decline in the rate of poverty measured in terms of the per cent of population falling below the upper poverty line. With high GDP growth over the past 10 years and good performance in agriculture, the incidence of hunger and food poverty has been reduced substantially. Thus, the poverty incidence fell from 48.9% in 2000 to 40% in 2005. It further fell from 31.5% in 2010 to 24.8% in 2015. Correspondingly, the percentage of chronic poor, defined as the population below the lower poverty line, fell from 34.3% in 2000 to 17.6% in 2010, and further declined to 12.9% in 2015. On dealing with extreme poverty, Bangladesh has, in many ways, led the way globally. Progress has also been made in reducing the depth of poverty. There has been a continuous narrowing of the consumption gap between 2000 and 2015. Thus, in 2000, the poor on average consumed 26% less than the basic needs consumption basket defined by the poverty line. This gap narrowed to 23% in 2005, 21% in 2010 and roughly to 19% in 2015.

In broad average national terms, it has been observed that the extent of per household benefit from SSNPs has been pretty small, and in some cases negligible. Their contribution to raising average household consumption, a critical indicator of the impact of social safety net benefits, has been widely reported to be insignificant (Osmani 2014; Ahmed 2015). Yet at the project level, specific programmes with proper targetting and implementation have produced tangible results, especially with regard to alleviating poverty and hunger. BRAC's TUP programme is a case in point. The programme has, in the recent past, substantially contributed to the first Millennium Development Goal (MDG) of eradicating extreme poverty and hunger. At the beginning of 2016, with an improved set of goals under SDGs, the programme is now looking forward to further expansion and effective alleviation of the poverty situation of Bangladesh. The TUP programme, which is playing a catalytic role, has attained global recognition as a tested method of graduating out of poverty. The programme, however, is dependent on intense attention to target households who are supported through asset grants, skills training, health and other support over an extended period. This would place a heavy demand on, among other things, resources and implementation capacity.

The disaggregated poverty profile by location, in terms of rural and urban and by divisions, shows substantial variations. This geographic variation in the distribution of poverty underscores the need to further refine the poverty profile by other characteristics, including gender, age, education, asset and employment, to layout an appropriate poverty reduction strategy and associated interventions. By association, the NSSS also needs to be aligned to the poverty profile based on a proper assessment of related risks.

7.9.2 *Social Protection and Inequality*

While lessons can be learnt on policies and programmes from country experiences, the individual country choices and their relevance will be guided more by the pragmatism of what is truly required, and what is feasible. Social protection policies and programmes are best realised through a well-coordinated and well-designed social protection framework.

The data indicates that the national, rural and urban Gini coefficient in Bangladesh have increased over the period 1973–74 to 2015–16 (Table 7.9). Throughout the period, the rural Gini coefficient was lower than the national Gini coefficient, whilst the urban Gini coefficient was higher than the national Gini coefficient.

Although the Gini coefficient is the most widely used measure of income inequality, it can sometimes fail to elucidate the extent of social injustice that is caused due to income inequality. Under such circumstances, it may be useful to look at the income shares held by the richest and poorest households in a nation.

Table 7.9 Income inequality in Bangladesh: 1973–74 to 2015–16

Criteria	1973–74	1983–84	1985–86	1988–89	1991–92	1995–96	2000	2005	2010	2015–16
Gini national	0.36	0.36	0.37	0.38	0.39	0.43	0.45	0.47	0.458	0.483
Gini rural	0.35	0.35	0.36	0.37	0.36	0.38	0.39	0.43	0.431	0.454
Gini urban	0.38	0.37	0.37	0.38	0.40	0.44	0.50	0.50	0.450	0.498

Source Authors' compilation based on the data from various issues of HIES and Statistical Pocketbook of Bangladesh, BBS

Table 7.10 Income share held by the poorest and richest (%)

Income share	1991–92	1995–96	2000	2005	2010	2015–16
Held by the poorest 5%	1.03	0.88	0.93	0.77	0.78	0.23
Held by the richest 5%	18.85	23.62	28.34	26.93	24.61	27.89
Income share held by the richest 5% as a multiple of the income share held by the poorest 5%	18	27	30	35	32	121

Source Authors' compilation based on the data from various issues of HIES, BBS

Data from the period 1991–92 to 2015–16 shows that the income share held by the richest 5% of households in Bangladesh increased from 18.85% in 1991–92 to 27.89% in 2015–16, whilst the income share held by the poorest 5% of households in Bangladesh fell from 1.03% in 1991–92 to 0.23% in 2015–16. The income share of the richest 5% households as a multiple of the income share of the poorest 5% households increased dramatically over the past few years. In 2010, the richest 5% households were 32 times richer than the poorest 5% households; but this difference magnified astronomically in 2015, when the richest 5% households were 121 times richer than the poorest 5% households (Table 7.10).

Given the persistent increase in inequality and the widening gap between the top and bottom 5% in the income spectrum, it is difficult to ascertain what role social protection programmes in Bangladesh have played as redistributive mechanisms. While in the case of poverty alleviation and income support, there is evidence to support that SSNPs have favourably affected specific groups and regions, it is not possible to establish such impact concerning inequality. There are indeed some SSNPs which target empowerment and enhancement of opportunities; for example, the initiative for development, empowerment, awareness and livelihood; investment component for the vulnerable groups; increased productivity and opportunity for employment of women, etc. These are, however, rather small and ad hoc, and would need to be scaled up in a major way.

The tax revenue as a percentage of GDP in Bangladesh has consistently been the lowest in South Asia, and one of the lowest in the world. As a result, scaling up SSNPs of the kind mentioned above will only succeed in generating additional fiscal pressure on the government. Nevertheless, the government has recognised the disconcerting rise in inequality and has given attention to the need for taking immediate steps to try and curtail inequality. The Seventh Five Year Plan (7FYP) was designed to shift budget allocations more towards social sectors (in particular, health and education), through curtailing subsidies in the energy sector and raising greater revenues. One has to observe how far such expenditure switching is likely to face constraints and political opposition. Meanwhile, inequality continues to grow and persist in Bangladesh, and the influence of the current SSNPs appears imperceptible.

7.10 The National Social Security Strategy: An Assessment

The NSSS was planned to be gradually implemented during the 7FYP starting from FY2015-16. The NSSS seeks to modernise the social security system in Bangladesh by combining tax-funded SSNPs with contributory social insurance and employment regulations to protect workers. This initiative has broadened the scope of social protection from the narrow safety net concept and included employment policies and social insurance. Implementation of this strategy was a major task of the 7FYP. The success of achieving social inclusion will largely depend on the way programmes under NSSS are designed, directed and implemented.

The NSSS is designed to address some of the limitations and weaknesses of the present social security system as identified above; in particular, undercoverage of regional dimensions, lack of access to the programmes, less than the full benefit of safety net programmes, leakages, etc. (GED 2015). Identifying the issues and broadening the scope of social security will ease the process of commissioning necessary steps towards safeguarding social security. As previously noted, there is no coordination mechanism in the present social security system that makes the system inefficient from various dimensions, including improper utilisation of resources, inappropriate targetting, etc.

The newly designed NSSS presents a mechanism to build an SPF, through identification and categorisation of the needs and priorities of social assistance and insurance according to different life-cycle groups. The NSSS suggests five core life-cycle programmes consolidated along with the life-cycle risks: (i) programmes for children; (ii) programmes for the working-age; (iii) comprehensive pension system for elderly; (iv) programmes for people with disabilities; and (v) special programmes for the freedom fighters. The mechanism will work well if it can be implemented in a systematic way, by checking overlap of the programmes and recipients and arresting leakages.

Based on the NSSS (GED 2015), Table 7.11 provides a bird's eye view of the critical challenges and mid-term priorities towards building a consolidated social security strategy, especially a consolidation of the life-cycle approach that is required to lay the foundations of an SPF. There are equally formidable challenges in financing the strategy, and in overhauling the coordination, implementation and monitoring system.

The NSSS has identified these broad challenges, as in Table 7.11, and the intent and broad objectives are noteworthy. Bangladesh's NSSS, with its life-cycle approach, has a potential to develop a platform that could eventually create an effective SPF, as spelt out by the ILO, which too focuses on a life-cycle approach. The SPF is a campaign towards establishing social protection guarantees, at nationally-defined levels, to support the poor, vulnerable and socially excluded. In this regard, the SPF proposes four guarantees as a minimum over the life cycle: (i) access to essential healthcare, including maternity care; (ii) basic income security for children, especially access to nutrition, education, healthcare and other necessary goods and

Table 7.11 Synopsis of Bangladesh's National Social Security Strategy

Issues in NSSS	Elements included in NSSS
Challenges	• Proliferation of programmes to consolidate • Inadequacy of the social security schemes • Serious gaps in addressing life-cycle-related risks • Targetting performance needs improvement • Dominance of food transfer and rural employment programmes • Focus on addressing the risks faced by the rural poor • Attention to marginalised and excluded groups • Climate change poses new vulnerabilities • Identifying the financing needs of a well-designed social security system and possible financing options • Absence of effective monitoring and evaluation (M&E)
Vision	• Build an inclusive social security system that effectively tackles and prevents poverty and inequality and contributes to broader human development, employment and economic growth
Mid-term priority/next five years	• A shift from current discretionary to a targetted universal approach • Expanding coverage of core schemes for the hardcore poor and most vulnerable people of the society • Progressive but substantive scaling up of the *graduation* programmes • Ensuring vulnerable women's income security and greater opportunities to engage in the labour market • Initiating a social insurance system that enables people to invest in their own social security • Expanding coverage to the residents of urban areas and to the socially excluded people • Ensuring that the social security system supports an effective disaster response system • Strengthening the delivery systems for priority transfers • Expanding awareness of the social security programmes for the beneficiaries and motivating potential contributors
Adopting a life-cycle approach to social security	• Programmes for children • Programmes for the working age • Comprehensive pension system for elderly

(continued)

Table 7.11 (continued)

Issues in NSSS	Elements included in NSSS
Other focuses and consolidation	• Social security for the socially excluded groups • Strengthening the social security system for the urban poor • Strengthening resilience in the face of covariate shocks • Consolidation of food transfer programmes • Consolidation of special programmes and small schemes
Financing instrument and source	• Social transfers are public expenditure financed • Social insurance is financed by contributions from employees • Labour legislation is financed by employers
Strengthening the delivery	• Institutional arrangement reinforcing and ensuring proper planning, implementation and M&E • Professionalisation of staff • Effectiveness in identifying recipients • Upgrading the management information systems • Strengthening payment mechanisms • Establishing an effective grievance redress

Source Authors' compilation based on the data from GED (2015)

services; (iii) basic income security for persons in active age who are unable to earn sufficient income, especially because of disability, sickness, unemployment or maternity; and (iv) basic income security for older persons.

The life-cycle system of social security of the NSSS (Table 7.11) corresponds closely to the above. Programmes in the SSNPs are intended to provide some of the above security, viz. old-age allowance, widow and destitute women allowance, maternal health allowance, stipend for disabled students, various allowances for freedom fighters, etc. However, the programmes are many and sporadic and are yet to be properly designed and articulated to spell out how such security (income security, health) is to be strengthened and attained as a universal target.

Although several programmes exist on SSNPs, the NSSS as a strategy, especially in its bid to extend various life-cycle guarantees, is in its infancy. As observed earlier, programmes and objectives are being reviewed and designed to conform to the life-cycle approach of the NSSS. However, it would be a long march to establish an appropriate SPF, as envisaged in the NSSS, and in conformity with the SPF above, and to attain the SDGs on social protection systems and measures for all, including floors (SDG Target 1.3) by 2030. The various challenges and some of the mid-term priority activities are well-marked in the NSSS (Table 7.11). However, given the constraints of resources and capacity, it is still unclear how these will be financed and implemented.

Financing of the NSSS would, in the long-run, be based on cost-sharing; that is, one part would be financed through public expenditure (i.e. transfers and subsidies) and the other by the private sector, based on social insurance and employment-based regulations. However, the proposed financing source of broader social security seems to be vague. There is no proper clarification on how the financing will take place and who will take responsibility. The social insurance component of financing is a negligible proportion; hence the NSSS will, for quite some time to come, have to be based on tax-financed transfers. Clear guidelines should be in place about financing of social security and how various ministries and departments will coordinate with each other to make the strategy work.

7.11 Moving Forward

As it currently stands, social protection in Bangladesh is almost synonymous with SSNPs, which are overwhelmingly focused on providing tax-financed transfer support to the poor and informal population and specific vulnerable groups. In the more recent period, these SSNPs have come to be associated with public measures on various dimensions of empowerment via improving access to health and primary and secondary education. In Bangladesh, where poverty is still fairly high, and the economy is largely informal, there is a constant need for income and employment support, i.e. an appropriate safety net and social protection measures. Various examples of public interventions and non-contributory social protection measures exist in Asia, especially in South Asian countries. In Bangladesh, increasing attention is indeed being paid to these, and currently, the NSSS has been formulated to consolidate these SSNPs, and reorient the social protection system towards an SPF, based on social assistance as well as social insurance.

As a starting point, the current SSNPs, and the entire gamut of transfer programmes which lack a framework, must be closely reviewed on an NSSS-coordinated platform. An appropriate rationale must be there to identify which ones deserve more attention and priority and which ones can be potentially phased out. According to the findings of the present study and several other studies, the following issues and limitations need to be addressed: (i) The vast number of SSNPs need to be reviewed in order to better establish the priorities of interventions, under the shifting economic and social profile of beneficiary households; (ii) A closer scrutiny is required of the SSNP beneficiaries and their relative prioritisation from various dimensions of vulnerability. This has to be done both at the programme-level and the sector-level that conducts the programmes. This would involve a comprehensive mapping of the most vulnerable groups that would help design SSNPs in keeping with the SDG commitment to *leave no one behind*.

One needs to balance priorities to address and build on processes that would reinforce the SPF goals and move the NSSS framework towards targetted universal goals, and move away from random discretionary SSNPs. The present study contends that the EGPP programme, with necessary modifications (e.g. better targetting of those regions and groups under high exposure to risks) and scaling up, has the potential to provide guarantee of minimum income to households (as in India's Mahatma Gandhi National Rural Employment Guarantee Act (MGNREGA)) whose members are *working poor* or are underemployed.

There is a skewed distribution of fund allocation among the SSNPs, with a few large ones and many small programmes. There needs to be a consolidation so that the interventions are effective, and can make tangible support to the beneficiary households in progressing towards the objective of the respective programme. As observed earlier, the pension budget is disproportionate to the rest of SSNP programmes. Furthermore, the social insurance component needs to be vigorously pursued through statutory provisions for the private sector enterprises, both formal and informal, as well as through innovative schemes where people invest in their own (income and health) security.

The review of the existing SSNPs needs to take into account some of the limitations identified in the study; viz. (i) better targetting, so that leakages and adverse selection are minimised; (ii) overlaps with other SSNPs and other NGO programmes are avoided; (iii) introducing finite planning with finite targets, so that an exit strategy is explicitly or implicitly incorporated.

Programmes need to be monitored and analysed within a comparable database and framework, so that the relative progress and comparative significance of the SSNPs are made transparent for future planning and resource allocation. Again, their orientation must be guided by the needs of gradually moving to the life-cycle approach.

There needs to be better coordination among the multiple ministries that administer the SSNPs in order to enhance efficiency and avoid turf war. This would allow scrutiny on whether programmes can be merged that could minimise administrative costs.

It must be noted that the SSNPs themselves cannot achieve SDG target 1.3. Apart from the measures mentioned above, and on the broader front, the design of social protection, its pervasiveness, and the realisation of the vision of the NSSS (especially attempts to merge the horizontal and vertical dimensions of social protection) will be contingent on three critical interrelated developments.

So long as poverty, inequality and vulnerability continue to persist in the economy, there will be continued pressure on the allocations and persistence of SSNPs. However, given that poverty has been declining, a fresh stocktaking is needed to redirect the SSNPs and required allocations. A first step would be to target extreme poverty and hunger, and the most vulnerable groups. This is significant to understand and reassess for whom the safety nets are intended, and by what measures and per capita allocations. In particular, this would help reorient SSNPs to attain the 2030 Agenda call to *leave no one behind* (Bhattacharya et al. 2017). Again, current SSNPs are, in aggregate terms, a minuscule addition to household income-consumption. Elimination of extreme poverty (SDG 1) and hunger (SDG 2) would require much more attention on a broader policy and programme front to ensure food and income entitlements, and to ensure access to various opportunities, e.g. jobs, skills, credit, etc. Inequality-averse growth would allow better prospects of poverty and inequality reduction in the economy.

Social protection policies towards the goal of full employment must be seen as critically interrelated in developing a strategy of inclusive growth. While the advanced economies, especially those in Western Europe, stand out as prime examples of how social protection and full employment policies go hand in hand towards institutionalising social welfare, this process has not been designed and pursued in the most developing countries. Even in the fast-growing East and Southeast Asian economies, which through their labour-intensive growth, attained near full employment, there has been less than proportionate emphasis on social protection measures (Lee 1998). An assessment of social protection and social safety nets is needed to ensure that alongside the goals of employment promotion, there are policies and an institutional framework to protect employment and incomes, especially of the vulnerable groups. Such an assessment would be a precursor to establish a universal SPF. Currently, there are numerous entitlement programmes which are rather fragmented, not well-coordinated, and have varied effectiveness.

Bangladesh, saddled with a high incidence of poverty and underemployment, and very low levels and coverage of social protection, would need to focus on an invigorated policy intervention to move towards a full employment goal. Productive and private formal sector jobs need to grow, which are potentially the precursor of the growth of social insurance and contributory finance. The gradual increase in such finance is likely to reduce pressure on SSNPs and simple transfers. Bangladesh has paid less than adequate attention on the weights that need to be given to employment generation, and less so, on the need to develop social protection mechanisms. Apart from the political commitment to develop such a strategy, the institutions—legal and administrative—that are necessary to safeguard the outcomes of these policies, need to be built as the economy progresses.

The fiscal challenge in Bangladesh vis-à-vis social security financing is enormous. Despite remarkable reductions in poverty, there are still nearly 47 million people in poverty, and 26 million in extreme poverty and more than three-fifths of the poor do not receive any social safety benefits. In this context, the pace of the realisation of the NSSS, and its vision to reach universal targets, would depend crucially on how the many elements of its programmes are financed and implemented. Although the design of the NSSS is to gradually encourage growth of social insurance and contributory financing, the latter would need a prolonged period of many developments before one can start envisaging a reduction in transfers and SSNP interventions, especially the steady growth in paid and protected jobs in the private formal sector. Nevertheless, the budget burden to finance the SSNPs will continue to be large, given the current levels of extreme poverty and vulnerability in the economy, especially of underprivileged groups and regions. Fiscal space will also need to expand to build the capacity and institutions needed towards implementation of the NSSS. Equally, statutory provisions that are likely to come with NSSS and the building of SPF (i.e. social guarantees of the life-cycle approach, targetted universal goals, etc.) will require financial provisions. For instance, attempts should be made to widen social insurance coverage in the informal sector and informal enterprises, and to make these effective, there will likely be the need to extend financial incentives and subsidies.

Fiscal space in Bangladesh is currently restricted by the very low revenue–GDP ratio (less than 10%), which is low not only compared to many of the Asian countries, but also many Sub-Saharan countries (average of 19%). Expansion of fiscal space is not only dependent on additional tax and non-tax revenues, but also on reprioritisation and better rationalisation of public expenditures (Ortiz et al. 2017a). More significantly, pressure on expenditures on SSNPs (i.e. transfers) in the long-run will diminish only when there is a steady job growth in the economy, especially in the private sector. The NSSS strategy to build an SPF will critically depend on how a rising employer–employee contribution (to social insurance) will supplement social assistance transfers, and eventually reinforce and institutionalise a public social insurance system that would be central to the realisation of SDG 1.3 and of the NSSS by 2030.

References

Ahmed, S. (2015). *Growth with equity: Contemporary development challenges of Bangladesh*. Dhaka: Bangladesh Institute of Bank Management (BIBM).

Ahmed, A. U., Hoddinott, F. J., Roy, S., Sraboni, E., Quabili, R. W., & Margolies, A. (2016). *Which kinds of social safety net transfers work best for the ultra poor in Bangladesh? Operation and impacts of the transfer modality research initiative*. Dhaka: International Food Policy Research Institute (IFPRI) and World Food Programme (WFP), Bangladesh Office.

Barkat-e-Khuda. (2011). Social safety net programmes in Bangladesh: A review. *Bangladesh Development Studies, 34*(2), 87–108.

BBS. (2011). *Report of the household income and expenditure survey 2010*. Dhaka: Bangladesh Bureau of Statistics (BBS), Government of Bangladesh (GoB).

BBS. (2017). *Preliminary report on household income and expenditure survey 2016*. Dhaka: Bangladesh Bureau of Statistics (BBS), Government of Bangladesh (GoB).

BBS. (2018). *Report on labour force survey 2016–17*. Dhaka: Bangladesh Bureau of Statistics (BBS), Government of Bangladesh (GoB).

Bhattacharya, D., Khan, T. I., Khan, S. S., Sinha, M. M., Fuad, S. M., Biswas, S., & Muzib, A. (2017). *Quest for inclusive transformation of Bangladesh: Who not to be left behind—executive summary*. Dhaka: Centre for Policy Dialogue (CPD) and Citizen's Platform for SDGs, Bangladesh.

Fiszbein, A., & Schady, N. R. (2009). *Conditional cash transfers: Reducing present and future poverty*. World Bank Policy Research Report. Washington, D.C.: The World Bank.

García, A. B., & Gruat, J. V. (2003). *Social protection: A life cycle continuum investment for social justice, poverty reduction and development*. Social Protection Series. Geneva: Social Protection Sector, International Labour Organization (ILO).

GED. (2015). *National Social Security Strategy (NSSS) of Bangladesh*. Dhaka: General Economics Division (GED), Planning Commission, Government of Bangladesh (GoB).

Holzmann, R., & Jørgensen, S. (2001). Social risk management: A new conceptual framework for social protection, and beyond. *International Tax and Public Finance, 8*(4), 529–556.

Human Rights Watch. (2011). *Failing its families: Lack of paid leave and work-family supports in the US*. New York: Human Rights Watch.

ILO. (2012, June 14). *R202-social protection floors recommendation, 2012 (No. 202)*. Geneva: International Labour Organization (ILO).

ILO. (2014). *World social protection report 2014/15*. Geneva: International Labour Organization (ILO).

ILO. (2016). *Maternity cash benefits for workers in the informal economy*. Social Protection for All Issue Brief. Geneva: International Labour Organization (ILO).
ILO. (2017a). *World employment and social outlook 2017—sustainable enterprises and jobs: Formal enterprises and decent work*. Geneva: International Labour Organization (ILO).
ILO. (2017b). *World social protection report 2017–19*. Geneva: International Labour Organization (ILO).
ILO. (n.d.) *ILO's social protection floors cost calculator*. Geneva: International Labour Organization (ILO). Retrieved January 17, 2020, from https://www.social-protection.org/gimi/gess/SPFCalculReport.action.
IMF. (2017). *The IMF and social protection: 2017 evaluation report*. Washington, D.C.: Independent Evaluation Office, International Monetary Fund (IMF).
Khatun, F., Khan, T. I., & Nabi, A. (2010). *Employment generation for the hardcore poor and national service challenges of effective implementation*. Draft Report. Dhaka: Centre for Policy Dialogue (CPD).
Khatun, F., Khan, T. I., & Nabi, A. (2012). *National budget for the ultra poor: An analysis of allocation and effectiveness*. Dhaka: Centre for Policy Dialogue (CPD) and BRAC Advocacy for Social Change.
Lee, E. (1998). *The Asian financial crisis: The challenge for social policy*. Geneva: International Labour Organization (ILO).
Mathers, N., & Slater, R. (2014). *Social protection and growth: Research synthesis*. Canberra: Department of Foreign Affairs and Trade, Government of Australia.
MSUK. (2013). *Improving the targeting effectiveness of social safety nets in Bangladesh*. Dhaka: Manob Sakti Unnayan Kendro (MSUK).
Ortiz, I., Cummins, M., & Karunanethy, K. (2017a). *Fiscal space for social protection and the SDGs: Options to expand social investments in 187 countries*. ESS Working Paper 48. Geneva: Social Protection Department, International Labour Organization (ILO).
Ortiz, I., Durán-Valverde, F., Pal, K., Behrendt, C., & Acuña-Ulate, A. (2017b). *Universal social protection floors: Costing estimates and affordability in 57 lower income countries*. Geneva: Social Protection Department, International Labour Organization (ILO).
Osmani, S. R. (2014). *Designing social protection for the rural poor: Learning from lessons on the ground*. InM Working Paper No. 31. Dhaka: Institute of Microfinance (InM).
Paitoonpong, S., Abe, S., & Puopongsakorn, N. (2008). The meaning of "social safety nets." *Journal of Asian Economics, 19*(5–6), 467–473.
Rahman, H. Z., Choudhury, L. A., & Ali, K. S. (2011). *Social safety nets in Bangladesh: Review of issues and analytical inventory*. PPRC-UNDP Research Initiative (Volume 1). Dhaka: Power and Participation Research Centre (PPRC) and United Nations Development Programme (UNDP).
SPFMSP. (2017). *Diagnostic study of maternity allowance (MA) and lactating mother allowance (LMA) programmes of Bangladesh: Implications for value-for-money in social protection interventions*. Dhaka: Strengthening Public Financial Management for Social Protection Project (SPFMSP), Finance Division, Ministry of Finance (MoF), Government of Bangladesh (GoB).
UN. (n.d.) *Goal 1: End poverty in all its forms everywhere*. New York: United Nations (UN). Retrieved January 17, 2020, from https://www.un.org/sustainabledevelopment/poverty/.
UNICEF. (2016). *The state of the world's children 2016: A fair chance for every child*. New York: United Nations Children's Fund (UNICEF).
UNRISD. (2010). *Combating poverty and inequality: Structural change, social policy and politics*. UNRISD Flagship Report. Geneva: United Nations Research Institute for Social Development (UNRISD).
US Social Security Administration. (2017). *Social security programs throughout the world: Asia and the Pacific, 2016*. SSA Publication 13-11802. Washington, D.C.: Social Security Administration, Government of the United States of America (USA).
Van Stolk, C., & Tesliuc, E. (2010). *Toolkit on tackling error, fraud and corruption in social protection programs*. Washington, D.C.: The World Bank.

World Bank. (n.d.). *World development indicators (WDI)*. Retrieved February 6, 2018, from https://databank.worldbank.org/data/reports.aspx?source=world-development-indicators.

Chapter 8
Governance, Growth and Social Inclusion

Muhammed Muqtada and Muntaseer Kamal

Abstract The significance of good governance for inclusive growth in Bangladesh is undeniable. This is particularly relevant, considering that despite remarkable progress in a number of development indicators, the benefits of growth are not distributed across various sections of the people due to weak institutions and poor governance. This chapter examines trends in some of the widely accepted governance indicators in Bangladesh, and seeks to assess their relationship in regard to growth indicators. It also investigates whether governance limitations can act as bottlenecks to future investment and growth of the country. Based on the analysis, the chapter identifies governance shortcomings that need to be addressed in order to facilitate inclusive growth in Bangladesh. In particular to foster social inclusion, governance would require additional considerations beyond the traditional indicators. The study contends that this would imply progress in the dispensation of rights, representation and rule of law. While this is tall order, these can be pursued gradually through, for example, choosing the *wrongs and rights in development* (Sen, Wrongs and rights in development. Prospect, 1995). It further contends that while strong institutions and improved governance are needed for long-term inclusive growth in Bangladesh, the importance of prudent and effectively implemented inclusive policies cannot be undermined.

M. Muqtada (✉)
Development Economist; Formerly a Director in the Employment Sector of the International Labour Organization (ILO), Geneva and a Visiting Fellow, Centre for Policy Dialogue (CPD), Dhaka, Bangladesh
e-mail: muqtada1@gmail.com

M. Kamal
Senior Research Associate, Centre for Policy Dialogue (CPD), Dhaka, Bangladesh
e-mail: muntaseer@cpd.org.bd

M. Muqtada (ed.), *Quest for Inclusive Growth in Bangladesh*,
South Asia Economic and Policy Studies,
https://doi.org/10.1007/978-981-15-7614-0_8

8.1 Introduction

Governance is undeniably an important consideration in the pursuit of inclusive growth. A significant part of the literature on governance, quite rightly, focuses on an understanding of the complexities and ambivalence that characterise it, and how to achieve good governance (as an *end*). There is equally a burgeoning literature on how far, and to what extent, governance is a *means* and is likely to influence growth, development and inclusion. The latter is largely based on extensive empirical research, made possible by the development, largely by the World Bank, of elaborate indicators and databases. Evidently recent discussions have often oscillated between whether governance should be seen as an end, or as an instrument towards achieving the various pillars of inclusive growth.[1] If it is an instrument towards achieving inclusive growth, how robust is its influence, considering that there are many other variables affecting growth and welfare? Can the relationship be endogenous, that is, would governance improve if there were sustained growth? It may be noted that the Sustainable Development Goals (SDGs), also referred to as 2030 Agenda for Sustainable Development, has a similar underlying pursuit; it calls for pursuing good governance and appropriate institutions as an end (SDG 16); on the other hand, the Agenda underpins its role as an instrument to achieve the other SDGs.[2]

Researchers and policy practitioners are impulsive to point that analyses and policies concerning growth are incomplete without factoring in *governance* (World Bank 2017b). As stated earlier, the role of governance is now seen as explicit and central to the discussions of the development agenda by both national and international stakeholders.[3]

The aforesaid issues have led to energetic discourses in the literature on governance, where opinions and empirical evidence are often strongly divided. Governance is an enigmatic and complex issue and much of the literature on its multiple dimensions hardly helps to secure a complete grip on it[4] and raises more questions than resolutions. What has broadly transpired in this burgeoning literature is that a good governance model, as the World Bank contends, appears in general to be associated with high-income advanced countries (Kaufmann et al. 1999); that few other developing countries have been able to consolidate growth and economic progress through foundations of appropriate *institutions* (Acemoglu and Robinson 2013; World Bank 2008), that growth and achievements can be derailed if institutions and governance are weak, as empirically examined.[5] Nevertheless, for a country like Bangladesh, the

[1] Rodrik (2008) warns that economists, in dealing with growth and related issues, need to refrain from getting into governance as an end, since much of the latter is a discourse best left to political and legal experts.

[2] UN (2015).

[3] Kaufmann et al. (1999, 2005).

[4] See among others, Acemoglu and Robinson (2013), North et al. (2008).

[5] Rodrik (1999), when he invokes failure of institutions in explaining 'Where did All the Growth Go?'.

above does not shed light on what constitutes good governance that is applicable at its current stage of development, or on how to go about achieving it without trade-offs.

In Bangladesh, there have been noteworthy achievements in several economic and social indicators of development in spite of a relatively low score in governance. Many experts have emphasised the need for urgent attention to address the more critical aspects of governance which are likely to pose threats and challenges to future growth.[6] In this study, some of the above issues, and some of the dimensions of governance that are key to attaining inclusive growth in Bangladesh, will be examined.

In the absence of a universally accepted guideline for governance indicators, this chapter attempts to reflect on some of the currently accepted data—e.g. Worldwide Governance Indicator (WGI) data—and anecdotal information for assessing governance in Bangladesh. The study also tries to observe whether there are improvements in some of the indicators; to assess their impact on and relationship to growth indicators; to explore how far governance and growth are endogenous; and whether governance limitations, unless improved, can impede future investment and growth; and to identify governance deficits that need to be redressed in order to facilitate inclusive growth in Bangladesh.

8.2 Examining the Issues

Several economic observers had expressed disappointment over the less than satisfactory growth rates that had been achieved during the 1980s and 1990s, especially in the backdrop of fairly sweeping reforms that were then undertaken in the framework of stabilisation and structural adjustment. In fact, some economists dubbed the 1990s as a lost decade (e.g. Easterly 2001). The elusive quest for growth, hitherto confined largely to policy reforms, had entered into the arena of governance. Such discourses have come from diverse sources, but mainly from the academia,[7] multilateral organisations,[8] and are often underwritten in pledges of donor aid.

Despite the burgeoning literature, and a measure of understanding on its broad attributes, there is hardly, in this discourse, anything definitive about *governance*, or consensual on its characteristics and measurement.[9] The terminology itself, often confined to the study of company/corporate behaviour, had been extended to wider

---

[6]Khan (2015).

[7]In the policy world, it has been reached more painfully, as a result of a long stream of reforms around the world that failed mainly because they did not pay attention to institutions and governance issues. See Acemoglu (2008).

[8]*Governance* is a frequent term in research and policy documents of the international financial institutions, United Nations Development Programme (UNDP) and other multilateral organisations. The World Bank, in particular, has spearheaded the research drive on governance—particularly in the construction of indicators that are now being widely used (World Bank 2017b).

[9]For an insightful survey of this literature, see among others, Kaufmann and Kraay (2003), North et al. (2008), Khan (2015).

tests in the context of national governance, and more recently, global governance.[10] Given that governance has come to be characterised rather randomly, and that empiricism has overtaken a conceptual ferment, the discourse has moved into a somewhat unchartered terrain. In fact, economic and political commentators are already apprehensive about its usefulness as an analytical tool.

The precise origins of the rise of governance as a principle objective of development, let alone inclusive growth, are difficult to trace. Meier and Stiglitz (2001) provide a schematic view of how governance issues are now at the centre of a development agenda.[11] Given that perceptions of governance are heterogeneous, and have emanated from different vantage points, it is difficult to agree on anything beyond the terse and very pertinent emphasis that *governance matters*.[12] Notwithstanding the ambivalence, governance is now being empirically tested by academics, by donor agencies/communities, and on specific self-selected indicators by various non-government organisations (NGOs).[13] The first systematic attempts at developing governance variables, from a large range of possible (subjective and objective) indicators, are much more recent, largely pioneered by the World Bank. The chapters that have been generated on quantifying governance indicators, and on establishing linkages with growth, have universally expressed caution regarding the use and interpretation of the database.[14]

8.3 A Governance Score for Bangladesh

To place a country on a governance scale is difficult and hazardous. The World Bank has devised a few indicators and a database to approximate those. Any alternative quantitative data on governance indicators that are consistent over time and comparable across countries hardly exists. The following empirical examination is thus based on the WGI database. Needless to say, each of the indicators would need to be explored further at the country level to be able to assess their true significance. This would require detailed, even anecdotal, narratives that are beyond the scope and space of the present study.

---

[10]Rodrik (2008).

[11]"To the first generation the government was an exogenous force, but the new political economy attempts to endogenise the decisions of politicians, bureaucrats, and administrators. It seeks to open windows in the black box of the 'state' by using various strands of thought: public choice, collective choice, transaction costs, property rights, rent-seeking, and directly unproductive profit-seeking activities" (Meier and Stiglitz 2001, p. 21).

[12]'Governance Matters' is also the title of an influential paper by Kaufmann et al. (1999).

[13]For example, a corruption index is monitored by Transparency International; similarly, Human Rights Watch and Amnesty International monitor the violation of human rights.

[14]Kaufmann et al. (1999).

The WGI[15] data report on six broad dimensions of governance for all countries since 1996 (Kaufmann et al. 2005). The dimensions include *voice and accountability, political stability and absence of violence, government effectiveness, regulatory quality, rule of law* and *control of corruption.*[16] Estimates give the country's score on the aggregate indicator, in units of a standard normal distribution that is ranging from approximately (−) 2.5 [negative] to + 2.5 [positive]. In Bangladesh too, in the absence of alternative databases, other studies have utilised the WGI data to plot progress and impact.[17] The following discussion provides a summary view of the trends in selected WGI indicators in Bangladesh as well as those in the comparator countries, with a focus on those that have relatively greater relevance to inclusive governance.

Among the six WGI indicators, one that deals more directly with *rights* is the *voice and accountability* indicator (Fig. 8.1). With regard to this, the conditions seem to have deteriorated in Bangladesh, especially compared to the 1990s. It is only India that has a positive record on *voice and accountability.* Interestingly, in most South Asian countries, barring Nepal and Sri Lanka, there had been an erosion of *voice and accountability* between 2015 and 2018. As can be evinced, Bangladesh has generally performed better than Cambodia, Pakistan and Vietnam. Nevertheless, in Bangladesh, various national and international observers have expressed serious concerns over the rising violations of human rights and curbs on the freedom of expression, be it from the opposition parties, the NGOs or media.[18] Recent regulations such as the Information and Communications Technology (ICT) Act, the Digital Security Act, have come under severe criticism, especially with regard to freedom of expression and freedom of media investigations.[19]

On political stability, Bangladesh has registered an improvement since 2005; although the score is still in the negative zone on the scale. As a matter of fact, in the more recent period between 2010 and 2018, there had generally been a marked improvement in both economic and political stability in the countries concerned, a

[15] World Bank (2019).

[16] *Voice and accountability* encapsulates perceptions regarding the degree to which citizens of a nation can take part in the government selection process, as well as freedom of expression, freedom of association and a free media; *Government effectiveness* delineates perceptions regarding public service quality, civil service quality and the extent of administrative liberty from political pressures; *Political stability* measures perceptions of the likelihood of political instability and/or politically-motivated violence, including terrorism; *Regulatory quality* captures opinions regarding the government's ability to create and maintain a sound policy environment that facilitates private sector development; *Rule of law* portrays perceptions of the degree of people's confidence in and willingness to follow the rules of society, and in particular, the quality of contract enforcement, property rights, the police, and the courts, as well as the likelihood of crime and violence; and *Control of corruption* captures assessment of the extent to which public power is misused for private gain, including both petty and grand forms of corruption, as well as capture of the state by elites and private interests.

[17] See for example, Roy (2006), Khan (2017).

[18] Iftekharuzzaman (2018).

[19] Bangladesh is ranked 146th out of 180 countries in the 2017 World Press Freedom Index (Reporters Without Borders 2017).

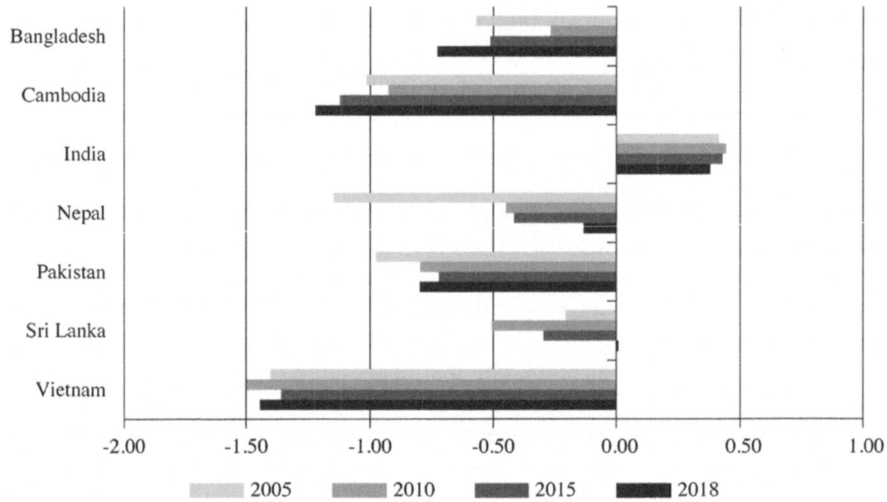

Fig. 8.1 Voice and accountability: Score of countries in South Asia. *Source* World Bank (n.d.b). *Note* (−) 2.5 [negative] corresponds to the lowest and (+) 2.5 [positive] corresponds to the highest state of governance

feature which is often associated with better growth performance of these economies (World Bank 2019). Nevertheless, political volatility will have different meanings and potency, and cannot be easily compared. In Bangladesh, despite the apparent improvements in *political stability*, the overall investor confidence is still shaky. In World Economic Forum's (WEF) competitiveness index surveys, political instability tops various other constraints to doing business (see for instance WEF 2015, 2016).

There are various other factors, besides political instability, that may be associated with the lack of improvement in the investment climate, especially in terms of private investment. One such factor is *government effectiveness*. In Bangladesh, government effectiveness, which can largely support business growth in the country, has mostly remained stagnant since 2010. Among the comparator countries, Bangladesh has a generally low score; sitting only above Nepal, it ranked the second lowest in 2018 (World Bank n.d.b). The general low score of Bangladesh on this account also suggests that the degree of independence of the bureaucracy and its ability to provide efficient public services are questionable.

A very similar picture emerges with respect to *regulatory quality* in Bangladesh. Among the countries compared, Bangladesh appears to have ranked the lowest in 2018 (World Bank n.d.b). Since 2010, there had been a stagnation on this account in Bangladesh. *Regulatory quality*, which essentially captures the government's ability to formulate and enforce policies and regulations, is a significant indicator of how the country provides support to the growth of the private sector and small enterprises in particular.

Together with indicators, *political stability* and *regulatory quality*, *rule of law* can produce tangible influences on investment and growth indicators, via its contribution

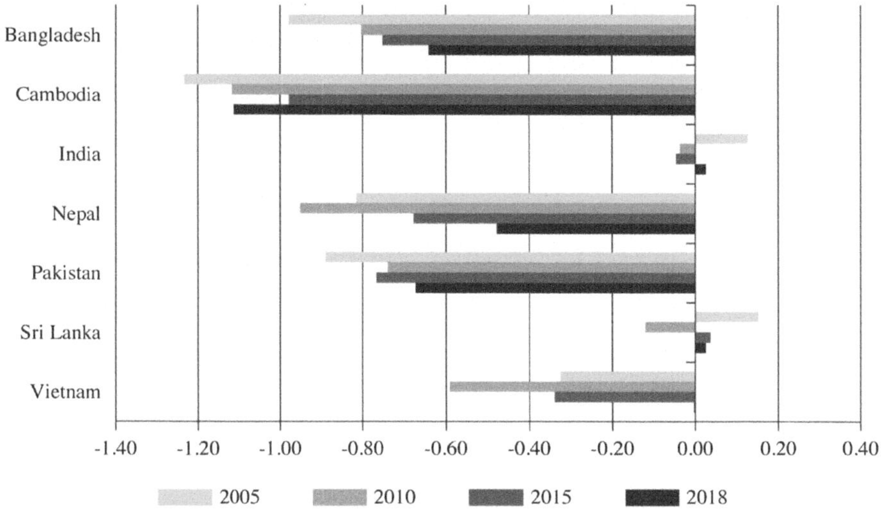

Fig. 8.2 Rule of law: Score of countries in South Asia. *Source* World Bank (n.d.b). *Note* (−) 2.5 [negative] corresponds to the lowest and (+) 2.5 [positive] corresponds to the highest state of governance

to sustaining stability. Experts have argued that the technical efficiency or the residual term in the Solow growth model often tends to vary according to the ways governance indicators influence investment and its efficiency.[20]

In particular, *rule of law* is the most significant in order to secure property rights, a condition that is central to regulated growth of the private sector and functioning of a market economy.[21] Figure 8.2 shows how every country, except for Sri Lanka and India, received a negative score on this account. India which had a negative score in 2015 went on to receive a positive score, implying an improvement in this aspect of governance. Bangladesh appears to have registered a better score than only Cambodia and Pakistan.

A weak score in the *rule of law* and *regulatory quality* create the perfect rationale for lack of *control on corruption*. Although it is alleged that this index has improved in Bangladesh over the years, its score is still among the lowest in the comparative countries, and the second lowest in South Asia (Fig. 8.3). Despite the existence of various laws and regulations,[22] corruption is certainly rampant in the country, as

[20]See Aron (2000), Acemoglu and Robinson (2013), Khan (2015).

[21]It is well-known, that reforms and policies towards growth and/or governance are certain to involve conflicts in interests among social classes, between capital and labour, between the state and market. If so, the process of selecting the indicators of rules of law would then be guided by how far these are effective in the management and mitigation of conflicts.

[22]BRAC Institute of Governance and Development (BIGD) states some of the recent anti-corruption reforms and legislations include the Anti-Corruption Commission (ACC) Rules, 2007; the Anti-Money Laundering Prevention Act, 2012; Government Servant (Conduct) Rules, 1979; Public Procurement Act, 2006; Public Procurement Rules, 2008; the Right to Information (RTI) Act,

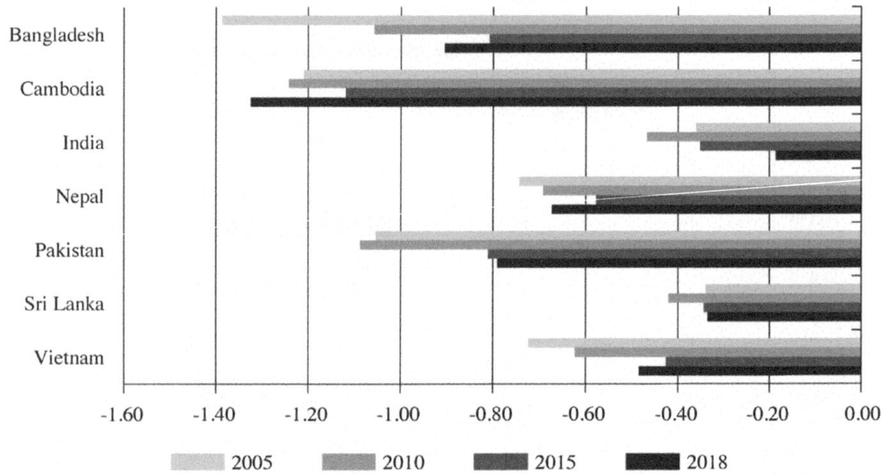

Fig. 8.3 Control of corruption: Score of countries in South Asia. *Source* World Bank (n.d.b). *Note* (−) 2.5 [negative] corresponds to the lowest and (+) 2.5 [positive] corresponds to the highest state of governance

voiced by national and international investors, and is a potential threat to future investment growth in the country (see Sect. 8.5). The linkages between corruption (governance) and growth need further in-depth characterisation and enquiry, so that what appears to be widespread perceptions (for instance, of corruption in Bangladesh) can be translated into indicators which can be measured and monitored.

There are very few studies that have analytically examined the state of governance as an end in Bangladesh. As noted earlier in the summary statistics, Bangladesh has achieved a rather low score overall on governance.[23] This is further reflected in its low position in the global rankings on several indicators, which implies that Bangladesh is still far from attaining acceptable standards of governance (Table 8.1).

Table 8.1 shows deterioration in *voice and accountability*, *government effectiveness* and *control of corruption* between 2012 and 2016, with fluctuations in *regulatory quality* and *political stability*, and improvements being in terms of *political risk* and *rule of law* for the same period. Table 8.2 provides a glimpse of the current perceptions by civil society at the country level. According to Transparency International's Corruption Perceptions Index (CPI) 2018, Bangladesh scored a paltry 26 points out of 100, and ranked 149th among 180 countries surveyed.

Bangladesh's strong economic growth and performance in social indicators are in contrast with the relatively poor perceptions of governance in the country. The most worrisome issue is the broad situation with political governance (that is including *government effectiveness* and *regulatory quality*) which exhibits no substantial sign

2009; Representation of the People's Order (RPO), 1972; and the Whistle-blower Protection Act, 2011.

[23] Asadullah et al. (2013), Roy (2006) and Khan (2017), using different time periods, have observed a relatively low score for Bangladesh on the six broad dimensions of governance.

Table 8.1 Global ranking of Bangladesh in selected indicators: 2012–2018

Indicator	Country coverage	Rank in						
		2012	2013	2014	2015	2016	2017	2018
Regional political risk index	100	86	87	83	82	80	81	79
Voice and accountability index	214	140	140	139	142	142	143	148
Political stability index	214	193	196	176	190	188	189	182
Government effectiveness index	214	161	162	162	159	156	163	164
Regulatory quality index	214	172	167	172	171	163	166	169
Rule of law index	214	175	169	160	155	151	150	150
Control of corruption index	214	167	168	169	163	170	169	174
GNI per capita (Atlas method)	213	184	186	181	183	176	150	151
GNI per capita (PPP)	213	177	175	169	173	168	144	147
Human development index	187	141	142	140	139	138	136	n/a

Source PRS Group (2018, 2019), UNDP (2014, 2015, 2016, 2018), World Bank (2013, 2014, 2015, 2016b, 2017a, 2018c, 2019, n.d.b)
Note GNI: Gross National Income; PPP: Purchasing Power Parity

Table 8.2 Corruption perception: Score of countries in South Asia

Country	CPI score (out of 100)	Ranking (out of 180 countries)
India	41	78
Sri Lanka	38	89
Pakistan	33	117
Bangladesh	26	149

Source Transparency International (2019)

of improvement.[24] In 2018, Bangladesh fared worse than India and Sri Lanka on all of the six indicators; than Vietnam and Nepal on five indicators; than Cambodia and Pakistan on three indicators. Bangladesh continues to have lower ratings in terms of *political stability*, *control of corruption* and *regulatory quality* than most other selected countries.

[24]See Roy (2006) for an elaboration on the scores of political governance.

Despite the relatively substandard quality of governance, social outcomes have improved in Bangladesh compared to its less corrupt neighbours (for example, India), providing evidence in support of the idea of a development surprise (Asadullah et al. 2013). Such paradoxes, however, need closer examination. Yet, among the developing countries of the world, and certainly among the least developed countries (LDCs), Bangladesh has been one of the better growth performers over the past decade. The Human Development Index (HDI) and gender empowerment indices have shown improvement. It can hardly be denied that there has been persistent attention given to, and resource allocation for (though not necessarily optimally), improvements in education, health, gender disparity and discrimination.[25]

While the analytical discussions on individual indicators seek to look for measures of improvement in each of these aspects, Sobhan (2004) finds recent overall trends in governance in Bangladesh as structurally flawed. Currently, as he dubs it, the *duopoly in the political market* of Bangladesh is creating governance tensions in multiple ways which have arguably been behind the amorphous attention to institution building, so vitally needed to consolidate economic gains and prepare for structural reforms and greater social inclusion.

8.4 Governance and Growth

8.4.1 Influence of Governance on Growth

Douglas North, in his influential writings, underscored the pivotal role of *institutions* in the process of economic and social progress of societies, and emphasised on various socio-political and cultural considerations that needed to be factored in a process of change.[26] The current response of writings on governance, which otherwise broadly cover concerns similar to North, largely depart form North's approach in two fundamental ways: first, there is a strong leaning towards the need for establishing links between governance and gross domestic product (GDP) growth[27] and growth-related variables; second, there is a growing tendency to measure and size-up governance, with a plethora of indicators being developed as proxies of good governance. In a sense, the *economics* domain of the sphere of governance has expanded through efforts to link it directly as a growth constraint. In this domain, the links between governance and inclusion are lightly explored.

The title of an oft-cited World Bank paper, 'Governance Matters',[28] sums up the tentativeness of the growth–governance literature in some ways. There can be no two

[25]Such concerted attention has indeed supported improvements in the Human Assets Index (HAI) and Economic Vulnerability Index (EVI), which in turn, has contributed towards Bangladesh meeting the eligibility criteria for graduation from the LDC status.

[26]North et al. (2008).

[27]Among others, see Kaufmann and Kraay (2003).

[28]Kaufmann et al. (1999).

opinions on the significant role that good governance is likely to play in unleashing the long-term potential of an economy; disagreements emerge on its details. The orthodox argument is a rather simple one: that per capita GDP is *causally* related to governance; a country with better governance will register better per capita GDP outcomes. The two broad propositions that result from the World Bank research on governance are: (i) governance matters, and *good* governance is likely to *cause* better growth performance; (ii) higher income growth does not necessarily lead to better governance (Latin American countries' examples are cited). Even if one were to accept the likelihood of these propositions, what is important to realise is that these propositions, if reversed, are not implausible either, viz. that: (i) growth matters, and that *good* growth is likely to improve governance indicators; and (ii) higher (better) governance may not necessarily lead to higher income growth, should there be various other binding constraints to growth. It is quite important to factor all these *mappings*. The World Bank's indicators and conclusions tend to address *governance* as a *supply-constraint*, which, if somehow eased or removed, would automatically lead to higher growth. This typical neoliberal stance tends to ignore the time dimension (North 1990), the dynamic processes that link the different aspects of development (Rodrik 1999) and that relations at stake can be a two-way phenomenon.[29]

In Bangladesh, there does not exist much analytical work on the governance–growth nexus, nor any detailed mapping of how the above indicators of governance can cause growth or is associated with growth-related variables. Hence, it is difficult to ascertain, in quantitative terms, how far the poor governance score, observed earlier in the case of Bangladesh, could be a constraint to growth. Two widely acknowledged observations on Bangladesh in this regard are: despite poor governance (i) the economy has registered a fairly strong rate of per capita GDP growth over a sustained period of time; and (ii) Bangladesh has registered substantial progress in several social indicators, especially health (e.g. child mortality); education (primary and secondary enrolment, especially for girls); and economic indicators (poverty reduction). In some of these social indicators, Bangladesh has scored above most of its South Asian neighbours despite having a lower per capita income level (Asadullah et al. 2013).

One needs to be cautious in interpreting governance and institution-building that tends to portray good economic and social progress despite low governance scores. Mahmud et al. (2008), which has dubbed good social progress in a milieu of low governance as a *development surprise*, provides possible explanations of the contexts where the two could coexist. These, among others, relate palpably to the spread of low-cost technology and innovative solutions in the fields of health and education, microfinance and critical catalytic role of NGOs.

Among the very few statistical exercises attempting to establish relationships between growth and governance, Roy (2006) finds that per capita income and governance dimensions, especially those related to political stability, institutions and technology have been, in the recent past, positively related—largely during the 1990s and

[29]Kaufmann and Kraay (2003) acknowledge all these difficulties, but rely on further data and vigorous methodology to come up with better understanding of causalities.

early 2000s. Rahman et al. (2000) finds a negative correlation between corruption and growth. These counterfactual studies essentially point out that had Bangladesh performed better with respect to individual dimension or collective governance scores, the economy would possibly have achieved higher GDP growth. In fact, the latter, claims that had the corruption score of Bangladesh been lower, for example, or similar to that in Eastern Europe during the 1990s, its GDP growth rate would have increased by 1.65 and 2.14 percentage points (Rahman et al. 2000). The above efforts on explaining the growth–governance nexus has come under criticism from various vantage points. The database on governance is too weak to yield any robust conclusions, especially in establishing the dynamics of how the various dimensions impact growth.

8.4.2 The Endogeneity Argument

By running two-way regressions between governance and growth, World Bank research contends that while governance leads to better growth, the converse may not be true. By way of implications, this would deny the existence of endogeneity in the relationship.

The growth–governance nexus is fuzzy and mired in several controversies, especially given that the database is either weak or non-existent; that there exist contrary historical country experiences; examples are drawn from several newly industrialising countries, such as South Korea, China and Mexico where growth spurts occurred amid widespread corruption. Furthermore, political instability and social disruption were not necessarily uncommon in the early stages of capitalist development.[30] All these feed into the debates on the chain and direction of influence, the endogeneity issue, and whether there can be a virtuous cycle of good governance and good growth. The complexity of the nexus often renders certain debates as misplaced, and warrants that the real issues are seen as country-specific and based on individual country historicity, intuitive reasoning and pragmatism.

The tentative nature of the conclusions that are derived lead one to a degree of ambivalence. Thus, in the context of Bangladesh, Fukuyama (2008) concludes that while fixing the problem of corruption and democratic accountability is a major challenge, Bangladesh has had just enough governance to continue to grow impressively, and that it may be better-positioned to reform its institutions in a decade or so, when it reaches a higher level of per capita GDP.

A critical issue in Fukuyama's observation is that with sustained growth, Bangladesh would have a better potential to improve its governance in the future. This observation that growth will lead to better governance is strongly refuted by Kaufmann and Kraay (2003) and others, who contend that there is no automaticity about a virtuous cycle of growth and governance.

---

[30]See for example, Khan and Jomo (2000), Kiely (1998).

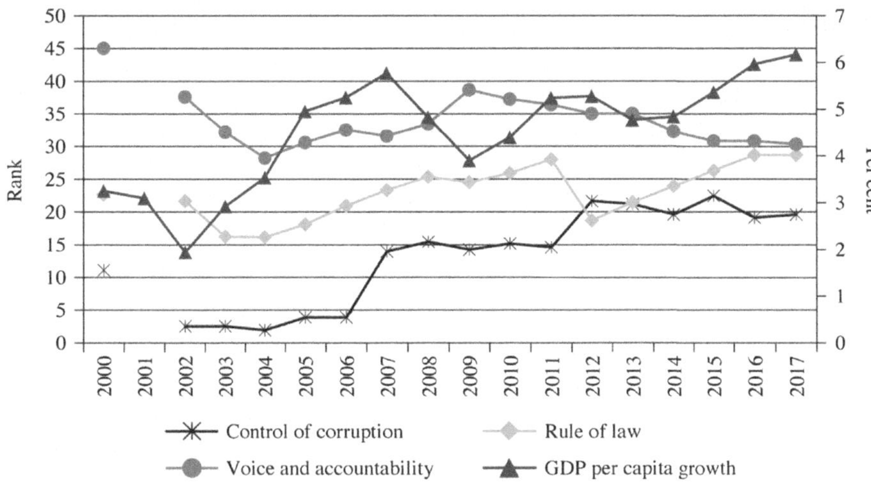

Fig. 8.4 GDP per capita growth and governance scenario in Bangladesh. *Source* Authors' calculations based on the data from World Bank (n.d.a; n.d.b). *Note* All the governance indicators are shown in a 100-country scale ranking. GDP per capita growth is shown in the right vertical axis. Data for governance indicators in 2001 is not available

Does the Bangladesh scenario reveal attributes that support the endogeneity hypothesis? There is no robust measure to ascertain whether the substantial growth momentum since 2000 led to any progress in good governance, or vice versa. In the absence of any established analysis, Fig. 8.4 traces the trends in per capita GDP growth along with trends in the global ranking of Bangladesh in three important indicators of governance (viz. rule of law, voice and accountability, and control of corruption).

It can be observed, that overall, the per capita GDP growth has hardly influenced the governance ranking in any significant way, nor has governance score, which has remained low and largely unchanged, thus far affected per capita growth. Thus, in the case of Bangladesh, there seems to be no perceptible evidence that growth has led to better governance, nor that poor governance, according to accepted indicators, has impeded growth. There are sporadic studies that have attempted to explore how Bangladesh has maintained a sustained growth rate despite poor governance overall. One of these contended that the political economy framework that has evolved through collusion between state actors and businesses, corruption (*deals*) and clientelism among others, need not necessarily be antithetical to growth-enhancing governance (Khan 2016). In any case, the empirical base for a contention remains fragile.

8.5 Slack in Private Investment: A Test of Governance?

The growth of private investment in Bangladesh has been lukewarm for a fairly prolonged period. The World Bank in pointing out relative stagnation in private investment, estimates that its contribution to GDP growth has declined from 1.5 percentage points to 1.3 percentage points.[31] One critical indicator is the near-stagnation of credit flow to the private sector. While credit flow to the private sector has been increasing recently, there has not been a corresponding rise in private investment.

While many factors exist that constrain investment growth, there are studies to suggest that several governance dimensions are likely factors that may have contributed to the slowdown in investment.[32] For instance, Roy (2006) contends that poor governance can be a constraint on domestic resource mobilisation, and account for a very low tax–GDP ratio, that in turn, are likely to inhibit public spending on social and physical infrastructure. Similarly, pervasive tax evasion, particularly by the richer income classes, and failure to recover massive non-performing loans (NPLs) and to punish fraudulent practices, are often attributed to poor governance.

While the governance–investment connection would require closer analytical and empirical scrutiny, the present study, in its limited scope, simply notes some developments that could potentially influence this nexus. These relate to developments that are likely to affect (i) transaction costs; and (ii) perceptions and expectations. If transaction costs tend to increase owing to poor governance (for instance, if business has to pay for a lack of property security or rule of law, as is often the case in Bangladesh), this would adversely affect investment. Similarly, a growing perception of palpable deterioration in governance and institutional support, which in turn would affect expectations, would tend to bring about investment uncertainties. The two are interlinked, and would affect not only domestic investment, but also foreign direct investments (FDIs). It may not be improper to consider the relevance of governance in ascertaining why FDIs are low in Bangladesh.

The present study, instead of cataloguing the lacunae and drawback in various aspects of governance, would like to foreground the current status of growth and investment in Bangladesh; and how transaction costs are being raised due to deteriorating traits in governance. There are, however, multiple factors that can cause transaction costs to increase. A few instances, albeit random, and which require further empirical analysis, are highlighted.

First and foremost, *rule of law*, in which Bangladesh has a relatively poor score, can produce tangible differences in investment and growth indicators, via its contribution to sustaining stability. Today, Bangladesh has a shaky enforcement of the existing regulations of property rights which is central to market-based functioning of the economy.[33] The lack of implementation and monitoring capacity, together

---

[31] World Bank (2016a).

[32] See Khan (2015), Khan (2017).

[33] North (1990) argues, with anecdotal evidence, that property rights and their enforceability, and acts to secure them have gone hand in hand with economic performance. If this observation is fully

Table 8.3 Estimated ranges for illicit financial flows in Bangladesh during 2005–2014 (% of total trade)

Illicit financial flows				Trade misinvoicing				BoP leakages		Total trade (billion USD)
Outflows		Inflows		Outflows		Inflows		Outflows	Inflows	
Low	High	Low	High	Low	High	Low	High			
12.0	17.0	4.0	12.0	7.0	12.0	4.0	12.0	5.0	0.0	446.2

Source Global Financial Integrity (2017)
Note BoP: Balance of Payments

with weak judiciary, have led to rampant malpractices in property transactions and property claims, whether this relates to real property or intellectual property. In the process, while the big businesses tend to *buy up* security through bribes, kickbacks and fraudulent practices,[34] the relatively small and vulnerable firms and traders are exposed to high risks. This not only hurts overall domestic investment, but foreign investment as well.

Another characteristic of the fragile *rule of law*, and closely linked to the above, is rampant corruption. There are widespread corruption practices, ranging from mega deals such as seen in trade and financial sectors; mega projects, for example infrastructure and energy, among others—to simple public sector job appointments. Various studies contend that such corruption takes place through political patronage, muscle power and extortions.[35] This has further been linked to alarming levels of capital flight from the country, carried out through multiple channels, including through trade misinvoicing (Table 8.3). Despite rampant corruption, there is no analytical exposition yet on how far this has adversely affected investment in Bangladesh. After all, there is a current complacency that bribes and kickbacks are taken as *speed money* to facilitate approvals, notwithstanding the fact that the benefits accrue largely to the big businesses and those close to political power (Iftekharuzzaman 2018). Some argue that corruption is a moral issue rather than an efficiency issue, and that tangible corruption existed, albeit in varying extent, in many countries in the early stages of development. Khan and Jomo (2000) and Khan (2017) argue one step further; they contend that collusion (patron–client relationship) and rent-seeking (corruption), within specific state policy/incentive structure, can have *transformational potential* as they did in South Korea and Taiwan-China.[36] While the evidence they draw on may underline such a potential, the *miracle* growth of East

valid, it would imply that rule of law, growth and development are historical processes, with one reinforcing the other. This would be an indirect manner to ascertain the links between rule of law and investment.

[34]Iftekharuzzaman (2018) of Transparency International Bangladesh (TIB), provides some disturbing insights—"Grabbing of land, forest, river and water bodies as well as perennial loan-default and other forms of plunder in banking and financial sector have been politically patronised.".

[35]See Khan (2017) for critical insights on the characterisation of corruption in Bangladesh and its likely association with investment non-performance.

[36]Also see, Rock and Bonnett (2004).

Asian economies has been contingent on many other factors, not the least of which has been the pursuit of an *inequality-averse* growth paradigm.[37]

A critical sector that is currently in *governance turmoil* is the banking and financial sector. Various experts, the World Bank, other international agencies and media have been vociferously drawing attention to the turbulence in the sector, and how adverse its effects could be on the economy. The World Bank, in its recent update, has raised an alarm on the increasing exposure to risks that are being caused by rising NPLs, which is around 10.6% on an average of all loans; nearly 4% of GDP (World Bank 2018a). More significantly, apart from creating uncertainties in the financial system, these developments are proximate factors affecting liquidity and lending rates, and private investment.

All the above factors not only affect transaction costs, but also indirectly affect the competitiveness index. WEF's country surveys for Bangladesh show that among the perceived hindrances to doing business, the governance dimensions are among the top-ranked (see for instance, WEF 2015, 2016). The World Bank's Ease of Doing Business index (World Bank 2018b) also shows the relative weaknesses of the incentive structure of Bangladesh vis-à-vis many developing countries of Asia.

Uncertainties and anomalies in the financial and capital markets are not only disincentives to domestic investment, but will also act as a hindrance on attracting foreign investment. The latter will have to assume increasing importance as Bangladesh graduates from its LDC status which will impel the country to forsake concessionary loans and grants, and source FDIs more aggressively.

8.6 Governance, SDGs and Social Inclusion: Additional Considerations

Governance and institutions are, however, not simply about enhancing investment and growth. As noted in the beginning of this chapter, it is equally seen as a strong factor that can affect distribution and other variables of social and political progress. In particular, governance has to take on added considerations when it comes to addressing inclusion, especially in the context of the multiple goals and indicators of an inclusive growth strategy (see Chap. 2). In this context, Bangladesh, in giving effect to SDG commitments on the participation of all (and *leave no one behind*), would confront challenges that go beyond growth–governance endogeneity issues; and issues that have hitherto remained confined to *economic governance*. While we have discussed Bangladesh's performance through largely the six WGI indicators, these do not necessarily capture many of the inclusion aspects of governance, especially, representation and participation. Furthermore, *participation of all* and *leave no one behind* would almost in definitional terms imply and underscore the need for

[37]Khan (2015).

dispensation of some rights and freedoms. Thus, the governance goal in an inclusive growth strategy of Bangladesh is as much an issue in economic governance as political governance.[38]

Thus, an inclusive growth strategy would need to seek alternative approaches that would integrate some of the basic inclusion dimensions of governance. The effort here is not to formalise any formula of governance, nor to seek firm parametric conditions, but to approach the critical governance issues, and the policies they signify, with a degree of pragmatism and sensitivity. One such approach is to ensure their appropriate integration in the comprehensive plan that Bangladesh has embarked on in attaining the SDGs in general, and SDG 16 in particular. One must note (i) although SDG 16 exclusively focuses on *peace, justice and strong institutions*, many of the other SDGs are equally significant and relevant in promoting inclusive growth[39]; (ii) as we shall note below, the various indicators of Goal 16 are not only immeasurable, but also do not necessarily add up to showing unequivocal progress on the goal and its targets.

The Sustainable Development Goals: Bangladesh Progress Report 2018 (GED 2018) provides Bangladesh's progress in different SDG Goals. The report discusses only nine out of the 23 indicators pertaining to Goal 16—mostly due to considerable data inadequacy. A closer inspection of the selected indicators reveals that most of them are linked to violence and related to death rates, abuse, exploitation, trafficking and violence against children; rule of law and equal access to justice; legal identity; access to information and strengthening of national institutions. The report does not spotlight on some key areas connected to governance, such as illicit financial and arms flows; reduction of corruption and bribery; development of effective, accountable and transparent institutions; promotion and enforcement of non-discriminatory laws and policies. Moreover, the data-centric approach of reporting failed to capture the nuances and intricacies related to a soft issue such as governance. In the context of the present study, additional considerations are required in a governance framework that would deliver progress in the inclusionary targets, such as SDG Targets 10.2 and 16.7. Regrettably, in the progress report mentioned above, these were hardly discussed, let alone adequately.[40]

---

[38]Khan (2017, p. 20) contends that it is the *political settlements* that determine and influence the governance structure. The political settlement, as we use the term, describes the "distribution of power across political and economic organisations." It helps us to understand how resources are being formally and informally (sometimes corruptly) allocated, based on the bargaining power of different groups.

[39]Note, for instance, the recent High-Level Political Forum (HLPF) 2019 discussed progress on six goals (viz. goals on quality of education; decent work and economic growth; reduced inequalities; climate action; peace, justice and strong institutions; and partnerships for the goals) under the theme, 'Empowering people and ensuring inclusiveness and equity.' For an account of progress in Bangladesh, on these, see Citizen's Platform for SDGs, Bangladesh (2019).

[40]In fact, of the three indicators of the aforesaid two targets, only one (indicator 16.7.1: Proportions of positions in national and local institutions, including (a) the legislatures; (b) the public service; and (c) the judiciary, compared to national distributions, by sex, age, persons with disabilities and population groups) was discussed partially. The exploration of indicator 16.7.1 was limited to a comment on female officers who received training overseas without providing any numerical figures. The SDG Tracker, i.e. the Government of Bangladesh's (GoB) initiative to monitor the progress in

In point of fact, the SDGs are in conformity with the imperatives of upholding human rights, principles of non-discrimination, participation and access to rule of law. It would be hard to imagine Bangladesh giving effect to the commitments above without undertaking some crucial reforms on governance, possibly in a minimalist approach, in order to strengthen rights, representation and the rule of law in the country. Such reforms, no matter how complex and difficult, would imply treating governance as an end, and perceiving such a goal as a fair pursuit. The World Bank, which had in the 1980s and 1990s largely concentrated on *rules to make markets work efficiently*, and abstained from the political dimensions of the growth–governance literature,[41] has, in its World Development Report 2017, clearly emphasised the need for political coalitions to enhance wider voice and participation (World Bank 2017b).

The present study contends that Bangladesh, in order to proceed towards the SDG goals stated above, would need to push reforms clustered around the following three themes: rights, representation and rules (of law). The three Rs are certainly interconnected, and are purported to contour the foundations of social inclusion in growth. In fact, much of the intent towards this *governance infrastructure* is laid down in the constitution, legal framework and various statutes that already exist in Bangladesh.[42] The practice of good governance has, however, been sloppy, and national and international watchdogs have been quick to point these out, whether in the field of human rights violation, lack of voice or absence of the independence of the judiciary.[43]

8.6.1 Rights

The recent upsurge in interest on *rights* has been emerging from various vantage points: *rights-based* approach to development[44]; empowerment of the poor[45]; rights

---

SDG indicators on a regular basis, does not provide any statistics as regards the indicators under Target 16.7. As for indicator 10.2.1 (Proportion of people living below 50% of median income, by sex, age and persons with disabilities), only 2018 data is available without any disaggregation.

[41]One may note that World Bank's foray into governance issues was led by a discussion paper in 1991 on 'Managing Development: The Governance Dimension'.

[42]See BIGD (2016) for an assessment of the current status of various dimensions of governance.

[43]BIGD (2016).

[44]The Declaration of the 2030 Agenda emphasises, "We resolve, between now and 2030, to end poverty and hunger everywhere; to combat inequalities within and among countries; to build peaceful, just and inclusive societies; to protect human rights and promote gender equality and the empowerment of women and girls; and to ensure the lasting protection of the planet and its natural resources" (UN 2015, p. 4).

[45]World Bank (2010).

as part of emerging negotiations on trade and investment; rights as value convergences, globally as well as in regional and bilateral agreements.[46] Although there is hardly any dispute on the need for greater progress on the human rights records, the devil is usually in the details of how to proceed. There are those that contend that better *rights* are achieved with economic and material progress, i.e. an evolutionary approach, and who draw upon the historical evolution of *rights* in the developed economies. There are others who take exception to this line of enquiry, stating that there are some *rights* which are central to the construct of a decent society, and that achieving such *rights* is an end in itself. The contention will continue to prevail, especially in the absence of a framework that supports the development and practice of a rights-led governance infrastructure, and one that goes beyond legal fiats and donor conditionalities.

In fact, a core element in fundamental human rights is the freedom of expression (United Nations (UN) Charter) and freedom of association (International Labour Organization's (ILO) Declaration). The realisation of such a right, and the legal framework needed to support it, is in any democratic country an end in itself. In Bangladesh, the Constitution, and various statutes clearly provide these guarantees. However, in assessing the rights issue in Bangladesh, one appears to confront a paradoxical situation where one observes palpable growth of reforms and statutes on rights and freedoms,[47] and yet an uncomfortable (anecdotal but fairly pervasive) evidence on suppression of individual and group freedoms by the state machinery.[48] Bangladesh has ratified, and is a signatory to, many of the international conventions on fundamental human and labour rights, such as the Universal Declaration of Human Rights. With strict reforms and political will, Bangladesh can vastly improve the *rights* dimension of the governance, not least through greater participation and redressing discrimination.

8.6.2 Representation

The political institution that encapsulates representation and constitutes a major global campaign is a free democratic society. There are innumerable studies to suggest how to measure it, and how these can be seen to influence incomes and welfare. Rodrik (2000), in his search for quality institutions, underscores the significance of participation, and attributes democracy as a *meta institution*, which is often linked to better economic and social outcomes (e.g. inequality).[49] Sen (1999) has

---

[46]Many bilateral agreements, for example, contain explicit considerations of rights, especially the core international labour standards.

[47]For instance, the Human Rights Commission, RTI Act, new Labour Code 2013, etc.

[48]The media and the press, which has in the recent years, increasingly come under intimidation, is currently wary of the curb in freedom via the ICT and Digital Security Act, 2017.

[49]Rodrik (2000), in particular, maintains decision-making through local-level participation leads to better economic and social outcomes.

Table 8.4 Democratic accountability: Score of countries in South Asia

Country	1990	1995	2000	2005	2010	2011	2012	2013	2014
Bangladesh	2.0	3.0	5.0	3.0	3.5	3.5	3.5	3.5	3.5
India	3.3	5.0	6.0	6.0	6.0	6.0	6.0	6.0	6.0
Pakistan	2.0	4.0	0.0	1.0	2.7	3.0	3.0	4.0	3.0
Sri Lanka	4.0	5.0	4.5	4.0	3.5	3.0	3.0	3.0	3.0
Vietnam	2.9	3.0	1.0	1.0	1.1	1.5	1.5	1.5	1.5

Source PRS Group (n.d.)
Note A score of 6 points equates to very low risk and a score of 0 points equates to very high risk

strongly argued that a free press (a critical characteristic of democratic societies) is associated with reduced incidence of large-scale famines and starvation. Inasmuch, as it fosters civil and political rights, democracy is also an extension of *rights* discussed earlier. However, the extent to which democracy influences growth and poverty reduction is an issue surrounded by controversy (World Bank 2017b). A large number of countries, with high incidences of poverty and varying *depths* of democracy, is often contrasted with countries that have registered satisfactory growth and poverty reduction under arguably less acceptable conditions of political and civil rights. Bangladesh appears to be among the latter group.

The Political Risk Services, the International Country Risk Guide (ICRG), provides some scores on *democratic accountability* (PRS Group, n.d.). It refers to a measure of not just whether there are free and fair elections, but how responsive the government is to its people. Here, countries are given a score of 0–6. Relative to the comparators, Bangladesh has a moderate level of democratic accountability, although this does not indicate the extent to which different sections and classes of people within the country perceive to be represented (Table 8.4).

Bhattacharya et al. (2013) has conducted an econometric analysis to argue that democracy has had negligible impact on economic growth, and suggests the country perhaps is yet to attain *the critical level of democratic stock* that could yield better impact. Sobhan's (2004) characterisation of the structural malaise in the democratic governance in Bangladesh has been noted earlier. Measures would be needed for a reordering of the *political settlements* (Khan 2017), and a strengthening of local level participation.

8.6.3 *Rule of Law*

As observed, the WGI indicators show that Bangladesh has a rather low score on *rule of law*, just ahead of Pakistan and Cambodia (Fig. 8.2). Again, a rules-based society is not easily defined. Several indicators, both subjective and objective, are used in the current literature (World Bank 2017b). Further, rules of law are likely to evolve into greater complexity as growth takes place, and to go beyond the initial details of underwriting rights and representation. As in any society, the Bangladesh population represents different groups and classes, unequal in income and asset ownership, with occupations that often represent conflicting interests. Governance is effectively a system of institutions underwritten by rules and values, to ease conflictual situations on the path to growth and its sharing, but also to safeguard fundamental rights and representation of the people. The weakening of roles of trade unions, labour market flexibility, growing inequality, unequal access to public services are a partial picture of this process.[50] In Bangladesh, rules and regulations exist aplenty, but a far heightened enforcement is needed not only in respect of supporting the weaker and vulnerable sections to access institutional support and public services, but also to arrest rampant corruption and political clientelism.

The World Bank in its 2017 Development Report (World Bank 2017b) makes a major departure from its earlier WGI-based writings, to acknowledge explicitly the critical role of political structures that could inhibit development and inclusion. In fact, any discourse on institutions and institution-building are, given their contents, political in nature. Thus, whatever the indicators used in the monitoring of governance and their linkages with (growth and inclusion) performance, the assessment must be seen and appreciated through the broader context of the political economy development. Improvements in any of these indicators cannot be realised, far less sustained, unless, as North et al. (2008) contended, the individual country's institutional and political cultures are factored in.

8.7 Challenges of Governance in Enhancing Inclusion: "Wrongs and Rights of Development"[51]

The above discussion essentially underscores that a pursuit of inclusive growth and the SDGs would imply the need to focus vigorously on reforms of the governance structure as a goal in Bangladesh, particularly in respect of rights, representation and rule of law.[52] A discussion of these reforms, largely political, is beyond the scope of this study. However, suffice it to say, there are narratives and widespread concern on the current political impasse, on unworthy developments in the democratic processes, on rampant rise in corruption, on collusion and clientelism, etc., which appear to be closely associated with lapses observed in the safeguard of rule of law, rights and representation.[53] In fact, these have created a skewed distribution of power

---

[50]One may recall that the past two decades of relentless pursuit of trade and market liberalisation was underwritten by the neoliberal goal of empowering markets, and of diminishing the influence of the state and the government.

[51]Sen (1995).

[52]This would tend to render Rodrik's (2008) dichotomy of economic and political governance inappropriate.

[53]See for example, BIGD (2016), Sobhan (2004); various publications of TIB on the issues at stake.

and privileges, where the poor and vulnerable sections of the population have weaker access to institutions, whether for public goods and services, participation, or justice.

Even within the framework of economic analysis, governance has been discussed extensively in areas beyond per capita GDP growth. Alesina and Perotti (1994) cast the governance problematique in terms of redistributive justice, and weighs alternative outcomes of fiscal stability and socio-political stability. Others posit a governance framework in order to tackle poverty and inequality, and covers a large gamut of economic management (fiscal in particular) and political participation issues.[54] Rodrik (2000) discusses governance in terms of developing *quality institutions* that are best fostered through a gradual process ("governance in the small"[55]) with local-level experiments, but developed within the broader framework of democracy (as a meta institution).

There is thus a plethora of perspectives on the very objectives of governance. Such objectives would then lead to the development of specific indicators to subserve the respective objective. Sen (1999), in his well-known treatise on *development as freedom*, provides forceful insights on how individual *capabilities*, freedom and democratic foundations of societies are intrinsically self-reinforcing. Governance can thus be as much about growth, as about distributive justice, reduction of poverty and inequality through specific interventions.

Given the ambiguous state of the debate on the governance–growth–inclusion nexus, Bangladesh will have to make hard choices to strengthen this nexus, based on evaluations of how the relationship has been unfolding, as well as important lessons from other developing countries. This would warrant pragmatism and identification of priorities, whether as implicit in the *unidirectional* or *endogeneity* narratives—or whether an economy pursues governance-for-development or development governance.[56] This is, however, not always a clear and uncontested path.

In this context, it may be useful to take cue from Sen (1995) who suggests possible pragmatic ways to strengthen the nexus of governance and inclusive growth. Referring to the contrasting goals and achievements of China and India, Sen points to the need for identifying the *wrongs and rights in development*. While different political orders will entail undertaking of alternative approaches to attaining growth and freedom, the contrasts are not always as polarised as is frequently made out.[57] With careful choice of priorities, one could calibrate policies that would go a long way

[54]See for instance, Khan (2007), Mahmud et al. (2008).

[55]This expression is due to Rodrik (2008, p. 17); while agreeing that good governance is both an end and a goal, he contends that it would be unwieldy to concentrate on a broad governance agenda, especially when there may be trade-offs between the governance-as-end and governance-as-goal. Given the discussion above, the present study maintains that both need to be pursued simultaneously, and address any trade-offs as appropriate.

[56]See Khan (2007) for an interpretation of development governance, and potential paths to move towards it, largely based on reordering the so-called *political settlements*. He accepts that the two may not necessarily be mutually exclusive.

[57]Sen characterises the development paths of India and China as essentially a contrast between postponability of social change and human development (POSH) and political unreadiness for speedy human rights (PUSH), respectively (Sen 1995).

in reinforcing the *rights* and de-emphasise the *wrongs*. In other words, the contrasts between progress in rights and representation and progress in economic and social development, unless appropriately addressed, can have unintended social costs. Can the so-called *Lee hypothesis* (Sen 1995) where rights and representation take a low profile in a growth strategy (but scores high on health, education and higher per capita GDP) prove to be a possible narrative for Bangladesh?[58] In the current state of the debate, a critical and straightforward question is whether Bangladesh can simultaneously *enjoy fast economic growth and political freedom*.[59] As Sen (1995) argues, with careful articulation of policies and institutions, these contrast between progress on rights and representations and progress in social development can be gradually narrowed down. A focus on such calibration will require strong political will, implementation capacity, and trade-offs in resource allocation.

Governance of inclusive growth in Bangladesh would, in the above pragmatic stance, depend on choosing the *wrongs and rights* in development, without necessarily confining to any comprehensive design of governance reforms, which is likely to flounder in the current impasse of the country's political malgovernance.[60] There are others (Rodrik 2008; Khan 2017) who argue in favour of a gradualist approach.[61] In a pursuit of strengthening the nexus of governance and inclusive growth, and following a strategy of nuanced and gradual strategy of identifying rights and wrongs, there can be many intervention areas. In view of the stated goals of inclusive growth strategy, the present study focuses below, by way of examples, on three such policy areas. A pursuit of these policies, though not directly linked to the three Rs of social inclusion stated above, will certainly enhance capabilities of the poor, and prospects of their economic and political freedoms.

8.7.1 Redistributive Measures

Bangladesh, over the past one and a half decades, has been witnessing a rapid and continuous rise in income inequality. Some studies contend that this may have contributed to the slowing down in the progress of poverty reduction during the more

---

[58] This refers to the well-known contention of Lee Kuan Yew, a former Prime Minister of Singapore. It is fairly well-known, that in Singapore, as well as in South Korea and China, in the early phases of their growth, property rights were not always secure, and there was a weak protection of human rights. These, some would contend, were however, *strong developmental states* that pursued pro-developmental rather than predatory policies (Khan 2015).

[59] Sen (1995).

[60] For example: "Our political settlements analysis suggests that implementable anti-corruption activities should have a low profile, and be based on an outcome-oriented and incremental set of policy proposals. The emphasis should not exclusively be on prosecution and punishment, but rather on finding policy combinations that create incentives for stakeholders in particular sectors or activities to behave in more productive ways" (Khan 2017, p. 39).

[61] Khan (2017, p. 7), in the context of anti-corruption policies in Bangladesh, argues that "an incremental approach to anti-corruption is the only feasible way forward.".

recent period.[62] In terms of wealth inequality, the scenario appears to be similar. Based on their analysis of the HIES data of 2005 and 2010, Bhattacharya et al. (2017) illustrated that wealth inequality in Bangladesh has been increasing.

A critical choice in the governance of inclusive growth would be a design of measures to resolve the challenges of the growth–inequality–poverty nexus,[63] viz. the prospects of enhancing growth while reducing both inequality and poverty. There are hardly any concerted measures in Bangladesh planning to consciously embed inequality-reducing measures in their otherwise conventional growth strategies.

Khan (2015), drawing on the development experiences of East Asian countries provides a strong rationale for pursuing an *inequality-averse* growth for Bangladesh. While the inequality-averse growth is not a frequently observed historical phenomenon,[64] there are no convincing reasons why such a strategy cannot be designed and pursued. In fact, the commitment to the SDGs towards inclusive growth can hardly be pursued without serious attempts to address growing inequality. Indeed, it may not be feasible for Bangladesh to recreate all the conditions behind the case of East Asian countries, especially various fortuitous circumstances. One must also recall the significant role that land reforms played in these countries, both to moderate inequality as well as to enhance agricultural productivity and growth. Nevertheless, there are several other considerations that could allow Bangladesh to associate its current high growth with greater job generation and egalitarianism. This would require closer review of its policy biases and the role of state and institutions.

Sobhan (2016) has identified the following as fundamental factors that tend to subvert equalisation in a growing economy, and to explain economic and social exclusion of the poorer segments of the population: inequitable access to productive assets; inequitable participation in the market; inequitable access to human development; and unjust governance.[65] These are characteristics of structural flaws which can be addressed only with major fiscal interventions and political will. Even if asset redistribution were a non-starter, a better governance structure could certainly provide the poorer and more vulnerable population with a far better access to resources and opportunities (in the public sector) and possible stake in the private sector profits and corporate shares.

---

[62] See, for example, Khan (2015). This has been borne out by the Household Income and Expenditure Survey (HIES) 2016, which shows that the income share of the poorest 5% had declined from 0.78% (2010) to 0.23% (2016). In contrast, the income share of the richest 5% had increased from 24.6% (2010) to 27.9% (2016) (BBS 2017).

[63] Refer to Bourguignon's triangle analysis in Chap. 2, which also provides a brief review of the challenges related to the nexus and the trade-offs.

[64] The other often cited example of equality with growth is of several Western European countries during the 1950s and 1960s when they introduced major welfare reforms.

[65] This inequitable and unjust social and economic universe is compounded by a system of unjust governance which discriminates against not just the resource-poor, but large segments of the less privileged sections of society, effectively disenfranchising them from the political benefits of a democratic process. These broader social groups, who may be collectively identified as the excluded, even where they are not directly oppressed by the machinery of state, remain underserved by available public services (Sobhan 2016).

Table 8.5 Incidence of poverty (cost of basic needs) by ownership of land

Size of land holding (acres)	National			Rural			Urban		
	2000	2005	2010	2000	2005	2010	2000	2005	2010
Lower poverty line									
All size	34.3	25.1	17.6	37.9	28.6	21.1	20.0	14.6	7.6
No land	30.4	25.2	19.8	48.8	49.3	33.8	22.3	17.8	9.9
<0.05	43.3	39.2	27.8	48.8	47.8	35.9	22.3	23.7	12.3
0.05–0.49	40.0	28.2	17.7	41.7	33.3	22.1	12.6	11.4	5.4
0.50–1.49	29.6	20.8	13.3	30.6	22.8	15.2	15.4	9.1	2.4
1.50–2.49	21.9	11.2	7.6	22.9	12.8	8.6	1.4	2.7	1.8
2.50–7.49	11.5	7.0	4.1	12.4	7.7	4.3	0.0	3.0	2.7
7.50+	4.0	1.7	3.7	4.1	2.0	4.2	0.0	0.0	0.0
Upper poverty line									
All size	48.9	40.0	31.5	52.3	43.8	35.2	35.2	28.4	21.3
No land	46.6	46.3	35.4	69.7	66.6	47.5	36.6	40.1	26.9
<0.05	57.9	56.4	45.1	63.0	65.7	53.1	38.3	39.7	29.9
0.05–0.49	57.1	44.9	33.3	59.3	50.7	38.8	27.3	25.7	17.4
0.50–1.49	46.2	34.3	25.3	47.5	37.1	27.7	27.4	17.4	12.1
1.50–2.49	34.3	22.9	14.4	35.4	25.6	15.7	10.2	8.8	6.6
2.50–7.49	21.9	15.4	10.8	22.8	17.4	11.6	9.1	4.2	5.5
7.50+	9.5	9.7	8.0	3.1	3.6	0.0	0.0	0.0	14.6

Source BBS (2005, 2010)

Chenery et al. (1979) had argued in favour of exploring policies that would maximise growth, but providing relatively greater weights to the growth of income of the lower percentiles. However, a diversion of investment resources to the poor would not succeed without some degree of change in the existing asset structure.[66] In Bangladesh, the issues of land and/or asset redistribution, apart from some land tenurial interventions, have never been on the policy agenda, largely due to the apparent scarcity of land. Yet historically, landownership and poverty have been inversely related (Table 8.5). In the absence of any asset redistribution, the policy focus has been on providing opportunities to enhance alternative forms of asset acquisition, and potential attainment of economic *freedoms* through, among other things, skills and technology; access to credit market; and more recently through financial inclusions. This would warrant a reorientation of redistributive measures, such as through wage policies, a more progressive tax structure and reprioritisation of public expenditures towards the poor and vulnerable.

[66]Chenery et al. (1979) proposed a maximisation of the weighted average of the rate of growth of the income of groups of different income classes-maximising $G = \sum_{i=1}^{n} w_i g_i$, where w_i are the weights of various income classes and g_i the growth rates of the different income groups, by attaching relatively greater weights to growth of income of the lower quintiles.

8.7.2 *Empowering the Poor Through Employment and Decent Work*

Empowering the poor in an inclusive growth framework is intrinsically related to their participation in the governance structure through devolution and decentralisation of decision-making and resources at local levels. As well-known and documented, the participation of the general public in the democratic process of the country is almost solely confined to voting.[67] There are studies that contend that, although there exists a plethora of rules and acts on decentralisation and local-level administration, there is little by way of local-level participation in either decision-making or resource control. These are mainly centrally administered. Although the local-level (upazila) elections (2013–14) were a step in the devolution of the democratic process, this has to be strongly complemented by greater autonomy of local bodies in the mobilisation and utilisation of resources. The local political and development space, which is still captured by the centre in multiple ways,[68] needs greater local-level participation.

Apart from ensuring participation, providing productive employment with a decent minimum wage and working conditions is a key measure of reducing inequality and empowering the poor, whose main asset is their labour and skills. The present study has contended that an inclusive growth strategy is best anchored on SDG 8 on achievement of a full employment in society. In Bangladesh, such a stance is missing in both the policy planning framework (e.g. plan documents still regard employment as a residual of growth targets), as well as in commitments. It may be noted that Bangladesh is yet to ratify ILO's Convention 122 which refers to a commitment to achieving *full, productive and freely chosen employment* (ILO 1964).

As available evidence suggests, the current scenario of decent work (as enunciated by the ILO) in Bangladesh lags far behind the standards it requires to ensure rights at work and to attain inclusive growth. Although Bangladesh is committed to the promotion of decent work, its substantive manifestations on the ground are less than encouraging. For achieving inclusive growth, the economy needs to vastly increase employment opportunities, ensuring an improvement in the various decent work indicators, some of which are mentioned above. The recent development in case of workplace safety in garment sector should be continued and spread over to other sectors. The allocation for social security targetting workers needs to be extended. Finally, the government has to create opportunities for effective social dialogue. In other words, an invigorated programme to attain the goals of decent work would also constitute a significant element in, and a testament to, the realisation of inclusive growth and good governance.

---

[67]"...participation does not refer simply to voting. Participatory processes must entail open dialogue and broadly active civic engagement, and it requires that individuals have a voice in the decisions that affect them" (Stiglitz 2002, p. 165).

[68]In fact, the amendment in 2009 of the Upazila Parishad Act, 1998 to designate a Member of Parliament (MP) as adviser to upazilas in respective constituency, marks centre's interference in local affairs.

8.7.3 *Public Policy and Public Goods*

Central to an inclusion-friendly governance structure is the role of the state itself. Notwithstanding the growing awareness and imperatives of an increasing private sector in the future growth of Bangladesh, the state will have to continue playing its part to ensure that inclusionary growth is not handicapped by market failures. Market failure, in particular relation to persistent growth in inequality and vulnerability as observed previously, provides adequate rationale for scoping greater provisions of public goods, and a strong public policy. Here, one must avoid distractions and the misplaced policy debate by conflating big government with a more effective governance framework. What must be avoided is over-bureaucratisation, and an over-regulated economy, which with its potentials of corruption and resource misuse, favours the rich and privileged, and throttles the opportunities of the small and the vulnerable. In effect, there has to be balanced governance that is informed by the critical needs of addressing market failures, but equally by the capacity of markets to deliver investment, skills and jobs. At the heart of public provisioning measures in a developing country like Bangladesh is the proposition that these not only enhance capabilities of the poor by lifting the economic and social standards of living, but also contribute to improving infrastructures (both physical and social), and to raising aggregate demand.[69]

Public policy and its framework will be defined by capacity and institutions, the commitment to inclusionary growth and fiscal capacity. In Bangladesh, the government has indeed played a significant role, both via growth and specific interventions in the improvement of average levels of living and of various social indicators, particularly related to health and education. Nevertheless, the incidence of the poor, the ultra-poor and the marginalised class in absolute numbers is still unacceptably high. While basic education and health facilities are expanding, there is still unequal access to these provisions.[70] Women's participation in the labour force is increasing, but still very low. There has been a relative stagnation/decline in resources directed towards the social sectors; especially expenditure on health and education has hardly been more than 1 and 2% of GDP, respectively. The COVID-19 pandemic and the economic crisis have thoroughly exposed the fragility of public policy systems and inadequacy of social expenditures in supporting and protecting the underprivileged population.

The size of many social safety net programme (SSNP) interventions are extremely low (especially as a proportion of per capita household consumption), while a National Social Security Strategy (NSSS) has been designed, the current coverage of social protection is almost negligible, and Bangladesh is far from creating a basic social protection floor (SPF). It is also not clear how the NSSS, comprehensive as it may seem, will be financed.

[69]"Modern economic growth requires a broad base and the mobilisation of such a broad base is impossible without the relatively widespread provision of some of the most basic public goods" (Acemoglu 2008, p. 5).

[70]See Osmani (2014), Khan (2015).

A central consideration is, of course, the fiscal capacity of Bangladesh which has, relative to many developing countries in Asia and Africa, a particularly low tax–GDP ratio. In the long-run, an inclusionary economy will have a large demand on public resources, especially as Bangladesh continues to build on its vision of a welfare state and on giving effect to the SDG commitments. In this regard, one will have to ensure the gradual enlargement of the tax base through enforcement of an equitable tax policy, enlarging the tax net, and more significantly by preventing the rich from dodging taxes. Equally, there should be corresponding uplifting of the expenditure–GDP ratio. Achieving the latter, in many ways, would be a close proxy for a *structural* social transformation in Bangladesh.

Furthermore, in order to pursue *inclusive growth* and the SDGs, especially in the milieu of a renewed vow to pursue the goal of full employment and decent work (SDG 8), the country's public investment, and public expenditures will need to be stepped up on a substantial scale. In other words, a budget allocation framework will need to internalise measures to achieve the SDGs. The soaring incidence of poverty and vulnerability due to the sharp economic downturn would require huge additional resources to ensure SDG targets remain on track. The massive infrastructure-building programmes as well the increasing need for provisioning of public goods (including education, health and employment/income entitlements) will warrant much higher resource needs. Of course, not all social goals can be engineered through public provisioning. Nevertheless, the fiscal stance would need to support a proactive employment strategy in order to achieve shared prosperity, through increased job creation and social protection.

8.8 Concluding Remarks

There appears to be overwhelming support, based on existing studies, the widely used WGI database, global rankings, and pervasive anecdotal evidence, that there are major deficits in various dimensions/indicators of governance in Bangladesh. Both in terms of trends in the indicators, as well as in its comparative ranking in South Asia or globally, Bangladesh has a relatively poor governance score. Despite these deficits, the economy has progressed quite remarkably, both on economic and several social fronts, which some experts dubbed as a *development surprise*. On the other hand, while there have arguably been marginal improvements in a few indicators, e.g. political stability and rule of law, it is unclear if the robust growth of 6–7% over the past decade and half has had any positive impact on improving governance.

As we have observed above, the governance–growth relationship, and the direction of the relationship is not always clear. There are at least two major reasons for this: first, there appear to exist scores of indicators to adjudge good governance[71] for which data may not be easily procured and covered by proxies; and second, there are

[71] One may note that behind the six broad WGI there are more than 300 sub-indicators.

ample contrary historical experiences that can be forwarded equally to confirm or negate a contention. Thus, while poor growth in the developing economies is often associated with low scores in governance, the case of Bangladesh, given its recent record on growth and social upliftment, apparently presents a challenge.

In Bangladesh, given the tenuous link between growth and governance, and the lack of any effective accountability in the current *duopolistic* political system, there has been ambivalence in respect of carrying out serious governance reforms. There are also growing concerns over the possibility of elites capturing influence over the shaping of laws, policies and regulations. Khan (2015) provides some sharp examples of these developments that would not only lead to entrenched rent-seeking but also potentially undermine future growth. These range from discriminatory rule of law[72] to rent-bearing policy distortions, such as observed in the excessive and biased support extended to readymade garments (RMG), and outright patronage and clientelism practised through deals and license distribution by sectoral ministries and agencies.

Moreover, a commitment to the pursuit of inclusive growth and to the realisation of SDGs would warrant a review and reform of not only the economic governance indicators (that relate to growth), but also several other dimensions of political governance. In particular, as argued in the framework of this study, an inclusive growth strategy would need to adopt measures that ensure a better platform for strengthening participation, voice and non-discrimination.[73] This would, in turn, imply that governance is not only a means to achieve better growth but also an end, since the above would require appropriate dispensation of rights, representation and rule of law.

In order to address governance as a goal in an inclusive growth strategy, it is necessary to have an effective understanding of the critical weaknesses of institutions that characterise governance in Bangladesh today. There are serious debates on what constitutes *good governance model*, on its measurements, on the costs and trade-offs involved, and on what its impacts are on various economic and social indicators. It is a tall order to provide a respectable account of these debates; the present study has tried to underscore the dimensions that warrant serious policy attention from the perspectives of inclusive growth in Bangladesh.

In moving towards a good governance framework, it may be difficult to push for and get results on all fronts (for example, curbing rent-seeking and corruption vs. attaining democratic accountability). Hence a clear positioning would be required to prioritise measures that are development-growth-friendly, and can be fiscally accommodated through sustained growth. For instance, the narrative in a previous section on the growing concerns on malgovernance, especially in the financial and banking sector, and on its likely impact on both domestic and foreign investment, is a case in point where certain specific measures could be adopted.

---

[72] For instance, the unorganised poor (whether farmer or entrepreneur) can hardly get access to their rights under rule of law, unless they pay bribes or have connections with ruling party men.

[73] See Chap. 2 on the outcomes and process dimensions of inclusive growth.

An ideal growth-inclusion governance framework in the context of a developing country is yet to be defined. Bangladesh does not have one, and hence, neither the reforms on how to achieve it. The present study argues, after Sen (1995), in favour of a pragmatic approach and a strategy that ably chooses *rights and wrongs* of a gamut of development issues that ranges from universal access to education and health to economic and political freedoms. This is perhaps a process of *governance in the small* (Rodrik 2008) that is likely to redress specific governance deficits in inclusive growth. In the context of Bangladesh, the present study in the light of its inclusive growth strategy advanced three focus areas (among others) which are interrelated measures of progress toward inclusion and growth. These relate to: (i) redistributive measures; (ii) empowering the poor through employment and decent work; and (iii) strengthening public policy and public provisioning.

Closely linked to the above governance–inclusion nexus is institution-building; that is to avoid, what Acemoglu and Robinson (2013) stressed, *extractive institutions* where a small privileged class exploits the rest; and instead, to encourage *inclusive institutions* which embrace broader cooperation and coalitions for better participatory decision-making. Any progress towards the latter, which will require huge political will, could help to address some governance limitations (Sobhan 2004), in particular, to an easing of the political uncertainties that Bangladesh is currently gripped in. It is imperative to stay alert, at a minimum, so that the conditions that currently characterise governance do not deteriorate further, and to ensure that Bangladesh does not swerve toward a predatory state, away from being the developmental state that (arguably) it is today. Meanwhile one must note that, while long-term inclusive growth in Bangladesh will firmly depend on improved institutions and governance, it will equally depend on how prudently and effectively inclusive policies are designed and implemented. Institutions matter for inclusive growth; so do policies.[74]

References

Acemoglu, D. (2008). Interactions between governance and growth. In D. North, D. Acemoglu, F. Fukuyama, & D. Rodrik (Eds.), *Governance, growth and development decision-making* (pp. 1–8). Washington, D.C.: The World Bank.

Acemoglu, D., & Robinson, J. (2013). *Why nations fail: The origins of power, prosperity and poverty*. London: Profile Books Ltd.

Alesina, A., & Perotti, R. (1994). The political economy of growth: A critical survey of the recent literature. *The World Bank Economic Review, 8*(3), 351–371.

Aron, J. (2000). Growth and institutions: A review of the evidence. *The World Bank Research Observer, 15*(1), 99–135.

[74]Botswana, for example, by avoiding *extractive institutions* and political play that governs them has achieved stability and remarkable growth. However, despite the accolades it has received (Acemoglu and Robinson 2013; World Bank 2008), it is among the most unequal countries in the world and has among the highest unemployment rates among the upper middle-income countries (UMICs). Hence, notwithstanding the creditable institutions that it has apparently achieved, its policy framework toward inclusive growth has remained shaky.

Asadullah, M. N., Savoia, A., & Mahmud, W. (2013). Paths to Development: Is there a Bangladesh Surprise? Brooks World Poverty Institute Working Paper No. 189. Manchester: Brooks World Poverty Institute, University of Manchester.

BBS. (2005). Household Income and Expenditure Survey 2005. Dhaka: Bangladesh Bureau of Statistics (BBS), Government of Bangladesh (GoB).

BBS. (2010) Household Income and Expenditure Survey 2010. Dhaka: Bangladesh Bureau of Statistics (BBS), Government of Bangladesh (GoB).

BBS. (2017). Preliminary Report on Household Income and Expenditure Survey 2016. Dhaka: Bangladesh Bureau of Statistics (BBS), Government of Bangladesh (GoB).

Bhattacharya, D., Dasgupta, S., & Neethi, D. J. (2013). Does Democracy Impact Economic Growth? Exploring the Case of Bangladesh—A Cointegrated VAR Approach. CPD-CMI Working Paper No. 5. Dhaka: Centre for Policy Dialogue (CPD) and Bergen: Chr. Michelsen Institute (CMI).

Bhattacharya, D., Khan, T. I., Khan, S. S., Sinha, M. M., Fuad, S. M., Biswas, S., & Muzib, A. (2017). Quest for inclusive transformation of Bangladesh: Who not to be left behind—Executive summary. Dhaka: Centre for Policy Dialogue (CPD) and Citizen's Platform for SDGs, Bangladesh.

BIGD. (2016). The State of Governance Bangladesh 2016: Regulation Process Performance. Dhaka: BRAC Institute of Governance and Development (BIGD), BRAC University, Dhaka.

Chenery, H., Ahluwalia, M. S., Bell, C. L. G., Duloy, J. H., & Jolly, R. (1979). *Redistribution with growth*. New York: Oxford University Press.

Citizen's Platform for SDGs, Bangladesh. (2019). Four years of SDGs in Bangladesh and the way forward: Looking through the prism of non-state actors. Dhaka: Citizen's Platform for SDGs, Bangladesh.

Easterly, W. (2001). The lost decades: Developing countries' stagnation in spite of policy reform 1980–1998. *Journal of Economic Growth, 6*(2), 135–157.

Fukuyama, F. (2008). What do we know about the relationship between the political and economic dimensions of development? In D. North, D. Acemoglu, F. Fukuyama, & D. Rodrik (Eds.), *Governance, growth and development decision-making* (pp. 25–33). Washington, D.C.: The World Bank.

GED. (2018). Sustainable Development Goals: Bangladesh Progress Report 2018. Dhaka: General Economics Division (GED), Planning Commission, Government of Bangladesh (GoB).

Global Financial Integrity. (2017). *Illicit Financial Flows to and from Developing Countries: 2005-2014*. Washington, D.C.: Global Financial Integrity.

Iftekharuzzaman. (2018, February 23). Bangladesh in corruption ranking. The Daily Star.

ILO. (1964). C122 - Employment Policy Convention, 1964 (No. 122). Geneva: International Labour Organization (ILO).

Kaufmann, D., & Kraay, A. (2003). Governance and Growth: Causality which Way? – Evidence for the World, in Brief. https://pdfs.semanticscholar.org/6ec6/772c537462ac023c1a8f462d616637fb3ca3.pdf?_ga=2.53885096.1052620127.1577617570-133060872.1577617570 Retrieved 10 June 2019.

Kaufmann, D., Kraay, A., & Zoido-Lobatón, P. (1999). Governance Matters. World Bank Policy Research Working Paper 2196. Washington, D.C.: The World Bank.

Kaufmann, D., Kraay, A., & Mastruzzi, M. (2005). Governance Matters IV: Governance Indicators for 1996–2004. World Bank Policy Research Working Paper 3630. Washington, D.C.: The World Bank.

Khan, A. R. (2015). *The economy of Bangladesh: A quarter century of development*. Basingstoke: Palgrave MacMillan UK.

Khan, M. (2016, February 20). Governance challenge on inclusive growth. Presented at the SANEM Annual Economists' Conference 2016 on Bangladesh: Way towards a Middle-Income Country, organised by the South Asian Network on Economic Modeling (SANEM), Dhaka, Bangladesh.

Khan, M. (2017). Anti-corruption in Bangladesh: A Political Settlements Analysis. ACE Working Paper No. 003. London: School of Oriental & African Studies (SOAS), University of London.

Khan, M. H. (2007). Governance, Economic Growth and Development since the 1960 s. DESA Working Paper 54. New York: United Nations Department of Economic and Social Affairs (UN DESA).
Khan, M. H., & Jomo, K. S. (Eds.). (2000). *Rents, rent-seeking and economic development: Theory and evidence in Asia*. Cambridge: Cambridge University Press.
Kiely, R. (1998). Neo liberalism revisited? A critical account of World Bank concepts of good governance and market friendly intervention. *Capital & Class, 22*(1), 63–88.
Mahmud, W., Ahmed, S., & Mahajan, S. (2008). Economic Reforms, Growth, and Governance: The Political Economy Aspects of Bangladesh's Development Surprise. Working Paper No. 22. Washington D.C.: Commission on Growth and Development.
Meier, G. M., & Stiglitz, J. E. (Eds.). (2001). *Frontiers of development economics: The future in perspectives*. New York: Oxford University Press and The World Bank.
North, D. (1990). *Institutions, institutional change and economic performance*. Cambridge: Cambridge University Press.
North, D., Acemoglu, D., Fukuyama, F., & Rodrik, D. (Eds.). (2008). *Governance, growth and development decision-making*. Washington, D.C.: The World Bank.
Osmani, S. R. (2014, June 20). Social protection for all: Learning from lessons on the ground. Presented at the First BEF Conference, organised by the Bangladesh Economists' Forum (BEF), Dhaka, Bangladesh.
PRS Group. (2018). Regional Political Risk Index. New York: The PRS Group. https://www.prsgroup.com/regional-political-risk-index-3/ Retrieved 28 September 2019.
PRS Group. (2019). Regional Political Risk Index. New York: The PRS Group. https://www.prsgroup.com/regional-political-risk-index-4/ Retrieved 28 September 2019.
PRS Group. (n.d.). International Country Risk Guide (ICRG). https://epub.prsgroup.com/products/international-country-risk-guide-icrg Retrieved: 28 September 2019.
Rahman, A., Kisunko, G., & Kapoor, K. (2000). Estimating the Effects of Corruption: Implications for Bangladesh. Policy Research Working Paper 2479. Washington, D.C.: The World Bank, South Asia Region.
Reporters Without Borders. (2017). World Press Freedom Index: Country Ranking—Bangladesh. https://rsf.org/en/bangladesh Retrieved: 10 June 2019.
Rock, M. T., & Bonnett, H. (2004). The comparative politics of corruption: Accounting for the East Asian paradox in empirical studies of corruption, growth and investment. *World Development, 32*(6), 999–1017.
Rodrik, D. (1999). Where did all the growth go? External shocks, social conflict, and growth collapses. *Journal of Economic Growth, 4*(4), 385–412.
Rodrik, D. (2000). Institutions for High-Quality Growth: What They are and How to Acquire Them. NBER Working Paper No. 7540. Cambridge: National Bureau of Economic Research (NBER).
Rodrik, D. (2008). Thinking about governance. In D. North, D. Acemoglu, F. Fukuyama, & D. Rodrik (Eds.), *Governance, growth and development decision-making* (pp. 17–24). Washington, D.C.: The World Bank.
Roy, D. K. (2006). Governance, Competitiveness and Growth: The Challenges for Bangladesh. ADB Institute Discussion Paper No. 53. Tokyo: Asian Development Bank Institute (ADBI).
Sen, A. (1995, October 20). Wrongs and rights in development. Prospect.
Sen, A. (1999). *Development as freedom*. Oxford: Oxford University Press.
Sobhan, R. (2004). Structural dimensions of malgovernance in Bangladesh. *Economic and Political Weekly, 39*(36), 4–10.
Sobhan, R. (2016, October 15–16). Towards an inclusive, just and peaceful society in South Asia: Who are the change agents? Paper presented at the Ninth South Asian Economic Summit: Reimagining South Asia in 2030, organised by the Centre for Policy Dialogue (CPD), Dhaka, Bangladesh.
Stiglitz, J. E. (2002). Participation and development: Perspectives from the comprehensive development paradigm. *Review of Development Economics, 6*(2), 163–182.

Transparency International. (2019). Corruption Perceptions Index 2018. Berlin: Transparency International. https://www.transparency.org/cpi2018 Retrieved 27 October 2019.
UN. (2015). Transforming Our World: The 2030 Agenda for Sustainable Development. New York: United Nations (UN).
UNDP. (2014). Human Development Report 2014—Sustaining Human Progress: Reducing Vulnerabilities and Building Resilience. New York: United Nations Development Programme (UNDP).
UNDP. (2015). Human Development Report 2015: Work for Human Development. New York: United Nations Development Programme (UNDP).
UNDP. (2016). Human Development Report 2016: Human Development for Everyone. New York: United Nations Development Programme (UNDP).
UNDP. (2018). Human Development Indices and Indicators: 2018 Statistical Update. New York: United Nations Development Programme (UNDP). http://hdr.undp.org/sites/default/files/2018_human_development_statistical_update.pdf Retrieved 11 June 2019.
WEF. (2015) The Global Competitiveness Report 2015–2016. Geneva: World Economic Forum (WEF).
WEF. (2016). The Global Competitiveness Report 2016–2017. Geneva: World Economic Forum (WEF).
World Bank. (2008). *The Growth Report: Strategies for Sustained Growth and Inclusive Development*. Washington, D.C.: Commission on Growth and Development, The World Bank.
World Bank. (2010). *World Development Report 2010: Development and Climate Change.* Washington, D.C.: The World Bank.
World Bank. (2013). Gross National Income per Capita 2012, Atlas Method and PPP. Washington, D.C.: The World Bank. http://ina.bnu.edu.cn/docs/20140606095459236642.pdf Retrieved 16 June 2019.
World Bank. (2014). Gross National Income per Capita 2013, Atlas Method and PPP. Washington, D.C.: The World Bank. http://scienzepolitiche.unipg.it/tutor/uploads/2014_wb_gni_cap_atlas_and_ppp.pdf Retrieved 19 June 2019.
World Bank. (2015). Gross National Income per Capita 2014, Atlas Method and PPP. Washington, D.C.: The World Bank. http://scienzepolitiche.unipg.it/tutor/uploads/2015_gnp_per_cap_current_and_ppp.pdf Retrieved 17 June 2019.
World Bank. (2016). *Bangladesh Development Update, April 2016: Moving Forward with Fading Tailwinds*. Dhaka: The World Bank, Bangladesh Office.
World Bank. (2016b). Gross National Income per Capita 2015, Atlas Method and PPP. https://astrofizyka.files.wordpress.com/2016/09/pnb-na-gc582owc499-wg-ppp-2015.pdf [Retrieved: 27 June 2019].
World Bank. (2017a). Gross National Income per Capita 2016, Atlas Method and PPP. Washington, D.C.: The World Bank. http://iplhq.org/icl/wp-content/uploads/2017/10/2.-2016-GNIPC-of-World-Bank2017.10.21.pdf Retrieved 29 June 2019.
World Bank. (2017). *World Development Report 2017: Governance and the Law*. Washington, D.C.: The World Bank.
World Bank. (2018). *Bangladesh Development Update, April 2018: Building on Resilience*. Dhaka: The World Bank, Bangladesh Office.
World Bank. (2018b). Ease of Doing Business in Bangladesh [data]. Washington, D.C.: The World Bank. http://www.doingbusiness.org/data/exploreeconomies/bangladesh Retrieved 25 October 2019.
World Bank. (2018c). Gross National Income per Capita 2017, Atlas Method and PPP. Washington, D.C.: The World Bank. http://www.ifs.se/IFS/Documents/Application%20Forms/GNIPC.pdf [Retrieved: 28 October 2019].
World Bank. (2019). Gross National Income per Capita 2018, Atlas Method and PPP. Washington, D.C.: The World Bank. https://databank.worldbank.org/data/download/GNIPC.pdf Retrieved 25 October 2019.

World Bank. (n.d.a). World Development Indicator (WDI) database. Washington, D. C.: The World Bank. https://databank.worldbank.org/data/home.aspx Retrieved 5 September 2019.
World Bank. (n.d.b). Worldwide Governance Indicators (WGI). Washington, D.C.: The World Bank. info.worldbank.org/governance/wgi/ [Retrieved: 24 October 2019].

The manufacturer's authorised representative in the EU is Springer
Nature Customer Service Centre GmbH, Europaplatz 3, 69115 Heidelberg,
Germany. If you have any concerns regarding our products, please
contact ProductSafety@springernature.com

Printed and bound by CPI Group (UK) Ltd, Croydon, CR0 4YY
01/10/2026
02226215-0003